D0898971

STRETCH

Coming of Age in Post-War Germany

by

GUNTER NITSCH

authorHOUSE®

AuthorHouse™
1663 Liberty Drive
Bloomington, IN 47403
www.authorhouse.com
Phone: 1-800-839-8640

First published by AuthorHouse   11/11/2010

ISBN: 978-1-4520-7929-5 (e)
ISBN: 978-1-4520-7927-1 (sc)
ISBN: 978-1-4520-7928-8 (hc)

Library of Congress Control Number: 2010914642

Printed in the United States of America

Also by Gunter Nitsch:

Weeds Like Us

DEDICATION

To Mary, Michael, and Frederick, who encouraged me to write this book.

ACKNOWLEDGMENTS

With appreciation to everyone who gave my manuscript a critical reading: Susan Barton, Caroline P. Cracraft, Annie Desbois, Lane Gutstein, Joseph C. Heinen, Sheila Ann Jones, Terry Jones, Marsha K. Konz, and David Vickrey.

My special thanks to my wife Mary for the editing and re-editing of my many drafts and to my sons Michael and Frederick for their invaluable contributions.

PROLOGUE

*I*n the aftermath of World War II, my family was among those relocated in what may have been the largest forced resettlement of a population in modern history — the expulsion of at least twelve million Germans and ethnic Germans from the former German provinces of East Prussia, Silesia, and Pomerania, as well as from long-established German-speaking enclaves such as the Sudetenland in Czechoslovakia. As a result, between 1945 and 1950, West Germany's population swelled with the arrival of millions of refugees, many of whom spoke with strange-sounding regional accents and often brought with them nothing more than a rucksack full of meager possessions. With housing already scarce, jobs hard to come by, and religious differences often setting them apart, it is perhaps no surprise that the newcomers were not always welcomed with open arms.

As I described in my first book, *Weeds Like Us*, my mother, brother and I had lived under Russian control in the former East Prussia from April 1945 to September 1948, followed by another two years in a West German refugee camp. By the time we arrived in Cologne in December 1950 to be reunited with my father, I was thirteen years old but had been in school for less than four years. Over the next thirteen years I would face the daunting task of getting an education, adapting to the unfamiliar customs of the Rhineland, and discovering firsthand the lingering traces of the Nazi mind-set. Most of my life so far had been a circuitous journey from East Prussia to Cologne. Now it was time for me to try putting down some roots.

CHAPTER 1

*T*he engine of Mr. Meyer's overloaded Opel clattered and strained under the unaccustomed weight of its five passengers and all of our belongings. It was shortly after my thirteenth birthday on a raw, gray Tuesday afternoon in December 1950, and my father's new boss was driving my mother, my father, my eight-year-old brother Hubert, and me, from Cologne on the Rhine towards the town of Bergheim. Except for the rickety taxi that had brought Mutti, Hubert, and me to the border during our escape from East Germany two years before, this was my first ride in any vehicle smaller than a Russian army truck.

A heavy carton packed with our two Bibles, my precious copies of *Huckleberry Finn* and *The Leather Stocking Tales*, my two atlases, and my stamp collection was crushing my lap. Hubert, who had barely managed to squeeze in between Mutti and me in the backseat, pressed against my side. He looked like an overstuffed piglet and breathed heavily. Occasionally I poked my elbow into his side and whispered, "Give me some space, will you?" but he would just glare at me and then nervously brush his straight blond hair off of his forehead.

Half an hour earlier our train had chugged slowly into the cavernous main railroad station where my father, without a trace of a smile, had waited for us on the platform. This was our second reunion since the

1

war ended. Our first, two years earlier, had ended abruptly after only ten days with my father's announcement that he was leaving us behind in a refugee camp near the East German border to take a job as a pastry chef in Cologne. In the two years since he had left us, my father had only been in touch through infrequent postcards and even more infrequent transfers of funds. From my perspective, his abandonment had begun long before that. When I was a small child, he had been away at war and rarely came home on leave. Now I knew that, as the war had neared its end and while Mutti, Hubert, and I were trapped in Russian-held territory in the East, my father had been captured by the British and had lived in relative comfort in the West. Then one day, out of the blue, this man, who was a virtual stranger to me, had sent us tickets so that we could join him.

My father had introduced us to Mr. Meyer moments after we stepped down from the train and the five of us walked outside together. Even though they were the same height, the two men could not have been more different. My father strode, stiff and fashionable, in his high-collared suit and heavy overcoat, but his steel gray eyes darted over the three of us anxiously. Mr. Meyer slouched alongside us in a crumpled gray suit. In contrast to my father's bald head and gaunt frame, Mr. Meyer's thick blond hair was combed straight back and his belt was nearly hidden beneath his protruding stomach. Laughter crinkled the corners of his blue eyes and he winked at Hubert and me as he had struggled to fit our belongings into the tiny trunk of his car.

My father sat in the front passenger seat and stared straight ahead. Mutti was seated behind Mr. Meyer and gazed glumly out the window as the car rumbled in the direction of Bergheim, which was twenty-four kilometers away. I couldn't see her face, but I was sure we were sharing the same thoughts. Had we just exchanged a hard life in the Bodenteich refugee camp for something even worse? At least in Bodenteich I could do pretty much as I pleased; I couldn't begin to imagine what it would take to please my father.

Rubble left over from the Allied bombing littered both sides of the road. The houses that were still standing were heavily pockmarked with bullet holes. The windows of some of the buildings had been walled shut with mismatched bricks scavenged from nearby ruins. Why would someone do that, I wondered. Were the owners trying to keep intruders out? Or were the bricked-up windows helping to keep the buildings from collapsing altogether? Had my father been a bit friendlier I would have asked him, but now I didn't dare.

Five long minutes passed without a word being spoken. Finally, Mr. Meyer cleared his throat. "Well, Frau Nitsch," he said, trying to make eye contact with Mutti in the rearview mirror, "what are your first impressions of Cologne?"

"It reminds me of Königsberg and Berlin," Mutti said after a moment's hesitation. "Terrible devastation everywhere you look."

"It's bad, that's for sure, but it's a paradise compared to the way the center of town looked in 1945. You know, around the main train station where we just were? Nearly everything over there was totally flat. It's a miracle the cathedral was spared."

My father turned to Mr. Meyer and said bitterly, "Every time I come through this part of town, I get angry at the British and Americans for what they did here."

"What we did to the Russians wasn't any better," Mutti protested. "The stories the Russians told me about their civilian casualties would make your blood curdle. And don't forget that *we* started the war."

My father craned his neck around and glared at Mutti. "Now you listen to me! You'd better forget all that Communist propaganda and get on with your life or you'll never fit in here. Germany's different now. We've put all that behind us."

"Well, you may be angry at the British and the Americans," Mr. Meyer said to my father, tactfully ignoring my parents' argument, "but the currency reforms they put through two years ago have really helped us get back on our feet."

"Well, I'll give them credit for that," my father said.

Mutti changed the subject. "I never thought to ask – which of the Allies is in charge in this area?"

"Officially, it's the British zone," Mr. Meyer replied. "But the troops stationed around here are all from Belgium. I'll point out their barracks when we drive past Ichendorf."

We left Cologne, passing through the villages of Königsdorf and Horrem. Up to that point, we had been driving on a rather high plateau, but now, straight ahead of us, lay a vast marshy plain divided into rectangular pastures; some were enclosed by thick hedges, and others, bordered by ruler-straight rows of tall poplar trees. Never in my life had I been able to see so far. To our right, however, the plateau continued. Mr. Meyer nodded in that direction. "There's a big deposit of soft coal over there. See the smokestacks just behind the hills? Those are factories that produce briquettes and electricity."

"Is that how the houses are heated around here? With briquettes?" I asked timidly.

"That's pretty much all we use," Mr. Meyer replied.

"Well then, at least I won't be chopping all that wood for the stove," I blurted out, thinking back to the backbreaking hours I had spent swinging an ax ever since I was barely eight years old.

"You'll have plenty of other chores to do, believe me," my father said sharply. "I'll see to that."

Color had rushed into Mutti's cheeks. She reached across Hubert to place a reassuring hand on my arm, but I could feel her trembling through my sleeve. Grabbing tight to the box of books on my lap, I slumped down in my seat as far as my long legs would let me.

"Now, Willi," she said to my father, measuring every word. "Günter has been looking after us ever since Opa died back in '46. You needn't worry about his carrying his own weight."

"Just so everyone knows who's in charge," my father snapped.

Mutti turned to me. With her free hand she pointed to herself and forced a smile.

Not long after that, we drove into a small town. "Well, this is Bergheim," Mr. Meyer announced, "and on your right, that's my café where we'll all have dinner later."

Mutti smiled gratefully and said, "That's very kind of you, Herr Meyer. We're certainly looking forward to it."

"Zieverich, where you'll be living, is just on the other side of the Aachener Tor, the old city gate ahead of us." From a distance the gate, with its two thick brick and mortar towers attached to an arched passageway, didn't look wide enough, but Mr. Meyer's Opel had no trouble passing through. As soon as we entered Zieverich we drove past a huge meadow on our right and a swamp on our left before crossing a wide cement bridge over the Erft River. Just beyond the bridge on the left, a driveway separated a Lutheran church from a three-story building with two separate entrances. Mr. Meyer made a U-turn on Aachener Strasse and parked in front of the entrance farthest from the church.

"So, here you are," he said. "This is it."

A meter-high stone wall separated the front yards of the two attached parts of the house. The left half of the building had a fresh coat of plaster and large windows with crisp lace curtains and dark brown shutters. A front walk crossed a garden and led to a flight of steps going up to the door. On the right side of the wall, six cement steps led down below the level of the sidewalk so that both the path and the first floor of the house on that side were well below street level. The right half also had smaller windows. There were curtains but no shutters. And the front wall was still deeply pocked with bullet holes and shrapnel scars.

Mr. Meyer opened the car door for Mutti and then went to the trunk to retrieve our things. Ignoring Hubert and me, my father joined him. I struggled desperately with the door on my side but couldn't open it. Mr. Meyer, noticing my predicament, put our possessions on the sidewalk and came over to let Hubert and me out. "It's a little tricky," he said soothingly as he opened the door. Why couldn't my father be like him, I wondered.

Mr. Meyer shook hands with both of my parents. "It's so nice to see your family reunited at last," he said. "Now I've got to rush back to the shop. I'll see all of you in an hour for supper."

"Well," my father said as Mr. Meyer drove off and we walked up to the front door, "we should let our landladies know we've arrived. At least one of the Lemm sisters should be home at this hour."

There were four doorbells. The bottom bell with the blank nametag was ours. Next up was Poltermann, then van Knippenberg. The Lemm sisters' bell, which my father now pressed twice, was on the top. After a minute or two, we could hear the tapping of high-heeled shoes in the hallway and then a middle-aged lady opened the front door. Miss Lemm was wearing a long-sleeved, dark-blue, ankle-length dress. A stickpin cameo brooch held her collar tightly closed. Her hair was pulled back into a neat bun.

"Frau Nitsch and children, so glad to meet you," she said, shaking each of our hands in turn. "I'm sorry that my sister isn't home to welcome you, too. Come in! Come in! No sense letting in the cold air and I'm sure you'd like to get settled."

We followed Miss Lemm into the narrow entry hall and she stopped at the first door on the left. As my father reached into his pocket for the key, we heard the sound of footsteps coming from the apartment across the hall. "Please be sure to let me know if you need anything," Miss Lemm said, wringing her hands nervously. She suddenly seemed anxious to herd us all into the apartment. At that moment, the door behind us was flung open and out popped a tall skinny man with an enormous handlebar mustache and stringy black hair that hung at least five centimeters over his shirt collar.

"Well, here we go again!" he boomed. "More damn rrrefugees! As if we didn't have enough already!" He intentionally mispronounced the word "refugees" by imitating the rolling "r" of the East Prussian accent.

"Now listen here, Herr Poltermann," Miss Lemm started to say, but Mr. Poltermann went right on.

"Don't take me too seriously," he said with a chuckle. "I can say whatever I like 'cause I'm a damn rrrefugee myself. Name's Poltermann. From the Sudetenland. Just got back today from my in-law's place in Fortuna."

"Nitsch," my father said, extending his hand.

"Well, well, well," Mr. Poltermann replied, looking the four of us up and down. "A hearty welcome to Villa Lemm! So you'll be living down here with us *Untermenschen* on the ground floor. I'm sure Fräulein Lemm has told you how to find your way to the shithouse at the end of the long brick path in the back. Refugees like us don't get indoor plumbing like the fancy-pants natives upstairs. Oh, no. We have to trek way out back through the snow in the dead of night and sit there freezing our asses off in the dark while the wind whistles through the…"

"Please, Herr Poltermann, I beg you! You know very well that this is only a temporary solution," said Miss Lemm.

"Well, you're a nice one! What do you mean, temporary? My family has been living under these primitive conditions for a year now!"

Miss Lemm turned to my parents. Her lower lip was trembling. "What Herr Poltermann has forgotten to say is that as soon as my sister and I have the money we'll install a toilet in the first-floor laundry room."

"Don't make me laugh," Mr. Poltermann said sharply. Then he grinned at us. "You'll see soon enough! *Auf Wiedersehen!*" And he ducked back inside his apartment.

Miss Lemm wrung her hands. "A very difficult gentleman, as you can see," she said, smiling weakly at Mutti. "The van Knippenberg family lives on the second floor and my sister and I live on the third floor. The van Knippenbergs are an old established family in this area, very refined people. They have three daughters. They lost their only son in a bombing raid in 1944. He was only fourteen, the poor dear." Miss Lemm barely paused to take a breath. "Herr van Knippenberg is the principal of the Catholic school here in Zieverich. I presume your boys will be attending there."

"The boys will go to the Lutheran school in Bergheim," my father corrected her.

"That's too bad," Miss Lemm said. "It's two kilometers each way, and a few days a week they'll have to go back and forth twice when the school has morning and afternoon shifts."

"I'm sure the walk will do them good," my father said. *That's easy for him to say*, I thought to myself, trying to imagine my chubby little brother walking eight kilometers a day.

"But at least you won't have far to go to get to church," Miss Lemm hastened to add. "It's right next door. Pastor Kampe and his family live in the other half of this building, by the way. Oh, and I almost forgot. We all use the other room on this side for doing laundry. You'll find the entrance back there by the staircase."

"Thank you so much for the information and good evening, Fräulein Lemm," my father said as he inched closer to the door of our apartment.

Miss Lemm nodded, smiled, and walked further down the hallway to the wooden stairs leading up to the apartment she shared with her sister. When she was out of earshot, Mutti asked my father, "Is that customary here to have such long conversations in the hallway?"

"There wouldn't have been space for all five of us to talk inside," my father replied as he finally turned the key in the lock and we got our first look at our new home.

I let out a low whistle. "It's not much bigger than our room in the refugee camp in Bodenteich!" I would have said more, but the angry look my father shot at me kept me quiet.

To our right, a row of clothes hooks attached to a thick wooden board had been nailed to the wall. A double bed took up all of the remaining space on that side. A sink and stove were to the left of the doorway. On the far left side of the room, a single window faced the front yard, and next to it, a couch, a rectangular table, and two stools completed the furnishings.

"I see what you mean," Mutti said. "There's barely enough space in here for the four of us. Where will the boys sleep?"

"Hubert can sleep on the couch and Herr Meyer gave me an old military folding cot that Günter can use. It slides right under the couch. We'll have set it up every night, that's all."

"Where?" Mutti asked, eying the narrow area between the table and the double bed.

"Oh, it'll fit all right. When the boys go to bed, we'll just have to move the table and chairs over there." He pointed to the cramped space in front of the coat hooks.

I looked up at the single ceiling light over the spot where my cot would be. I took a deep breath and said to my father, "Could I ask you something? When I go to bed, will that light still be on?"

"Of course it will," my father snapped. "Do you think your mother and I are going to spend our evenings in the dark?"

"Don't be so hard on Günter," Mutti objected. "He has the right to ask a simple question."

"Now you listen to me, all of you," my father replied. "This isn't going to be easy for any of us, but there's a housing shortage and we'll just have to make the best of what we have." Not another word was said as Mutti unpacked a towel from her bag and we all washed our hands over the kitchen sink before setting out for Café Meyer. We left the house, climbed the cement steps that led up to the sidewalk, and turned in the direction of Bergheim.

As we walked, I thought about the fact that, by 1950, my parents had been married for fifteen years but they'd only actually lived together for fewer than four. Although they now walked side by side, my father kept his hands firmly in his coat pockets. He and my mother never so much as glanced at each other. As Hubert and I dawdled along behind them I tried my hardest to imagine how they might have acted as newlyweds in the years before the war. Living here isn't going to be easy for Hubert and me, I decided, but how much worse must it be for Mutti!

After crossing over the river and passing the meadow and the swamp, we walked through the pedestrian passageway on the right side of the Aachener Tor. We passed the Frambach clothing shop and the Stüssgen Food Market before reaching the café.

The sign on the door said, "Closed" but the lights were on inside. Mr. Meyer was waiting to greet us together with a tall, ash blond lady with a charming smile and big dimples.

"Allow me to introduce you to my wife," Mr. Meyer said. "Dear, this is Herr Nitsch's wife and these are his two boys, Günter and Hubert."

"So nice to meet you, Frau Meyer," Mutti said shyly, trying her best to smile. "I must apologize for how the boys and I are dressed. We didn't have time to change."

"There's no need to apologize!" Mrs. Meyer exclaimed, her eyes sparkling. "We're just happy to welcome you to Bergheim! Josef and I have lived here all our lives and we really love this place. Once you get settled in, I'm sure you will too. But let's not waste time on small talk. You must all be starving after your long trip. Excuse me just a minute." She turned around and shouted towards the back of the shop, "Maria, our guests are here!"

Mrs. Meyer led us past several small marble top tables to a larger table set for six. Atop an embroidered white linen tablecloth were six heavy porcelain plates decorated with blue and white painted wildflowers. Each of us had been provided with two spoons, two forks, and two knives. I tried to imagine how any one person could use so much silverware. Throughout the meal I carefully observed my parents and Mr. and Mrs. Meyer to be sure that I was using the right utensil at the right time.

Since, for the past two years, my supper had been limited to two slices of rye bread spread with lard and onions and one slice of bread with sugar beet syrup, I was totally unprepared for the meal that followed. We started with a thick vegetable soup, followed by sauerbraten with red cabbage, and mashed potatoes soaked with real butter. Ignoring all conversation, I proceeded to stuff myself. Then, when I was just about ready to burst, Maria brought out the dessert, together with real coffee for the adults and hot chocolate for Hubert and me.

Mr. Meyer beamed. "Boys, I want you to know that the tart was made by your father. Isn't it beautiful? And I'll tell you a secret – it tastes even better than it looks."

The fruit tart really was a piece of art. Peach slices circled the outer edge. Semi-circles of a pale yellow fruit nestled between the peaches and the four banana halves; in the center, a whole ring of the mysterious pale fruit was garnished with bright red cherries. I knew my father was a pastry chef, but I had no idea that he could make such a beautiful dessert.

"I recognize the bananas, peaches, and cherries, but what's the other fruit?" I asked, looking shyly from my father to Mr. Meyer.

Mr. Meyer beamed. "That's Dole pineapple, imported from Hawaii! It's a bit expensive, but I think you'll find that it's well worth it."

I put a big dollop of whipped cream on the slice of tart Maria served me and ate very slowly, savoring every bite. Hubert finished his piece first and we were both relieved when Mrs. Meyer insisted that he and I have seconds. Maria also brought Hubert and me another cup of hot chocolate, but instead of more coffee for the adults she brought out four crystal wine glasses and a bottle of wine.

"How about a little Kröver Nacktarsch to cap off the evening?" Mr. Meyer said. He held up the bottle so that we could all see the picture on the label of a little boy, his short pants pulled down to the top of his knee socks, getting spanked on his bare bottom by a vintner. My father surprised me when he burst out laughing.

Even Mutti started to giggle. "I can't remember when I last tasted wine but I've never seen a bottle like that," she confessed.

"It's one of our favorite Mosels," Mr. Meyer said. "Guaranteed to liven up any occasion." Then he winked at Hubert and me. "Sorry, boys, this stuff's off-limits for children!"

By the time the adults had finished off their third bottle of wine, they were all chatting away like old friends.

"So how does your new place compare with where you were before?" Mr. Meyer suddenly asked Mutti. "Pretty cramped space for four people, I'd say."

"Now, Josef," his wife began, but Mr. Meyer went right on.

"If you can keep this under your hats," he said, leaning across the table and grabbing my father's sleeve, "when I ran into Fräulein Lemm a few days ago in the butcher shop she hinted that she was trying to get the Poltermanns out so that your family could have two additional rooms."

"I wouldn't mind that at all," Mutti chimed in. "I couldn't believe how insulting Herr Poltermann was to Fräulein Lemm this afternoon."

"That's just his sense of humor," my father said. "He's perfectly harmless."

"Well, I wouldn't put up with it," Mutti replied firmly.

"Actually, he's got the law on his side," my father explained. "The way I understand it, once someone rents space to refugees, it's pretty hard to evict them."

"All the same, I'll let you know if I hear anything more about it," Mr. Meyer added as he leaned back in his chair with a conspiratorial grin.

****

Mutti was a little wobbly on the walk back to Zieverich, and almost without thinking, she grabbed onto my father's arm to steady herself. The

12

Kröver Nacktarsch and the fine meal had certainly worked wonders. By the time we got back to our room, all four of us were talking at once.

My father held up his hand to get our attention. "Now let's see how fast I can put Günter's cot together," he said, as he carried the small rectangular table and the two stools to the opposite corner by the door. Then, reaching down, he dragged a bulky olive green canvas pack out from under the couch as Hubert, Mutti and I sat down to watch.

"I had lots of practice with these when I worked in the military hospital in Berlin," he said to me, "but it took me a while to get the hang of it. I want you to watch what I'm doing so that you can do this yourself in the future." Within minutes he had unfolded the canvas cot on its three pairs of crossed wooden legs. Mutti put a folded blanket and a sheet on top. It was the first time in my life I could remember seeing my parents working together as a team.

"Give it a try," my father encouraged me in a friendly voice. "I hope it's long enough. Just be careful not to get pinched by the frame."

The cot was surprisingly comfortable except for the sharp edges of the six square wooden pegs connecting the legs to the sides. And it was even better when Mutti added my pillow and the lumpy feather comforter I'd brought from the refugee camp. After Hubert and I had washed up and brushed our teeth over the sink, Mutti asked us to close our eyes so that she and my father could undress for bed.

My parents had bickered from the Cologne railroad station until we got to Café Meyer. Our room was a bit cramped and the idea of living with my father was something I'd have to get used to. But my father had softened as the evening wore on. *Maybe things won't be so bad after all*, I thought. I fell asleep before my parents turned off the light.

CHAPTER 2

"**I**t's 6:30. Time to get up for your first day of school!" Mutti gave my shoulder a hard shake. Hubert was already crawling out from under his comforter on the couch.

"Where's Vati?" he asked, rubbing his eyes.

"He left for work at four o'clock."

Hubert stifled a yawn. "Is he going to do that every day?"

"Every day except Monday. That's his day off."

"He works on Sundays, too?"

"Sundays, too. C'mon boys, let's have some breakfast! Frau Meyer was nice enough to give us these rolls with margarine and jam, and then we have to get going. You've both missed so much school that you'll have a lot of catching up to do. There'll be no more interruptions in your education if I have anything to say about it."

On our way to the school, the three of us walked, once again, through the Aachener Tor and along the main street of Bergheim past Café Meyer. We crossed over the Little Erft River before cutting off to the left onto Bethlehemer Strasse. The road climbed steeply and Hubert was forced to take frequent breaks. One more turn at the top and the shrieking of the children in the schoolyard led us directly to the front entrance of the large school building. Even without making allowances for Hubert, it had taken us a good half hour to get there.

Mutti took Hubert by the hand and the three of us went inside to enroll at the Bergheim Lutheran Elementary School. We found the principal in a small office. Mr. Reitberg was tall and skinny and his head reminded me of an egg, wide at the bottom and narrow on top.

"Let's see," Mr. Reitberg said, looking over the registration forms. "Hubert will be in the lower class, grades one to four. Günter will be in my classroom, grades five to eight. Just so you know, I teach everything except German and history. That's the job of Herr Schulz."

"Oh, there aren't separate classes for each grade?" Mutti asked.

"We have to be grateful for whatever we can get, Frau Nitsch. Let me put it this way. I have one student, Krienke, from Thuringia, in East Germany and two other boys who were born here in Bergheim. But all of the other children arrived in the last few years from Soviet- and Polish-occupied areas like East Prussia, Pomerania, Silesia and the Sudetenland. This is an overwhelmingly Catholic area. We're lucky that the Catholic Elementary School administrator was kind enough to let us use two of their classrooms at certain times of the day."

"I understand," Mutti said.

"Why don't you take Hubert to his class. Günter can come along with me."

Mr. Reitberg led me upstairs to a large converted attic with such a sharply sloping ceiling that I couldn't stand in the back without bumping my head. Small windows had been installed below the slope of the roof. Even though the room was furnished with sixty wooden desks and chairs bolted together in pairs, more than half of the available floor space was empty.

"You can sit next to him," Mr. Reitberg said, pointing to an empty chair towards the middle of the room.

"Jochen Krienke," my seatmate whispered.

"Günter Nitsch," I replied.

"No talking in class!" Mr. Reitberg boomed. "For the benefit of our newcomer here, I'll repeat this just one more time. If any of you wants a smack, I have a hand and I'm not afraid to use it!"

At midmorning, when we broke for recess, I followed Jochen downstairs. A small section of the playground, marked off by a chain link fence, was set apart for the Lutheran students.

"So what did you think of Reitberg?" he asked me.

"I can't seem to get away from idiot teachers like that," I replied with a grin.

"At least with him you know what to expect. Just wait 'til you meet Schulz. Most days he's in a good mood, all dressed up in a fancy dark blue three-piece suit, a white shirt, and a tie. He always starts his classes at 8 A.M. by making us sing a silly song."

"Sounds harmless enough to me."

"The trouble is," Jochen continued, "at least once a week he shows up drunk. You can tell right away because he'll be madly crunching on big handfuls of Dr. Hiller's peppermint drops to try to cover up the smell of schnapps." Jochen was quiet for a minute to let me digest this news. "Hey, so are you from Zieverich or Bergheim?"

"Zieverich. We just moved in there yesterday."

"We live in Zieverich, too! We can walk back and forth to school together."

Four days a week, including Saturday, our section had classes from eight in the morning until one in the afternoon. But twice a week we had two shifts, the first from eight to eleven and the second from three to five. For me the best part of the school day was *Schulspeise*, a free breakfast compliments of the American government, served during the midmorning recess. As long as we provided our own container and a spoon, we could eat as much oatmeal with milk and raisins as we wanted. Two days later, when I was just about to bring over the German army mess kit my father had given me to ask for seconds, Jochen held me back.

16

"Not yet," he whispered. "Wait about three more minutes and she'll tip the big pot over to one side. That way we'll get mostly raisins!"

****

On Christmas Eve, 1950, the pastry shop stayed open late and so we ate our supper without my father. The next morning, while Mutti, Hubert and I listened to Pastor Kampe's Christmas sermon, my father chose to stay home and cook. When we got back from church we all sat down to a delicious dinner of Wiener schnitzel, mashed potatoes, and carrots and peas. Everyone was in good spirits.

I waited for a break in the conversation to share my news. "You know my friend, Jochen Krienke? He's going to the *Gymnasium* when the new school year starts in April."

"Oh, how nice! How old will he be when he starts?" Mutti asked.

"He'll be twelve."

"You know, Willi," Mutti said slowly, "I've been wondering whether Günter shouldn't also take the entrance exam for the *Gymnasium* or at least the one for the Middle School."

My heart skipped a beat. Even though I doubted that I could pass the test, I really wanted a chance to try. But my father shook his head.

"Out of the question. Let him get through the seventh and eighth grades and learn a trade. Besides," he went on, "look at him! He's thirteen. That's way too old to apply. Most children take the test when they're ten or eleven. Pastor Kampe's son is Günter's age and he's been going to the *Gymnasium* for two years already."

"I just thought it could be a way for him to make up for lost time," Mutti countered. "And maybe then he could get an office job some day. Do you really want him to end up working twelve or fourteen hour days like you?"

My father sighed. "I just don't see it. You're filling the boy's head with a lot of nonsense. End of discussion!"

17

We cleared the table and washed the dishes in silence. We didn't even sing Christmas carols. I was angry with my father for having spoiled the day. And yet, even though I was upset about what he had said, I was afraid he might be right. When the other children had reached the age to be tested, I had still been living under the Russians, begging for food and stealing potatoes. How could I possibly hope to catch up?

CHAPTER 3

*O*n New Year's Eve, Mr. and Mrs. Meyer invited the bakery staff to a dance party at a local hotel. After my parents left for the evening, Hubert and I forced ourselves to stay awake until the radio announcer had welcomed in 1951. Then we both dozed off. When my parents came home several hours later, their loud voices woke me up. I lay face down on my cot with my eyes closed and listened.

"You were dancing way too often with that young salesgirl Adele," Mutti was saying. "How could you embarrass me like that? Are you starting something again?"

"You're out of your mind. I was just having a little fun! This is the Rhineland. People around here aren't so formal. Get used to it!"

"Not so loud. Keep your voice down. You'll wake up the boys," Mutti whispered. "It's just that it wouldn't be the first time…"

"And I suppose you want me to believe that you were always alone from the end of the war until now."

"I never looked at another man in all those years. You can ask my sister Liesbeth!"

"Oh yeah, a nice impartial witness she'd be," he sneered.

I heard my parents get into the double bed and the room was quiet for a few minutes. Then my father whispered, "If you can't trust me, maybe we should get a divorce."

"That's exactly what you want, isn't it? To be free to fool around."

The same discussion was repeated often in the weeks that followed. As I lay there in the dark, night after night, listening to my parents argue about divorce, I felt like yelling, "Go ahead! Why don't you?" I was sure that we would all be better off without him.

****

When I had first met our neighbor Mr. Poltermann, for some reason I imagined that his wife would be short and frumpy. I couldn't have been more wrong. Raven-haired, vivacious, and sweetly perfumed, Mrs. Poltermann looked as though she'd stepped right out of one of the American movie posters in front of the Apollo Theater on Hauptstrasse in Bergheim. On the rare occasions when I had seen her in the hallway going back and forth to the laundry room, she always greeted me in her singsong local dialect and my heart would skip a beat. In my opinion, Mr. Poltermann was a very lucky man.

One day towards the end of January when Hubert and I came home from school, Mutti told us to hurry up and take off our coats and boots and wash our hands. "I've been visiting back and forth with Frau Poltermann over the past few days," she explained, "and she's asked all three of us over there for a visit."

The entrance to the Poltermanns' living room was directly opposite our room. Once inside, a wide door made of opaque glass led to a second room towards the back of the building opposite the laundry room.

"We don't spend that much time in Zieverich," Mrs. Poltermann explained as she poured coffee for Mutti and herself and put down a plate of cookies for us, "but I wanted you boys to meet my children. Peter! Bärbel! Come over here and say hello to Günter and Hubert. Peter's starting first grade in April."

"Will he be going to Bergheim with us?" I asked.

"Actually, Peter will be going to the Catholic elementary school in Fortuna, so the children and I will be spending even more time at my parents' place." She stopped to sip her coffee. "It's silly, really, separating schools based on religion, don't you think? My parents in Fortuna are very religious, but I only go to Mass because of the children; my husband thinks the whole thing's a big joke," she admitted with a laugh. "But with us away in Fortuna, my husband will be able to get a lot more of his work done here at the apartment."

Mutti took one of the cookies and put it on her saucer. "What kind of work does your husband do, if I may ask?"

"He's a partner in a small advertising agency in Cologne. That's where you see him going every morning on his motorcycle. But he often has to bring extra work home with him on the weekends."

"Excuse me, Frau Poltermann, but what does an advertising agency make?" I asked.

"Well, they don't exactly *make* anything. They try to get people to buy things. For instance, you know those advertising slides they show before the main feature at the Apollo?" I nodded politely, although I'd never been inside the theater. "He designs them, not just for the Apollo but for a lot of the other movie houses in this area. In fact," she added, almost as an afterthought, "he's so busy lately that he may start bringing his assistant to work here in our apartment. She commutes to Cologne from even farther away. So that should save them both a lot of travel time."

After we'd returned to our apartment, I considered asking Mutti what she thought about Mr. Poltermann's work-at-home plans, but I was afraid that doing so would remind her of the girlfriend my father had left behind in Uelzen. Instead, I decided to wait and see what happened.

CHAPTER 4

According to the big clock in the front of our classroom, it was 8:14 and Mr. Schulz still hadn't appeared. Somewhere behind me, a boy was launching spitballs. "Where's Schulz?" yelled another boy from the front of the room. Just at that moment, Schulz strode into the room, his chest heaving from having raced up the stairs. He was dressed, as usual, in a fancy dark blue suit, a crisp white dress shirt with French cuffs, and a deep yellow tie.

He glared at all of us, and without a word of apology, took a book out of his desk. "Now who can tell me where we left Joan of Arc yesterday in Schiller's *Die Jungfrau von Orleans*?" But no one moved to open a book. We were all staring at the long white thread that hung from just below Mr. Schulz's belt to down between his knees. The girls covered their mouths and giggled; the boys chuckled; but no one laughed harder or louder than Jochen who was doubled over in his seat.

"What's the meaning of this uproar?" Schulz demanded, storming over towards Jochen and me. "Krienke!" he shrieked. "What's wrong with you? What's so funny?"

But Jochen was laughing so hard that he couldn't talk. He was holding his freshly inked steel-tipped pen in his right hand, so he used his left hand to point at Mr. Schulz's crotch.

Mr. Schulz's face turned a bright shade of crimson. "Of all the impertinence!" he shouted as he raised his hand to strike Jochen across the face. Jochen instinctively defended himself by lifting his right hand. As if in slow motion, I watched Schulz's palm come down just as the point of the pen came up. Schulz screamed as a dark mix of blood and ink spurted all over his French cuff. The class was suddenly quiet.

"You damn hooligan!" Schulz screamed, while wrapping his bleeding hand in his snow-white handkerchief. "There will be consequences!"

I wondered whether this incident would disqualify Jochen from attending the *Gymnasium*, but in April when the new term started, he changed schools as planned. Another of my new friends, Dieter Henkelmann, who lived across the street from us, went off to the nearest middle school, thirteen kilometers away in Kerpen.

"Stop moping," my father said when I complained about being left behind. "It's not the end of the world. Just one more year of grammar school and you can start an apprenticeship. Maybe you can even become a pastry chef like me. Anyway, I wouldn't want a son of mine to turn into an egghead. You know what I always say, 'Reading too many books makes people stupid.'"

An hour later, when my father went to the back to use the outhouse, Mutti took me aside. "I don't think it's fair, either," she whispered. "Let me see what I can do."

****

The van Knippenberg family occupied the entire floor above ours. Supplementing the information we had first been given by Miss Lemm, Mutti had learned in the meantime that two of the van Knippenbergs' daughters, twenty-seven year old Anneliese, who was a nurse, and nineteen year old Agnes, who was studying to be a teacher, lived at home with their parents. Margret, the middle daughter, was also a nurse. She lived in a suburb of Cologne and came home only on weekends and holidays. The van Knippenberg's son, Matthias, had been killed in a bombing raid in December 1944, just months before the end of the war.

"So Matthias died while we were still living on Opa's farm in Langendorf?" I asked, thinking back to the time when the war had hardly seemed to touch us.

"Right. And a few weeks later the Russians overran East Prussia," Mutti replied.

By this time Mutti, Hubert, and I had gotten to know Mrs. van Knippenberg quite well. Tall, frail, and badly crippled by arthritis, she walked slowly and winced when someone tried to shake her hand. We went to her apartment at least once a week, since she kindly allowed Mutti, Hubert, and me to use her bathtub every Saturday night. (My father used the shower in the spacious apartment over Café Meyer where the six journeymen bakers lived.) The Poltermanns were not given the same privilege.

"Frau van Knippenberg can't stand that man," Mutti explained one night over supper. "And she's told me she doesn't want him anywhere near her daughters."

Late the following afternoon, while my father was still at the café, Mutti went upstairs to the second floor to talk to Mr. van Knippenberg about my schooling.

"Since he's a school principal, I figured he would have some good ideas," she told me later.

What Mr. van Knippenberg had suggested was that I try to get into a *Handelsschule*, a two-year commercial school where subjects such as business English, business German, German literature, accounting, typing, and stenography were taught. With a certificate from a *Handelsschule*, I could make an apprenticeship in a company or a government office.

"Of course you'd have to study extra hard and do a lot of reading to pass the entrance exam."

"But what about Vati?"

"If you pass the exam, I think I can convince him that attending the *Handelsschule* would be the best thing for you," Mutti assured me. "In the meantime, let's keep quiet about this, until you've actually passed the test, all right?"

"It's a deal."

****

Of course, Mutti's idea of "reading" wasn't exactly the same as mine. A few days after she'd spoken to Mr. van Knippenberg, I joined some boys who were searching for scrap metal in the huge garbage dump near the Aachener Tor. Mr. Hammerschlag, the scrap dealer, paid me a whole Mark for the precious copper wire I found. Early the next morning on my way to school I stopped in to Langnickel's Bookstore and exchanged the Mark I'd earned for two *Billy Jenkins* dime novels.

That Saturday afternoon, I ran into Mr. Poltermann in the courtyard of our building. He was walking with a statuesque young blond in a tight-fitting, knitted outfit and the tallest high heel shoes I'd ever seen.

"Have the two of you met?" he asked. "No? This is my assistant, Fräulein Leichtsinn. She's working with me this weekend in my apartment. Heidi, this is Günter Nitsch."

I blushed as she shook my hand.

"Your mother tells me you're still reading that *Billy Jenkins* trash," Mr. Poltermann said. "Look at me when I'm talking to you, young man!" I reluctantly turned in his direction. "Don't waste your money on that crap! Did you know that Langnickel's has a lending library in the back? That's where I get my reading material. Come inside with us and I'll let you have a couple of books you can try. Langnickel's a friend of mine so he won't mind if I keep them past the due date.

"The wife and kids are spending the weekend in Fortuna," he continued. "So Fräulein Leichtsinn and I can get a lot accomplished." He went over to a small table and picked out five books. "Keep them for a day or two to decide which one you want to read and give me back the rest."

"Thank you, Herr Poltermann!"

"Oh, and before you go, I want you to see my latest gadget." He pointed to a large brown box. "It's a record player." I stared at him blankly. "Let me show you how it works. Do you like jazz?"

I nodded. "Yes, I do. Especially Louis Armstrong. I've heard him on the radio."

Mr. Poltermann took a flat black disk out of its case, lifted the cover of the machine, and placed the disk inside. "You put the record on the turntable like this," he said. "And then all you have to do is move the needle arm over to the edge and listen!"

As if by magic, the sound of the "St. Louis Blues" came out of the machine. Half way through the song, Mr. Poltermann lifted the needle and turned off the record player.

"When I have more time you can listen to some more, but right now Fräulein Leichtsinn and I have to get down to business."

"August," Miss Leichtsinn said, "haven't you forgotten about your other new gadget? You know," she giggled, pointing to another box behind us.

"Oh, right!" he smiled at her. "Actually, this one's even more amazing!" He reached over to turn on the other machine just as Mutti knocked at the door.

"Hello, Frau Nitsch, were you looking for your son? I was just about to show him my tape recorder. But first let me introduce to you my assistant, Fräulein Leichtsinn. Heidi, this is Günter's mother, Frau Nitsch."

"Nice to meet you," Mutti said, but there was a slight hesitation in her voice. As she and I both knew, it was certainly not customary for a boss to be on a first name basis with an assistant. "You've whetted my curiosity," Mutti said. "We've been away from civilization so long that I have no idea what a tape recorder is."

Mr. Poltermann laughed. "Hold it right there!" He pushed two buttons in quick succession.

"We've been away from civilization so long that I have no idea what a tape recorder is," the machine repeated. Mutti looked up in amazement. "Is that the way I sound? Oh, my goodness."

"I must tip my hat to you, Frau Nitsch. Most people take much longer to figure out what's going on. My wife's always annoyed with me when I buy expensive new gadgets but I actually need this one for work." Miss Leichtsinn nodded in agreement. "But I haven't dared tell her yet that I'm getting a bigger motorcycle with a sidecar." As Mutti and I got up to leave, he added, "I'm lending Günter those books. Maybe they'll take his mind off *Billy Jenkins.*"

"Thank you, Herr Poltermann. That's very kind of you. *Auf Wiedersehen!*"

"It was funny to hear your voice on the tape recorder," I said to Mutti as we crossed the hallway, "and he's got a record player, too. I'm sure he'll show it to you sometime."

"He's a real wizard when it comes to those things," Mutti agreed. "I don't know about the new motorcycle though; Frau Poltermann hinted recently that he makes good money, but he spends it just as fast."

"His assistant's very pretty, isn't she?" I asked coyly.

Mutti gave me a sharp look but ignored my question. "I've got to pick up Hubert," she said with a sigh. "Why don't you have a look at those books while I'm gone?" As she left the room, I heard her mutter under her breath, "The nerve of that man!"

I flipped the pages of several of the books before deciding on a biography of Johann Friedrich Böttger, an alchemist. After failing in his attempts to transform base metal into gold, he turned his attention to discovering the secret process for making porcelain. I soon learned that, although Europeans had tried for centuries to find out what the Chinese had known how to do for nearly two thousand years, it was Böttger who finally created the formula that led to the opening of the first European porcelain factory in Meissen in 1710. I was fascinated by the story but just as thrilled by the account of the passionate romance between Böttger and his first serious girlfriend.

I had no idea that books could be so interesting! So when Mr. Schulz assigned us an essay on Goethe's play *Hermann und Dorothea*, I screwed up my courage and spoke to him after class.

"Excuse me, Herr Schulz," I said, my voice barely above a whisper. "I was wondering whether I could write a book report about a biography I just read instead. It's about the inventor of Meissen porcelain."

"Out of the question!" he snapped. "You have to write a report on the play. Let's say four, five, six pages. That should do it." As my shoulders slumped in disappointment Mr. Schulz tapped his fingers on the desk. "Of course," he went on, "I'd have nothing against it if you were to write an *extra* report on the Böttger biography. If you do, I promise to read it to the seventh and eighth grades after I've corrected it. But be sure to do the Goethe report first. There'll be points off if it's late."

"Yes, Herr Schulz, and thank you!"

Had I promised too much? Now I had to write two papers instead of one. But I needn't have worried. Mr. Schulz gave me a good grade on the Goethe paper, and the day after I turned in my book report on Böttger, he asked me to stay after class to go over his corrections.

"You've done a nice job, Nitsch," he said. "You can tell your mother that you probably won't have a problem passing the essay portion of the Commercial School entrance exam. Of course, I don't know about your other grades. How's your math?"

"I'm working really hard at that too," I stammered. "I'll be sure to tell my mother what you said. Thanks so much for the extra help!"

Up to that point, I had rarely gotten any encouragement from my teachers. Nearly every day during our geometry lesson, Mr. Reitberg drummed the same message into our heads, "You're so dumb! You'll all end up as ditch diggers!" But maybe I wasn't so stupid after all. When Mr. Schulz read my paper to the class, some of the boys snickered. A few even called me a "brown noser" after school. But when I thought about what Mr. Schulz had told me, I just grinned and ignored them.

CHAPTER 5

*T*he pastry shop opened later on Sundays, so my father was able to join us for breakfast. After he left for work, Mutti, Hubert and I went to the service at the adjacent Lutheran church. The women in the congregation, including Mutti, were quick to admit that Pastor Kampe cut a dashing figure. Whether driving around town in his 1931 Audi or delivering a sermon, he was always dressed to kill in a neatly pressed dark suit, a starched white shirt, and a tie. He had salt-and-pepper hair, thick in the middle and trimmed short, military style, at the sides. And when he spoke to you, his eyes would lock onto yours as though he could see right into your heart.

Pastor Kampe had married well. His father-in-law was a director of the Rhenish Power Company & Soft Coal Mines. The Kampes' son, Detlef, a tall, skinny boy my age with glasses, attended the *Gymnasium* in Bergheim together with Jochen Krienke.

Since he lived right next door, Detlef and I often spent time together, kicking around a soccer ball or climbing trees. But more often than not, his mother would call him back inside to do his homework.

"Just ten more minutes!" Detlef would beg.

"Günter may have plenty of time to play," she'd reply with a pitying glance in my direction, "but *Gymnasium* students have to knuckle down!"

****

Jochen, Detlef, and I were all taking confirmation classes in a large room annexed to the side of Pastor Kampe's house. But on Wednesday evenings the chairs were pushed back and the classroom was transformed into a clubhouse for the Lutheran Youth Group. Under the supervision of Erwin Landmann, an eighteen-year-old *Gymnasium* student, the twenty-two of us boys, ranging in age from twelve to sixteen, learned hiking songs, played board games, and challenged one another to table tennis matches. But when the group went off on weekend bicycle trips, I was left behind. I didn't own a bike and even if I had owned one, I wouldn't have had any idea how to ride it.

Of all people, it was my father who came to my rescue. He had bought an old bicycle frame, a pair of second hand wheels, new inner tubes, and an old handlebar. In the little bit of spare time that he had, he built me a bike and with surprising patience spent time each evening teaching me to ride while Mutti and Hubert cheered me on.

Over the next few days I practiced in the driveway. Time after time I would wobble along unsteadily for a few meters before tipping over. Before long, my knees were badly scraped and my elbows were bleeding. As if this weren't humiliating enough, Detlef would always manage to come outside to laugh at me.

"I can't believe my eyes," he heckled as I picked myself up for yet another attempt. "You're the oldest boy I ever saw who didn't know how to ride a bike!"

"I'd like to see how you'd do if you'd lived in a refugee camp like me!"

"Oh, c'mon. Don't get your nose all out of joint," he said. "I figure ten more crashes like that one and you'll get the hang of it."

And then, before I could reply, he scooted off behind the church.

****

Over the first long vacation of the school term, our Youth Group left for a camping trip in Lohmar an der Agger, a village in a hilly area some twenty kilometers southeast of Cologne. Pastor Kampe hired a truck that we loaded with tents, stakes, spades, hammers, pots and pans, and rucksacks before clambering aboard ourselves. The pastor led the way in his old Audi.

We pitched our tents on the outskirts of town, lit a roaring campfire, and at a safe distance, dug a latrine. Our huge triangular tents were like the Indian teepees described in the *Billy Jenkins* stories, with a narrow opening at the top to let out the smoke. One tent was set aside for cooking.

The first two days went smoothly. We took hikes, cooked soup, and sang songs around the campfire. The following night brought heavy rain, and with it, colder temperatures. Three days later it was still raining when the pastor drove off to spend the weekend in Zieverich so that he could deliver his Sunday sermon. He left our group's leader, Erwin Landmann, in charge.

During the day, we huddled together in our tents, struggling to keep warm and dry. But the firewood was as wet as we were and we choked on the heavy smoke. The nights were even worse. Very few of the boys had sleeping bags; some boys slept on thin pieces of canvas; the rest of us lay on a "blanket" of twigs that barely covered the rain-soaked ground. No one stayed up to stoke the fires and as the last of the embers from the fires in our tents died away, we were chilled right down to the bone.

It was hardly surprising that most of us caught colds. But one boy, Karl-Heinz, a refugee from the Sudetenland, developed a hacking cough and soon was too weak to walk to the cooking tent. As we took turns bringing him hot soup and bread, I noticed that Erwin Landmann was constantly scanning the road for the pastor's Audi. When Pastor Kampe finally returned, he carried Karl-Heinz to his car, wrapped him in the dry blanket he kept on the back seat, and drove off with him to the Maria-Hilf Hospital in Bergheim, leaving the rest of us behind in the rain.

The day the sun came out was the day the truck arrived to bring us all home.

"I'll tell you about it tomorrow," I said to my parents and Hubert as I wolfed down my supper that evening, "but right now I want to lie down on a warm, dry bed." Not five minutes after we cleared away the table and stools and set up my cot, I was sound asleep, dreaming of *Billy Jenkins* and the hardships of the frontier.

When I came home from school a few days later, Mutti sat me down next to her on the couch. "I just heard some terrible news. It's about Karl-Heinz. You know, the boy Pastor Kampe took to the hospital. He died of pneumonia this afternoon." She paused to let her words sink in.

"I hope people aren't blaming Erwin Landmann," I finally said. "He did his best."

Mutti shook her head. "No, not Erwin. From what I hear, people are blaming the pastor."

****

The following Sunday my father was about to leave for work at twenty minutes to nine while Mutti, Hubert and I were dressing for church.

"I don't know why you waste your time with that church," my father said, "especially after what just happened. I'll bet it'll be extra crowded today, what with everyone wondering what the pastor will say about the boy's death." He paused. "He can't just ignore it."

At that moment, our bell rang. Mutti and I went to the window to see who it was. Two young men were waiting outside. Both were wearing suits but neither had on a necktie. They were each carrying a Bible.

"I think it's those Seventh-Day Adventists that people have been telling me about," Mutti whispered.

That was enough for my father. As the color rose in his cheeks and the veins on his neck bulged, he stormed out into the hallway and pulled open the front door. The young men took two steps back.

"Who the hell do you think you are, disturbing my family on a Sunday morning?" my father screamed. "Don't ever come back! Is that clear?" He clenched his right fist. "Next time I won't waste my time talking!"

As the young men beat a hasty retreat, the door of the Poltermann apartment flew open and Miss Leichtsinn stuck out her head. She was wearing a gauzy pink nightgown. "Is everything all right?"

Mr. Poltermann, uncombed and still in his pajamas, joined her. "I saw the whole thing from my front window. Great job, Herr Nitsch! You showed them! They woke us up, too. Next time it'll be my turn to deal with them."

My father grinned. "Maybe we can both go at them together," he said, and with that, he grabbed his briefcase and headed off to the pastry shop.

Mr. Poltermann turned to Mutti, who was still standing in the hallway fighting back tears. "No need to be upset, Frau Nitsch," he said soothingly. "That's the only sure way to get rid of fanatical blabbermouths like that. Have a nice day!"

Mutti shut the door behind her and turned to face Hubert and me. "I sometimes feel like crawling into a hole when your father explodes like that," she said. Her hands were shaking. "I hope with all my heart that the two of you never develop his temper."

Apart from a brief eulogy, Pastor Kampe didn't mention the boy who died. Instead he launched into a lengthy oration on Leviticus 19:18: "Do not seek revenge or bear a grudge against one of your people, but love your neighbor as yourself. I am the LORD." As he spoke, I thought about Karl-Heinz shivering with pneumonia in his tent. I thought about my father's verbal assault on the Seventh-Day Adventists, but I especially thought about Mr. Poltermann in his pajamas and Miss Leichtsinn in her sheer pink nightgown. It was the first time I couldn't really concentrate on what Pastor Kampe had to say.

CHAPTER 6

*A*fter the disastrous camping trip, it was hard to settle back down in school but I forced myself to study hard so that I would be ready when the time came for the Commercial School entrance exam. Still, I couldn't help envying Jochen Krienke. At the *Gymnasium* he had a different teacher for almost every subject and there were only twenty-four students in each class, in contrast to the fifty-four children in the one large room set aside for the fifth through eighth grades in my elementary school. Even so, I was glad I didn't have to take Latin, which Jochen hated just as much as Detlef Kampe did.

When I mentioned Jochen's complaints about his Latin homework to my father, he grinned. "I'm glad you don't study that stuff. The Romans are all dead anyhow. So why bother?"

But no matter which school we were attending, all of us were given a day off on the 24th of May.

"It's a Catholic holy day," Mr. Reitberg explained.

"What for?" the boy behind me called out.

Mr. Reitberg glared. "Freischmidt! Where are your manners? Raise your hand if you want to talk to me. And if I call on you, you stand up and say, 'Excuse me, Herr Reitberg.' Then, and only then, may you ask your question." He tapped his pencil impatiently against his desk. "Well?"

Freischmidt's face was red as a beet as he slowly raised his hand.

"Yes, Freischmidt, what is it?" our teacher barked. "On your feet! Speak up!"

"Excuse me, Herr Reitberg," Freischmidt mumbled. "What kind of holiday are they celebrating on Thursday?"

"It's called Corpus Christi," Reitberg snapped, and left it at that.

I walked home from school with Wilfried Plath, a refugee boy from Pomerania whose family lived on the second floor of the scrap dealer's half-finished cinder block house in Zieverich. We both slowed down to give Wilfried's twin sister, Erika, a chance to catch up to us.

"Do either of you know what Corpus Christi is all about?" I asked.

"Beats me," Wilfried confessed.

Erika shook her head. "We've been living in Zieverich less than a year so we weren't around for the last one. But I hear there'll be some sort of a procession."

****

On Thursday morning, it looked as though the entire population of Zieverich was walking down Aachener Strasse in the direction of Bergheim. Curious, I joined them. A roadblock had been set up at the Aachener Tor, diverting all of the Cologne-bound auto traffic away from the main street. Only pedestrians were allowed to pass through the city gate. In the center of Bergheim several thousand people, all dressed in their Sunday best, lined the sidewalks, craning their necks to the left.

From my spot along the curb in front of Café Meyer, I could just barely make out the start of the procession. At first I thought it was a band of women, but as it got closer, I realized that the people in the ornate robes were actually priests. Following them were young boys in gowns so long they dusted the pavement. They were swinging ornate silver containers that gave off fragrant puffs of smoke.

But the priest who got all of the attention was bearing an ornate cross. Around the cross metal spokes gleamed like the golden rays of the sun. As he passed us, followed by a crowd of worshippers, the people all around me fell to their knees and made the sign of the cross. I was the only one left standing.

"Show some respect," a white-haired lady next to me whispered as she reached up and tugged on my sleeve.

Somewhere behind me, a boy shouted, "Eh, you with the fat head! Get down!"

There it was again. The dreaded mention of my large head. I had first been called Fathead in Plötzin in East Germany and then again during the nearly two years I'd lived in the Ammo refugee camp outside Bodenteich in Lower Saxony. But never, until that moment, had anyone said it in Bergheim.

I pulled away from the old lady, and trying hard not to cry, I somehow made my way home by weaving through the crowd. In the past, Mutti had often reassured me that my head was in perfect proportion to my body, but how could I believe her now?

The next day I ran into Mrs. van Knippenberg in the hallway, and leaving out the Fathead part, I told her what had happened at the procession. "So, if you wouldn't mind, since you're Catholic, I thought maybe you could explain what the holiday was all about."

"I don't suppose you met many Catholics growing up in East Prussia," she began.

"There was a Polish scrap dealer in the Ammo Camp in Bodenteich who may have been Catholic. That's about all that I know of."

"Well, in this area it's always been just the other way around. But now that refugees are moving in, we really have to learn to live together. Don't you agree?" I nodded. Then Mrs. van Knippenberg went on to explain that the smoke was from the incense used in the Catholic Mass and that the priest was carrying a consecrated wafer symbolizing the body of the Lord Jesus. "To us Catholics, the wafer is a very sacred thing," she added. "So Günter, should you ever see a procession like that again, I'd suggest that if everyone else kneels down, you should too. You will, won't you?"

"Yes, and thank you for the advice, Frau van Knippenberg." I replied, but I wasn't sure I would.

****

News travels fast in a town like Bergheim. The next morning as I headed up the hill to the elementary school, four boys blocked the way.

"Is this the guy?" one of them asked, grabbing hold of my shoulder.

"Yeah, that's him! He was standing right in front of me."

"Let's teach him a lesson!" Without further warning, the largest of the four punched me with full force just above my elbow.

"You've been warned," the gang leader snapped as I rubbed my sore arm. "Are you listening to me, you stinking refugee?"

"Yes," I murmured. It was four against one and I didn't stand a chance.

Even worse was yet to come. During recess, I saw the same four boys on the Catholic side of the chain link fence that separated our smaller Lutheran play area from theirs. They were pointing in my direction and whispering. I was sure they were talking about me and I tried my best to ignore them.

"Eh, Fathead, how's your arm?" the shortest of them yelled through the fence, loud enough for everyone to hear.

I cringed as Gottwald, a twelve-year old from my class picked up the cue. "Hey," he shrieked. "Fathead! What a great nickname! It goes with your huge noggin."

And once again, the name stuck.

****

That night over supper when I described my encounter with the Catholic boys, my father stared at me in disbelief. I expected him to bawl me out for not fighting back but I was mistaken.

"Do you mean to tell me that the school yard has a small separate area for you and a larger area for the Catholics divided by a wire fence?"

Mutti answered for me. "Willi, you didn't know that?"

"It's the first I've heard of it and it's absolutely outrageous! It was bad enough that they make you boys go to school in Bergheim. But this nonsense with the fence! It's like living in the Middle Ages. Who dreams up this crap? Is it the local clergy? They're a bunch of damn hypocrites! I don't know how the people around here can live with themselves."

However strongly my father felt about the locals, Mr. Poltermann outdid him. Late one afternoon, he cornered Mutti, Hubert and me in the entrance hall.

"The people in this area are really stupid," he began in a voice so loud the van Knippenbergs must certainly have heard him upstairs in their apartment. "They can't even speak proper German, just that awful *Kölsch* dialect. If they ever get as far as Cologne, they think they've been around the world. And when they take a bus excursion, where do they are go? To the shrine at Kevelaer, that's where!"

Mutti tried to get a word in edgewise, "I'm sorry to disagree with you, but…"

Mr. Poltermann ignored her and kept right on talking. "It's inbreeding, that's what it is. Think about it. Every tenth person you meet in Bergheim is named Schmitz. And all their children are named either Joseph or Maria. They don't even have any imagination! These people ought to thank God that we refugees came here to bring in some new blood."

"That's not exactly why we came here," Mutti protested. "Are you forgetting that we had no homes to go back to and they took us in?"

"Say whatever you like," Mr. Poltermann continued. "For hundreds of years all kinds of people settled in the Eastern provinces – Russians, Poles, Jews, Austrians, Dutch, Huguenots, and Lithuanians. We got the best genes from everyone. That's the reason why we're smarter and have more damn fire in our bellies than these lazy half-wits."

Mutti shook her head. "I should point out that the Russians came one time too many. That's why we can't go back to East Prussia."

"I'll give you that," Mr. Poltermann conceded reluctantly.

"Anyway, you don't really believe this nonsense do you, about the locals I mean?"

"You bet I do! I'll give you an example. Just the other day I went to my father-in-law's house in Fortuna. He works a twelve-hour shift in the mine and his wife wasn't home. So I used my spare key to let myself in. There was a frying pan on the stove and lying in the pan was a note my mother-in-law had left for her husband." He took out a pencil and scribbled a few words on a piece of paper. "This is what it said."

We studied the paper he held out to Mutti: "Fix yoself sum egs, but dont eet dem awl."

When we'd all had time to decipher the message, Mr. Poltermann continued. "First I laughed about the spelling and then I decided to fix some of those eggs for myself. But guess how many eggs I found in the fridge? One. One lousy egg. The poor slob works twelve hours and doesn't even get a proper dinner. I tell you, if I were him, I'd send my wife right to hell. Not that he doesn't give her grief. I've seen him stagger in late on a Friday and mumble that he lost his paycheck in the pub." We heard someone on the staircase. Mr. Poltermann grinned. "I've got to go. Let's continue this discussion some other time."

It was Miss Lemm who had come down. After we greeted her, we went into our room and closed the door.

Mutti sat us both down. "Isn't he something else? I'm never sure when he's joking and when he's serious. But he was wrong to say those things about the native Rhinelanders. Sure they talk a bit funny, but so did your Oma and Opa back home in East Prussia."

"His in-laws don't sound like the brightest bulbs," I commented.

"Well, that may be so. But it's certainly no reason to assume that everyone else around here is just as ignorant." She glanced over at the alarm clock on the shelf over the sink and jumped up. "Six o'clock already! I'd better get started on supper before your father comes home."

CHAPTER 7

*T*he routine was always the same. My father left for work at four in the morning Tuesday through Saturday and around eight-thirty on Sundays. He often worked Mondays too, even though that was his official day off, but he usually got home in time to join us for our evening meal of lard and bacon or bologna sandwiches. I would have liked to talk to my parents during supper about my school day. I'm sure that Hubert felt the same way. But somehow, my father always managed to steer our conversation to Mr. Meyer's pastry shop.

"I don't know how long I can last there," he would grumble. "Meyer knows how good I am, but he watches over me like a hawk."

For the first time, I understood exactly what he meant. That afternoon I had stopped by the pastry shop to pick up my father's laundry. He was just about to pour a warm gelatin coating over five fruit tarts when Mr. Meyer walked over to my father and said, "When the sales rep comes by tomorrow, be sure he adds five dozen extra cans of pineapple. I've just lined up orders for two weddings." As he talked he reached into one of the fruit tarts and clawed out three tiny bananas. "We can't make a profit if we pile on the fruit like that. Just cut them in half lengthwise."

"But Herr Meyer, they're so small. I didn't want them to look skimpy."

Mr. Meyer was busy extricating the bananas from the second tart. "I repeat, half slices from now on."

"Günter saw what happened," my father fumed as we started our supper. "Meyer's an idiot sometimes. I had to heat up more gelatin and start from scratch, as if I had nothing else to do. I know my stuff! I'll bet he was still doing his apprenticeship when I had my own pastry shop in Königsberg."

"But that was before the war," Mutti would remind him. "Times are different now. At least he's hired that policeman's son to help you."

"Rudi Meinertz?" My father shook his head. "I wanted a journeyman, someone with real experience. And what do I get? A beginner, an apprentice, someone who can't even talk without stuttering!"

"But you've told me that he's a hard worker so he must be some help."

"I guess so. The poor guy does work hard," he reluctantly admitted.

Even though my father knew next to nothing about soccer, on Monday nights he always turned to the sports section first to check the Toto soccer betting results. As Hubert and I helped Mutti clear the table, he would reach over to take the latest issue of the *Kölner Stadt-Anzeiger* from his briefcase and mumble, "Well, let's see if my ship has come in." Since winnings depended on the weekend scores from the German Soccer League, he would carefully compare his two Mark betting slip with the actual outcome of the games. Except for the two times when he won three Marks, he always tossed the paper down in disgust. "*Scheisse!* Lost again!" A few minutes later he would be fast asleep on the couch.

The following Monday was different. Even before we sat down, he waved the newspaper at us. "You're not going to believe this. Rudi Meinertz's father just won 384,000 Deutschmarks in the Toto! Can you imagine? No one's ever won a prize like that. The lucky bastard!"

"How's Rudi taking it?" Mutti asked. "His head must be spinning!"

"He didn't even bother to show up for work today and I don't think he'll be coming back."

"Of course he will. Even rich people go to work; besides, he needs to be trained for a job. That money won't last forever."

Mutti was wrong. The next day Rudi came into the pastry shop and quit his job.

"So I'm back to doing it all on my own," my father said with a sigh. "Meyer's not likely to replace him. The funny thing is, despite all that money, I actually feel sorry for Rudi. He's only two years older than you are, Günter. That's way too young to quit training for a skilled job, and I've got to admit, even though Rudi had some problems, he caught on fast. I'm pretty sure I could have made a good pastry chef out of him if he'd only stuck it out."

CHAPTER 8

When our summer vacation started in the middle of July, I made up my mind to spend part of my free time working to improve my grades. Mr. Poltermann continued to offer me an assortment of books from the lending library and Mutti helped me select the best ones to read in preparation for the upcoming school admission test.

Mutti also gave me another kind of assignment. Every evening for as long as she could remember, Mrs. van Knippenberg had walked the half-kilometer to the Grootendieck farm to fetch two liters of milk. But now she was so crippled with arthritis that she could no longer go that short distance.

"She was wondering whether you'd be willing to get the milk for her," Mutti explained. "She even offered to pay you for doing it."

"Sure!" I agreed. "It'd be nice to do something for Frau van Knippenberg for a change."

"Actually, you can do something for us at the same time. This morning I had a nice chat with Frau Grootendieck and she and I made a deal at a very fair price. So when you go, you can pick up two liters for us, too. She'll expect you to bring the money for the van Knippenbergs and for us once a week on Saturdays."

"Should I start tonight?"

"Sure, off you go!" As I reached the door, she called me back. "Of course, I told Frau van Knippenberg that she docsn't have to pay you anything for fetching the milk for her since you have to go anyhow. You understand that, don't you?"

"That's fine with me."

A short time later I was standing in Mrs. Grootendieck's kitchen waiting for her to fill two large aluminum jugs with milk. Through the wide door on the far side of the room I had a good view of the living room where the furniture sat somewhat unevenly on two thick layers of mismatched carpets, one piled on top of the other. Mrs. Grootendieck explained that the carpets came from cash-strapped customers who used them to barter in exchange for meat, butter, and milk. During the following weeks, whenever I delivered the milk to Mrs. van Knippenberg, I would report on the latest addition to the pile of carpets. Eventually, there were six of them on the stack, of all different sizes. And nearly every time I stopped by, Mrs. van Knippenberg would reward me for my help with a slice of cake. Sometimes she even slipped a fifty-pfennig coin into my pocket. "Don't tell your mother," she'd say with a wink. "Let this be our little secret!"

****

Summer also gave me the chance to get better acquainted with the neighborhood boys who attended other schools. One of them was Dieter Henkelmann, whose father administered the Schlenderhan stud farm directly across the street from us. The Henkelmann family lived in a spacious brick residence attached to one of the stables.

Mr. Henkelmann was a slim, muscular, mean-spirited man with buckteeth. His wife was decidedly overweight. She had a double chin and her squinty eyes were set deep within her pudgy face. Mr. Henkelmann was a man of few words. Mrs. Henkelmann prattled endlessly in a high-pitched voice. Their marriage was not a happy one.

During the school term, Dieter commuted by train to the Middle School in Kerpen and when he got back home, his parents forced him to stay in his room while he did his homework. But during summer vacation he was allowed to spend more time outside.

To earn some extra spending money, Dieter, Jochen Krienke, and I scoured the garbage dump next to the Aachener Tor for scrap metal. On nice days we sometimes rode our bikes out into the countryside, or we went for a swim in the swirling waters of the Erft River floodgate near the five hundred year old mill where Jochen's family lived. And of course, we traded stories.

"My father was a cook in the *Luftwaffe* so he didn't see any real combat 'til the last few months of the war," I confided.

"Then I suppose he goes easy on you and Hubert," Dieter replied. "My old man was a Master Sergeant in the cavalry and he's got a nasty temper. It doesn't take much for him to beat the crap out of me with his riding whip. He even hits my little sister."

"You're wrong about my father. He smacks Hubert and me all the time. And if he owned a whip, he'd probably use it. I think it was the war that made them so mean."

Jochen spoke up. "You can't blame the war. Just look at my dad. He was a Major in the cavalry so he saw action the whole time. Then after he came back home, he got arrested when some Communist in our village tipped off the East German authorities that he'd been an officer. He spent the next six months in the jail run by the Soviet secret police in Bautzen and then another four years in a Russian work camp. I admit he's no angel, and he loves his liquor, but he's never hit my sisters and me." He shook his head firmly. "Not once."

****

My parents and Dieter Henkelmann's parents didn't socialize much. But the Krienkes soon became our close friends. Since our room was too small to accommodate everyone, the four of us would walk over to their place whenever we got together. The first time I met Mr. Krienke he gave me a firm handshake and a friendly pat on the back. I liked him instantly. He always had a twinkle in his eye, and it was clear to see, he was still deeply in love with his dark-haired wife Elli. Mutti called Mr. Krienke "a gentleman of the old school."

When he went to work, Mr. Krienke carried himself with the rigid posture of a Prussian military officer, in keeping with his position as the supervisor of the German security staff at the Belgian barracks in nearby Ichendorf. He got a fresh buzz cut at the base barbershop every week. But on his days off, he switched to casual clothes and didn't mind getting dirt under his fingernails and grease on his shirt. He knew something about everything: carpentry, cabinetmaking, house painting, gardening, and especially, auto mechanics. He went on endless quests for spare parts for his thirty-year-old jalopy and spent up to eight hours at a time tinkering under the hood until the engine started up, only to have the old wreck sputter to a stop after an hour or two. This explains why he always rode his bicycle to work. But no one is perfect. As Jochen had mentioned, his father loved his wine, cognac, and beer. When he got tipsy, he would cheerfully regale us with war stories.

"I knew Hitler and his big-shot staff were a bunch of morons," he always said. "And when they decided to invade Russia, I knew that was the beginning of the end!" Then he would take another swig of cognac. "Did I ever tell you about the time in occupied France when we liberated a castle?" And then, as always, without waiting for a reply, he would retell the story for the umpteenth time. "We all took as many bottles of wine as we could carry from the wine cellar, and the next morning…" he paused to build up the suspense even though we all knew what was coming, "the next morning *I brushed my teeth with red wine!*"

CHAPTER 9

*J*ust before school reopened in the fall, the boys' and girls'
Lutheran youth groups joined up for a weeklong religious retreat
in Blankenheim, a small town in the Eifel Mountains. The leaders of
the boys were again Erwin Landmann and Pastor Kampe. The leader of
the girls was Traute Willig, who taught Lutheran religion and German
literature at the *Gymnasium* in Bergheim.

The sixty of us grudgingly attended daily Bible classes and hymn-
singing sessions. In our free time we wandered the streets of the town,
admired the half-timbered houses and the castle, went for swims in
a crater lake, and took hikes. But the highlight for all of us was the
food – three meals a day in the dining hall and snacks of hot chocolate
and cake in the afternoon. At lights out we climbed under the covers
in our bunk beds; Alfred Unruh, Detlef Kampe, and I appreciated the
comforts of life.

"You don't know how good you have it," I told our friend, Lothar
Moser, who had not been with us on the ill-fated, rain-soaked trip to
Lohmar.

Still, after two days, we were bored silly.

"We've been leaving camp to get some excitement," Lothar confided
to Alfred and me that evening when Detlef had gone to wash up. "But
the real action is right in front of our noses."

"What do you mean?" Alfred asked.

"My sister tipped me off to keep an eye on Pastor Kampe and Traute Willig. All the girls are talking about how the two of them always manage to slip off together after supper."

"C'mon," Alfred protested. "She's half his age! And ugly, too!"

"Yeah, but she sure has a good figure!"

"So you really think there's hanky-panky?" Alfred still looked doubtful.

"Why don't you watch and see?"

It was true. Once we'd finished the evening meal, Traute Willig would put an older girl in charge of the girls and Erwin Landmann was left in charge of the boys. Then the pastor and Traute Willig would go off on long walks together, or they would drive away in Pastor's car, returning long after sunset. Of course, there was no proof that anything was going on between them. As Alfred put it, "They could just be discussing the next day's Bible lesson."

But I wasn't willing to give Pastor Kampe and Traute Willig the benefit of the doubt. There was something about the way the two of them acted when they were together that reminded me of how my father flirted with the shopgirls in the bakery or how he had charmed the baggage claim clerk in the Uelzen railroad station right after we crossed the East German border to join him. I couldn't put my finger on it exactly. I just knew it was there.

The gossip spread like wildfire on our return from the retreat, but none of our mothers believed it. Of all of the women attending Bible study with Pastor Kampe, Mutti was perhaps the most adamant. "You should know better than to listen to those silly girls," she scolded. "Pastor is a wonderful person and I don't want to hear another word about it!"

"Mutti's right," my father was quick to add. "What did the girls actually *see*? Nothing. It's all in their imaginations." I wanted to protest that you had to have *been there*, but I bit my tongue.

51

A few days later Pastor Kampe offered Mutti a job at the church.

"You see what a good person he is?" she gloated. "He knew we could use some extra spending money and he came through for us."

Mutti was responsible for cleaning the inside of the church after every service, baptism, wedding, and funeral, as well as for sweeping the front churchyard, once a week in the summer, winter and spring, and twice a week when the leaves were down in the autumn. On winter mornings she was supposed to shovel briquettes into the basement furnace between 6 A.M. and 8 A.M. to warm up the building before the congregation arrived. In return, she received sixty-five Deutschmarks a month. Compared to what my father was making it was only a drop in the bucket but every little bit helped.

To my surprise, even though Sunday was the only work day when he could sleep a little later, my father offered to help Mutti with the furnace in the winter.

"It's a man's job," he said. "When the time comes I'll shovel in the briquettes at 6 A.M. and 7 A.M., but Günter has to take on the 8 A.M. shift when I leave for work." In addition to promising to help my father with the briquettes, I volunteered to help by raking the gravel during the summer, sweeping away the leaves during the fall, and shoveling snow during the winter in the front churchyard.

"What can I do?" Hubert asked, obviously feeling left out.

I glanced over at his flabby arms and knew he couldn't do any heavy lifting. "You can make sure I don't miss any of the leaves," I replied with a sympathetic smile.

****

When I came home from school a few weeks later, Mr. van Knippenberg was talking with Mutti in the entrance hall.

"I certainly understand how you feel, Frau Nitsch," he was saying. "Crowded together like that in one little room. But keep in mind that the sixteen thousand refugees who arrived here in the last five years increased the local population by nearly twenty percent. And they keep on coming. We've got the jobs they need: soft coal mining, power plants, sugar beet farms, textiles, linoleum, the Arminius AG chemical plant. So, of course, we have a housing crisis."

Mutti sighed. "You're right, Herr van Knippenberg. We just have to make the best of things under the circumstances."

Mr. van Knippenberg lowered his voice. "Are the Poltermanns home?"

"No, I don't think so."

"Then I can speak my mind. I've got nothing against those people, mind you. Frau Poltermann is a charming lady and her husband is an excellent businessman. But his behavior sometimes...I won't go into details, but I'm sure we understand each other, Frau Nitsch. My wife and I have often talked about how much better off we'd all be in this house if the Poltermanns would move out and your family could have their apartment. But perhaps I've already said too much. Good afternoon, Frau Nitsch."

"I know just what you mean, Herr van Knippenberg. Please give your wife my regards!"

****

When the four of us sat down to supper Mutti repeated the conversation she'd had with Mr. van Knippenberg. "First the hint from Herr Meyer and now from him. I don't know where they're getting the idea that the Poltermanns may be moving out, but it sure would be nice to have the extra space."

"He's certainly right about the housing shortage," my father agreed.

"What about Pastor Kampe?" I suddenly blurted out.

"What on earth does he have to do with this?" Mutti asked.

I knew I was on dangerous ground so I chose my words carefully. "Every Sunday just before the ushers come down for the collection, he reminds us that 'God loves a cheerful giver'. Well, why doesn't he practice what he preaches? Fifteen people live in our half of the house but on his side, it's just the Pastor with his wife and Detlef. They have plenty of room to take in a few more."

Mutti had heard me out with a stony face, but now she exploded. "That's enough now. Hold it right there. How dare you talk that way about Pastor Kampe! He needs the extra space for his work for the church: the youth groups, confirmation classes, my Bible study. It's outrageous to compare his situation to ours. This subject is closed. I don't want to hear another word about it. Is that understood?"

"Yes Mutti, but…"

"No buts, this is it!"

"Yes, Mutti."

I glanced over at my father who looked torn. Uncertain with whom to side, he chose to keep silent. Later that evening I lay awake thinking about the injustice of our situation. Surely Pastor Kampe's family had some space to spare. As I fell asleep, my mind drifted back to the rumors about Pastor Kampe and Traute Willig in Blankenheim. Mutti could think whatever she wanted, but in my book at least, the man was certainly no angel.

****

If I had my doubts about Pastor Kampe's character, my opinion of his son was even worse, and with good reason. Whenever Detlef showed up, trouble followed. One day when I was helping Mutti in the laundry room, we heard a series of sharp pings coming from the backyard. Through the window we could see Mutti's wooden clothespins split apart and fly off the line. I threw open the backdoor and looked up. Sure enough, there was Detlef, leaning out of a second-story window, shooting air rifle pellets over the wall. He gave me a smart salute before ducking back inside.

"His parents let him get away with everything," Mutti complained to my father.

"You know what they say about pastors' children," he replied with a chuckle. "They never amount to anything good."

I shook my head. "I don't think it's funny. Anyway, shooting clothespins is bad, but what he does to me some Sunday mornings is even worse. The whole congregation thinks I'm an idiot."

Mutti nodded. "You mean with the church bell? I can't believe he gets away with that!"

In addition to my other chores, Pastor Kampe had asked me to ring the huge church bell for the ten minutes before the service started on Sunday mornings. This wasn't an easy job. The heavy bell with its long thick rope was set high in the steeple out of sight. The rope's loose end started out curled at my feet on the platform where I stood. At the appointed time, I would pull down on the rope; this action caused my feet to lift off the floor as the weight of the bell pulled the rope back up. Once the rope reached its highest point, I would repeat the process. Sometimes I had to repeat these steps as many as ten times before the bell made any sound. After that, it was easy to keep it swinging enough to produce a steady rhythmic clang.

It was strictly against the rules to pull on the rope when it was half way up or half way down since this caused the bell to ring wildly out of control. The problem was that every so often, the pastor asked his son to help me, and whenever Detlef came into the tower, he managed to "help" by intentionally pulling on the rope at the wrong time. When he and I came back down, I would slink into the pew next to Hubert and Mutti as half the congregation glared at me. Detlef, on the other hand, looked as innocent as a newborn baby as he proudly took his seat up front next to his mother.

CHAPTER 10

*T*he railroad line ran behind our house, less than half a kilometer beyond the stone wall surrounding our backyard. In February 1952, two months after my fourteenth birthday, I walked to the Zieverich station and waited in the cold for the local train to Horrem, which was thirteen kilometers away. The dreaded day of the Commercial School entrance exam had arrived. The half-day test would cover a wide range of subjects: math, geography, and German history, together with a long essay to evaluate my writing skills. A few days earlier Mutti had told my father about my plans, and to my relief, he had supported me. But now I worried about letting both of them down if I were to fail.

Once at the school, I squeezed into one of the few remaining seats in the third row just as the proctor started passing out the questions.

"Psst, G-g--ünter," someone whispered behind me. "How-how d-d-do you feel about this t-t-test?" Before I turned around I knew it was Rudi Meinertz, my father's former apprentice at the bakery. He grinned at me.

"I wish it was over with! Good luck!"

"G-g-good l-l-luck to you!"

Each part of the test was handed out separately. After tackling the essay, struggling with the math problems, and doing my best to handle

56

the history section, the proctor started to distribute the geography questions. He had passed my row and Rudi's and was still working his way to the back of the room. Meanwhile, Rudi had glanced over the question sheet. He tapped me on the shoulder.

"Quick, t-t-tell me, when going from C-c-cologne to K-k-königsberg does one g-g-go v-v-via M-m-munich?"

I shook my head. "Via Berlin! Not Munich, Berlin!" I whispered. Poor Rudy. At least he'd remembered that Königsberg was my hometown. He probably had even less of a chance to pass than I did.

"Silence!" the proctor screamed. "Anyone who talks from now on will automatically fail the exam!"

I hunkered down and finished the test. After handing in my answer sheet and boarding the train for the return trip, I ignored the other boys and girls who were playing cards or whooping it up in celebration. My heart was heavy with a sense of impending doom. I was convinced that I had flunked.

Two weeks later during recess I overheard two girls saying that they'd received acceptance letters from the Commercial School. Within minutes, a small circle of jubilant students, Catholic as well as Lutheran, had gathered along both sides of the playground fence. All of them were about to start the new term together in Horrem in April. Although the boys would be in one classroom and the girls in another, for that morning at least, they were joined together as one happy incoming class.

My feet dragged as I walked home alone. *It was probably the math problems that did me in*, I thought to myself as I crossed the bridge over the Erft River. *I never could get the hang of them.* Mutti was standing on the sidewalk waiting for me, waving the letter clutched in her hand. "Why so glum? You're in! Congratulations!" and she gave me a hug.

"Are you sure? Let me see!" My hands were shaking as I took the letter from her and read it over slowly.

"Oh, and I almost forgot," Mutti added as we walked along the front path together. "I hope you don't mind but I already told the van

Knippenbergs, and guess what? Herr van Knippenberg said since you'll need a quiet place to study, they've offered to let you sit at their dining room table to do your homework, provided Frau van Knippenberg is home and they don't have visitors."

****

For the next two months I relished the thought of transferring to the Commercial School. Then reality set in. In addition to the subjects I'd been studying in the elementary school, my course load would now include accounting, business administration, algebra, merchandizing, English, economic geography, industrial arts, typing, and stenography. And the competition with my classmates would be stiff. Because my education had been interrupted during the years I'd spent in Russian-occupied East Prussia, I had only had a total of four years of schooling up to that point. All of the other boys had spent twice as long in elementary school. Some had even attended the *Gymnasium* for four or five years before being expelled for failing grades in Latin or advanced math.

There was one glimmer of hope. Rudi Meinertz had also passed the test. If he can make it, I said to myself, then I have a chance. Rudi's arrival at the school on a brand new motorcycle created a sensation. His departure at the end of the five-hour school day was even more dramatic. As all of us approached the Bahnhofplatz, he would screech to a stop. Letting the motor run, he would stand proudly alongside his gleaming motorcycle surrounded by a bevy of admiring girls, one of whom, if she were lucky, would be offered a ride home.

Our teachers were Mr. Blum, who taught English; Mrs. Roda, who taught German literature; Herr Direktor Müllmann, who taught mathematics, and Herr Dr. Knops, our homeroom teacher, who taught the remaining subjects. In addition, the Catholic students had one hour of religious instruction a week with Chaplain Fuchs. During that time the rest of us had a study hall.

Herr Direktor Müllmann was a redheaded man with a substantial paunch and a thick pink neck. If he and I stood side by side, the top of his head didn't quite reach my shoulders. With fingers the shape of small sausages he constantly tugged at his collar as if he were struggling for air. Despite his porcine shape (or perhaps because of it) he delighted in making sarcastic remarks about the appearance of the students in his classes.

Math with Herr Direktor Müllmann was the ultimate torture. For the students who had been to the *Gymnasium*, algebra was a breeze. But to me the jumble of numbers and letters just didn't make sense. One day four weeks into the term we had our first test. Herr Direktor Müllmann returned the graded papers. Four boys had failed. I was one of them.

"So, Nitsch," he growled after I'd had a chance to glance over my results. "Tell the class how you should have solved question number six."

I shook my head. "I still don't know, Herr Direktor Müllmann."

"Well, then, I'll show you!" Striding briskly to the back of the classroom, he grabbed me by the hair and pulled me out of my seat. Still firmly gripping my hair, he yanked me down to his level. Then he led me to the blackboard, all the while reciting a little rhyme:

"There was a man in Syria land

Who led a camel by the hand"

When we reached the front of the classroom, he released me while he wrote a formula on the board. Poking me in the chest with a pudgy finger, he shrieked, "Do you get it now?"

"I think so," I stammered.

Müllmann's eyes narrowed. "No you don't, you idiot! You're lying!" and he smacked me hard across my face. Then, reaching up, he grabbed me again by my hair, and while repeating the same awful camel ditty, he paraded me back to my seat past my horrified classmates.

CHAPTER 11

*T*o reward me for helping out at the church, my father decided to give me an allowance of five Deutschmarks a month out of the money Mutti earned.

"That way you won't have to scrounge for scrap metal to earn a few pfennigs," he explained. "Your mother and I are always jittery when you boys rummage around in the swamp over by the railroad tracks. There are bound to be a few unexploded bombs buried under there."

"We don't look in the swamp that much. We've had much more luck in the garbage dump on the left side of the Aachener Tor."

"I don't want you digging around there either!"

"Vati's right," Mutti added. "I already spent two years worrying that you'd blow yourself up in the Ammo Camp in Bodenteich. Let's not start again here!"

Despite the restrictions my father put on my activities, for the first time in my life I had a regular supply of my own money. As soon as school let out for the summer break, I headed straight to the sporting goods store to buy myself a pair of dark blue fins. Although Bergheim only had a population of eight thousand people, the town had an outdoor sports complex with an Olympic-size swimming pool. Built during the Third Reich, the pool was a monument to the Nazis' enthusiasm for rugged physical exercise. My goal for the summer was to use the fins to swim the entire fifty-meter length of the pool under water.

After spending the entire afternoon practicing in the pool, I came home at suppertime and proudly showed the fins to my parents. "The next thing I plan to buy is a used sports handlebar for my bike," I announced.

My father banged his fist on the table so hard that the dishes rattled. "Are you out of your mind? Wasting your money like that? You don't need fins! And don't you dare get that handlebar! I want you to return those fins tomorrow."

Before I could say a word, Mutti spoke up. "Willi, please calm down. It's not good for your health. Besides, it's his money. It's the first time he's bought anything like this. He can't bring the fins back because he's already used them."

"You keep out of this. I'm talking to Günter!" Then he turned to me again. "Next time you think about buying something crazy like that, I expect you to ask my permission first. Keep the damn fins but you can forget about the handlebar. The handlebar on your bike is fine. Is that understood?"

"Yes, sir," I replied.

Since I needed to blow off some steam after supper, I invited Hubert to join me for a walk along the bank of the Erft River. Once we reached the street, Hubert looked up at me and rolled his eyes. "Sometimes I think he's nuts. It's your money. You worked for it. Why shouldn't you spend it on something you like?"

I kicked a pebble with the tip of my shoe and watched it skitter off into the river.

When I didn't reply, Hubert added, "He yells at me like that pretty much every day. 'Don't shuffle when you walk. Stand up straight. Cover your mouth when you yawn.' I can't seem to do anything right."

"I guess no matter what we do, it's never going to be good enough."

****

By trying to make her household money last as long as possible, Mutti set a good example for me in her own way. There was rarely any room for special treats or extras of any kind. But all that changed three days later when, out of the blue, we received a huge CARE package from Dan and Naomi Peachey, our Mennonite guardian angels from Pennsylvania who had sent Mutti and me twenty CARE packages while we were living in the refugee camp in Bodenteich. The four of us gathered around the table to unpack the contents together: ham, lard, raisins, flour, corned beef, spam, cocoa powder, cheese, canned fruit salad, and a two-pound can of real coffee!

"It's a godsend!" Mutti exclaimed. Even my father managed a smile.

In her long letter, Mrs. Peachey apologized for not having sent the CARE package sooner; she had misplaced our new address in Zieverich. And then, to my astonishment, she invited me to come to America and spend a year or two on their farm.

"I'm sure you'd like to go," Mutti said.

"You bet I would!"

"Sorry, Günter, but even though you're already taller than your father, you're still only fourteen and you need to finish your education."

And when Mutti wrote back to thank Naomi Peachey, that's exactly what she told her. Then, after talking things over with all of us, she added a postscript.

"We can never express how much your CARE packages have meant to us," Mutti wrote. "But now that our family has been reunited and both my husband and I are working, we should be able to manage without them. I'm sure you'll find another family who needs them more than we do. God bless you and let's please keep in touch!"

****

The next morning, Mutti, Hubert and I walked into Bergheim. After stopping on the way to drop the letter to Naomi Peachey into the mailbox, and with it, my dashed hopes of a trip to America, we headed for Frambach's clothing store where Mutti exchanged the Peachey coffee for new underwear for the entire family. Mr. Frambach, a man in his early sixties, had two daughters. The older one, who was in her mid-thirties, was squat and hunchbacked. The younger girl, Alice, was an adorable brown-skinned five-year-old.

"How did Alice get to look like that?" Hubert asked Mutti after we'd left the store.

"Herr Frambach adopted her," Mutti said without further explanation.

"The kids in school say she's actually his granddaughter," I chimed in. "And that her real father was an American occupation soldier."

"I don't want you spreading those silly rumors," Mutti scolded.

"Well, that's what they're saying all the same."

That afternoon, as I was cutting across the shallow wading pool in the Bergheim sports complex on my way to the lap lanes, I hit the water so hard with my foot that I accidentally splashed little Alice who was sitting along the other edge of the wading pool.

"Hey," she yelled up at me, "you got me all wet, you dirty *Neger*!"

"Sorry! I didn't mean it," I started to apologize, but Alice was already running away.

Later I told Mutti what had happened. "It was such a strange thing to say. She must be called names like that all the time."

Mutti nodded. "The poor dear. I can't even begin to imagine what she must have to put up with. People can be so cruel!"

CHAPTER 12

As the summer holiday drew to a close, Mutti talked me into taking another trip with the Lutheran Youth Group, this time to the picturesque little town of Linz on the Rhine River.

"The camp is so inexpensive, we couldn't feed you at home for the same money!" was how she put it and I couldn't argue with her.

After three weeks in Linz, hiking every day, sleeping in tents at night, and a summer filled with swimming, reading, and chores at the church, I dreaded going back to school. Two days before the start of classes, I arranged to meet Dieter Henkelmann among the stand of old-growth trees between the edge of Schlenderhan's stud farm and the Erft River. We had decided to build ourselves a *Huckleberry Finn* style raft and Dieter had promised to bring the necessary tools.

Like an Indian scout, I climbed up high in the branches of a big chestnut tree, shaded my eyes with my hand and watched for Dieter. But when he still hadn't come after what seemed like an hour, my thoughts drifted back to the love scene in the romance movie I had seen the previous Sunday, and from there, to the pretty girl with long brown braids whom I admired every morning on my way to the Commercial School. One time when I had sat directly behind her on the train I caught the scent of her lilac perfume, but I had never dared to speak to her.

How would it feel, I wondered, if I were to embrace her and hold her close to me?

I scoured the horizon but saw no one approaching. There was no sound except the occasional chirping of a bird or the buzz of an insect as there, in my high perch, for the first time in my life I gave in to temptation. Then, minutes later, trembling with a mixture of excitement and shame, I waited for God to strike me dead before starting to climb back down. My legs were wobbly and it would have been easy to return to the ground branch by branch just as I had gone up. Instead, when I reached a thick branch nearly two meters off the ground, I took a flying leap. In the past, I had made the same jump with ease, but this time, just as the ball of my left foot hit the ground, my left heel struck the sharp edge of an exposed tree root. I felt the bone inside my leg crack and I crumpled in a heap, sure that God Himself had put that root there to punish me for my sin. Would He now abandon me to die in that lonely place? There was only one way to find out. Gathering all my strength, I hollered for help at the top of my lungs.

Just when I was sure that all was lost, my screams caught the attention of a horse groomer who hurried over to me accompanied by Mrs. Henkelmann. I knew better than to expect any sympathy from her.

"What on earth have you been up to?" she scolded.

"I was waiting for Dieter and I fell from the tree. I think my leg is broken," I moaned.

"A boy your age climbing trees!" She shook her head in disgust before adding, "Dieter is confined to his room reviewing his math."

The groomer was sent to get Mutti, and half an hour later, I was lying on a stretcher being X-rayed in the Maria-Hilf Hospital in Bergheim. After it was determined that both bones between my ankle and my knee were broken, my leg was put into a cast and I was wheeled into a large ward. Eight other boys, ranging in age from eight to sixteen, were already patients.

I was gently lifted onto the bed in the back corner along the wall on the right side of the ward. As I lay gritting my teeth, trying to act brave for Mutti, an elderly nun approached us. She was wearing a floor-length black habit. A bulky silver crucifix hung on the thick chain around her neck. Below her enormous black hat, a starched white cloth tightly encircled her face, pressing against her fat jowls. A rectangular piece of crisp white linen perched on top of the hat. She looked like an overfed squirrel with a sail.

"I'm giving you two of these," she explained to me, pointing to the pills on her small tray. She turned to Mutti. "Visiting hours are over for now, Frau Nitsch. Anyway, I'm pretty sure your son will fall asleep once he's taken the medication."

Just before I dozed off I suddenly remembered that classes were about to start in Horrem. "What about school? When can I go back?"

"I'm afraid you'll be staying here for a little while," the nun said. "We have to get your leg fixed up first."

Toward evening, the nun returned. "All right, boys!" she announced in a loud voice, waking me up. "Let us pray!"

The other boys folded their hands in prayer, and in unison with the nun, they began to chant, "Hail Mary, full of grace..." Endless other unfamiliar prayers followed. At last everyone recited the Lord's Prayer. My Opa had taught me the words and I gladly joined in but when I got to the lines "For Thine is the Kingdom, and the power, and the..." I suddenly realized that everyone else had already stopped.

The nun glared at me and some of the boys started to giggle as the prayers continued. "Amen!" Sister Adele finally proclaimed. "Supper will be up in a few minutes," and she marched out of the room.

"Does she do that every night?" I whispered to the boy in the bed next to mine.

He lifted himself up on one elbow and turned to look at me. "Since you have a different version of the Lord's Prayer, I take it you're not Catholic?" I shook my head. "Well, if they keep you here you'll be

66

praying too, four times a day, once before every meal and again at bedtime. I hate it. But trust me, you'll get used to it!"

"You're joking, right?"

"Just wait and see. What happened to your leg?"

"Broke it, both bones. You?"

"I just had my appendix out."

After forcing myself to eat a shriveled frank, some watery mashed potatoes, and a lettuce salad flavored with lemon juice, I fell back to sleep only to be awakened once again several hours later by another call to prayer.

The nun's "little while" turned into five long weeks. Five weeks of tasteless food, stinking unemptied bedpans during interminable prayer sessions, and boredom, all under the watchful eye of unattractive nuns like Sister Adele.

"That's why they became nuns in the first place," one of the boys joked. "They knew they'd never find a husband."

"Not true," another retorted. "They're all married…to Lord Jesus!"

I had been idly scratching inside my cast with a long knitting needle but this information caught my attention. "You're not making this up, are you?"

"Nope. My parents told me the nuns belong to an order called the Poor Handmaidens of Jesus Christ and they're all married to Him."

"All of them?"

"Every single one."

****

At long last, on a Friday afternoon in early October, my cast was taken off. To my horror my left leg was decidedly thinner than the right. Worse, the blond hair on my injured leg had turned a ghastly shade of black-brown.

"You understand that you'll have to practice using those crutches for a week or two before you can go back to school?" the doctor admonished as he signed the discharge papers.

I nodded in agreement but I wasn't really paying attention. Instead, I kept staring down at my leg. "Will it always look like that?"

"Give it time," he reassured me, "and it will get back to the way it was."

****

After five weeks flat on my back, I spent the weekend on my crutches hobbling slowly up and down the hallway between the Poltermanns' apartment and our room. On Sunday evening I felt confident enough to go out back to watch Hubert and little Peter Poltermann kick a red rubber ball back and forth across the uneven brick surface.

"Hey, Stretch!" Hubert yelled, using the family nickname my father had recently given to me. "You wanna kick it? Give it your best shot!"

Without giving it a second thought I gave the ball a sharp kick with my right foot, and as I did, my left leg crumpled out from under me and I went down like a dead weight. At first Hubert and Peter froze where they were standing. Then they both ran back inside to get my parents.

"You're an idiot!" my father said when he saw me sprawled out on the stone walkway. And for once, I had to agree with him.

Early the next morning as I lay in the same bed in the same ward I'd left only two days before, my parents and Hubert came to see me accompanied by Dr. Spickernagel, the chief doctor at the hospital. The veins in my father's neck were bulging and his eyes were steely with anger.

"Let me explain this to you again as best I can," Dr. Spickernagel said, gently examining my re-injured leg. "In all likelihood your son's bones are weak due to his years of malnutrition under the Soviets in East Prussia, especially since he's so tall for his age. My colleagues and

I all agree that the best plan would be to insert two long silver nails here and here, to hold the bones together."

"Now you listen to me!" my father shouted. Mutti tugged on his sleeve and pointed to the other patients; he nodded and lowered his voice a notch. "I still have Russian shell splinters in my back from the battle at Schwedt an der Oder in February 1945. Every time there's a change in the weather, my back hurts like hell. My son is only fourteen years old and as far as I'm concerned, his bones will heal without your damn silver nails!"

"Are you willing to take responsibility for the consequences?" The doctor looked first at Mutti and then at my father. They both nodded. "Well, you're his parents. We'll just put another full cast on his leg and hope for the best."

An hour later, just as soon as the plaster had hardened, I was wheeled back upstairs.

"You must really like it here!" one of the boys yelled at me but I ignored him. I was trying too hard not to cry. The doctor had just told me I'd have to stay until at least the middle of November.

Once a week a black-frocked priest came by. Although he talked to all of the other boys, he just nodded and smiled at me, I guess because I wasn't Catholic. I wished Sister Adele would also keep away from me because whenever she leaned over my bed to adjust my pillow, I came face to face with her fuzzy brown mustache.

Just when I had concluded that all nuns were old, fat, and ugly, Sister Monika, a novice nun, arrived on our ward. At least forty years younger than Sister Adele, Sister Monika had dark brown eyes, big dimples, and a sunny disposition. She was a beautiful ray of sunshine in our daily routine.

One night, six of us boys kept talking long after we were supposed to be asleep. Whenever that had happened before, Sister Adele would storm into the ward and scream, "Quiet! I want you to be quiet *right now*!" But on this particular night, to our utter astonishment, in came

Sister Monika. She was already dressed for bed in a floor-length white nightgown, her long brown hair flowing loosely down her back. As she stood in the middle of the room in the bright moonlight, the six of us stopped talking and gaped as she whispered, "Boys, you have to sleep now. Please, do me the favor and go to sleep. Good night." With that, she tiptoed out of the ward.

Past experience taught me that the nuns always came back to check on us one more time after all was quiet. So, from my vantage point facing the door, I lay as still as I could while keeping watch through half-closed eyes. Sure enough, back came Sister Monika about a half an hour later. Starting at the bed to the left of the door, she walked slowly around the ward, leaning down at each bed to make sure that boy was really asleep. Finally my turn came. *It's now or never* I said to myself, and before she had a chance to react, I reached up, grabbed her neck with both of my arms, and kissed her right on the mouth.

She pulled away and shook her head in disbelief. "Günter, don't you ever do that again!" she gasped and she ran from the room.

Although everyone pretended to be asleep, the older boys, awake like me, had all seen what had happened. The next morning some of the boys even congratulated me, but Josef, who'd been there during my first stay, hinted that there would be repercussions. From that day forward until I was sent home again weeks later, the older nuns shunned me as if I were the Devil himself. Only Sister Monika was as nice to me as she had been before I kissed her, at least as long as none of the other nuns were around. I had no regrets.

CHAPTER 13

*W*hen I finally returned to the Commercial School in Horrem on November 24, 1952, just nine days before my fifteenth birthday, it wasn't only math that I found difficult; I was also behind in every subject and despaired of ever being able to catch up. Most afternoons after school I limped slowly upstairs to Mrs. van Knippenberg's dining room, spread out my books, and tried to master the nearly three months of course materials I had missed. Over the Christmas holidays I spent even longer hours on my studies while Mrs. van Knippenberg hovered nearby like a concerned mother hen. Hardly a day went by when she wouldn't look in on me and say, "You look hungry," before bringing in a plate with a cheese sandwich, or a ham sandwich, or a tasty piece of cake together with a tall glass of milk, for which I was immensely grateful.

"I know you can do it!" she'd encourage me. Mutti also gave me daily pep talks but even so, I felt like I was at the bottom of a deep pit with no ladder to climb back out.

Meanwhile, I was getting mixed signals from my father. Although he supported my efforts, he never missed an opportunity to let me know how disappointed he was in Hubert and me.

"You're slobs!" he would scream. "Look at those filthy fingernails! Wash your hands! Stand up straight! Look at me when I'm talking to

71

you!" Then he would give us both a slap in the face and add, "When will you two ever become civilized?"

On New Year's Eve my parents were once again invited to the Meyers' staff party. It must have been long after midnight when they came home, turned on the light, and woke me up. My father clung to the doorframe for a minute before staggering into the room. Clutching the wall for support, he worked his way over to the sink and promptly threw up. The sickening smell of half-digested sausages filled the room. I pushed past my father, who was desperately trying to squeeze big chunks of vomit down the drain, and rushed to the outhouse. My pajamas offered no protection against the bitter cold in our backyard; even so, I waited a few minutes before coming back inside. When I crawled back under the covers on my cot, my father was snoring like a truck with a broken engine.

****

As if I didn't have enough problems at school and at home, by the beginning of February the pressure was also building up in my confirmation class. Our confirmation was scheduled for the end of March, but Pastor Kampe didn't feel that we were ready. To step up the pace, he brought in Mr. Molitor, a forty-year old ruddy-faced bachelor who taught religion and Latin at the *Gymnasium*. Mr. Molitor's lesson plan consisted of trying to beat the Good Book into us by slapping anyone whose mind happened to wander. Since Mr. Molitor was far from scintillating, that meant pretty much all of us. With the exception of a plump boy named Wilhelm who sat up straight while defiantly eating a liverwurst sandwich, the rest of us slouched in our chairs wearing expressions of utter boredom.

During a break, Mr. Molitor excused himself and left the room for five minutes. Looking around at all the glum faces, I decided to liven things up by singing a song that had been popular among German soldiers on the Russian front: "In der Heimat angekommen, fängt ein neues Leben an, und 'ne Frau wird sich genommen, doch die bringt der Weihnachtsmann!" ("Having arrived back home to start a new life, I'm looking for Santa to bring me a wife.") Some of the boys were humming along and the girls were giggling when Mr. Molitor stormed back in.

"You impertinent boor!" he shrieked, slapping me twice across my face. "This is a confirmation class! How dare you sing such an outrageous song?" I needed all of my self-control to keep from hitting him back.

After class I thought of the loving, gentle Lord Jesus to whom my Opa had introduced me. Clearly, Mr. Molitor and *that* Lord Jesus had never met.

Fortunately for all of us, by the following week Pastor Kampe was back in charge of the class. "The ceremony will take place in front of the whole congregation," he explained. "I want the girls to wear black dresses. The boys should wear dark blue suits. Here, in a nutshell, is how it will proceed. The girls will sit together on the left side of the sanctuary and the boys on the right. Then I'm going to call you up two at a time and ask you questions about the Bible. It's nothing to worry about. We've spent weeks going over the questions and the answers, so it's really like an open-book test. There's no way anyone can fail."

The pastor then proceeded to pair us up. "Günter, I want you and my son Detlef to walk up front together." Detlef would hardly have been my first choice, but of course, I agreed. When I told my parents what the pastor had said, they both decided that buying me a dark blue suit for this one occasion would be a needless extravagance.

"Trust me, I'll find you something to wear," Mutti promised. True to her word, the next day Mutti visited the local funeral director who donated a hand-me-down black suit for the occasion. When I got home from school, Mutti took me to the nearby shop of master tailor Keip for a fitting. As soon as he saw me in the suit, he shook his head.

"Your son's tall and skinny," he said as he encircled my waist with his tape measure. "And whoever owned this suit before must've had an even bigger beer belly than mine. I'll do my best to take it in for you, but I'm no magician."

On the big day Detlef Kampe showed up in a brand-new dark blue suit. Feeling like a poorly dressed scarecrow with over-wide shoulders, I slunk over to take my place next to him on the driveway. At least the extra folds of worn material at the seat of my pants weren't visible, but that was only because my double-breasted jacket was way too long.

"Nice suit," Detlef sneered just as Mutti rushed over. I was sure he had been watching from the window as my father snapped my picture just before we'd left for church.

"Hello, Detlef, how are you?" Mutti said breathlessly. "Has either of you boys seen the Krienkes? Everyone's here but them."

My father joined us. "They're coming in now, but there's something's wrong with Jochen."

With his father supporting him on one side and his mother on the other, Jochen stumbled towards us. His eyes were glazed and his mouth hung open in a twisted grin.

"What on earth?" Mutti said as we gathered around the Krienkes.

"He's totally plastered!" Mr. Krienke replied. "We left a big bowl of strawberry punch to cool on the windowsill and he climbed up a ladder to get at it."

"Fred made the punch with four bottles of Mosel wine and a whole bottle of champagne," Mrs. Krienke added by way of explanation.

"It wush delishush," Jochen mumbled, licking his lips.

"He can't walk on his own and he's definitely in no condition to pass a Bible test," Mr. Krienke went on. "Detlef, would you be willing to pair up with Albert, Jochen's partner, and Günter, you're a big guy, could you make sure Jochen gets to the front of the church without falling down? All right? I'm relying on you boys! Now I'm going to see whether Pastor Kampe would be willing to address all of Jochen's questions to Günter when the two of you are called up."

74

Detlef and I locked arms with Jochen and led him to a seat between us in a front pew. Had we not pressed tightly against him, he would have tipped over to one side or the other. The pastor took his place and began calling up the confirmands two by two. When Detlef and Albert were called up, I did my best to anchor Jochen in place on my own.

By the time Pastor Kampe finally called out, "Günter Nitsch and Jochen Krienke," Jochen was snoring with his head resting on my shoulder. I shook him awake and pulled him to his feet. Slipping my right arm around his back, I grabbed hold of his left elbow in an iron grip. As we walked slowly to the front, there were a few gasps and some muffled laughter from the congregation behind us. Pastor Kampe asked me several questions to which I gave the answers. Then he blessed and dismissed us. There wasn't a single person in church who didn't stare at us as we returned to our seats in the pew. At least, I thought to myself, I could be thankful to Jochen for one thing; no one was paying any attention to my ill-fitting suit.

CHAPTER 14

*T*he twelve weeks I'd spent in the hospital had taken a terrible toll on my schoolwork. Despite all of the extra hours studying at Mrs. van Knippenberg's dining room table, my grades had slipped in almost every subject. In late March, shortly before the end of the term, Dr. Knops made an announcement in homeroom. "König! Nitsch! You're both wanted in the principal's office."

Minutes later the two of us stood in front of Herr Direktor Müllmann's giant desk like two traitors facing a firing squad. The principal addressed König first.

"König, you don't have enough brains to fill a pea. I don't want you back here. What are you going to do?"

König looked down at his shoes. "I guess I'll try to get an apprenticeship."

"As what?"

"Electrician."

"Good. *Auf Wiedersehen.* Out you go."

Leaning back in his chair and clasping his fleshy fingers behind his head, Herr Direktor Müllmann now turned his attention to me. My heart was pounding so hard I could hardly breathe.

"Nitsch, you're just as dumb as König, and if it were up to me, you'd be following him out the door. But your other three teachers have asked me to give you another chance. So I'm giving you two choices. If you stay, you'll have to repeat the entire first year when classes start again after Easter vacation. Or you can leave right now which would please me no end. What do you want to do?"

I thought about how Herr Direktor Müllmann had led me by the hair down to the blackboard. Did I really want two more years of that? It would have been so easy to cut and run! But then I'd never get an office job. I might even end up working long hours like my father.

"I haven't got all day!" the principal shrieked at me, drumming his fingers impatiently.

Between suffering Müllmann's torture for two more years and working my entire life for someone like my father, the choice was suddenly clear. "I want to stay."

He shook his head, clearly surprised by my decision. "Well, then, we'll just have to wait and see if the other teachers' faith in you is justified," he said. "And now get out of here. I'm busy!"

"Thank you. *Auf Wiedersehen*, Herr Direktor Müllmann," I stammered before rushing outside. My classmates had already started walking to the train station.

"So Nitsch, do you have to quit like König?" one of them asked me.

"No, but I have to repeat the whole year."

"It's no big deal," he consoled me. "I had to repeat the third year at the *Gymnasium*."

I knew he meant well but his comment was hardly reassuring, since repeating the third year at the *Gymnasium* had apparently not been much help. Otherwise he wouldn't have ended up in the Commercial School in Horrem.

In the train, I worried that my father might disagree with my decision and force me to get an apprenticeship, but he was surprisingly supportive.

"Cheer up, it's not the end of the world," he encouraged me. "You'll graduate in another two years and then you can look for the job you want."

Easier said than done, I thought. Now that I knew he expected me to succeed, I wasn't so sure that I could.

****

A few days later Mutti ran into Jochen's mother in Café Meyer. Mrs. Krienke invited all of us over to their apartment in the old water mill that evening after supper. As soon as we arrived Mr. Krienke put down his glass and greeted me with a warm smile.

"Jochen told me what happened to you at the Commercial School. Did I ever tell you that I once had to repeat a class? I'll let you in on a little secret. Once you have your diploma nobody's going to give a rat's ass how long it took you to get it. All anyone wants to see is that piece of paper."

He poured wine for my parents and apple juice for Hubert, Jochen, and me. "To make sure you boys can walk straight afterwards," as he put it. Then he turned back to me. "Now, let me ask you a question. Why haven't you joined Jochen's Boy Scout troop?"

Mutti answered for me. "Günter's still a member of the Lutheran Youth Group at church. It's right next-door and it doesn't cost any money. The scouts meet over in Quadrath, don't they? And we've heard that their trips are pretty expensive."

"Well, I think Günter's missing a great opportunity. First of all, boys his age shouldn't be sitting around a campfire doing Bible study. They should be roughing it and having fun."

My father grinned but Mutti still looked skeptical.

"And secondly, if Günter joins now he'll be able to travel with the scouts when they go to the Tyrolean Alps for three weeks in August. I'm sure we can talk to the Scoutmaster about the cost if that's a concern.

Friedel Meuser's the kind of guy who'd give you the shirt off his back."

"Willi, what do you think?" Mutti asked. She was clearly wavering.

"I think it's a terrific idea!" my father exclaimed, much to my relief. "Other than the army, scouting's the best way to turn a boy into a man."

Mutti nodded. "All right then. So long as Günter can keep up with his schoolwork."

****

When the new term started at the Commercial School after Easter there were a few changes that made my life more bearable. For one thing, I had the advantage of knowing what to expect. Even Herr Direktor Müllmann didn't seem as threatening somehow, especially because he'd pounced on another boy to torment instead of me. When I heard that Chaplain Fuchs didn't give Bible lessons, I started attending his class instead of sitting with my Lutheran classmates in an unused classroom. Chaplain Fuchs triggered lively discussions based on news stories from the *Kölner Stadt-Anzeiger*. We even had heated debates about the pros and cons of regaining the lost provinces of East Prussia, Pomerania, and Silesia.

Since my friend, Wilfried Plath, and his twin sister, Erika, were just starting their first year studies, the three of us could get together to tackle difficult homework problems. But the most important improvement in my life was my membership in the Boy Scouts. By the time the new school term started, Jochen, Wilfried Plath, and I had already biked together several times to the village of Quadrath, nearly five kilometers from Zieverich on a busy road, to attend scout meetings. More than half of the boys in our troop attended the *Gymnasium* or the Middle School. Many had come from even farther away than Zieverich. The reason was clear. Our scoutmaster, Friedel Meuser, was an extraordinary young man. Whether he was teaching us catchy hiking songs, accompanying us on his guitar, or leading us on overnight biking trips forty kilometers into the countryside to explore the Eifel Mountains, his good nature never flagged. If one of the boys thought the road was too steep or the ride was too long, he found just the right words to encourage him to continue. When disagreements arose between the Lutheran scouts and the Catholic scouts, or between the *Gymnasium* students and those of us attending the Commercial School, he was the peacekeeper. He knew how to predict the weather, pitch a tent, dig a latrine, repair a bicycle, and cook delicious meals over the campfire.

All of us lived for the day when our trip to Austria would begin. On August 1, 1953, Mr. Krienke drove Jochen and me to the main railroad station in Cologne where the other boys were already waiting with Friedel Meuser on the platform. I had held my breath the whole way there listening for telltale signs of engine trouble but on that occasion at least, Mr. Krienke's old clunker held up just fine. The overnight train brought us to Munich in time for an early breakfast and several hours of sightseeing before we caught another train to Kufstein in Austria. From there a bus brought us to the village of Sölden in the Tyrolean High Alps.

For the next three weeks we slept in tents at night and took exhilarating daylong hikes above the tree line to the tops of towering snow-covered mountains. Every fourth day we stayed in camp to rest. On one particular Thursday three boys had been hard at work cooking up a thick pea soup in the iron cauldron hanging over the fire on a tripod. At Friedel Meuser's suggestion, each of us had dug into our knapsacks to contribute chunks of cheese or salami, slices of stale bread, and margarine to make the meal tastier and more nourishing. When the mouth-watering soup was ready, two boys put a flexible stick through the handles of the pot and lugged it over to a small rocky patch of flat ground to let it cool. With hunger gnawing at our stomachs, we started an improvised soccer game on the meadow to make the wait go faster.

"Our soup!" Jochen shrieked, and we all turned towards the campsite. A large brown cow, her legs slightly spread, stood with her rear end backed up to the steaming pot. As we watched in horror, her scraggly tail started to move up in rhythmic jerks like the hands of a giant clock. Click! Seven o'clock. Click! Eight o'clock. You didn't have to be a farm boy to know that once the tail reached eleven o'clock, our meal would be ruined. Rushing to the rescue, eight of us heaved against the poor creature so hard that she nearly tipped over. But our soup was safe! From that day forward, "cow look-out" was added to our other camp responsibilities.

Since Jochen and I were among the youngest boys in the troop it was our job to scrub out the greasy soup kettle with fine sand in the ice-cold water of the nearby creek. In the mornings we brushed our teeth and washed our hands and faces in the same frigid water.

After several days Jochen poked me. "Have you noticed that the older scouts always head upstream to wash?" he whispered. "What do you suppose's wrong with the water right here?"

"There's one way to find out," I replied.

The next morning, Jochen and I trailed the older boys uphill along the edge of the swift-flowing creek. After a five-minute walk, we solved the mystery. A dozen people – young men and young women – had set up camp alongside the creek. The six giggling women in the group, clad only in the skimpiest of two-piece swimsuits, were bending over to wash themselves under the admiring eyes of my fellow scouts.

"They're French," one of the older boys explained as we walked back down to our campsite. "I guess you've just seen your first bikinis!"

A short time later, as we started on our hike, I was lost in thought, trying to imagine Sister Monika in one of those tiny outfits, her long, dark hair concealing whatever the bikini revealed.

Jochen poked my arm. "Cat got your tongue?"

"Huh?"

"I was asking what you thought about those bathing suits."

"Pretty nice."

"That's all you've got? You're blushing!"

I grinned and put my arm around his shoulder. "Did I ever tell you about the time I kissed a nun?"

CHAPTER 15

As our group boarded the train for the trip home, I thought of how much our Austrian adventure had brought all of us closer together. When we had gone off on hikes or pitched our tents or rescued our soup or ogled the French girls in their bikinis, no one had cared who was a native and who was a refugee; who was Catholic and who was Lutheran; whose father was a lawyer, or a doctor, or an engineer, and whose father was a pastry chef; we were all Friedel Meuser's boys. But the closer I got to Zieverich and the cramped room my family shared, the more I began to envy the scouts whose families were better off than mine.

Most of the boys had already left the train at other stations before it pulled into Zieverich. Jochen and I shook hands before going our separate ways. It was already well past suppertime when I approached our house. Mutti had seen me from the window and she, my father, and Hubert all came out to greet me. From their broad smiles, I knew something was up.

"Hey, Stretch!" my father greeted me. "Didn't you get any food in Austria? You're skinny as a rail."

"We ate like horses but I guess we worked it off." I looked from one of my beaming parents to the other. "Did you win the soccer Toto?"

"Even better than that!" Mutti replied. "The Poltermanns found a bigger place in Fortuna and we'll be getting their rooms on September first!"

"In ten days?"

"That's right," my father said. "We're planning to put two beds into the back room for you and Hubert."

"And a table and chair," Mutti added, "so you can do your homework. We've already thanked the van Knippenbergs and told them you won't need to use their dining room anymore."

"It'll be great to have two rooms instead of one!"

"Actually," my father corrected me, "it'll be three. Your mother and I are keeping our bed right where it is. That way we can use the Poltermanns' front room for entertaining."

Three rooms! I thought to myself as I lay down later on my cot. *And a real bed!* Just before I dozed off, I also considered what it would mean to my parents to finally have some privacy. Things could only get better from now on. I slept like a log.

The Poltermanns' front room soon became our living room, complete with our couch and several new armchairs. Now my parents could invite their friends over for coffee and cake or a glass of wine in the evening.

And Miss Lemm was true to her word. Within ten days workmen demolished the outhouse and installed a flush toilet in the back corner of the laundry room. Admittedly, the situation was far from ideal. Since the wooden partition enclosing the cubicle only extended part way to the ceiling, if one of us was sitting on the toilet there was no way to prevent the sounds and smells from escaping into the room. This was particularly awkward when Mrs. van Knippenberg or Miss Lemm came downstairs to do their laundry. Still, compared to the outhouse, it was a definite improvement.

Most important to me, I had my small table next to the back window to do my schoolwork. Determined to let nothing stop me, over the next

several months I pushed on despite a long succession of broken bones
– first a finger, then an arm, and then several broken ribs. But when I
broke my collarbone, Mutti decided that enough was enough. She and
I sat down with Dr. Ute Klemm, our family doctor.

"Let me see," Dr. Klemm began, leafing through my thick file.
"How old is Günter now?"

"He turned sixteen in December."

"Then I imagine he's having a growth spurt and that puts extra
pressure on his bones." Mutti and I looked at her expectantly. "Actually,
I've seen this a number of times with refugee children. It's the result of
Günter's having starved under the Russians in East Prussia; his bones
didn't get the calcium they needed."

"Well, he can't go on like this," Mutti replied. "I'm afraid one day
he'll just break apart."

The doctor's remedy was torture for me. Every morning for the
next several months I had to eat half an eggshell that had been soaked
in lemon juice overnight. It was all I could do to force the awful stuff
down, but it worked.

****

At the beginning of April 1954, despite my mediocre grades, I was
promoted to the next class at the Commercial School. Together with my
friends Wilfried and Erika Plath, I joined in my classmates' celebration
in a café in Horrem before heading home.

Report card in hand, I burst into our living room to share the news
but stopped in my tracks. Mutti was sobbing as Hubert sat helplessly at
her side. I sat down on the arm of the couch and reached over to take
Mutti's hand.

"Please tell me what's wrong!"

"Do you remember the woman your father was living with in Uelzen
when we crossed the border to join him?" I nodded and waited for her
to go on. "She's invited him to her daughter's First Communion."

"And he said *yes*?"

"He's dead set on attending."

"That doesn't make any sense." Then another thought struck me. "You don't suppose it's his child?"

"He says it isn't."

The three of us sat in silence for a few minutes.

"What're you going to do?" I finally asked.

"That's just what I've been asking myself ever since he told me his plans last night." She put her arm around Hubert and tried to smile up at me. "I'm sorry to burden you boys with this, but I'm at the end of my rope."

"The two of you have discussed divorce. Perhaps the time has come."

"When did you hear anything like that?"

"When we all shared a room and you thought I was asleep."

Mutti gave me a strange look and got up from the couch. "I'm going next door to fix supper," she said. "If you both don't mind, I'd like to be alone for a while."

When my father came home, he chatted briefly with Hubert and me about the pastry shop, but he ignored Mutti entirely. It was only when we all sat down at the table and were about to eat that Mutti looked my father straight in the eyes. After taking a deep breath, she broke the almost unbearable tension.

"Willi, just so you know. I've told the boys everything and I've also made up my mind. If you go to Uelzen, I'm filing for divorce!"

Still clutching his knife and fork, my father rose slowly from his chair. "Are you nuts?" he snarled. Then he threw the utensils into the sink, put on his coat and stormed out, banging the door behind him. Hubert, Mutti and I finished our meal and cleared the table in silence. Then the three of us took a long walk. It was dark when we got back, but my father was still not home.

The next morning was the first day of our spring school vacation so Hubert and I slept later than usual. When we crossed the hall to the kitchen, Mutti smiled as she gave us our breakfast. Then with a steady hand she poured herself a cup of coffee and sat down to join us, a glint of triumph in her eyes.

"The problem's solved," she said calmly. "Your father's not going anywhere."

****

Not long after I thought that things had settled back down at home, my father began attending regular meetings of the East Prussian Club in Bergheim.

"Our president, Herr Klinger, is an amazing man!" he boasted one evening. "He's determined to help us get back the Eastern provinces we lost in 1945."

"What on earth for?" Mutti asked. "Who in their right mind would want to go back there if the Russians and Poles ever gave them back?"

"We all would!"

"Not me. After what the boys and I suffered there under the Russians, you can count us out!"

To my surprise, my father backed down. "I suppose you're right. But I'm still going to the meetings. It's a nice group of people. Actually, I've invited Herr Klinger and his daughter over here for a glass of wine on Saturday after supper."

On Saturday evening my father insisted that Hubert and I put on our best clothes in honor of our guests. The Klingers arrived right on time. Since only a few white tufts of hair encircled the edges of his shiny scalp, Mr. Klinger reminded me of the portrait of Otto von Bismarck in my history book. He was a huge bear of a man with a fleshy nose and a booming voice loud enough to wake an entire neighborhood in the middle of the night.

His daughter, Annemarie, could have come from a different planet. She had an hourglass figure and was dressed to kill in high-heeled shoes, a tight-fitting navy blue business suit and a low-necked white blouse. She had long eyelashes, bright red lipstick, and flowing jet-black hair. As soon as she walked in, the entire living room smelled of her perfume. And it was soon apparent to everyone, but especially to Mutti, that my father was paying Miss Klinger an inordinate amount of attention.

When the Klingers finally left, Mutti boiled over. "So that's why you go to those meetings! The way that woman dyes her hair and pushes up her bosom, it's absolutely tasteless."

"Don't be ridiculous! She's a nice young woman that's all. You and your damn suspicions."

At a signal from my father, Hubert and I went into our bedroom and closed the door but we could still hear our parents arguing in the living room.

"You've given me plenty of reason to be suspicious," Mutti snapped. "Your own sisters told me how you bragged about all the women you had in Paris during the war. Then Uelzen and now this! What am I supposed to think?"

"You can think whatever you want but I intend to invite the Klingers over here any time I want to and that's that."

****

My father seemed determined to make everyone's life miserable at home. When he wasn't criticizing Hubert or me for some imagined fault, he was arguing with Mutti or sulking on the couch. At least the scouts gave me a temporary means of escape.

Over Easter weekend we pitched our tents on a plateau at the edge of the Fortuna Forest overlooking Bergheim. Early on Sunday morning, while most of the other boys slept snug and warm in their military sleeping bags, I crawled out from under my olive-green woolen blanket and hopped up and down to bring the circulation back into my arms and legs. By the time I had gotten our campfire going, the aroma of freshly brewed barley "coffee" brought the other scouts out of their tents.

On that chilly mid-April morning our breakfast of margarine and jam on rye bread tasted better than any fancy Easter dinner with my parents at home. As an extra treat, one of the boys cut off slices of the hard salami sausage his mother had slipped into his rucksack as a surprise, and gave some to each of us. While many of us were munching on the salami, a man suddenly yelled from the top of the small hill.

"How're you doin', boys?"

"Oh, no!" Jochen muttered under his breath.

Looming above us, Jochen's father sat straight as an arrow astride a majestic horse. Then, with the skill of a retired major in the cavalry, he guided the skittish creature down the rocky path towards our campsite. Basking in the admiration of the group, he tipped his hat and leaned down to shake Friedel Meuser's hand before reining in his horse in front of Jochen.

"Glad to see everything's under control here! I'll see you tomorrow night," he exclaimed and he took off down the trail at a full gallop.

The effect on the other scouts was sensational. The effect on Jochen was decidedly less so.

"I wish I could've crawled under a rock when he showed up," he whispered to me.

"Hey, Jochen!" an older boy called out. "Why didn't you tell us your father owns a race horse?"

Jochen's shoulders sagged. "Because he doesn't. He borrowed it from Schlenderhan's stable."

Once we had cleaned up after breakfast, Jochen steered Wilfried and me to a small grove of trees out of the earshot of the other boys.

"What was *that* all about?" I asked. "Your father looked like he came straight out of *Billy Jenkins*."

"When he told me yesterday what he planned to do, I begged him not to. So what does he do? He shows up anyway and embarrasses the hell out of me. The thing is, he'd like nothing better than to quit his job at the Belgian military barracks and join the cavalry again."

"What's he got against the job in Ichendorf?"

"When you've reached the rank of Major, I guess it's hard to take orders from a lowly Belgian sergeant who barely speaks German. But that's not the real reason. The real reason is he wants to be a cavalry officer in the new German Army. That's all he talks about at home."

"Do we still even *have* a cavalry?" Wilfried asked.

"That's what my mom keeps telling him. He's living in the past. And riding around Bergheim on a borrowed horse like he's the Emperor of China is about as close as he's going to get."

"Boy, you think you have a problem? What about my father?" I exclaimed. "You know the *Lastenausgleich* money the government is loaning to refugees who lost their possessions in the East? He actually believes he's going to get some of that money and open his own café because he's tired of being told by Meyer what to do."

Wilfried shook his head. "Maybe you're being too hard on your fathers. At least they have something to hope for. Who knows what nutty ideas we'll get when we're that old?"

CHAPTER 16

A brown Grundig radio was perched on the high shelf in our living room. If my father wasn't too tired in the evening, he would sit on the couch and listen to a broadcast of an operetta, although he preferred military march music. But when he was at work, I would reach up and change the dial to the popular tunes on the American Forces Network (AFN) or to Chris Howland's show on the British Forces Network (BFN). Speaking in a comical German with his thick British accent, Chris Howland introduced my classmates and me to the complex rhythms of Louis Armstrong, Ella Fitzgerald, Jack Teagarden, Benny Goodman, and Mahalia Jackson. But sometimes, if I let my guard down, my father would come home early and catch me listening to jazz.

Regardless of who the performer was, his reaction was always the same. "Don't you have anything better to do, you lazy bum? Turn off that crappy *Negermusik!*"

In late November, 1954, Heinz Orem, a classmate of mine from the Commercial School, sat down next to me after class. "Have you ever heard any music by Glen Miller?" he asked.

"I don't think so. Does he play jazz?"

"He plays swing, sort of like Goodman. Real smooth stuff."

"I'll listen for him on Chris Howland's show."

"I've got an even better idea," Heinz confided. "There's a movie house in Cologne where they're showing *The Glenn Miller Story*. Wanna go with me?"

I took a minute to think over his suggestion. On the one hand, ever since my father had bawled me out for buying the swim fins, I'd tried to be frugal with my pocket money. Going into Cologne would mean roundtrip train fare, a movie ticket, and missed time when I could have been doing my schoolwork. But on the other hand...

"Sure why not! Let's go on Thursday when our classes get out at noon. I'll just tell my parents I have an afterschool study group."

After I saw *The Glenn Miller Story*, whenever Chris Howland put "In the Mood", or "Moonlight Serenade", or "Pennsylvania 6-5000" on his turntable, I imagined myself in a fancy jazz club in New York City, a thick wad of dollars in my pocket, and a June Allyson lookalike on my arm. And much to my surprise, whenever Chris Howland played a Glenn Miller tune on his radio program, I noticed my father's foot tapping along with the music. It may have taken me seventeen years, but he and I had finally found one thing we had in common.

****

My visit to the movie theater in Cologne with Heinz Orem made me realize that the fifty-year-old Apollo Theater in Bergheim was actually a dump. Judging from the coming attractions, patrons in Cologne could see a timely succession of first-run movies. In Bergheim we got films that were at least two or three years old. And since the same motion picture played for weeks at a time, we always knew the inevitable moment would come when the film would sputter to a stop and have to be spliced back together. Then the lights would come back on; we would whoop and holler in our seats, and the projectionist would try to fill the time by showing slides we'd seen a dozen times before. "Buy your radio at Elektro-Schiffer!" "Dress shoes on sale at Schuhhaus Creutz!" Not to mention the dueling ads for the two local funeral parlors. The solemn message "Trust us to make things easier for you in your time of loss!" was always accompanied by a chorus of boos.

But then again, Cologne didn't have Alex, the good-natured man in his mid-thirties with wire-rimmed glasses and thick graying hair who stationed himself like an eternal fixture in front of the Apollo box office. According to Alex, he had seen most of the films at least twice, and if you had the bad judgment to linger more than fifteen seconds in front of a movie poster before buying your ticket, he would corner you to reveal the entire plot – beginning, middle and end. Actually, he didn't stop there.

"See that picture of Grace Kelly?" he would boast, pointing to a poster for *The Bridges of Toko-Ri*. "I slept with her. And with Rita Hayworth. And Lana Turner. All of them!"

"How about Betty Grable?" Jochen asked, trying to keep a straight face.

"Her too, and, and, and also, what's her name?" Alex replied.

Jochen guessed, "Audrey Hepburn?"

"Yeah, yeah, she really liked me," he assured us.

In all those years I never saw Alex unhappy, whether he was hanging out in front of the movie house during the week, or before a Sunday afternoon matinee. The same couldn't be said for anyone who had the bad luck to actually watch a movie with him since his running commentary was always louder than the soundtrack.

CHAPTER 17

*W*hen I came home from school ten days before the Christmas holiday in 1954, Mutti greeted me with some big news.

"Guess what? Oma's coming to live with us."

My heart sank. Hardly a day had gone by during the years we'd lived together under the Russians in East Prussia when my grandmother hadn't found a reason to slap me into shape with her wet dishrag.

"Why doesn't Aunt Liesbeth take her in? She probably has more room than we do at her place in Bavaria."

"No, it's up to us. I've already talked to Vati about it."

"But isn't Oma a bit too old to be sneaking across the border like we did?"

"She doesn't have to. The East German government is actually encouraging its old people to go to the West so they don't have to pay for their old age pensions and health insurance. It's pretty cynical, but what can you expect from the Communists? In any case, she's arriving by train next week."

"And she'll stay with us here?" I could already imagine losing the bedroom Hubert and I shared.

"Just for a few weeks. I've already started looking for a furnished room for her in Bergheim. We want her to be within easy walking distance of Dr. Klemm's office, just in case."

94

Oma had definitely mellowed. When she arrived just in time for Christmas, she gave Hubert and me big hugs, and I suddenly recognized in her the gentle, loving person she had been before the Russians came. And Mutti's prediction was correct. Using his connections, Mr. Meyer soon found Oma a furnished room on Hauptstrasse near the Aachener Tor.

Six weeks after Oma came to Bergheim, we received a postcard from Uncle Ernst, my mother's brother. He was attending a meeting with executives of the AGFA Company in Leverkusen just outside of Cologne and would come to visit us over the weekend. Mutti was overjoyed. She, Hubert and I had last seen Uncle Ernst at his home in East Berlin in November 1948.

"It's at least five years longer than that for me," my father calculated. "I think it was 1943 when he and I were both on leave in Langendorf together. Looks like we'll have to break open some really good bottles of wine!"

"But how is Uncle Ernst crossing the border?" Hubert asked.

"Oh, I imagine it's no problem for him. He's a big shot in the East German photography industry so they let him travel to West Germany for business meetings," Mutti explained.

"Right," my father added. "But he has to leave the rest of his family behind every time."

Uncle Ernst arrived on Saturday. After kissing Oma and hugging Mutti, he shook my hand and looked me up and down.

"Boy, oh boy, look at you. You must be at least ten centimeters taller than I am!" Then he turned to Hubert who was not only overweight, but also suffering from a bad case of acne. Still, Uncle Ernst found just the right words. "Can this be Hubert? When I last saw you, you were just a little boy and now you're a fine young man!"

Reaching into his overnight bag, he pulled out gifts for all of us; mine was the book *Erwin Kisch, the Flying Reporter*. We talked over supper, sometimes all at once, and later on, after Oma had been brought home and Hubert and I went off to bed with our new books, the conversation continued long into the night.

Since my father had Monday off, my parents invited the Krienkes over on Sunday evening. After supper the adults started on the wine. Before the third bottle was empty, all of the men were addressing each other with their former military titles. Uncle Ernst became Herr Master Sergeant; Mr. Krienke was Herr Major and my father, Herr Staff Sergeant.

"Shouldn't Günter have a glass of Mosel in honor of the occasion?" Uncle Ernst suddenly asked.

"Now, Ernst, it's a school night!" Mutti protested but she was quickly overruled.

My father gave Uncle Ernst a sharp salute. "*Jawohl*, Herr Master Sergeant." He reached over to fill my glass. "Just following orders!"

As soon as Hubert went to bed, Herr Major Krienke issued an order. From that point forward, anyone planning to tell a dirty joke had to remove his dentures first.

"Here, I'll show you how it's done."

Mutti, Mrs. Krienke and I burst out laughing as Mr. Krienke placed his false teeth on his cake plate. Uncle Ernst promptly did the same. But when my father reached into his mouth to remove his upper and lower partial dentures, I had had more than enough and I escaped to the bedroom. When I woke the next morning to get ready for school, Uncle Ernst was already on his way back to East Berlin.

****

It didn't surprise me that my father and Uncle Ernst could joke about their wartime experiences. After all, my father had served as a cook in military hospitals and had seen very little action until the last weeks of the war, and Uncle Ernst had trained recruits. But I couldn't understand how Mr. Krienke, who had spent significant time on the front lines, could laugh right along with them.

When I asked my father about it, he handed me a copy of the latest issue of the *Kölner Neue Illustrierte*. Although he wasn't much of a reader, he looked forward every week to the latest chapter from Hans-Helmut Kirst's trilogy *08/15*. The serialization of Kirst's books had created a sensation, turning what had been a glossy gossip magazine into one of the first publications to write about the war. Kirst's first book, *In the Barracks*, was full of amusing stories. The tone shifted in his second book, *In the War*, with its brutal description of battles from the point of view of the common soldier.

"Read Kirst," he advised, "if you want to know why all of us soldiers have a common bond. Don't you think so, Gretel?"

"Vati's right," she agreed. "But if I were you, I wouldn't read it at bedtime or you won't be able to sleep."

"Is there anything in his book about concentration camps?" I asked. "From what I've been reading in the newspaper, some former camp guards from the *SS* are on trial right now for murdering a lot of Jews in Poland."

My father shook his head. "Kirst's no idiot. He won't put stuff like that in if he wants to sell his books; nobody would want to read about that sort of thing."

CHAPTER 18

*O*ur graduation from the Commercial School was scheduled for March 24, 1955, and by the end of January we were all scrambling to get apprenticeships. My grades continued to range from fair to middling, but at least I was passing all of my subjects. Still, I cringed whenever I added a copy of my transcript to my applications. Several of my classmates had already lined up positions at insurance companies and manufacturing firms as my rejection letters kept pouring in.

Ford didn't want me. Neither did Allianz-Versicherung and Gerling nor a slew of others. Only Arminius AG, a Swiss-owned chemical plant near Bergheim, had invited me in to take a written test along with eighteen other applicants. But with only two positions available, my chances seemed bleak.

A few weeks later, three letters arrived for me on the same day. The first was another rejection but the second letter was an offer of a three-year apprenticeship from a large insurance company in Cologne.

"They want to start me at seventy Deutschmarks a month!" I exclaimed, handing the letter to Mutti to read.

The third letter was from Arminius AG. "Another rejection," I predicted.

"But it doesn't matter now," Mutti comforted me. "You already have a job."

With trembling hands I opened the last letter. "I don't believe it! They want me too, but they only pay sixty Deutschmarks a month for the first year."

"Let me see," Mutti said taking the letter from me. "Actually, I think the offer from Arminius AG is a better deal. If you factor in the price of the monthly commute to Cologne, you'd end up with less in your pocket. You can get to Arminius AG on your bike. You could even walk in the winter if necessary. I've talked to some of the women who work there and they all seem to like their jobs. Anyway, you have to make your own decision, but why don't we wait to see what Vati says when he gets home?"

My father read the two letters before we sat down to supper. "I'm proud of you," he said. "As for my opinion, I'd go with Arminius AG. In my book, people who work for insurance companies are just as bad as those high-pressure Bible thumpers who come around here sometimes. But I'll support you no matter what you decide."

After supper I put on a warm coat and my woolen cap and took a walk into Bergheim to think things over. When I got back, my parents and Hubert all looked at me expectantly. "I'm going to write an acceptance letter to Arminius AG tomorrow morning!" I announced, surprised at how fast my heart was pounding.

"Congratulations!" My father shook my hand, Mutti gave me a big hug, and even Hubert did a little dance.

My father picked up the letter and read it again. "So you start on April 1st?"

"Yes!"

"On April Fools' Day?"

"C'mon, Willi," Mutti hastened to say. "It's nothing to joke about. All of the apprenticeships start that day."

CHAPTER *19*

*O*n that first Friday in April, summoning all my courage, I stepped off the bus and walked over to the two men in the little guardhouse on the left side of the wide entrance to the Arminius AG Chemical Plant.

"Good morning. My name is Günter Nitsch. I'm the new apprentice and I'm supposed to report to Herr Beutelrock."

The younger man replied, "I'll accompany you, just a minute." He ducked back inside the booth to check off my name on his list. "This way. Follow me!"

I expected him to bring me across the driveway to the vast, three-story administration building that I'd seen many times when I'd pedaled past the plant on my bike. Instead, he escorted me to a smaller, reddish building behind the guardhouse. We walked along a long entrance hall cluttered with boxes, passing two huge grey machines and a table stacked high with stiff cardboard cards filled with seemingly random rectangular punch holes. The door of the office on the right was open but the guard reached in to knock anyhow. A short well-dressed man with a protruding belly stood next to the desk pushing out his suspenders with his thumbs. He looked up at us through the dark plastic frames of his thick eyeglasses.

"Good morning, Herr Beutelrock. This is your new apprentice, Günter Nitsch."

Mr. Beutelrock looked me up and down. His first question came as a surprise. "Good grief! How tall are you?"

"I'm 1.91 meters, Herr Beutelrock."

"Please sit down," he said to me, taking a seat behind his desk and dismissing the guard with a wave of his hand. "You'll be starting your apprenticeship right here with me in the Payroll Department. My staff and I calculate the weekly wages for the firm's eight hundred factory workers. Then we put the cash into brown envelopes and distribute them to the various departments of the factory. It's been pretty routine stuff up until now, but that's about to change. Over the next few months we'll be converting our whole operation so that it will run on the two IBM computers you saw on your way in. Any questions so far?"

"No, sir."

"Oh, before I forget, we work from 8 A.M. to 5 P.M. Monday through Friday with thirty minutes for lunch. On Saturday our hours are from 8 A.M. to noon."

He stood up and I did the same. "Am I correct in assuming that you're originally from the East?"

"Yes, Herr Beutelrock, from Königsberg, East Prussia."

"Really? I was stationed in East Prussia in 1939. I'm from the Sudetenland myself."

As we talked Mr. Beutelrock started walking with me down the corridor outside his office, eventually stopping at a large office with fourteen desks. On top of each desk was a heavy black mechanical calculator.

"Good morning everyone! This is Günter Nitsch, our new apprentice. Frau Plaumann, please introduce him to your colleagues and then take him on a tour of the administration building." He started to leave, but turned back to Mrs. Plaumann. "By the way, Günter Nitsch is from Königsberg, just like you."

Mrs. Plaumann, a pleasant blond lady in her late forties shook my hand and greeted me with an East Prussian accent, "Welcome to the Payroll Department!"

I tried my best to remember everyone's names but only the first three stuck in my mind: Mr. Mohr, clearly the oldest member of the team; Mr. Hendricks, a skinny, balding, intellectual type with a handlebar mustache; and Mr. Batz, a broad shouldered, heavyset pipe smoker with a noticeable limp whose shirt pocket bulged with an excessive number of pencils.

Mrs. Plaumann assigned me to the only free desk. "What's in your briefcase, a sandwich?"

"Yes, Frau Plaumann."

"Just so you know, we have three canteens in Arminius AG. The large cafeteria is for the factory workers. It's self-service. Then there's a dining room with waitress service for the white-collar workers like us and another one set aside just for management. You can eat in either of the first two. If I were you I'd go to the white-collar dining room where you'll get to meet the employees from the other departments." She lowered her voice to a whisper. "As one East Prussian to another, I'll let you in on a little secret. The lunch prices are so reasonable, you can eat there for less than your mother's sandwich costs."

"Thank you, Frau Plaumann. I appreciate the advice."

"Now," she continued, "if you follow me I'm going to introduce you to the people in the main administration building. By the way, don't worry if you can't remember who everyone is at first. There are just too many of them. The important thing is to try and remember the names and locations of the major departments because Herr Beutelrock will be sending you over there on errands pretty much every day."

We crossed the two-lane road beyond the guardhouse and headed up the twenty steps leading to the marble entrance of the administration building.

"Could I ask you something, Frau Plaumann? Do you happen to know why all of the buildings are painted that odd shade of red?"

"It's not paint. It's bauxite dust from our chemical plant back there. Gets into everything, as you'll soon find out, your eyes, your clothes, everything!"

We went through a glass door leading to the small addition to the right of the main entrance. A short corridor led to a second glass door beyond which was a high-ceilinged office with two large windows.

The desk on the left side along the wall was empty. On the right side two men sat facing each other at desks placed back to back in front of one of the windows. The younger man was busy on the telephone.

Mrs. Plaumann brought me over to a slim, middle-aged man of medium height whose slicked back black hair was graying at the temples. "This is Herr Kopf, the manager of the Transportation Department. The young man over there is Herr Miele, his assistant."

Mr. Kopf got up to shake my hand. "Pleased to meet you. When you've finished your time in Payroll, you'll be coming here next." He winked at Mrs. Plaumann. "In case Herr Beutelrock runs out of work for this young man, he can join us here any time." He turned back to me. "We have way too much work, and as you can see, your desk is already waiting for you."

In the meantime Mr. Miele had gotten off the phone and he came over to shake my hand. "Happy April Fools' Day and welcome aboard! I'll second Herr Kopf. We can certainly use all the help we can get around here!"

As soon as Mrs. Plaumann and I got back to the Payroll Department, I sketched a rough diagram with the names of the most important departments on the ground floor: Transportation, Bauxite Purchasing, the Mail Room, Statistics, Accounting, and Sales. Then I added the location of the offices of the executive secretaries to the two directors, Dr. Haubold and Mr. Senf. It was hopeless to remember the names of the technical departments on the two upper floors.

Mr. Mohr had been running his calculator while humming loudly to himself, much to the evident annoyance of his co-workers. As soon as I returned to my desk, he stopped working and walked over to me. "Nitsch, since you have to start somewhere, here are three hundred payroll slips. I want you to sort them alphabetically."

"Yes, Herr Mohr."

Once I finished my first assignment, I ate my lunch at my desk. Mrs. Plaumann came over to me as soon as I took the last bite of my sandwich.

"Let me show you how to work your calculator," she said. "Each of these metal dials has a little lever at the top. Let's say the number you want to enter is 945. You first pull the lever over the third dial to turn it to the 9, then you pull the lever for the second dial to the 4, and finally the first dial gets set to the 5. Once all the numbers are lined up, be sure to push the crank on the right side back and forth to store the completed number before going on to the next one. Are you with me so far?"

"Yes, I think so."

"The next step is to press a lever to indicate what you want to do with the number, add, subtract, multiply, and so forth. Then you're ready to enter the next number. And at the very end, you press the lever over here to get your total. All of the results have to be written down by hand. The machine doesn't store them." I gave the machine a try. "As you can see, it's a slow process," Mrs. Plaumann conceded. "We each have a calculator on our desks but most of us old timers discovered a long time ago that we can figure out the results faster in our heads."

"I couldn't believe how boring it was," I reported to my family that evening over supper. "Everyone sat hunched over those awful little machines. The fourteen of us hardly exchanged one word all afternoon."

"Give it time," my father assured me. "You should never judge a job by the first day. Trust me, it'll get better."

****

Thursday brought a change in the routine. Putting aside our calculators, we spent hours counting out the weekly wages of each factory worker in amounts ranging from sixty to one hundred twenty Deutschmarks. The money was then slipped into little brown envelopes and passed along to someone else who would recheck the contents before storing the envelopes in a long narrow tray. Although the work required a great deal of concentration, the people in the department somehow managed to talk to one another while doing it. It was as if they had kept their personal news bottled up all week long and couldn't bear to wait with it any longer.

During my second week Mrs. Plaumann and three young women who had been attending IBM courses in Cologne started to input the payroll information onto IBM punch cards which Mr. Hendricks then fed into the two huge IBM card processing machines. Since it was only a dry run, the rest of us continued to enter the same data on our mechanical calculators. The numbers matched and Mr. Beutelrock and Mr. Hendricks were delighted with the results. The same process was repeated the following week. Once again, the numbers matched.

However, in the third week, when the computer did all of the work on its own, the result was a disaster. According to the computer, some factory workers were entitled to more than a million Deutschmarks for the week, others to as little as seventeen pfennigs. Mr. Beutelrock wrung his hands and glared at the numbers through his thick lenses muttering over and over, "How could this have happened?" while Mr. Hendricks paced nervously back and forth, his few long strands of black hair dangling precariously out of place.

"Well, let's try to sort out this mess!" Mr. Beutelrock finally exclaimed. "Not you, Nitsch. You're only seventeen so I can't keep you here past five o'clock, but for the rest of us I expect it's going to be a very long night."

****

To break the monotony, the staff of the Payroll Department seized on every possible excuse to celebrate a birthday or the saint's day of one of the Catholic employees. On those occasions I was given money from the petty cash box and told to bike over to Café Meyer in Bergheim to buy slices of chocolate cream, fruit, and hazelnut tarts; assorted Danish pastries filled with cherry, apple and marzipan; and a bowl full of freshly whipped cream. While I was gone Mrs. Plaumann brewed a huge pot of coffee so that, as soon as I got back, the party could begin. Everyone participated; everyone, that is, except Mr. Beutelrock, who would stop by for five minutes at most before excusing himself with a terse, "Sorry, but I have work to do."

Inevitably, just when the party was getting into full swing, Mr. Mohr would rap on his desk with his ruler for attention. Then, whether we liked it or not, he would burst into song. He had a rich tenor voice, but the schmaltzy old folksongs he chose didn't go down well with the younger employees.

"Outside the gate's a fountain and an old linden tree," he would warble. "Under its shady branches my dreams were sweet and free..." When he reached the last line I started to applaud, but Mr. Hendricks pulled on my sleeve to stop me. "He's just warming up," he whispered. "Don't encourage him!" Sure enough, Mr. Mohr's impromptu concert went on and on. Several of my co-workers groaned, two or three retreated to the washroom, but Mrs. Plaumann, clearly enchanted, waited breathlessly to hear "Ännchen von Tharau," an old East Prussian folk song with which Mr. Mohr always concluded his performance. For people of my parents' generation, the song was as close to a national anthem as East Prussia ever had, and when he sang, "Should you be torn from me wandering alone, in desolate land where the sun is scarce known..." tears welled up in Mrs. Plaumann's eyes.

When everyone had finally returned to work, Mr. Beutelrock called me into his office. "Just so you know where I stand," he began, "I hate this endless partying. People here in the Rhineland don't take their work seriously enough. Just wait until Carnival starts and the entire staff goes bonkers. Not just the Catholic natives, even refugees who would never have acted crazy like that back in East Prussia or the Sudetenland. If I can manage it, I try to take my vacation the week before the start of Lent; nothing gets done around here that week anyway." I nodded, not sure where the conversation was headed. "Oh, I almost forgot," Mr. Beutelrock went on, "this is what I wanted to tell you. Right after I finished my studies at the *Gymnasium* I was drafted into the army, and when the war was over I had to look for a job. I would've liked nothing more than to be able to attend a university, but of course, that was impossible under the circumstances. You should do everything you can to get a Masters Degree in Business or Economics; otherwise you'll wind up stuck in a routine job looking for any excuse to party like your co-workers down the hall."

"Thank you, Herr Beutelrock," I answered. "I'll do my best." But I wondered whether he had forgotten what was in my personnel file; with the little bit of education I had, I had no hope of following his advice.

****

Among other things, my low position on the totem pole required me to fetch snacks for the other members of my department. Mr. Beutelrock in particular regularly sent me over to the cafeteria to buy him a Coke in the morning or in the mid-afternoon. Late one Friday, shortly before five o'clock, Mr. Hendricks called me over.

"Here's some money. Would you please get me a cup of coffee because I have to work late tonight?"

When I had gone to the cafeteria during the workday it was nearly deserted, but this time it was packed with men from the factory in their sweaty work clothes. Every last one of them was guzzling a glass of beer with a chaser of dark brown schnapps. I tapped a burly middle-aged man on the shoulder. "Excuse me, sir, but what's the reason for the celebration?"

"Where do you live? On the moon? It's payday!" he bellowed. His boozy companions lifted their glasses to him and shouted, "*Prost!*" and the toast was repeated a hundred times over across the vast cafeteria. When I finally fought my way up to the sales counter, I had to shout to place my order with the harried salesgirl. With even greater difficulty I wove my way back through the drunken crowd, carefully balancing a pot of coffee, a small container of milk, and two wrapped lumps of sugar on the small metal tray. To my great relief, I made it safely back to Mr. Hendricks.

"Here you are, sir. Sorry it took so long, but..."

He held up his hand. "No, I should apologize to you. I'd totally forgotten that it's payday."

"Is it really like that every Friday afternoon?"

"If you think the cafeteria's bad, you should see what goes on in the bars over in Kenten and in Quadrath. Some of the wives actually station themselves at the doors around a quarter to five to head their men off before the damage is done. Anyway, thanks for the coffee. See you tomorrow!"

****

A few days later Mr. Batz limped over to me and leaned his cane against my desk. "I've just talked with Herr Beutelrock. There's a job you need to do for me that might take a day or so." I looked up at him expectantly. "See those rolling file cabinets over there in the corner? I want you to sort all those files into two categories, one box with all the files from before May 15, 1945, and the others from May 15, 1945 forward. Be sure to keep them in alphabetical order. Any questions, you know where to find me."

"Yes, Herr Batz." I wheeled the two large file cabinets over to my desk and pulled out all of the files starting with the letter A. They landed on my desk in a cloud of dust.

"What's Nitsch doing with that old junk?" Mr. Mohr asked Mr. Batz.

"The personnel files from the forties? He's separating them into two sets," Mr. Batz replied.

Mr. Mohr clearly wasn't satisfied. "Why don't you just throw all that old stuff away?"

"Management is planning to create an Archive Department where all this information will be stored."

"Oh, for heaven's sake! What's next? First these damn computers, and now an Archive Department? I wish they'd give us a raise instead," Mr. Mohr grumbled before starting up to work, and to hum, once again.

Each worker's stiff manila record was accompanied by a small headshot. As I picked up each file I glanced at their gaunt faces and the hunger in their eyes. I knew all too well the look of starvation and hardship from my years under the Russians in East Prussia, and seeing it in the Arminius AG personnel files made me wonder what the lives of these men must have been like. I thought of the haggard factory workers, their clothes caked red with bauxite, with whom I talked at the end of the workday as we all used old rags to wipe the red dust off our bikes. Whenever I was sent on an errand to the production hall, the heat and the acrid stench of the acid used to process the ore had made me appreciate the term "hazard bonus" on the payroll slips. But there was something about these wartime workers that was even worse, something I couldn't quite put my finger on.

Once the files were separated by date, I began to verify that each set was in proper alphabetical order. Since I wasn't in any hurry to get back to my tedious payroll work, I took my time, studying the handwritten information entered on each card as I processed it. Many of the workers had foreign-sounding names but even more puzzling was the disparity in their hourly pay; some received only a few pfennigs per hour, while others had gotten substantially more.

I took several of the personnel cards over to Mr. Batz to ask him about them.

Mr. Batz smirked. "Oh, that's easy to explain," he replied, lowering his voice. "The ones who only got pennies per hour were *Untermenschen*; some people call them 'forced laborers.' Just look at those ugly mugs. They've got nothing in common with us. Look in the mirror! Do you look anything like them?"

"If I were starving again like I did under the Russians and had to work in the factory, I probably would," I replied.

"No, you wouldn't!" he insisted, gazing at me admiringly. "Tall, blond, steel-grey eyes. In my book, a perfect candidate for the *SS*." He took a book of matches out of his pocket and relit his pipe. After taking a few puffs he looked back up at me. "Any other questions?"

I was rattled by Mr. Batz's answer. How could he still be thinking of the *SS* after all these years? But after a moment's hesitation, my curiosity got the better of me. "Where'd they come from? Where'd they live while they worked here?"

"From all over Europe, wherever our brave German soldiers were fighting. They were held in a camp over in Kenten. Hell! Can you imagine? Those creeps had a better life than our boys did on the Russian front!"

"Thank you, Herr Batz," I replied. With a sick feeling in my stomach, I retreated to my desk to try to digest what he had told me.

Later that evening, I reported the incident to my parents. "Besides all that, the man's really creepy. I have the feeling that even when it looks like he's working, he's actually listening in to everything that's being said in the office."

My father shook his head. "I know that amputees can be bitter. But this Batz guy seems to have really gone off the deep end. I'd try to stay away from types like that if I were you."

"Thanks for the advice, but that's easier said than done while I'm still assigned to his department. By the way," I added, "you were right. It's definitely not dull at work any more."

CHAPTER 20

By the end of June 1955, the chaos in the Payroll Department caused by the introduction of the IBM computers had subsided. The giant machines regularly spewed out reports faster and more accurately than anyone on the staff had ever done by hand and the department was being streamlined as a result. Mr. Mohr was due to retire by the end of July and several other members of the staff were being transferred to other departments. When I was called into the office of Mr. Schmelzer, the Personnel Manager, I assumed I would be moved to the Transportation Department, but he had an unexpected request.

"So, young man, how would you like to take your annual vacation now, in July?"

"What about my start in Transportation? Herr Kopf is expecting me."

"I've talked to Herr Kopf and it's fine with him if you start there on August first."

Of course my co-workers in Payroll used my departure as another excuse for a party. After listening for the last time to Mr. Mohr's schmaltzy folksongs to the accompaniment of half-hearted applause I went down the hall to say good-bye to Mr. Beutelrock in his office.

"Don't forget my advice," he repeated. "From what I've seen you're definitely not cut out to be a pencil pusher in some back office. You need to work with people in sales or marketing, something along those lines. Think about continuing your education, maybe night school. Work your way up to an MBA degree. Don't get left behind the way I did." Mr. Beutelrock reached over to shake my hand. "Sorry I didn't have more time for you these past few months what with the IBM changeover and all. Good luck!"

****

Weeks earlier Jochen Krienke had asked me to hitchhike with him to Copenhagen over his school vacation but I'd been stalling him because of my apprenticeship. Now it was only a matter of convincing my parents. To my surprise, they both supported the idea. Saturday evening I absentmindedly hummed "Ännchen von Tharau" while packing spare underwear and socks, a shirt, a sweater, a rubber poncho, a toiletry kit, and a towel into my *Wehrmacht* rucksack, a gift from Friedel Meuser. Three thin leather straps on the outside of the rucksack secured the long roll of my second-hand sleeping bag and my half of a small tent. The name and military unit of the former owner of the rucksack were inscribed in neat handwriting inside the wide, light brown cowhide flap. Every time I opened the rucksack and saw the soldier's name, I wondered how old he had been and whether he had survived the war. To complete my preparations I carefully stowed a half loaf of rye bread, a plastic tub of margarine, one can of sardines, and one-third of a hard salami wrapped in aluminum foil into my army-surplus, green canvas food bag along with a military canteen filled with water before strapping it onto my belt.

Early on Sunday morning Mr. Krienke dropped Jochen and me off near an Autobahn entrance ramp in Cologne. Both of us were dressed in our usual hiking outfits: short *Lederhosen*, navy blue shirts with rolled-up sleeves, and yellow boy scout scarves with blue borders. Minutes later a sleek Mercedes stopped and the driver rolled down his window. Classical music was playing on the car radio.

"Where do you want to go?"

"Hanover," we both said at the same time.

"Hop in. I can give you us a lift as far as Bad Oeynhausen."

From Bad Oeynhausen it took us only two more lifts to get to Hanover where we stayed over with my Aunt Käte and my Uncle Hermann with whom Mutti, Hubert and I lived for four months in December 1948 after my father had abandoned us in a refugee camp. Aunt Käte served us a delicious supper -- assorted cheeses and breads with garden salads in dill dressing on the side.

"So," Uncle Hermann asked me when the dishes had been cleared, "how's your education coming along?"

"I graduated from a commercial school and was hired as an apprentice at the Arminius AG chemical factory near Bergheim."

"And how about you, young man?" he asked, turning to Jochen.

"I'm studying at the *Gymnasium*, sir, but I'm not sure I want to stick it out."

Uncle Hermann leaned forward in his armchair. "Let me tell you boys something. There's nothing more important than a good education. If I were in your shoes I'd try to get as much of it as I could. It's dog eat dog out there and that's the only way to keep ahead of the pack. Take our son Siegfried, for example. He still had two years to go when the Party muck-a-mucks handed him a high school diploma just so they could make him an officer cadet. So when the war was over he was a second lieutenant without skills. And then, instead of continuing his education he decided to become a bricklayer. Can you imagine?"

"Is that what Siegfried is still doing?"

"He got promoted so now he supervises the teams on the construction sites and makes a good living, but I'm sure he's always regretted not going to the university after the war. Aunt Käte and I were certainly disappointed that he didn't go on. Don't make the same mistake he did."

****

Fortified with Aunt Käte's scrumptious breakfast of scrambled eggs and toast, Jochen and I set out again in clear, sunny weather the next morning. Over the next few days we had no trouble hitching rides, first to Hamburg and then to Flensburg near the Danish border. Everyone, it seemed, was happy to give us a lift. That changed as soon as we walked across the border where nineteen other hitchhikers were already gathered at the side of the road waiting for rides. After waiting several hours, a young Danish businessman pulled up in a Volkswagen beetle and took us as far as Aabenraa, a picturesque fishing village on a large inlet of the Baltic Sea.

"You know," our driver warned us, "Denmark has been overrun with hitchhikers from all over Europe so you may have a tough time getting any further."

Even though it was still early, Jochen and I treated ourselves to an early lunch of raisin rolls and milk before strolling to the edge of town. At least twenty-five other hitchhikers, some of whom had been waiting since the night before, were standing dejectedly along the main road. Hours passed and some of the young men drifted away on foot only to be replaced by hopeful new arrivals. By six o'clock in the evening our enthusiasm was definitely flagging.

"I've been thinking," Jochen said grudgingly. "If we don't get ourselves a room at the youth hostel pretty soon, they'll run out of beds."

Our walk back into the village took us past the harbor where a small freighter was being loaded at the dock. I grabbed Jochen's arm. "Would you look at that? That boat's going to Kiel! Should we forget about going to Copenhagen and go back to Germany instead?"

"Are you kidding? You want to hitch a ride on a *boat*?"

"Why not? It's worth a try." I walked closer to the dock and yelled over to a man in a crisp white uniform leaning against the railing on the main deck. "Excuse me, sir, are you heading back to Kiel? If so, would you mind giving us a lift?"

"If it's just the two of you, sure, why not? Come on board. We sail in two hours!"

We walked up the gangplank in a state of disbelief. This had to be a hitchhiking first!

The man at the railing saluted us. "Captain Rasmussen. Welcome on board the *Suevia*. Where do you boys hail from?"

"From a small town near Cologne."

"I was there once during carnival a few years back. Too many people; too much noise. Couldn't wait to get back out to sea!" He looked us up and down. "I suppose you're both hungry. You'll find some leftover rice and curry beef in the galley. Then you can bunk down in the ship's infirmary. The two wooden beds in there aren't being used. Just put your sleeping bags on top."

"We don't mind staying up," Jochen protested. "It's only for a few hours."

The captain chuckled. "A few hours! We'll be sailing all night. I don't expect to dock in Kiel before eight in the morning." He pointed down to the hold of the ship. "Oh, by the way, in case you're wondering, we're transporting livestock."

After supper we sat on a bench on deck and watched the stars until nearly midnight before heading off to bed in the cramped, red-upholstered infirmary, falling asleep to a strange mixture of scents and sounds: salty sea air, antiseptics, and the muffled grunts of hundreds of hogs.

CHAPTER 21

At 7:55 A.M. on Monday, August 1, 1955, just one week after returning from my hitchhiking trip with Jochen, I reported to Mr. Kopf in the Transportation Department.

"Good morning and welcome. I hope you had a nice vacation," he greeted me, shaking my hand. Then he turned to Mr. Miele. "What've you got to start him on?"

Mr. Miele was a solidly built twenty-six-year-old who reeked of an overpowering aftershave lotion. "He can do the monthly statement and compile the railroad freight bills." He led me over to the empty desk along the wall, its surface covered with a fine coating of red dust. "Have a look at this batch of freight bills while I have my coffee. Then I'll tell you what you need to do."

"But before you start with that, I have a question for you," Mr. Kopf said. "Has anyone over at Payroll ever bothered to tell you what we're doing here at Arminius AG?"

"No, sir, I can't say that they have."

Mr. Kopf sighed. "Why am I not surprised? Arminius AG is a subsidiary of Helvetia Chemie. Basically, we're a chemical company. We buy thousands of tons of bauxite from countries like Yugoslavia, French Algeria, Jamaica, Indonesia, and Australia. It's shipped by sea to

Rotterdam, brought up the Rhine to Cologne on barges, and transported to our factory by rail. It takes eight tons of soft coal, which we get right here in Fortuna, to produce two tons of aluminum oxide powder from four tons of bauxite. We ship the powder to Rheinfelden, a town near the Swiss border, where our sister company produces one ton of aluminum from every two tons of aluminum oxide. Follow me so far?"

"Yes, sir."

While Mr. Kopf was talking, Mr. Miele took a mirror on a little stand out of his top drawer and placed it on his desk. After adjusting the mirror to the correct angle, he leaned over and proceeded to pop a tiny yellow pimple on his chin. I tried my best to ignore him.

"Herr Miele and I are responsible for negotiating the most favorable freight rates for the ocean liners and the Rhine barges, so we'll be spending a considerable amount of time on the phone."

I was jotting down some notes before returning to the stack of railroad freight bills on my desk when a homely man wearing a dark blue smock came into the office. He had curly red hair, a wrinkled, pockmarked face, and crooked teeth.

"The name's Kratzer," he said to me. "You used to be in Payroll, right?" I nodded. "I thought so. Well then, here are some more freight bills for you to work on. I'll be bringing them to you pretty much every day."

As soon as Mr. Kratzer was out of earshot, Mr. Miele turned his attention to me. "Kratzer may be a bit crude," he said, while still holding a tissue to his chin to stop the bleeding, "but you'll get used to him. The worst thing about him is his illegible scrawl. If you can't read his handwriting, I'll try my best to help you decipher it."

My job in the Transportation Department turned out to be fairly routine. Every day I had to telephone for information, compile statistics, and type a few letters to shipping companies. Mr. Kopf, Mr. Miele and I worked hard until about 10 A.M. and then I was sent to fetch a cup of coffee for Mr. Kopf from the cafeteria. Once I got back, the three of us shot the breeze about everything except work. I soon learned that Mr. Kopf and his wife were regular patrons of the opera; Mr. Miele and his fiancée preferred spending their weekend evening in nightclubs in Cologne. Mr. Kopf and his wife used public transportation; Mr. Miele's fiancée, whose parents owned a beauty salon in Quadrath, had a Volkswagen at her disposal. But one thing both men definitely had in common was their contempt for the company director, Dr. Haubold. Whenever Dr. Haubold was traveling, our coffee break lasted almost until lunchtime, only interrupted, much to everyone's annoyance, by an occasional phone call for Mr. Kopf or Mr. Miele. But when Dr. Haubold was in town, Mr. Kopf was constantly on the lookout for his approach from the courtyard, ready at a moment's notice to give a warning signal.

Dr. Haubold had been the captain of a minesweeper during World War II and he continued to run a tight ship. Letters to large freight forwarding and shipping companies which Mr. Kopf dictated to one of the ladies in the typing pool had to be signed by him before two o'clock. It was then my responsibility to bring the letters, each carefully placed between sheets of blotting paper in a special folder, to Miss Ruth Goldschmidt, Dr. Haubold's attractive secretary, so that Dr. Haubold could co-sign them. While the letters were under review, Mr. Kopf would pace back and forth, sharpen all of his pencils, tap his fingers on his desk, and stare at his telephone. We all knew that there were two possible outcomes, a good one or a bad one.

If Miss Goldschmidt or her assistant phoned Mr. Kopf an hour or two later to let him know that the mail could be picked up, he would beam triumphantly as if he'd just received an Olympic gold medal. "Thank you! Thank you so much. I'll send Herr Nitsch over right away for the folder!"

But when, as was more often the case, Miss Goldschmidt would say, "Herr Dr. Haubold wants to see you," the color would drain from Mr.

Kopf 's tanned face, his shoulders would slump, and he would leave the office like a beaten dog.

The first time this happened in my presence, Mr. Miele called me over to his desk. "Just between you and me, the Old Man's totally nuts. He probably found some word in the letter he didn't like or a comma out of place and now there's hell to pay. Poor Kopf. I wouldn't want to be in his shoes right now." He stopped a minute and looked up at me. Then he grinned. "I have a job for you. You know the hallway counter in front of the mailroom and supply office? Go find a spot there and wait for Heller. Take your time. He's always busy so, with any luck, he won't get to you for a while. If he asks, tell him I need," he paused and looked into his desk drawer, "five pencils and five pads. Oh! And while you're hanging around there, you might just happen to overhear the tongue lashing the Old Man's giving Kopf in his office." When I hesitated, he added with a wink, "Come on! I really need those supplies!"

I left our office and went into the main building, passing the Bauxite Purchasing Department, the secretarial pool, and the controller's office. Just before arriving at the mailroom counter, I heard angry shouts from behind the double doors of Dr. Haubold's office. The mail clerk, Mr. Heller, a short, skinny one-armed man with a perpetual grin, was folding a letter with his right hand and stuffing it into an envelope faster than most able-bodied men could have done. At the desk behind him Mr. Rutkowski, the telephone operator, hung up the receiver and remarked to both of us in a low voice, "Kopf is the Old Man's fourth victim today."

Mr. Heller shrugged and turned to me, "Nitsch, what can I do for you?"

"Herr Miele would like to have five pencils and five pads."

After getting the supplies from a large closet, Mr. Heller leaned across the counter to hand them to me, keeping his voice at a whisper. "You want some advice? I can't afford to quit. Who else would hire someone like me? But you have everything going for you. Once you

120

have some experience under your belt, if you ever get a boss like that, run for your life!"

"So," Mr. Miele greeted me on my return to our office, "did you hear anything?"

Before I had a chance to reply, Mr. Kopf stormed back in. His hands were trembling and his face was flushed a deep shade of red. "He's a madman!"

"What'd the old nitpicker get you for this time?" Mr. Miele asked. "A quotation mark? A semi-colon?"

"First he blasted me for using an exclamation point, but what really got him going was the letter I wrote to the Rhenus Shipping Company in Cologne. 'Too lenient', he said. 'You should have given them hell,' he said. Does he have any clue how important they are to our operations?"

Mr. Miele interrupted him, "Hey, Herr Kopf, calm down. Take a deep breath. You should be used to it by now. If he bawls me out I just look right back at him and don't say a word. Try it next time. I've done it. It works for me."

Mr. Kopf sat down, clasped his hands behind his head, and leaned back, "I've tried. Believe me I have. But your method doesn't work for me. I have to fight back!" He turned to me. "Don't get me wrong, Herr Nitsch. If an employee makes a mistake, he should expect to be criticized, reprimanded even. That's the prerogative of a superior, even someone like Herr Dr. Haubold who's ten years my junior. But it should be done in a *constructive* way like our deputy director, Herr Senf, does. Haubold's tirades are going to run me into an early grave."

"While we're on the subject of difficult people, if you don't mind my asking, what do both of you think of Scharwerker, the comptroller?" I inquired. It was from Mr. Scharwerker that I picked up my meager paycheck around the first of every month. To describe Mr. Scharwerker as ugly would be giving him too much credit. He had a shock of gray hair on top of his oblong-shaped head, a high forehead, cadaverous, sunken-in cheeks, and an upper lip too short to cover his yellow buckteeth. On top of that, he laughed like a Billy goat.

"Worst brown noser I ever met," Mr. Kopf replied. "When he talks to the Old Man it's 'Yes, Herr Dr. Haubold', 'Of course, Herr Dr. Haubold', 'You're entirely correct, Herr Dr. Haubold.' But he treats everyone under him like dirt."

"If you ask me," Mr. Miele added, "I think he'd be an even worse director than Haubold."

Mr. Kopf gave that comment some thought. "It would certainly be a toss up," he finally conceded.

CHAPTER 22

Rain or shine, I biked over to the Bergheim pool complex on my way home from work to unwind. Swimming five or six laps at a time before stopping to rest, I let my mind drift to thoughts of hiking, Boy Scout meetings, Sister Monika, anything other than Arminius AG.

Our family physician, Dr. Ute Klemm, was the advisor to the Bergheim Girls' Swim Team, and so she was usually there at the same time coaching her daughters, Silke and Gesine. Dr. Klemm had been a top national athlete in her youth, and despite being the mother of five, she still had the figure to prove it. Tall, slim, brunette, and undeniably feminine in her swimsuit, she swam in the summer and went skiing in the winter, which explained her year-round tan. A former leader of the League of German Maidens, physical fitness was her passion. In contrast to the young women who spent hours in front of the make-up mirror and then teetered around Bergheim in high-heels, Dr. Klemm only used lipstick and wore practical, flat-soled shoes. She was one of those unusual, persuasive people who could talk and smile at the same time.

As I climbed out of the pool and grabbed my towel, Dr. Klemm came over to me. "Günter, I've been watching you for a while now. You've got a good strong breaststroke, but you're not taking advantage

123

of our Olympic-sized pool by swimming short distances like that. If you really want to build up your endurance, you need to do at least ten laps without stopping and once you can do five hundred meters, then aim for a thousand and then two thousand."

"I'll give it a try!" I promised.

"Actually, I've got an even better idea. Why don't you talk to our swimming instructor, Herr Hansen, about taking a lifesaving course? He's looking for young men like you. What do you say?"

"I'd been thinking about it. Sure! Why not?"

"And while you're at it," the doctor added, "I'm starting a six-week-long Red Cross class at the Catholic elementary school. You should join that, too."

By the end of the day, I had signed up for both. How could I say no?

****

Thirty-three teenagers, two-thirds of them girls, attended Dr. Klemm's Red Cross class. We met for two hours every Wednesday night. At the first meeting, I scanned the group for familiar faces. Other than Dr. Klemm's two daughters, there was only Marlene Bodden, a tall, blue-eyed girl with a long blond ponytail who had attended the Commercial School in Horrem at the same time I did. Marlene's father owned Metzgerei Bodden, the largest butcher shop in Bergheim, and both he and Marlene's brother drove around town in shiny Mercedes cars. Even if Marlene had not been in a separate class in Horrem, there were three reasons why I never had had the nerve to approach her. She was rich, she was beautiful, and she was a girl! And now, there she was, only two rows away.

Over the following six weeks the customary invisible barrier between teenage boys and teenage girls continued to hold. If one of the boys dared to throw an admiring glance in their direction, the girls disdainfully ignored him. The free-flowing beer and wine at the graduation party for classmates and guests in the Zur Krone pub changed all that. To the soft sounds of Caterina Valente's latest hit, "All Paris Dreams of Love," inhibitions crumbled as we crowded together around the lavish platters piled high with sandwiches stuffed with cold cuts and cheese, potato salad, and franks, compliments of the German Red Cross. Lale Anderson's old standby "Blue Night in the Harbor" had just dropped down from the stack on the turntable when Dr. Klemm called for our attention.

"The next record will be a Polonaise," she announced, "and I want to see all of you out on the dance floor."

Her announcement started a stampede as some of the boys rushed over to choose a partner. I took a deep breath and headed straight for Marlene Bodden.

By the time I had asked, "May I have this dance?" my armpits were wet with sweat and I was sure she could see my heart pounding through my shirt. With a smile Marlene took my right hand and together we followed the first four couples in the slow march step. I hadn't been aware of how tall she was! In her high-heels she was my height and I was the tallest of the boys. The first couple took the lead, holding up their joined hands to form a tunnel. We all ducked through, the boys turning to the left and the girls to the right until we had all circled back together again. At the very end of the dance the boys had to swoop their partners into their arms and carry them for several rounds.

"I'm glad you chose me," she murmured as her left arm clung round my neck and the sweet scent of her perfume tickled my nose. "None of the other boys could've carried me so easily!"

"You're light as a feather!" I boasted, wishing I could carry her another thousand meters, when, just then, the Polonaise was replaced by a Viennese waltz. As I gently set Marlene back down, some of the girls were already waltzing with each other as the outnumbered boys retreated to the buffet.

"Do you know how to waltz?" Marlene asked.

Oh, how I wished that I did. "Sorry, no."

"That's too bad," she said. "Thanks anyway," and she wandered off to look for another partner.

I sulked all the way home, but when I confessed to my parents what had happened, Mutti made a practical suggestion. "Why don't you take dancing lessons? That way you'll be more confident next time."

My father seconded the idea. "You're almost eighteen years old. I knew all the steps long before I was your age."

So, every Monday for the next eight weeks I put on my leather-soled shoes, gritted my teeth, and attempted to master the intricacies of the waltz, the foxtrot, the tango, and the cha-cha-cha under the watchful eye of a diminutive dance master and his equally short wife. They didn't take to me kindly.

"Look at that klutz!" that perverse little man would call out, pointing a skinny finger at me. "Make sure the rest of you don't dance like that!"

But his insults were harmless compared to the humiliation I'd felt when I lost my chance with Marlene Bodden. No matter what it took, the next time a beautiful girl asked me if I knew how to waltz, I would be ready to sweep her off her feet.

CHAPTER 23

*T*he first of December fell on a Thursday. Just before lunchtime I put aside the piles of freight charge slips I'd been working on all morning and walked over to the counter in Mr. Scharwerker's office to get my paycheck. He was hunched over his desk, pen in hand. I cleared my throat and said, "Good morning, Herr Scharwerker."

Mr. Scharwerker scribbled some entries in a journal, moved his appointment book from one side of his desk to the other, and evened up the edges of the letters awaiting his signature. The minute hand on the electric wall clock behind him moved slowly around the dial. I shifted uneasily from one foot to the other. One minute. Two minutes. Three minutes. He looked up.

"So, Nitsch, as you can see I'm swamped with work but I suppose I have to squeeze you in." He stood up, twiddled the dial on the safe, and took out my money. Then he ambled over to me and counted it out in a loud voice, bill for bill and coin for coin down to the last pfennig.

"Is it correct?"

I picked up the money and added it up silently. "It's correct."

"Of all the impertinence!" he snapped. "'It's correct.' How dare you! Next time be sure you say, '*Jawohl*, Herr Scharwerker, it is correct.' Is that clear?"

What was it that Mr. Miele had said? *Just look right back and don't say a word.* I stuffed my money into my pocket, turned on my heels, and stormed out.

"Arrogant pig!" I muttered to myself when I got back to my office.

Mr. Miele had just started eating his sandwich. "What's gotten into you, young man? You're blushing like you just saw a naked virgin in the hallway!"

"I'm probably going to get fired."

"How come?"

"I took your advice. I just stood up to Scharwerker."

"Well, well, well." He rose from his chair and came over to shake my hand. "You won't get fired. Right, Herr Kopf?" Mr. Kopf took a gulp of his coffee and nodded in agreement. "You should get a medal for bravery! Someone has to teach that man that he's no longer a captain in Hitler's army. Here's an idea! Next time you go to his office you march right up to that counter, salute, and say, 'Apprentice Nitsch reporting for duty, Herr Scharwerker, sir. Request permission to fetch my money!' Then click your heels and stand at attention."

Mr. Kopf burst out laughing. "Seriously, Herr Nitsch, the man can't help it. For him the war's still going on. Ask him where he was in 1943 and he'll scratch his head, gaze off into space, and say something like, 'It must've been Yugoslavia because after our campaign to eradicate the partisans, I was promoted to First Lieutenant.' The way I figure it, if you count up all the times he says he was promoted, it's a wonder he wasn't running the whole damn War Office single-handedly."

****

Mr. Kopf, Mr. Miele and I could talk so freely because the small vestibule outside our office enclosed by its two glass doors served as an early warning system. No one could pop in on us unannounced. By the time any visitor reached the second glass door, we could switch at the drop of a hat from trashing Mr. Scharwerker or Dr. Haubold to an intense discussion of comparative shipping charges. This special feature of our office had two other advantages.

First of all, Mr. Kopf used our safety zone to read aloud to us every morning from the most sensational front-page stories in the *Kölner Stadt-Anzeiger* and the *Frankfurter Allgemeine Zeitung* whether or not they had any relevance to Arminius AG. Once a month, he would bring in the latest issue of *Reader's Digest* and regale us for several days in a row with the best articles and jokes. But more importantly, he would go off on fascinating tangents, describing in vivid detail an opera he had seen the previous weekend, complaining about the influx of job-seeking Poles, East Prussians, and Silesians into Bergheim before the first World War, chuckling over his adventures as an apprentice in a Cologne law office, bemoaning the financial struggles his parents faced during the Great Depression. Mr. Kopf always tried to be fair-minded. Although he resented the flood of refugees from East Prussia and the other lost Eastern provinces, he admired the work ethic of someone like my father who wanted to open his own store. He may have objected when Catholics were attacked in the press, but he readily conceded that Bavarian Catholics played a major role in the top hierarchy of the Nazi party. Intentionally or not, he was by far the most interesting teacher I had ever had.

Our office also served as a secure confessional for several of the other department heads who stopped by to pour their hearts out to us whenever the Old Man raked them over the coals. One of our steady visitors was Mr. Stommel, the bald, stocky middle-aged man with dark eyes, bushy eyebrows and horned-rimmed glasses who managed the Sales and Export Department. Mr. Stommel was a Rhinelander with an eighth-grade education. Over more than four decades, he had fought his way up through the ranks, advancing from lowly apprentice to department head.

"He treats me like an old sock," he complained bitterly to us one afternoon.

"Dr. Haubold giving you a hard time?" Mr. Kopf asked, knowing full well that he was.

"He's ignoring me."

Mr. Miele shook his head in disbelief. "The Old Man isn't calling you in and you're *complaining* about it?"

"Oh, he calls me in, all right, if the shit hits the fan. But recently if he just wants to discuss what's going on in the department he sends for my snot-nosed export manager, you know who I mean."

"Rupert Mayer? He seems like a fine young man to me," Mr. Kopf replied. "Is it true that he once studied for the priesthood at a Jesuit University? And he knows Latin, English, and French?"

"Yeah, yeah, yeah. And he was a prisoner of war in France when he was only sixteen. But what's that got to do with it! Hell, it's my department. If the Old Man needs to speak to someone, it should be me!"

"I still don't see what's bugging you. The less I have to do with Old Man Haubold the better," Mr. Miele declared.

"It's not just Haubold," Mr. Stommel continued. "Some of our best customers have started calling Mayer instead of me. And have you seen the way he drives to work in his fancy Volkswagen? He's lording it over us; that's what he's doing. He should walk to work like me or ride a bicycle."

Mr. Kopf held up his hand. "Come on, Herr Stommel; hold it right there. Herr Mayer is a young man. Why shouldn't he drive a car? You have a wife and five children to support. He's a bachelor and at his income level he can't go looking for a bride while riding on a bicycle."

"He doesn't have to look too far," Mr. Stommel grumbled. "Two of my secretaries and at least four other women from the firm are all chasing after him."

"More power to him!" Mr. Kopf exclaimed. "But be realistic. Forget about Rupert Mayer for the moment. Let's face it, Herr Stommel, we old timers have to accept the fact that nowadays a higher education counts more in the business world than years of experience. I hope our young apprentice is listening to what I'm saying. What about your own son? The one who works for a German company in Rio de Janeiro?"

"What about him?"

"Isn't he about the same age as Rupert Mayer? Twenty-eight? Twenty-nine? Weren't you bragging to us only last week that your son was on the verge of pushing out an older, more experienced Brazilian manager? What's good for the goose is good for the gander."

"Yeah, Herr Stommel, what do you say to that?" Mr. Miele mocked.

"I suppose you're right," Mr. Stommel reluctantly conceded.

From my desk I had been listening to the conversation while keeping on eye on the double glass doors. "Psst! Someone's coming!"

Rupert Mayer rushed into our office. "Herr Stommel! Herr Dr. Haubold wants to see you in his office right away!"

Mr. Kopf got up and patted Mr. Stommel on the back. "You see? The Old Man can't manage without you."

****

It was the beginning of December 1955, right after my eighteenth birthday. The engine of Dr. Haubold's sleek Mercedes limousine was purring and his uniformed chauffeur was ready behind the wheel as I rushed next door to deliver some documents to Miss Goldschmidt's office. Just as I opened the big glass door to the administration building, Dr. Haubold came barreling down the hallway in his black felt Fedora hat and heavy winter coat, bulging leather briefcase in hand. I held the door for him and had to take a step back to avoid being trampled. He ignored me and ran down the steps to the waiting car.

Not far behind Dr. Haubold, Mr. Kratzer was strolling towards the exit, whistling, hands in the pockets of his factory smock. He nodded at me as I continued on to the office Miss Goldschmidt shared with her assistant. The door was open but the office was empty.

"Excuse me, please. Hello? Is anybody here?" I called out in a loud voice.

I heard Miss Goldschmidt's voice from inside the open connecting door to Dr. Haubold's office. "Come in here, young man."

Both ladies were on their hands and knees, picking up files, documents, pads, pencils and assorted knickknacks from the floor and putting them back on Dr. Haubold's massive desk.

"Did you see Herr Dr. Haubold leave?" Miss Goldschmidt asked as she grabbed onto the edge of the desk to pull herself back up.

"I watched him get into his limo so he must be gone by now. Is it too late to give you these documents?"

"No, not at all, I'm sure they can wait until he gets back."

"Excuse me, Fräulein Goldschmidt, I hope you don't mind my asking, but what happened here?"

She gave me a tortured smile. "He had another one of his tantrums. Happens all the time. He gets angry about nothing and just shoves everything off his desk. I don't know how much longer I can take this!"

I bent down to help but Miss Goldschmidt shook her head. "That's all right, thanks. We can manage."

When I got back to our office, Mr. Kratzer was sitting at my desk. He yielded back my seat with obvious reluctance. "So, Nitsch, you must've seen the Old Man on his way out."

"You mean Herr Dr. Haubold?" I asked cautiously. "Yes, I did." Then I reported to Mr. Kopf. "I gave Fräulein Goldschmidt the documents. Apparently he didn't need them for this trip."

"She must be relieved that he's gone for a few days," Mr. Kopf said.

"I'm sure you're right about that. When I left his office she and her assistant were crawling around on the floor retrieving the stuff from his desk."

Mr. Kopf shook his head but Mr. Kratzer burst out laughing. "Serves her right! That arrogant Jew bitch. The company would be better off without people like her."

"I'll thank you not to talk like that in this office," Mr. Kopf said in an icy tone. "Just because Fräulein Goldschmidt speaks High German doesn't mean she's arrogant. In my book she's a very refined lady with excellent manners. And I don't see what difference it makes whether she's Jewish or not."

Mr. Kratzer glared. "I just don't like to be around those people."

"Is there anything else Herr Kratzer? Otherwise I think we should all get back to work, don't you?" Mr. Kratzer shrugged and headed out the door. As soon as he left, Mr. Kopf shook his head. "What an idiot! Talking about Fräulein Goldschmidt like that." Then he addressed me. "I'm sorry you had to hear all that garbage, Herr Nitsch. Kratzer may be a good factory manager, but his personal prejudices disgust me. From what I understand, as soon as Hitler got into power, he was one of the first in Bergheim to join the Storm Troopers. He somehow got to a pretty high level in the County organization during the war and he's still spewing hatred. By the way, just so you know, Fräulein Goldschmidt regularly attends Sunday Mass. She's not even Jewish."

Mr. Miele nodded in agreement. "If you look closely at Kratzer's face, you can still see the scars he got when his band of thugs brawled with the Communists. He's an incorrigible old Nazi, and if you ask me, when it comes to anti-Semitism, he's as crooked as his teeth."

****

Another regular visitor to our "secret confessional" was Mr. Immervoll, Arminius AG's chief bauxite buyer, whose office was two doors down the hall in the main administration building. A tall, slim man in his mid-forties with a scarlet complexion, a rum-blossom nose, thick lips, and dark bags under his bloodshot eyes, Mr. Immervoll usually wobbled unsteadily into our office shortly after ten o'clock in the morning reeking of booze. In contrast to Mr. Kopf and Mr. Stommel, he didn't waste much time criticizing Dr. Haubold; rather he entertained us with an endless stream of outrageous stories about the playboys he met among Greek shipping magnates, international bauxite mining executives, and transportation industry big shots from Antwerp to Rotterdam.

One morning Mr. Immervoll showed up in our office even more tipsy than usual with an announcement. "Guess what? That hopeless idiot just left on a four-day business trip to Hamburg and Stockholm. How d'ya like that? So, in other words, we can relax a bit." Since we didn't have an extra chair, he leaned against the edge of my desk to steady himself. "Did I ever tell you the story about Karapoulos, the Greek tycoon?" He didn't wait for a reply. "No? Well, a few weeks ago I got an irate phone call from the manager of the Vier Jahreszeiten Hotel in Hamburg. 'Herr Immervoll,' he said, 'your customer just showed up here with four fancy call girls in tow.' Four hookers! Imagine that! Then he told me, and I quote, 'Herr Immervoll, as much as we value your business, this man's behavior is totally unacceptable. I insist that you try to straighten him out. Otherwise, we will no longer accept any future reservations for you or for him.'" He slapped his knees and roared with laughter.

After Mr. Immervoll left, Mr. Kopf shook his head. "Immervoll knows his stuff but his drinking's getting out of hand. And this Karapoulos story. It's the third time I've heard it."

"He's married, right? You'd think his wife would try to keep him in line," I commented.

Mr. Miele snorted with laughter and I looked to Mr. Kopf for an explanation. "She's an even bigger lush than he is. She was the cocktail waitress at the nightclub he frequented when he was stationed in Danzig during the war."

"Just to give you an idea," Mr. Miele added. "He recently bragged that the two of them can polish off an entire bottle of Courvoisier on a Saturday night."

Only a day later, about an hour before lunch, Mr. Kopf rushed back to our office from a meeting in the Sales and Export Department. "Herr Nitsch, drop everything you're doing. I want you to sit at Immervolls's desk and answer his incoming phone calls!"

"What should I say?"

"How about, 'I'm sorry, but Herr Immervoll is in a meeting,' or something along those lines."

"And if someone comes in?"

Mr. Kopf shrugged. "Think of something. Anything. Tell them he's not feeling well."

"Let me guess," Mr. Miele said in a mocking voice. "He's out cold in his office again."

Mr. Miele had guessed right. Mr. Immervoll lay sprawled like a dead man in a thickly padded leather armchair, snoring like a buzz saw. In his lower right-hand desk drawer, half-empty bottles of Asbach Uralt brandy and Pott rum were lined up next to a brown pottery jug of Steinhäger gin.

"Can you imagine?" I complained to my family later that evening. "He woke up two hours later, phoned for a cab, and took the rest of the day off. So now, instead of doing my own job, they've got me covering for a drunk who works a two-hour day and probably makes ten times what I do. It's not fair!"

"So you think it's unfair, do you?" my father said. "Welcome to the real world."

"Don't be such a grouch," Mutti teased. "It's nearly Christmas and we have some exciting news to share with the boys. Do you want to tell them, or should I?"

"What your mother means to say is that I've had more discussions with the city officials in Bergheim about getting a *Lastenausgleich* loan so that I can open my own pastry shop. They actually sounded encouraging, especially since Mutti and I had leased a café in Königsberg before the war."

"When do you think it will happen?" Hubert asked Mutti.

"Soon, we hope, but nothing's settled yet."

"But getting back to Arminius AG for a minute," my father said. "In my opinion, nothing ruins a person's job prospects faster than spreading gossip about management. You can learn a lot by listening, but if I were you, I wouldn't put in my own two cents worth. You can't believe how fast stuff like that travels back up the chain of command." I nodded in agreement. "There's one more thing. We have an early Christmas present for you. Starting next month Mutti and I have decided that you can keep your entire apprenticeship paycheck; you don't have to give any of the money to us. If Herr Beutelrock thinks you should get more education, maybe you can use that money to register for an English-language course or something."

I was stunned. All of the apprentices I knew had to turn over nearly every pfennig they earned to their parents. "Wow! Thank you so much. I'll do just that!"

CHAPTER 24

*T*wice a month a bookkeeper from the Accounting Department would wend his way down the long hallway of the Arminius AG administration building to bring Mr. Miele new questionnaires about freight-volume statistics. A self-important, chinless little man, 1.51 meters tall in his stocking feet, Mr. Schmitz had deep-set slanted eyes, which peered out from a miniature skull reminiscent of the shrunken heads from the South American rainforest. An impeccable dresser, he obsessed about his appearance, from the unusually tall hat he wore over his sleek comb-over right down to his polished elevator shoes. Behind his back everybody in the firm called Mr. Schmitz "Little Uncle."

If Mr. Kopf didn't cut him off, Mr. Schmitz could rant for half an hour about German politicians, rarely having a good word for any of them. When he wasn't putting someone down, he was building himself up. One blustery day in the middle of January 1956, he strutted over to Mr. Kopf and Mr. Miele and puffed out his chest.

"I want you gentlemen to know that our department has collected more booze, wine, and champagne for *Weiberfastnacht* this year than ever before!"

Mr. Miele rolled his eyes. "Well, bully for you. Imagine that. A record stash with three weeks still to go 'til we celebrate the end of Carnival. I'm sure you'll all get some kind of prize."

"That's quite an accomplishment," Mr. Kopf agreed, his voice dripping with sarcasm. "But now, if you don't mind, we have actual work to do."

As soon as Mr. Schmitz had gone through the second set of glass doors, Mr. Miele shook his head. "Pompous little fart. I don't know where such a tiny man has room for such a big ego."

"Of course what he conveniently forgot to mention was that all that alcohol probably came into the Accounting Department in the form of bribes from craftsmen wanting company contracts," Mr. Kopf added. "I think the guy really has a Napoleon complex. From what I've heard, during the war he put a giant map of Europe up on the wall in his office and every day he'd climb up on a stepladder and move bright-red push pins around to mark the progress of the German front in Russia, all the while bragging, 'Today we captured such-and-such place and tomorrow it's on to Moscow!'"

"So what did he say after Stalingrad?" Mr. Miele wanted to know.

"You got me there. But the fanatic Nazis still believed in the final victory until the very end."

Just then Mr. Kratzer walked in. "Did you just say 'final victory'? It breaks my heart to hear that phrase. We would've had the best army in the world if weren't for those traitors who refused to fight to the death for the Fatherland. And all that materiel the Americans supplied to the Ivans to keep them going? The whole thing was financed without any doubt by the Jews!"

Now Mr. Kopf exploded. "Herr Kratzer, I told you weeks ago that we don't want to hear any more of that nonsense. Not now. Not ever. Since you've given those railroad freight bills to Herr Nitsch, there's no reason for you to hang around here."

When the three of us were alone again in the office, Mr. Kopf took a deep breath. "There must be a full moon or something. First it's that crazy Little Uncle and now Kratzer, the fanatical Jew baiter. You know, since the Old Man is away for another two days, this may be as good a time as any to give you both a little history lesson. Many people who've lived around here all their lives have no idea about what I'm going to tell you. I'm damn sure Kratzer doesn't." Mr. Kopf took a sip of his coffee and cleared his throat. "It was a Jewish industrialist named Adolf Silverberg and his son, Paul, who made the area around Bergheim into an economic success. The father was the first to recognize the importance of our natural resources. Together with the Salomon Oppenheim Bank, he bought up the soft coal mines in Fortuna, and later he founded the power company there. He's also the one who established the wool and the linoleum manufacturing plants in Bedburg. When Adolf Silverberg died, his son took over the family business. Dr. Paul Silverberg was a lieutenant in the Bavarian cavalry and even though he converted to the Lutheran faith, he financed the building of a Catholic Church with a connected kindergarten and school over in Oberaussem. The Pope even awarded Dr. Silverberg a medal for his good works. Just imagine!"

"Sorry, Herr Kopf," I interrupted. "But what does all that have to do with Schmitz and Kratzer?"

"Easy. What idiots like Schmitz and Kratzer don't seem to realize, is that this whole region owes its economic development to one Jewish family. The son eventually became the Chairman of the Association of German Industry and the President of the Cologne Chamber of Commerce, that's how respected he was."

"Did he somehow survive the war?"

"I understand he moved to Switzerland in 1934 when he saw the handwriting on the wall. What a loss to this area! If you ask me, we need more men like the Silverbergs, but try telling that to someone like Kratzer. You might as well argue with a lump of clay."

****

"How're things back at the old Elementary School?" I asked Hubert the first weekend in February as he and I shoveled snow in front of the Lutheran Church.

"Pretty much the same as usual. I can't wait until I'm fourteen next year so I can get an apprenticeship!"

"Speaking of that, did I tell you I finally got a chance to spend some time with Josef Reinike, the apprentice who started at the same time I did? He and I work in different departments so we hardly ran into each other until about two weeks ago."

Mr. Schmelzer, the Personnel Manager, had called Josef Reinike and me into his office in late January. "Gentlemen," he announced, "Arminius AG is always trying to find ways to improve the health of our employees. And from what I hear, you can never underestimate the health benefits of exercise combined with a good dose of Vitamin D. So, I'm urging you both to spend fifteen minutes three times a week in our brand-new solarium. Our company nurse will be glad to schedule the sessions for you."

"They've advised my father to use the solarium, too," Josef informed me as we headed over together for our first appointment. "He moved recently to the Drying Department. You know that peculiar chemical odor over there? It still clings to his skin hours after he's changed out of his work clothes. According to him, the solarium is a great fringe benefit."

Since Mr. Kopf sent me over to Mr. Kratzer's office at least once a week, I regularly passed the various production departments where thick red dust hung in the air and the men worked in unbearable heat as harsh fumes cut deep into their lungs. The worst of them all was the Acid Department, a steamy hellhole where workers sloshed through puddles of acid in their thick rubber boots.

Now Josef and I, together with a dozen lean, middle-aged men from those departments, their skin as pale as cottage cheese, donned dark goggles, stripped down to our briefs, and entered the solarium. In that huge, dark room, sunlamps in continuous thick glass tubes snaked around the floor forming a maze. Other tubes were attached to the walls at shoulder level. Still others hung from the ceiling. As we silently padded around the circuitous path in our bare feet while keeping an eye on the wall clock, every part of our bodies was exposed to the supposedly life-affirming benefits of Vitamin D.

"So," Mr. Miele asked when I got back from my first session. "How many young women in panties did you see in the solarium?"

"Not one, I'm sorry to say. I guess you've never been."

"I'm afraid we can't go," Mr. Miele said. "The solarium is reserved for the factory workers and our apprentices. Unfortunately, it's off limits to us white-collar folks."

Because Josef worked in accounting and I was in transportation, we were on different work schedules, so he and I went to the solarium at different times after that. I didn't particularly enjoy the visits and would have given up after the second time but my father, who had worked in military hospitals during the war, encouraged me to continue, insisting that the sunlamps would do me good.

Late one afternoon at the end of the week, I ran an errand to the Accounting Department. There, to my horror, was Josef, who had been transformed from a dark-haired eighteen-year-old boy into a shriveled-up old man with wrinkled skin and swollen eyelids.

"What on earth happened to him?" I whispered to Mr. Schild, the office manager.

"As best I can piece it together, he was alone in the solarium and sat down on one of the chairs to rest. Next thing he knew, someone was waking him up and carrying him in here. They're going to bring him to the doctor."

I ran into Josef in the cafeteria when he returned to work a few days later. His face was slathered with a greasy ointment; his lips were cracked; brownish-yellow leathery skin covered the backs of his hands, and he grimaced with every step he took.

"You still going to the solarium?" he asked me through clenched teeth.

"Not if you paid me a million Deutschmarks!"

Josef's eyes flashed. "If it were up to me, Arminius AG would take their wonderful fringe benefit and shove it up their ass!"

****

On Wednesday afternoon, February 8, 1956, the eve of *Weiberfastnacht*, I was puzzled to see young women throughout Arminius AG, but especially those working in the typing pool and the Accounting Department, decorating their offices with colorful flower wreaths, balloons, and red, blue, green, and yellow paper streamers.

"Is something troubling you, young man?" Mr. Kopf asked me when I returned to my desk.

"It looks like there'll be a big party around here tomorrow. I was just wondering. Does Herr Dr. Haubold know about all this?"

Mr. Kopf smiled. "Herr Nitsch, may I remind you that this is the Rhineland? On *Weiberfastnacht* the women rule the roost. Tomorrow, even Haubold will be powerless. He may not have been born around here but he knows enough not to interfere. There's nothing he could do about it anyway. By the way, don't expect to get much work done between now and Ash Wednesday."

"Thanks for the information."

"Oh, one more thing. If you're not too hungry when you get up tomorrow, I'd suggest that you skip breakfast. You'll get a much better one here!"

Over supper that evening I related the day's events to my family. When I'd finished talking, my father looked suddenly serious.

"Stretch, may I make a suggestion? From what I've heard, a lot of heavy drinking goes on at office parties on *Weiberfastnacht*. Do me a favor and go easy on the beer. And stay away from the hard stuff. You're only an apprentice and you don't want to make a bad impression."

The next morning, forgoing my usual breakfast of roasted barley coffee and sliced bread spread with margarine and jam, I biked over to Arminius AG, arriving at twenty minutes to eight. Mr. Kopf and Mr.

Miele were already busy making phone calls to freight forwarding and shipping companies. Mr. Kopf put his hand over the receiver and said, "So, Herr Nitsch, if I were you, I'd do whatever you have to do now, because in less than two hours this place is going to come to a stand still."

Shortly after 9 A.M. I brought a file over to Mr. Stommel in the Sales and Export Department. To my astonishment, the normally sedate Mr. Stommel was wearing a woolen turtleneck sweater with alternating light green and dark red horizontal stripes. His bright yellow bowler-shaped party hat clashed with the hat worn by Mr. Mayer, a pointed white cone covered in purple polka dots and topped with an orange paper plume. Both men were on the phone, Mr. Stommel speaking in German and Mr. Mayer in French. Each held a telephone receiver in one hand and a half-empty glass of white wine in the other.

After I put the file on Mr. Stommel's desk, I noticed Miss Bonacker, one of the secretaries, leaning heavily against the frame of the connecting doorway. She waved me into the adjoining office. "A young man like you must be hungry," she said. "Fräulein Neumann and I are fixing sandwiches. Feel free to help yourself!" She pointed to a huge tray stacked high with buttered rolls that had been cut in half and filled with ham, or cheese, or sausage. Thanking her, I helped myself to a cheese sandwich.

"How 'bout a glass of wine or a beer to wash it down?" Miss Bonacker asked me, her voice somewhat slurred.

Miss Neumann covered her mouth with her hand and giggled. "Are you sure he's old enough to drink?"

When I walked back into my office a few minutes later munching on the roll, a bottle of beer in my hand, Mr. Miele called out, "Atta boy, Herr Nitsch! That's the spirit! You know what? You've made me thirsty and we still have to make a few phone calls. Could you please run over to the Accounting Department where they have all the good stuff and bring us back two bottles of DAB?"

"DAB?"

"For heavens sake. You mean to say you turned eighteen in December and you still don't know what DAB is? It's Dortmunder Actien Bier. Try it. You'll like it."

In each of the gaily-decorated offices along the hallway on the way to the Accounting Department, the staff was already eating, drinking, and generally frolicking. However, not everyone was joining in the fun. When I walked by the office of Mr. Kohlhofer, the humorless manager of the Statistics Department, he beckoned me to come inside. Mr. Kohlhofer's over-sized head was nearly bald. In his early forties and a confirmed bachelor, he had the peculiar habit of pushing his milk-bottle-thick eyeglasses back up onto the bridge of his short nose with the index finger of his left hand. When he ate the sandwich he brought from home every day for lunch at his desk, he licked that same finger and used it to pick up spilled breadcrumbs and pop them into his mouth. It was his custom to wear a snow-white, starched smock like those worn by the employees in the Chemical Laboratory Department. According to his assistant, Miss Brockhaus, from time to time Mr. Kohlhofer would come across a long-forgotten, moldy sandwich in the back of his desk drawer, cut away the spoiled parts, and eat the rest as a snack. His table manners might explain why, even though he was fastidious about changing his dress shirt every day, the food-stains on his tie read like a miniature cloth menu of his recent meals.

"Nitsch, come in here for a moment!" he called out to me over the din. "You've probably heard I'm from the Sudentenland, right? And you're from East Prussia?" I nodded. "So what do you make of all this? Isn't it outrageous? Good thing the factory workers are still on the job or the whole production process would grind to a halt." Miss Brockhaus, a Rhinelander, grinned at me, turned her back on her boss, and defiantly flounced out of the office. "They're all nuts! It's a wonder Herr Dr. Haubold puts up with this. It's chaos!" Just then, Dr. Haubold stopped by the open door to wave and smile at us. He was wearing an elegant

144

black top hat; a red paper rose was pinned in the lapel of his dark blue suit. Mr. Kohlhofer threw up his hands in disgust. "Forget it, Nitsch. We should discuss this some other time. Go! Enjoy yourself! Oh, and please close the door on your way out."

The Accounting Department had ceased to be a workplace and had been turned instead into one big party room and dance hall. When I arrived, a record player was blasting the carnival song "You Can't Be True Dear" at top volume. Two Schild brothers worked in Accounting. The younger one, tall and skinny as a rail, had his arm around the waist of a dark-haired secretary. His corpulent older brother was the office manager. I pushed my way through the crowd and tapped him on the shoulder.

"Excuse me, Herr Schild!" I yelled at the top of my voice. "May I have two DAB beers, please?"

"Don't even ask, Nitsch," he screamed back at me. "Just take whatever you need, and tell my pals over in Transportation to hurry up and join us over here!"

At lunchtime, I wandered from department to department stuffing myself with food before heading back over to Accounting where the party had heated up considerably. Since it was *Weiberfastnacht* – the Thursday before Ash Wednesday – most of the time it was ladies' choice. After three of the secretaries had asked me to dance, one of my former classmates from the Elementary School who worked in Purchasing took me by the hand and pulled me over to the side of the room. Jutta was a refugee like me; her family had been expelled from Silesia.

"Check out the Schild brothers!" she hissed, pointing towards the back wall. "Those girls are half their age." Some couples were dancing cheek to cheek but the Schild brothers had gone one step further. They were both clinging so tightly to their dance partners that they practically melted together. "Some people are saying they should get a room! It's disgusting."

"Or at least have the decency to take off their wedding rings."

"Anyway, this whole scene is making me uncomfortable. I'm going back to my department."

I left the Accounting office soon after Jutta did, passing by the Bauxite Buying Department where Mr. Immervoll was stretched out on the couch sound asleep with his party hat covering his face, and stopped in to say hello to Mr. Mayer in Sales and Export. He was on the phone.

"Yes, sir, I know it's Thursday afternoon." He put his hand over the receiver and waved me in before continuing his conversation. "Uh huh. I can appreciate your position, but there's nothing I can do. This is the way things are in the Rhineland."

"Hello, Herr Mayer," I said once he hung up the phone. "You're one of the few people still working around here."

"Someone has to try to explain to our customers why they can't get through to us. So far today I've talked to people in Bremen, London, Marseille and Antwerp, and they all think we're crazy."

"In all of the other offices, if the phone rings random people just grab the receiver and yell, 'We're celebrating carnival!' and hang up."

"I know, but I figure someone around here has to act civilized," Mr. Mayer said with a sigh as he reached over to take another call.

Our office was empty, and since Mr. Miele's briefcase was missing, I presumed he had gone off to join his fiancée at the carnival party her parents were hosting in the beauty salon. I would have liked to leave too but didn't dare, so I walked back to Accounting where the action was. Little Uncle, looking dapper in a bright green top hat with silver trim, was standing on his toes in a futile attempt to tower over two secretaries who were sitting in swivel chairs enjoying his jokes. While he talked, his squinty little eyes darted around the room, noting everything that was going on. He glared at me when I came in. Since I suspected he was jealous of my height because he called me "Beanpole" behind my back, I kept my distance so that I wouldn't steal his thunder.

I had just poured myself a glass of beer when Miss Gimborn, a tall brunette my age I knew from the telex room on the second floor, flashed me a smile and said, "Let's dance." It was a schmaltzy song, and before I knew it, the two of us were cheek to cheek. Three more records dropped onto the turntable before we finally took a break. I poured Miss Gimborn a glass of white wine and then she and I sat down together to talk while I cooled off with the rest of my beer.

"Is it my imagination, or is the younger Herr Schild leering at us?" Miss Gimborn complained after a few minutes. "He's creepy."

"That's for sure," I agreed. "Let's go over to the secretarial pool office and see if they have any leftover food." But as soon as I stood up, I knew I was going to be horribly sick. "I'm awfully sorry," was all I could say before I made a mad dash to the men's room.

As soon as I closed the door to the toilet stall, I started to vomit so violently that I thought I would die. After my stomach had rejected all of the food and beer I'd consumed throughout the day, I sat down on the toilet seat, exhausted, and must have passed out for I don't know how long.

"Hey! Are you gonna be in there all day?" someone shouted while pounding on the door. With the room spinning crazily around me, I grabbed onto the walls for support and got up. The man brushed me aside, leaned over the toilet bowl, and threw up. All the other stalls were occupied; everyone in them was sick. I dragged myself over to the sink and washed my hands and face before staggering back to my office. Mr. Kopf was just about to leave.

"You're an awful shade of green," he commented. "Someone told me you were sick. What happened exactly?" He listened sympathetically to my account. "It looks like someone must've poured a few shots of vodka into your beer while you were dancing. Vodka's tasteless, you know. Take my advice. From now on, never leave your drink alone during carnival." Mr. Kopf took my arm and walked me outside into the fresh air. "The way you're feeling, I'd suggest leaving your bike here and taking the bus home. See you tomorrow!"

"Thank you, Herr Kopf."

While my parents and Hubert had supper, I moved my chair away from the dinner table so that I wouldn't have to watch them eat.

"So," my father said to me once the dishes had been put away, "you didn't listen to my advice and now you've had to learn the hard way."

"I didn't mix my drinks," I protested. "Someone mixed them for me."

"That may be, but your stomach obviously couldn't tell the difference."

The next morning in the office Mr. Miele greeted me with, "So, how's our champion puker doing today!" Then he lowered his voice. "Actually, I'm glad you felt up to coming in to work. From what Herr Kopf told me, I didn't think you'd make it."

"I'd like to strangle the person who did it to me!"

"Now, don't quote me, 'cause I can't prove it; the skinny Schild brother has spiked the drinks of some of our young apprentices in the past. But this time my money's on Little Uncle! Either way, if I were you I wouldn't go anywhere near Accounting for the next few days."

I interrupted him. "You mean the party's still going on over there?"

"Not like yesterday. Half the staff won't even bother to show up for work today aside from the ones who've taken official vacation days through Saturday, and Monday's a legal holiday. But for the ones who do make it in, they have a motto over in Accounting. 'When it comes to booze: No leftovers!'"

"C'mon, Herr Miele. You're pulling my leg!"

"Just wait and see," Mr. Kopf said. "The staff won't really get back down to business until Ash Wednesday."

And that's what happened. The partying continued right until the close of business the following Tuesday. On Wednesday morning, as most employees showed up ready for work with ash crosses on their foreheads, only a few forlorn streamers, some trash baskets filled with empty bottles, and a faint smell of vomit were all that was left of the celebration.

****

"Well, this beats everything!" Mr. Miele said as he returned to our office from the administration building the following week. "All of the department heads, and that includes you, of course, Herr Kopf, are going to get a buzzer for your desks. So, when the little light turns red and the buzzer goes off, you'll be expected to hotfoot it over to the Old Man's office."

"Is this some kind of joke? Because, if so, it's not very funny," Mr. Kopf retorted.

"Sorry, I wish it were. I just got the word from our colleagues over in Sales."

That same afternoon two electricians showed up to install a buzzer next to Mr. Kopf's telephone. That poor man had always nervously anticipated the dreaded phone calls from Miss Goldschmidt calling him into Dr. Haubold's office, but the buzzer had a far worse effect on him. Whenever the Old Man was in the building, Mr. Kopf would sit and stare at the buzzer. And when the red light came on and the buzzer sounded, his hands shook so hard that his coffee sloshed out of the cup. Then he would grab a pad and pencil and run out to meet his fate.

"This isn't good for his health," Mr. Miele predicted as we watched him go.

A week after the system was installed, the buzzer sounded and Mr. Kopf raced out of the office only to return a few minutes later.

"Back so soon?" Mr. Miele inquired.

"The Old Man is losing it. There's no doubt in my mind. When I rushed over there, nine of us – Immervoll, Stommel, Mayer, Kohlhofer – well, you know who they are. All of us arrived at the same time. We were practically falling all over each other to get inside. And once we were at his desk, what does he do? He stands there screaming at the top of his lungs, 'I just wanted Muckenberg. The rest of you get the hell out of my office!' Poor Muckenberg was on his way in as the rest of us scrambled for the door."

Just then the phone rang. Mr. Kopf picked up the receiver, listened, smiled, hung up and said, "That was Fräulein Goldschmidt who called to apologize because, and these are her words, 'Herr Dr. Haubold may have pushed most of the buttons at the same time by mistake.' Some mistake! I think he just wanted to see who'd get there the fastest."

****

A few days later word got around that Dr. Haubold would be away for a week. The department heads were all looking forward to some peace and quiet, none more so than Mr. Kopf. I had just come back from the cafeteria on the other side of the wide truck lanes opposite the administration building. Carrying a pot of coffee, sugar and cream on a tray, I was about to go up the wide staircase when I saw Mr. Kopf waiting impatiently on the top step. The moment he saw me he called out, "Psst! Herr Nitsch! Has the Old Man left already?"

Just then Dr. Haubold came up right behind Mr. Kopf. "No!" he sneered. "The Old Man is still here!"

Mr. Kopf, his cheeks blazing red, whirled around and stammered, "Herr Dr. Haubold. I beg your pardon! My apologies. I didn't mean to say that," and then he rushed into our office.

In the meantime I had reached the platform. "Good morning, Herr Dr. Haubold."

"Is that coffee for Kopf?" he snapped.

"Yes sir."

"Tell him I hope he chokes on it!"

When I entered our office Mr. Kopf was standing near the window staring out through the curtain. He looked back over his shoulder. "The coast's clear. He just got into the car!" He sat down at his desk, added cream and sugar to his coffee, and lifted the cup with a trembling hand.

"I was wrong about Haubold's effect on Herr Kopf's health," Mr. Miele said to me with a chuckle. "Our Herr Kopf must have the constitution of a horse. I would've died of a heart attack if it'd happened to me."

CHAPTER 25

On April 2, 1956, I was officially transferred to Mr. Stommel and Mr. Mayer in the Sales Department for the remainder of the year. Since they didn't have a desk for me, I was given a small wooden table alongside my bosses' giant adjoining desks. Except for some light filing and an occasional errand, I didn't have much to do, so I spent most of my time listening to telephone calls. Stommel concentrated on customers in Germany; Mayer handled calls from English- and French-speaking customers. I soon noticed that whenever Mr. Mayer was speaking a foreign language, Mr. Stommel, consumed with jealousy, would find some excuse to leave the office. After a few weeks I was able to meet in person some of the executives from Holland, Belgium, France, England, and Switzerland whose names I had heard so often on the phone. They drove up to Arminius AG in their flashy American cars with gleaming chrome fins, and parked in front of the cafeteria, dwarfing the Volkswagen Beetles owned by our employees.

"I'm starting a night school English course," I confided to Mr. Mayer. "We studied English in the Commercial School but I really need to improve."

"Well, I'll certainly be glad to help however I can."

"If you don't mind my asking, Herr Mayer, but where did you learn to speak French?"

"I'd studied it in the *Gymnasium* but I really improved when Arminius AG sent me to our sister company in Marseille for three months a year or two ago. That's the best way to learn a language. Classroom French is fine but having to use it every day makes all the difference. And it's not just the language. You learn about the culture."

Mr. Stommel had come back to the office while Mr. Mayer was speaking. "You're not going to tell Nitsch your French story, I hope? I've heard it so many times already."

"Well, Herr Nitsch needs to have his horizons broadened, don't you think?" He winked at me. "My second week in Marseille I came back to the office early from lunch and was chatting with two young secretaries when one of them asked me, '*Voulez-vous un bonbon?*'"

"Which means..."

"It means, 'Would you like a candy?' Well, I took the bonbon and as I started unwrapping it, I noticed the two ladies watching me intently and trying not to laugh. Turns out it wasn't a candy at all. It was a little rubber cap *pour faire l'amour*! And that, Herr Nitsch, is the French sense of humor!"

"Now if you don't mind my interrupting your storytelling, Herr Mayer," Mr. Stommel said in a sharp tone, "we have work to do and I need Nitsch to pick up some sales statistics from Kroll."

I had been in Mr. Kroll's office many times when I had to pick up reports from him for Mr. Kopf. Old Mr. Kroll had two double chins, and at 1.95 meters and more than four hundred pounds, he was by far the biggest man in Arminius AG, perhaps even in all of Bergheim. If Mr. Miele were to be believed, when he was an apprentice one of his jobs had been to tie Mr. Kroll's shoelaces because the poor man couldn't reach over his enormous belly to tie them himself.

"And if you think he's fat," Mr. Miele had added, "you should see his wife. I won't mention any names, but one of our employees is a neighbor of theirs. He told me when Frau Kroll waddles from Kenten to

Bergheim, she leans so far forward her face arrives in Bergheim while her rear end is still in Kenten."

Even Mr. Stommel, who normally didn't badmouth anyone except Dr. Haubold in front of me, had once told Mr. Kopf in my presence, "This Kroll guy has a face the size of a wall calendar and he's got terrible B.O. I try not to breathe in his office."

"The same here," Mr. Kopf had readily agreed. "The poor man obviously can't reach all the places he needs to wash."

Mr. Kroll also managed to butcher the German language, jumbling tenses, mispronouncing words, and often ignoring the agreement of subject and verb. He and Mr. Poltermann's mother-in-law must have learned grammar from the same source.

Meanwhile I had gone upstairs and was approaching Mr. Kroll's office. The door was wide open and I could hear him speaking on the phone.

"Are you the real estate guy? Listen here, I inherited sumpthin I wants to get rid of. Huh? What is it? It's a shack. A house. Whatever. Can you unload it for me?" The moment Mr. Kroll saw me he covered the receiver with his hand. Sweat was pouring off his great blobs of fat and he was breathing heavily. "The reports ain't ready yet. Can't talk to you now. Come back later. I still hafta take care of the diverse."

"Take care of the diverse" was Kroll's favorite expression. He threw it into every conversation, undeterred by the fact that no one, including him, had the slightest idea what it meant.

My parents and Hubert eagerly awaited my stories from the office every night so I was looking forward to telling them about Mr. Mayer's misadventure in Marseille and my latest encounter with "Fat Kroll" but that evening, judging from the glances my parents were exchanging, I suspected they wanted to inform Hubert and me about something important. My father was the first to speak, even before we sat down for supper.

"Can your mother and I trust you boys to keep a secret?"

"Of course," Hubert and I readily agreed.

"You know the Buchholz family? They have a pastry shop on Hauptstrasse."

"I don't know the parents," I replied, "but their son Rainer and I were in the same classroom in elementary school before he transferred to the *Gymnasium*."

"Well, as you both know, we've been trying for a while to get the financing to lease a pastry shop but the authorities have given us a runaround because we didn't have a concrete project. Now this is the part you have to keep under your hats. We just heard that Mr. Buchholz isn't in good health and may have to give up his shop. If he decides to close, then we'd have a chance to take over his business."

"I hate to benefit from someone else's misfortune," Mutti added. "But if we don't get the shop, someone else will. Let's all keep our fingers crossed. And please don't talk about this to anybody."

****

The sniping between Mr. Stommel and Mr. Mayer was never-ending. In the middle of June I was helping Miss Bonacker and Miss Neumann with some filing in the secretarial office when Mr. Kopf stormed into the sales office next door.

"You're not going to believe this," he confided. "The Old Man is having an air conditioning system installed in his office. Can you imagine? He must be suffering from megalomania. Does he think we're in the middle of Africa or the Amazon jungle? No one needs air conditioning around here. He's just throwing money out the window."

Mr. Stommel agreed instantly with Mr. Kopf but Mr. Mayer had a different opinion. "Air conditioning? Actually, that's not such a bad idea. I wish we'd all get it. When I was working at our sister company in Marseille, the whole building was air-conditioned. So people could keep their windows closed and no one had to breathe in the bauxite dust."

Mr. Stommel, as expected, objected, "Nonsense! I've coped with the bauxite dust for forty years. The Old Man should take the money he's wasting on his air conditioning system and give us some fat raises instead."

Three graduate students served as summer interns at Arminius AG. In the summer of 1956 we had an engineering graduate student from the Technical University in Aachen and two graduate students from the University of Cologne, who were economics majors. Since there were three of them and the tables in the dining room for white-collar employees seated four, I made it my business to sit with them at lunchtime at least once a week. I was still thinking about the discussion in my office when I walked over to ask if I could join their group.

"Of course," the curly-haired economics major said as he snuffed out one cigarette and lit another. "What's new?"

"There seems to be a difference of opinion about installing an air-conditioning system into Dr. Haubold's office. I was wondering what the three of you think about it."

The two economics majors at our table scoffed at the idea, calling it, "A waste of money!"

But Justus Reichenbach, the engineering student, disagreed. "Come on, guys. You have to think outside the box. You know I spent a year studying at M.I.T.? Well, the climate in Massachusetts isn't all that different from ours but nearly all of the office buildings over there, from the executive suites down to the mailroom, were air-conditioned. It's the wave of the future so you might as well get on board."

The future economists raised their beer glasses in a mock toast. "Cheers! Our expert on America has spoken!"

"Wait and see," Justus Reichenbach responded. "Just wait and see."

"Since you must know English, mind if I ask you a question?"

"Sure, why not?"

"I've just started taking an English class at an adult education program in the Hansa-*Gymnasium* in Cologne. It's a small group; there are only fourteen of us. I'm the youngest; the oldest is sixty-two. Even though our teacher spent a year in England and he promised we'd only speak in English, he keeps slipping back into German because most of us have no idea what he's talking about half the time. So I was wondering, when I finish that course, if you could suggest a better way to improve my English."

"You should look into studying at Berlitz. They only use native speakers and some of their teachers don't even speak German so it's pretty much total immersion. The only drawback, it's kind of pricey, but that's the fastest way I know to learn a language in a relatively short time."

One of the economics students nodded in agreement. "I've heard about Berlitz. Their small class size really appeals to me, not like at our university where as many as two thousand students cram together in lecture halls. Even my smallest class has several hundred."

"I guess I got spoiled at M.I.T.," Justus Reichenbach said. "Many of my courses had only twenty students and the lectures had a hundred, tops."

"Are you serious?" the curly-haired student exclaimed. "Maybe I should have given more thought to studying in the States."

It was time for me to get back to work. "Thanks for the advice, Herr Reichenbach! I'll look into Berlitz, and who knows, maybe I'll get to sit in on one of those American university classes some day!"

****

Ever since the end of Carnival, the employees at Arminius AG had been looking forward to the annual company outing.

"They pull out all the stops," Mr. Stommel had promised me in what turned out to be a major understatement.

The company had rented an entire train for the day, and shortly after sunrise on the last Saturday in June, nearly one thousand of us, white collar and blue collar workers and top management alike, took our assigned seats in the six-person compartments for the trip to Cochem, a picturesque town on the Mosel River in the heart of the German wine country. Shortly after we left the station, uniformed waiters passed through the aisles offering complimentary soft drinks, coffee, wine, and beer, as well as gouda cheese and salami sandwiches on buttered rolls. With my *Weiberfastnacht* disgrace still fresh in my mind, I kept a firm grasp on my bottle of Coca Cola, not letting it out of my sight even for a minute. Despite the early hour, my colleagues had already begun to drink much stronger stuff.

We had been given lunch vouchers, so once we arrived in Cochem, we split into separate groups and headed out in different directions to find our assigned restaurants. By the time my group reached Zum Schwarzen Adler it was already packed with Arminius AG employees, their voices raised in drunken conversation amid half-empty bottles of Mosel wine. They lifted their glasses and cheered as we took our seats. The party was in full swing long before we were served our platters of Sauerbraten and red cabbage. Arms wrapped around each other's shoulders, we swayed from side to side, singing at the top of our lungs. While we were eating, an oompah band started to play and soon couples were twirling on the dance floor. I danced with Miss Bonacker and Miss Neumann and then several times with Miss Gimborn, until someone from the Accounting Department cut in. Throughout the afternoon, ignoring the jeers and taunts from my companions, I stuck with mineral water.

Around four o'clock Arminius AG employees staggered arm in arm out of restaurants all over Cochem and wobbled unsteadily back to the train. No sooner had we rolled out of the Cochem railroad station than the waiters returned, offering more food and liquid refreshments. Since two men were sprawled across the seats in my compartment sound asleep, I positioned myself in the corridor outside where I had to flatten myself against the window to let groups of revelers squeeze by.

Josef Reinike, still bearing the scars from his disaster in the solarium, pushed through the crowded aisles and leaned over to shout in my ear. "Günter, come back with me to Accounting. You've gotta see this!"

The corridors in several of the cars were slick with vomit, and in compartments throughout the length of the train, many of the fine men and women of Arminius AG, their disheveled hair stringy with sweat, were clasped in tight embraces sharing mushy kisses.

"It's like *Weiberfastnacht* on wheels," Josef joked when he got back to his seat. "See you Monday!"

Two cars back, I peeked through the partially drawn curtains of another compartment. On one of the seats three women leaned together, unconscious, their heads lolling forward. On the facing seat, Mrs. Vollweg, one of the secretaries from the typing pool, lay on her back under a bare-bottomed, curly-haired researcher from the chemistry lab. *What a phony!* I thought. How often had I admired the family picture of her husband and her two adorable children prominently displayed on her desk?

Josef Reinike and I met over lunch the following week to compare notes. "You only saw the one couple?" he scoffed. "Maybe you need glasses. Should I name names?"

"No thanks," I replied. "I'd rather not know."

****

Ever since I was assigned to the Sales Department, one of my responsibilities was to go over to the mailroom twice a week to help Mr. Heller, the one-armed mail clerk. Between four in the afternoon and half-past five, I had to collect the mail from all the departments, fold the letters into envelopes, figure out the postage, and run the envelopes through the postage meter. Mr. Rutkowski, the one-legged telephone operator who shared the office with Mr. Heller, had to catch a bus that departed at five o'clock sharp. Late one Tuesday afternoon, after Mr. Rutkowski had left for the day and Mr. Heller had stepped out to the men's room, the telephone rang. I picked up the receiver and said, "Mail room!" The caller snapped, "Puschtappole," and hung up.

Mr. Heller came back. "Any phone calls, Nitsch?"

"Just one, Herr Heller. Someone named Herr Puschtappole called, but unfortunately he hung up on me."

Mr. Heller burst out laughing. "That was Herr Brunnenbauer, our Chief Engineer. He's Swiss and what he said to you was *Post abholen!* (Get the mail!). Now run up and get it. Don't worry, he won't bite your head off."

Mr. Brunnenbauer turned out to be an elderly, white-haired gentleman whose pungent pipe tobacco drifted out the door and into the hallway. He handed me two folders of mail while asking me a long question in a deep, raspy voice. The only words I was able to make out were, "new apprentice?"

"Do they all talk like that in Switzerland?" I asked Mr. Mayer the next day.

"I'm afraid so. Maybe once you've improved your English and studied some French you'll tackle Swiss German next," he replied with a chuckle.

In the middle of July around a quarter to five on a Thursday Mr. Heller called me from the mailroom. "Nitsch, you can't go home. I know it's not your turn today but we need you now."

"Yes, Herr Heller, I'll be right there," and I raced over.

Dr. Haubold was pacing back and forth in the corridor, clenching and unclenching his fists, as Mr. Heller cowered behind the counter, nervously tugging at his collar.

"It's about time you got here!" Dr. Haubold growled at me. "I want you to go to every department on this floor and collect all, and I mean ALL, the hole punchers, with their contents. Then bring them back here and tell Heller the department they came from. Start in Transportation and work backwards. If anyone asks, just say Herr Dr. Haubold sent you and not one word about why! All right, off you go! And make it snappy!"

While Dr. Haubold was giving me his instructions, Mr. Heller's eyes kept darting back and forth between my face and Dr. Haubold's fancy black felt hat on the light-yellow countertop, a hole-punch sized hole in its brim. Now I understood what all the fuss was about.

In office after office, terror-struck employees searched their desk drawers for hole punchers.

"What does he want with them?"

"Sorry, I can't explain!"

"Are we in some kind of trouble?"

"Sorry, no time to talk!"

Running back and forth between the various departments and the mailroom, I stopped from time to time to check on the ongoing investigation. Mr. Rutkowski was busy prying open one hole puncher after another while Mr. Heller carefully sifted through the contents.

After half an hour Dr. Haubold rejoined us. "So? Did you find the culprit?"

"I'm afraid not, Herr Dr. Haubold. We've done our best but we've come up empty," Mr. Heller humbly replied.

"What an impertinent coward, punching a hole like that!" Dr. Haubold fumed as he picked up his damaged hat and examined the brim. But then, to our surprise, he broke into a smile. "As my buddies in the Navy would say, 'May whoever did it be struck by lightening while taking a crap!'" He tipped his hat to us, cheerfully wished us a "Good evening," and strolled out of the building.

****

"How come you're home so late?" my father wanted to know. "Sorry, we didn't wait for you. We've already eaten supper."

"I had to work late in the mailroom today. It's a long story. Perhaps I should eat first."

"By all means go ahead. Enjoy your meal!"

Mutti had fixed three different kinds of sandwiches and had even peeled an orange for me. I hadn't seen my parents so relaxed and happy in quite some time.

"Any idea what's going on?" Hubert whispered to me. I just shook my head.

"Your mother and I have some news," my father announced, looking over at Mutti who nodded. "We've talked to you boys before about Herr Buchholz, the refugee from Pomerania who owns the café on Hauptstrasse. Buchholz called me into his shop this evening for a chat. It seems that his son Rainer disappeared about ten days ago and then he phoned home from Paris to say that he'd enlisted in the French Foreign Legion for five years. The Buchholzes followed Rainer to Paris and hired a French attorney with the help of the German Embassy, but by the time they got there, Rainer had already shipped out to Sidi Bel Abbès in French Algeria. Apparently it was all perfectly legal and there was nothing they could do about it."

"That must've been devastating for Rainer's parents," I said, "but what does it have to do with us? There's more to the story, I can tell!"

"You're right. For Buchholz this was the last straw. His health is failing, as you know. Now his son has run off. He told me he can't go on like this any more and he's willing to lease us his store."

"Can you imagine?" Mutti added. "Because a boy runs off to the Foreign Legion, we may get a pastry shop. Life certainly takes strange turns sometimes."

"How soon will you get the store?" Hubert asked.

"Let's not count our chickens!" my father replied. "There's still the red tape with the *Lastenausgleichsamt*. It might take months!"

Mutti turned to me. "So, Günter, what happened to you today?"

I launched into an account of Dr. Haubold's hat. When I'd finished my father shook his head. "I had no idea they used that expression in the Navy. The boys in the *Luftwaffe* used it all the time."

"Some education you're getting!" Mutti commented. She was trying not to smile. "And from the director of the company at that."

"Speaking of Dr. Haubold," I added. "I was thinking about what happened on my way home. Remember when he brushed everything off his desk? And when he pushed all the buttons for the buzzers? It wouldn't surprise me if he punched the hole himself!"

CHAPTER 26

Hubert, who was now thirteen, was an even worse student at the Lutheran elementary school than I had been. All too often Mutti would receive a letter from Mr. Reitberg asking her to come in for a conference to discuss Hubert's poor grades or his behavior problems, foremost among which were the imaginative excuses he invented about his missing homework.

To make matters worse, Hubert was grossly overweight, a problem triggered by his being force-fed fatty foods during the two years he spent in a tuberculosis sanatorium while Mutti and I were living in a West German refugee camp. Since even the mildest exertion made him gasp like a fish out of water, he was hopeless at sports compared to the other boys his age. He had few friends. And he had the worst case of acne of anyone I'd ever met.

Spending time with my younger brother was not one of my priorities. So it was without much enthusiasm, and only after weeks of constant nagging by my parents, that I helped Hubert join my Boy Scout Troop in the summer of 1956.

At the beginning of August I took some vacation time from Arminius AG, and with Hubert in tow, left by train for a Scout camping trip to the Bavarian Forest in southeast Germany near the Czech border. Replacing

Friedel Meuser as troop leader was a twenty-four-year-old office clerk named Anton Merz who worked for the Ford Motor Company in Cologne. Anton's brother Bert and my brother Hubert were the youngest members of our group of eighteen. Hubert was by far the heaviest in his age group.

After spending a night in the Passau Youth Hostel, we set out, weighed down with heavy rucksacks, our tents, small spades, and pots and pans, on a twelve-kilometer hike through dense forests and past low mountains to our first campsite. We had barely gone five kilometers before Hubert collapsed on a rotten log, his face bathed in sweat. From the back of the group I could hear him pleading, "Günter, I can't do this! Günter!"

A few of the older boys started chanting, "Crybaby! Crybaby!" If Hubert had been someone else's brother, I might have joined in, but I had promised my parents to look out for him. Swallowing my pride, I walked with Hubert to the side of the road, put out my thumb, and hitchhiked with him to our campsite where Hubert promptly collapsed in a heap.

Exhaustion must be contagious. By the following day more than half of the boys were suddenly too tired to hike. Over the next week, the number of hitchhikers in our group continued to rise. While a few hardy souls sneered at us and grimly set out on foot, the rest of us spread out along the road waiting for lifts, much to Anton's disgust. There was no hitchhiking possible on Tuesday, August 14th when we climbed to the top of the Grosser Arber, at 1,456 meters the highest mountain in the region. From our vantage point on top we enjoyed a spectacular view across the border into Czechoslovakia before being drenched by a heavy downpour.

"Well done, boys!" Anton congratulated us after we'd returned to the valley to pitch our tents and dry out around the fire. "You've earned a day off. No hiking tomorrow!"

On Wednesday afternoon Anton sent Jochen Krienke, Wilfried Plath, and me into the nearby village of Bodemais to buy four loaves of bread, dry salami, noodles, potatoes, and milk. The bakery display window was empty. A sign on the door read, *"Geschlossen"* (closed). We passed two shops specializing in crystal and glassware, also *"Geschlossen,"* before reaching the food market. It was our last hope and it was closed like the rest.

"What's the matter with this place?" Jochen grumbled. "It's the middle of the week!"

A young couple window-shopping in their Sunday best overheard him. "How long have you boys been in the woods?" the young man asked. "It's August 15th, the Assumption of the Blessed Virgin Mary. You won't find a single store open in all of Bavaria." He tipped his hat to us as they walked away.

Jochen reacted first. "Now what? I've got nothing to eat except a small piece of stale bread and some margarine."

"Same here," I agreed.

Next it was Wilfried's turn to grumble. "Anton's Catholic. Shouldn't he have known about this holiday? I'll bet if Friedel Meuser had been in charge, this wouldn't have happened!"

As we walked back, empty-handed, to our campground, I suddenly got an idea.

"The solution's right here! See those plants with the thick, bluish leaves? That's yellow turnip. What some people call rutabaga. My Oma used the root to make soup when we were living under the Russians in East Prussia."

Jochen looked skeptical. "Are you sure people can eat that stuff?"

"Trust me! You're in for a real treat. We used to eat it plain but it'll be even better if we add some margarine, a few slices of stale bread, and the leftover salami."

After making sure no one was watching, the three of us dug up nine of the heavy, globe-shaped roots, and without stopping to remove the stems or to brush away the dirt, we returned to camp feeling like heroes coming to the rescue. Anton listened to our explanation.

"Sorry, I should've known about the holiday. And I know you boys mean well, but what makes you think those roots are edible? The farmers in the Rhineland feed rutabagas to their cows."

Jochen and Wilfried looked to me for a reply. "Not to worry. We ate rutabaga soup in East Prussia all the time," I boasted. "I'll show you how it's done!"

While Jochen, Wilfried and I cut off the stems, peeled the uneven earth-crusted skin of the turnips, and cut them into cubes, the rest of the scouts rummaged through their rucksacks searching for bread crusts, margarine, lard, sausage ends, and a few pieces of cheese to add to the mix. Once we had washed the cubes in a near-by creek, we added all of the ingredients to the heavy iron cauldron and set it to boil over the campfire. The soup was delicious and I basked in glory as most of the boys lined up for seconds.

"How about a cheer for Günter?" Anton exclaimed. "Picking those rutabagas was a stroke of genius!"

I wasn't a hero for long. Shortly after midnight I woke up with a terrible stomachache and rushed outside in the rain, barely reaching the bushes before I was violently ill. And I wasn't alone. Except for two boys who had refused to try the soup, we were all out there in the dark in various states of distress.

Over the next two days we remained in camp, too weak to hike. Several of the boys lay moaning in their tents. Those who ventured out to get some fresh air gave me a cold stare. No one cared anymore that Hubert had been unable to keep up the pace. All of the blame for the disastrous trip fell on my shoulders and now it was Hubert's turn to stand up for me.

"They must have a different kind of rutabaga in East Prussia," he insisted.

"Yeah, right," one boy mocked. "Maybe Günter should've thought of that beforehand." No one was willing to give me the benefit of the doubt, and in a way I couldn't blame them. The teasing continued throughout the all-day trip from Passau to Cologne.

After sending Hubert on ahead to Zieverich, Jochen Krienke and I left the train in Quadrath to stow the tents and the cauldron in Friedel Meuser's house. My father was watching for me from the kitchen window when I got back and my whole family came out front. "So, Stretch," my father greeted me. "Welcome home!"

"I made stuffed cabbage in honor of the occasion," Mutti added. "It's in the fridge. I just have to heat it up. Hubert's already told us all about the scouting trip."

"Even the soup?"

"I gather from Hubert that you were a real hero!" my father exclaimed. "He's been bragging about you ever since he got home."

"Is that what he told you?" I studied their faces to see if this was a joke, but my parents seemed to have swallowed Hubert's whitewashed version of the story hook, line, and sinker. "Well, whatever Hubert may have said, just in case I ever need it again I'm going to stop by Oma's apartment on my way home from work tomorrow to get her recipe for rutabaga soup."

CHAPTER 27

Rupert Mayer was always finding ways to help me with English. When he had English-speaking visitors, he made a point of introducing me to them and letting me sit in on their meetings. At his suggestion, I bought a copy of *The Old Man and the Sea*.

"You were right, Herr Mayer!" I reported back a few days later. "I read the whole thing already."

"Well, in that case, you should make a point of buying the *Reader's Digest* every month. Not the German edition, the real one in English. If you read it aloud, you should do just fine. And while you're at it, when you go into Cologne for your class, be sure to stop in to the British Library and the Amerika-Haus. They have great lectures, English-language films, and plenty of good reading material." After a few visits to Amerika-Haus, it didn't take me long to discover *Life* and *Ebony* both of which not only improved my English, but also opened up new worlds to me. The two magazines had similar advertisements showing attractive families living in fancy houses, eating wholesome foods, and driving flashy cars; the only difference was that in *Life* the families were always white, and in *Ebony* the families were always Negro. There were many more layers to America, it seemed, than the Wild West of *Billy Jenkins* and the Technicolor fluff I saw in the movies.

In the middle of November Mr. Mayer was talking on the phone when I came back from an errand. He hung up the receiver, thought for a moment, and then said, "Herr Nitsch, I was wondering whether you have any plans for tomorrow night."

"No sir, I don't. Do you want me to work longer?"

"No, not at all. It's just that something unexpected came up and I can't use my subscription ticket to the theater in Düsseldorf. I think I mentioned that I go there once a month with a busload of folks from Bergheim? They're putting on *Die Katze auf dem heißen Blechdach* by Tennessee Williams and I was wondering if you'd like to have my ticket."

"Would I ever! Thank you so much, Herr Mayer."

"Too bad you won't have time to read the play in English before you go but you should try to get a copy at the Amerika-Haus next time you're there. Once you've seen it done in German, the English should be much easier to read."

"Excuse me, sir, but what's the title in English? I understand 'cat' and 'hot' and 'roof' but I don't know the English for 'Blech'."

"That's what reference books are for," he said cheerfully, handing me his well-worn German-English dictionary. "If you look it up yourself, you won't forget it."

The only time I had come even close to a live stage performance was the school Christmas pageant in Plötzin in the Russian-occupied Zone. Our makeshift stage had been set up in the front third of a large classroom, and in the weeks leading up to my eleventh birthday I had painstakingly practiced my lines as the Magi Balthasar while admiring the ease with which my friend Gudrun handled the starring role of Mary. But since Mutti had picked the day of the dress rehearsal for our escape to the West, I never got to see Gudrun in her Virgin Mary costume. I never got to perform in the play. I never even had the chance to say good-bye. Now nearly eight years later, in a Düsseldorf theater, a uniformed usher led me to my assigned seat in a plush armchair under a sparkling chandelier among an elegantly dressed audience in front of a real stage with a real curtain.

"I couldn't believe it!" I confided to my parents the next evening after supper. "Maggie, one of the main parts, was played by a beautiful woman in a revealing white slip. I actually felt sorry for her. Her husband was an alcoholic and her father-in-law was a real brute."

"What was Herr Mayer thinking, giving you a ticket to that kind of show?" Mutti protested. "That was no place for an eighteen-year-old."

My father snickered. "C'mon, Gretel. Stretch is nearly nineteen. Let the boy grow up. He must've seen much worse things than that!"

He was right, of course. Mutti might have fainted if I'd described the sickening behavior of some of the Arminius AG employees on the way back from the company outing. But this was different somehow. There was something so appealing about the vision of Maggie in that skimpy slip that, for a second night in a row, I lay awake and fantasized about her long after everyone else was sound asleep.

****

When I came home from work on Monday, December 3, 1956, my parents and Hubert had already started supper. After I had washed my hands and sat down, my father greeted me warmly, "So, how's the birthday boy?"

"Great, thanks. It seems like just about everyone at Arminius AG congratulated me today, which is why I'm a little late." I was about to launch into a report of the day's events when, to my astonishment, my father reached over and took Mutti's hand. I looked from one of them to the other. "Something's going on here! What am I missing?"

"You tell him, Willi," Mutti said.

"The loan came through today and we signed the lease for the café. We're moving into the apartment over the store on Wednesday!"

"So, Stretch, what do you think of our news?" Mutti asked. "Isn't it exciting?"

"It looks like you're the ones to be congratulated! When are you going to tell Herr Meyer at the bakery?"

"I told him as soon as I heard. As of today, I'm not working there any more."

"And I've quit my job at the church. Pastor Kampe was very understanding," Mutti added.

"It's good for me, too, don't forget!" Hubert chimed in. "I'll have a much shorter walk to school!"

"Here's to Café Nitsch!" I said, raising my water glass. "If there's any way I can help, please let me know."

"Thanks, Günter. I may have to take you up on that. Even though I can't wait to be my own boss again, we're not under any illusions," my father admitted. "It'll mean working fifteen hours a day, three hundred sixty-five days a year, and we'll have to hire staff and still make enough to pay back the loan. But your mother's going to run the shop while I handle the baking so I'm sure we can make a success of it."

"Just like we did in Königsberg before your father got drafted in 1939," Mutti added. She squeezed my father's hand. "We made a good team back then, didn't we, Willi? I'm glad we're finally getting a second chance."

****

First thing the next morning I pedaled over to Arminius AG to ask Mr. Stommel for two vacation days so that I could help my parents with the move. They were already at the new store when I got back to Bergheim. Craftsmen were hard at work installing the sign, renovating the shop window, and replacing the sales counter with a new one of gleaming chrome.

The pastry shop was on Hauptstrasse and shared a covered entryway with Elektro-Schiffer, an appliance store. Beyond the room with the sales counter was a café with fourteen small tables and thirty-four chairs.

Mutti was busy dusting the shelves. "Oh, hello, Stretch. Welcome to Café Nitsch! Let me show you what's behind the scenes." A door at one end of the sales counter led into a kitchen. "This is where we'll have our meals," Mutti said, pointing to the two built-in benches in one corner. "Our table should fit nicely there and you and Hubert can push your stools underneath it during the day to make more space. And through the door behind that huge dishwasher is the bake house where Vati will be spending most of his time." She opened the door and I followed her inside. The oven was in one corner of the small room, and on the opposite wall, my father had placed a brand-new radio on the narrow windowsill above the worktable.

"There's barely enough room to turn around," my father greeted me. "But after cooking for the military, I'm used to working in cramped spaces. Have you seen our apartment yet?"

"I'm taking Günter up there now," Mutti replied. "And then I'm going to put him to work!"

"Give me a minute and I'll join you!"

Mutti and I walked back into the kitchen. "That door next to the benches leads to the inside building corridor but I can also buzz people into the main part of the apartment house. Here, let me show you." I went back outside to the street entrance and Mutti pressed the buzzer behind the counter, unlocking the door to the inside corridor of the building. "The washroom for our café guests is behind those stairs at the end of the hall," Mutti explained when she rejoined me in the corridor. "So if anyone needs to use it, they just have to step outside the shop and wait until I buzz them through the other door. There's a sink in there, too." She pushed open the door. The washroom was small but clean and well stocked with toilet paper and paper towels. I peeked out the window and could see the railroad tracks in the distance.

"Is this the toilet we'll be using, too?"

"Only when we happen to be downstairs or when Vati and I are working in the shop, but there's a full bathroom with a tub in the hallway on the third floor. We'll just have to share it with the Grafs, the couple who have the apartment next to ours. He's a retired *Gymnasium* teacher who taught Latin and Ancient Greek. They're both very nice."

"Who lives on the second floor?"

"The Päslacks, also very pleasant people. They own the building and have the entire second floor to themselves."

My father came out from the kitchen through the side door and the three of us headed upstairs.

The wide window in the living room of our new apartment faced Hauptstrasse.

"I'm going to have a desk to do my bookkeeping on the right-hand wall next to the window. And Mutti wants to have a cabinet on that same wall for our wine glasses. The living room furniture will fit nicely in the opposite corner and we're planning to buy a couch for the long wall on the other side."

"Vati forgot to mention that we're getting a telephone with a private number for his desk up here in addition to the two down in the shop." We hadn't had a telephone since we left Opa's farm in Langendorf in a covered wagon just ahead of the advancing Russian front right after my seventh birthday. I had actually never made a phone call until the start of my apprenticeship in Arminius AG so this was exciting news. There was more to come.

"What's going into the space at the other end of the window?"

Mutti smiled. "Just as soon as we've moved in, your father and I are going next door to buy a television set at Elektro-Schiffer and put it right over there! We've talked about getting one for a long time but we didn't want to bother with it in Zieverich."

"Wow! Does Hubert know about it?"

"Not yet. But one thing's for sure. He'll have to finish his homework downstairs in the kitchen before he'll be allowed to come upstairs to watch."

Just beyond the living room was the tiny bedroom Hubert and I were going to share.

"Pretty small, isn't it, especially for a tall fellow like you," my father said. "But not to worry. Mutti and I have already ordered an extra long, custom-made bunk bed for the two of you. That'll leave just enough room for your desk along the same wall as the bed, right next to the glassed-in balcony. And you can have an armoire on the wall facing the bunk bed."

Our bedroom had a narrow window facing Hauptstrasse on one side and a glass wall leading to a glass-enclosed balcony on the other.

"The balcony can't be heated in the wintertime," Mutti explained, "but it's nice to have the extra space, don't you think?" When we stepped outside, I was already imagining myself curled up on the balcony with the latest book by Heinrich Böll once the weather got warmer. I glanced out past the glass wall at the far end of the balcony. Just below us were vegetable gardens, and off to the left I caught a glimpse of the Bergheim railroad station. Looking straight ahead, beyond the railroad tracks, lay a flat stretch of seemingly endless meadowland, interspersed by straight rows of poplar trees.

Mutti followed my gaze. "It's a nice view, isn't it? Still, whoever designed this place must've had a good sense of humor. To get to the door to our bedroom we have to go through your room and onto this balcony. But I'm not complaining, mind you. We have enough space for our double bed and there's even a small sink in the corner where we can wash up and brush our teeth."

"What's that other door in your bedroom for?"

"If the weather gets too cold, it leads from our bedroom directly out into the hallway, right across from the bathroom."

"Enough sightseeing," my father announced. "Let's get back to work!"

****

My parents wasted no time getting the business up and running. My father purchased the ingredients to make his specialties: cherry puff pastries, Florentina sugar nut cookies on a chocolate base, hazelnut, mocha and marzipan tortes, cream puffs, and éclairs. He also arranged with a bakery in the old part of Bergheim to deliver fresh bread and rolls to the shop so that they could be sold early each morning. Meanwhile, after interviewing a succession of applicants, Mutti hired Ursula to work in the café as a waitress and Waltraud to assist her behind the counter.

The hardest position to fill was that of dishwasher. From the time the café opened at breakfast time until the last customer left at night, dirty dishes, utensils, cups, and glassware had to be loaded into the machine and then, when they were taken back out sparkling clean and steaming hot, they had to be dried by hand while the next load was running. It was a monotonous job and the first young woman Mutti hired to do it quit after two days. To replace her, Mutti found full-figured, strawberry blond Anna Gudat whose family, like ours, had come from East Prussia. Anna had a broad face, a pug nose, and red cheeks. She actually enjoyed the repetitive work, which she attacked with incredible speed. The only drawback was that she was always drenched in sweat, and even though Mutti bought her a deodorant, the corner of our kitchen where the dishwasher stood always smelled of Anna.

One night Hubert and I sat down to supper holding our noses in protest but my father refused to budge. "Look, boys. I understand how you feel. But the dishwasher job always has a big turnover. In Café Meyer they never kept any dishwasher for more than a few months. So, as long as Anna is willing to do the work, I'm willing to keep her on, sweat and all."

"Anyway, look on the bright side," Mutti added cheerfully. "As soon as the weather gets warmer, we can keep the kitchen window open."

That Sunday when Anna's family came to the café for coffee and cake, she dried her hands on her apron and went out front to greet them. Mrs. Gudat was a larger version of Anna, with the same broad features and snub nose. Her father and her three brothers, all of whom worked in the Fortuna mine, were cut from the same mold. When the five of them lumbered over to the counter to pick out their pastries, I noticed a vivacious blue-eyed girl with long blond braids standing behind them patiently waiting her turn.

Anna tapped me on the shoulder. "That's my sister Eva. She'll be going to the *Gymnasium* in the spring!"

Later that evening I asked Mutti about Eva. "You saw her? She's so different from the others. She's as tall as they are wide. It's like night and day."

"Can I trust you with a secret?"

"You know you can."

"Anna told me the story after her family went home. A Russian officer in East Prussia raped Mrs. Gudat in 1945 while her husband was in an American POW camp and Eva is the result. The whole thing brought back such awful memories. Do you remember the elderberry juice and flour I put on my face at night so those drunken Russians would think I had typhus?"

"You scared Hubert half to death. How old was he then? Two? And then Oma and I actually got typhus. How could I forget all that?"

"I guess," Mutti said, almost to herself, "we can never really put those things behind us, can we?"

****

The news that my parents had opened the shop traveled fast at Arminius AG. A week later Mr. Stommel gave me enough money so that I could pedal over to the café to buy three slices of hazelnut cream torte, three Florentina cookies, and a dozen Holländer Kirsch cherry puff pastries "to help launch Café Nitsch" as he put it. As soon as I got back, while Mr. Stommel distributed pastries to the ladies who typed for our department, Mr. Mayer invited Mr. Kopf and Mr. Miele to stop by to share in the festivities.

"So," Mr. Miele said after choosing the hazelnut cream, "Isn't it amazing what miracles the *Lastenausgleich* loans can create? If this trend continues the refugees will soon be doing better than the natives!"

Mr. Kopf, wanting to protect my feelings, shot back. "Herr Miele, I'm sure Herr Nitsch's father got a loan with favorable interest rates, that's all. It'll take years of hard work to pay it back."

"Don't mind me, I was just kidding," Mr. Miele said as he licked the last crumbs off his fork. "Anyone who can make pastry like this deserves to succeed."

Before we ate supper at home that evening my father shook my hand. "Thanks, Stretch. Mutti and I really appreciated the order from Arminius AG. When you're just starting up, every sale is a real boost, and word of mouth is so important. If you can steer any other orders this way, that'd be great."

"Actually, it was Herr Stommel's idea but I hope others will follow his example."

"There's another favor I want to ask you. It's a struggle for me to carry the fifty-kilo sacks of flour up from the basement to the bake kitchen. I've done it a few times already this week and my back is killing me. Can you take over that job from now on?"

"Sure, I'll get you one now."

We went down the steep staircase to the storage room in the basement. Assorted cans and bottles with colorful labels lined the shelves and there was a distinct aroma of vanilla in the cool, damp air. I had no trouble lifting the sack of flour but getting it up the stairs was quite another matter. In that cramped space there was no room to carry the flour sack on my shoulder. Instead I had to clutch it to my chest while bending my head to one side to avoid knocking against the low beams.

"Thanks, Stretch," my father said once we reached the kitchen. "I'll be asking you to bring those sacks up for me a few times a week, at least until Hubert starts his apprenticeship here."

Every time my father alluded to his plans for Hubert's future, my poor brother winced. I really couldn't blame him. Hubert was a mediocre, unmotivated student, with a tendency to bend the truth, whereas my father was a rigid, humorless perfectionist. The two of them frequently argued about Hubert's schoolwork, his appearance, and his attitude. I couldn't see how they could get along in that tiny workroom in back of the kitchen. I certainly couldn't imagine Hubert fitting his chubby frame into the narrow basement stairwell while lugging up a heavy sack of flour. However unlikely the arrangement sounded, I somehow doubted that Hubert would find an apprenticeship anywhere else.

****

Toward the end of December, as my assignment in the Sales Department was coming to an end, Hubert and I spent all of our free time helping my parents meet the demand for holiday orders. To save Mutti some time, Hubert helped out in the kitchen while I took over the job of writing Christmas cards and letters. The letters were shorter than usual since for the first time in twelve years, we were able to pick up a telephone and speak directly to our faraway relatives. Our new television set was rarely turned on. The novelty had quickly worn off and there wasn't all that much worth watching anyway. When the shop closed for the day on Christmas Eve, Hubert and I went to the Lutheran service in Zieverich alone. My parents were too exhausted to go.

Right after New Year's, I reported to Dr. Muckenberg in the Accounting Department to start the next phase of my apprenticeship. Dr. Muckenberg was a bespectacled man in his forties. His black hair, graying slightly at the temples, was parted right down the middle with the same precision he used to keep the company finances in balance and to oversee the thirty members of his staff. Originally from Berlin, he disapproved of the easygoing Rhinelanders. He was one of those who made a point of taking a vacation each year at Carnival time.

My new job consisted of comparing long columns of figures against receipts, alphabetizing files, running numbers through the calculator to verify results, and making sure that debits and credits balanced. As if this weren't boring enough, my work also brought me into closer contact with Mr. Kohlhofer in Statistics to whom I was assigned for a week in early February. As Mr. Kohlhofer searched his desk drawers for leftover sandwiches, I struggled to prepare the charts for a seemingly useless report on the length of cord that workers used to tie jute sacks full of calcinated alumina in the Production Department.

"Excuse me, Herr Kohlhofer. May I ask you a question?"

"Ah, here's one!" he exclaimed in triumph. "So, Nitsch, what's your question?"

"Why should it matter whether a piece of cord is thirty centimeters long or fifty centimeters long? That's not much of a difference."

Mr. Kohlhofer shoved his thick glasses against the top of his short nose and glared. "Let me make one thing clear to you, Nitsch. Whatever you do in business, you have to be exact. Otherwise someone's going to get screwed. And you know who usually gets the worst of it? The workers, that's who. Just look at the idiotic carnival season. The white-collar workers drop everything and act like damn fools for a week while the poor slobs in the factory work themselves to death." He paused to lick his finger and rescue two breadcrumbs from his desktop before turning back to me. "What was your question again?"

"The length of the cord..."

"Right, the length of the cord. Twenty centimeters isn't much of a difference you say? Now you listen here! Arminius AG uses several hundred thousand jute bags a year. Multiply that by the cost of those twenty extra centimeters and that makes one *hell* of a difference. A company that can't figure out the cost of production is on dangerous ground." He was shrieking by now. "Do you understand what I'm telling you? You have to be precise! You have to be exact!"

"Yes sir!"

I thought he was finished but he was just warming up. "Nitsch, while we're on the subject, you were upset recently when I criticized you for reading a newspaper ten minutes beyond your lunch hour. Get this through your thick head. 'Time is money'! If every one of the one hundred twenty employees in administration were to take ten extra minutes lunch time every day, that's one thousand two hundred minutes, which is the same as twenty hours or, to put it another way, two entire working days stolen from the company. Now multiply that figure by the number of annual working days and the result is horrifying. That's no longer cheating, that's a crime!"

"I see. Thank you, Herr Kohlhofer. It won't happen again."

"Time is money, Nitsch. Time is money!"

He pushed his eyeglasses back up and returned to work.

On a Monday only four weeks later, Miss Brockhaus returned from a doctor's appointment at one in the afternoon to discover her boss, Mr. Kohlhofer, in an elegant dark suit deeply absorbed in his work at his desk.

"Herr Kohlhofer! I didn't expect you back so soon. May I be the first to congratulate…?"

Turning a deep shade of red, Mr. Kohlhofer jumped up. "Oh, for heavens sake!" he spluttered. "Look at the time! I completely forgot. My fiancée has been waiting for me at the Marriage License Bureau for at least half an hour."

"So," said Miss Brockhaus with a chuckle when she repeated the story for perhaps the twentieth time, "I called him a cab and he raced out like a madman. I'm amazed his fiancée was still waiting for him when he got there. Just imagine, of all people in Arminius AG, he's the last one I'd expect to lose track of time!"

CHAPTER 28

With the exception of the drunken carnival parties at the end of February, work in the Accounting Department continued its dull routine. By the middle of May 1957, I would have accepted a transfer to just about any other department. But you have to be careful what you wish for.

"So," the younger Schild brother greeted me one Monday morning. "Are you looking forward to working for the Woodlouse?"

"Is this some kind of a joke? Who on earth is the Woodlouse?"

"Oops!" Mr. Schild threw up his arms in mock alarm. "I guess I wasn't supposed to tell you. Dr. Muckenberg is assigning you to help out Batz the last two weeks of May."

I swallowed hard. "Thanks for the warning. Last time I worked for him, Herr Batz had me sort personnel files when I first started my apprenticeship. That was right before he was put in charge of the Archives Department."

"Never mind 'put in charge.' He *is* the Archives Department."

By then everyone at Arminius AG knew that the "Archives Department" was just a fancy name for the two basement rooms where Mr. Batz worked. Yellowed file folders lined the shelves of the first room where Mr. Batz had his desk and a folding worktable that had been set up for me. Beyond that room behind a thick drape with a black lining was a darkroom. Here Mr. Batz stood hour after hour in front of a humming machine as the glow from a single red light bulb reflected off his thick eyeglasses and the smoke from his pipe took on a rosy tint. The acrid odor of the acid used in processing photos permeated both rooms and made my stomach queasy.

"Oh, there you are, Nitsch!" he had shouted at me over the noise of the machine when I peeked behind the curtain to announce my arrival. "Don't you think it's a crime to put a disabled veteran who fought for the Fatherland into a hellhole like this?" I nodded politely, unsure what to say. Mr. Batz fished out a dripping photo from a flat, acid-filled tray. "Damn! That one's a piece of crap. Now I'll have to start all over again. Damn!"

"If you don't mind, Herr Batz, before you get back to work, could you please let me know what I'm supposed to do?"

"Didn't those idiots upstairs tell you?" He came out through the curtain and pointed to a stack of cartons in the corner of the room. "You need to alphabetize those old files from the Sales Department and when you're finished, I'll tell you what to do next."

While Mr. Batz made copies in the darkroom, I worked my way through the stacks of yellowed Sales Department files, all the while inhaling a nauseating mixture of dust, pipe tobacco, and acid fumes. If any clerks came downstairs with work to be copied, I had to shout through the drape at the top of my lungs to get Mr. Batz's attention over the whirring of the machines. Other than that, he and I rarely interacted.

Finally, after several days, the alphabetizing was complete. "I'm ready for the next step, Herr Batz," I reported to him when he next emerged, blinking, into the light of the outer office.

"Well, then, let me get you started. Remember the files you sorted for me two years ago? These five big cartons have all of the cards from before May 15, 1945. I want you to shred them, one at a time."

"Just to be sure I understand. You mean tear each personnel card into tiny pieces?"

Mr. Batz shook his head. "No, that won't be necessary. We got a new gadget to do that." He brought me over to a machine that resembled a giant, square trashcan. "It's a paper shredder. Once each cardboard personnel record goes into that slot, no one's ever going to be able to put it back together. That's the whole point, to make sure these files get completely destroyed." He showed me how to operate the machine. "Remember to feed the personnel cards in one at a time; otherwise the damn thing's going to jam up. Any questions, ask them now. I can't hear you when I'm in the other room."

"Thank you, Herr Batz. I understand what I have to do."

I watched him disappear into the dark room and then set to work. As I picked up the individual records, I paused long enough to read each name and to study the emaciated face on the identity photo that went with it. Most of the workers had unpronounceable Polish and Russian names. But a few had beautiful German names like Apfel, Birnbaum, Blumenberg, Goldberg, and Himmelfarb. One by one all of them slid into the shredder and disappeared forever.

Mr. Batz limped out of the darkroom two hours later, took his glasses off, rubbed his eyes, and muttered, "Terrible, this combination of acid smell and darkness!" Then he sighed and sat down at his desk, his wooden leg stretched out in front of him.

"Excuse me, Herr Batz, but is this a good time to ask you a question? I wondered if you could tell me who the forced laborers were with the German names? You know, like Goldberg and Himmelfarb?"

"Are you some kind of idiot? You really don't know? They were all Jews, of course. But don't let the names fool you. They didn't just come from Germany. They were from all over Europe – Poland, Lithuania, Hungary, Romania. By the way, you can't tell from the pictures, but many of them were lawyers, judges, politicians, doctors. Real big shots! And there were plenty of Communists among them, too." He leaned forward in his chair and relit his pipe. "You know, Nitsch, I'm willing to bet that for most of those Jews, Arminius AG was the first place in their lives they ever had to do an honest day's work. Really worked up a sweat, if you know what I mean! And if you ask me, between the Slavs and the Jews, the Jews were by far the worst. They were born cheats, the whole lot of them. But they couldn't cheat here at the factory; no sir, they couldn't cheat anybody here." He rubbed his hands together gleefully. "You know what I find funny? We made those lazy Jews help with our war effort. The aluminum they produced went into our weapons and planes. We put them to work for the Fatherland! That was the ironic beauty of it."

During Mr. Batz's rant, I glanced down at the next batch of cards. There were so many still to be processed, box after box of them.

"Just to be sure, Herr Batz. You really want me to destroy *all* these files?"

"That's exactly what I want you to do. Every last one!" and he hobbled back behind the thick drape.

Since Mr. Batz came back out every so often to check on my progress, I worked with a steady rhythm. Read the name; glance at the face; insert in slot; shred. Read the name; glance at the face; insert in slot; shred. I wished I could have lingered longer over the photos of the hollow-eyed, sunken-cheeked workers on the identity cards. Did some of them survive the war I wondered? Did their families ever learn what happened to the ones who died? Once the records were gone, how was anyone ever to find out?

By the end of May, when all traces of the forced laborers were gone, I walked over to Mr. Scharwerker's office to pick up my monthly paycheck.

"Good afternoon, Herr Scharwerker," I said as humbly as I could and then I waited for him to acknowledge my presence.

"Hey, Nitsch, still on that special project for Batz?"

"I just finished there, sir. I'm going to Purchasing next."

"So!" he said triumphantly. "I take it the wartime records are all gone?" I nodded. "From what I hear, most of the workers were Russians and Poles. But those Jews! They were all shysters! Rag dealers! Lousy peddlers! I knew those types all too well."

"Excuse me, Herr Scharwerker, but Herr Batz told me many of them had been lawyers and doctors and the like."

"Batz is from Cologne so he has no idea about those Yiddish-speaking caftan Jews around Danzig where I come from. They were the scum of the earth, the whole lot of them!" He glared at me as I shifted uneasily from one foot to the other. "You came for your money I suppose?"

He handed me my paycheck and when I slipped it into my pocket, it somehow felt like blood money.

****

"We had a great day today," Mutti announced when we all sat down to supper that evening. "Remember the order we got for tarts, cakes, and pies for that wedding three weeks ago? Where we made about half our average day's take in one fell swoop? Well, today two more couples came in, one before lunch and one right after, and placed *their* wedding orders. It seems that the first couple had recommended us. So things are really taking off!"

"And all of them had been long-time customers at Café Meyer," my father added with grim satisfaction before turning to me. "So, Günter. Are you still working for that idiot in the basement?"

"This was my last day down there. The Purchasing Department is next."

"Then why so glum?"

"A week ago Batz was gloating about the forced laborers. But today it was Scharwerker's turn over in Payroll. He gave me a whole speech attacking so-called 'caftan' Jews around Danzig. Frankly, I don't see how it much matters whether they came from the city or the countryside. Their cards all ended up in the shredder."

"Well," my father said, "this Scharwerker guy may have been on to something. If a Jew was a lawyer or a doctor in a place like Cologne, he looked like everyone else. But the Eastern Jews dressed in strange robes and kept to themselves. In my opinion, they weren't really German."

"Still, Günter's right," Mutti cut in sharply. "When you get right down to it, it doesn't make a difference. Anyway, the war's been over for twelve years and it's high time people stopped talking like that, wouldn't you say?"

"And *thinking* like that," I added with a defiant stare at my father.

"That," my father said, meeting my gaze, "is easier said than done. Let me tell you how things are in the real world. They just had a funeral for Keip, the former *Kreisleiter* of Bergheim."

"You mean the tailor who took in my confirmation suit?" I asked in disbelief.

"That's the guy. And when they lowered the coffin several dozen men raised their arms and shouted 'Heil Hitler!' I got the story directly from Herr Drescher when he came by this morning to deliver the bread. That must've been a sight!" He chuckled.

"I don't see anything funny about it," Mutti snapped. "What a bunch of idiots! Herr Drescher must have a vivid imagination."

"Far from it. He actually toned the story down. According to the local paper some of those old Nazis even brought along swastika flags." Then he looked directly at me. His face was twisted into a nasty grin as he said, "And you thought you could change the way people think!"

CHAPTER 29

O n the first of June I reported to Mr. Gierig, Manager of the Purchasing Department. A former army captain, he was a short-statured, corpulent man with a commanding voice.

"Oh, it's you, Nitsch," he snapped when I walked into his office. "Before you even get started, Schmelzer down in Personnel wants to have a talk with you."

The Personnel Manager greeted me with unexpected respect. "Ah, Herr Nitsch! Just the person I want to see. I've been pleased with the excellent evaluations I've been getting, especially from Herr Kopf and Herr Mayer. And as a result, we've decided to shorten your apprenticeship by six months. In other words, as soon as you finish your rotation in Purchasing, you'll be promoted to a regular salaried employee. Effective October 1, 1957, you'll become an official part of the Arminius AG team."

"That's wonderful news. Thank you, Herr Schmelzer!"

My head was spinning as I walked back to the Purchasing Department. I had heard about two other apprentices from the Commercial School who'd been hired before the end of their apprenticeships but I hadn't dreamed it would happen to me. Since the promotion would triple my monthly pay, I wondered whether my parents would start to charge me for my room and board. Or would they be different from the other parents I knew and let me keep the money? I still hoped to be able to afford those English classes at Berlitz that one of the summer interns had told me about. Maybe this would be my chance.

"So, did Schmelzer give you the good news?" Mr. Gierig asked when I got back.

"Yes, sir!"

"I've already instructed my deputy, Herr Auer, to give you an overview of our activities and then you can get down to work. If you have questions, don't come bothering me. Go ask Auer!"

"Yes, Herr Gierig."

"Oh, one more thing, Nitsch, before you go. Just because you're getting a promotion in October, don't think you'll get any special treatment around here. You're still an apprentice and I expect you to act like one!"

I left Mr. Gierig's office, crossed the large room where the purchasing staff was hard at work, and poked my head into Mr. Auer's office on the opposite side of the room. "Good morning, Herr Auer. Herr Gierig asked me to see you about getting started."

"Asked you? Ordered you, more likely," he said with a wink. "Well, no sense hanging in the doorway, Herr Nitsch. Please come in and have a seat!"

Mr. Auer needed an hour to describe the workings of his department but then he turned the conversation to more personal matters, asking me about my parents, my education, as well as possible plans for my future before telling me something about himself.

"I was stationed in East Prussia at the beginning of the war," he began. "But later on I was sent to fight in North Africa under Rommel. That's where the Americans caught me."

"You were in a POW camp in North Africa?" I asked.

"Not for long. The *Amis* put us on a boat and brought us to the States. For the next two years we worked picking fruits and vegetables

189

in Louisiana and Mississippi. We were good at it too, even faster than the Mexican girls picking tomatoes right alongside of us. And since our captors gave us 'free room and board' and the girls had families to support, we sometimes added our tomatoes to their baskets to help them out. We got along so well with those Mexican girls that, every so often, one of them returned the favor, if you know what I mean."

"How was it?" I asked and then I blushed. "Let me rephrase that. How was it *being in the States?*"

"It may sound strange considering why I was there, but I loved it. Everyone was friendly to us and we had more sunshine in one month than we have here from April to September. To be honest, I've often regretted that I didn't move to the States after the war. Maybe in a couple of years you should consider working over there for a while. It would really widen your horizons. Anyway, I guess you need to get started around here. If you follow me, Herr Nitsch, I'll introduce you to the other people in our department."

I followed Mr. Auer into the large room outside his office where, together with the nine other members of the purchasing staff, it was my job to search through the more than ninety thick directories and the hundreds of catalogues the Purchasing Department used to find items required by the factory. Even with all the sources available to us, it often happened that the chemical and production engineers would ask for items that weren't readily available. Then endless telephone calls were required to find a manufacturer for a particular item or to persuade a manufacturer to develop and make a particular item. I worked closely with Mr. Funke, a tall, skinny soft-spoken Rhinelander who parted his thinning hair at the side, and with Mr. Gierig's efficient and long-suffering personal secretary, Mrs. Binting, a divorcée in her mid-forties who wore heavy make-up, and in my estimation at least, must have been a real beauty in her younger days.

No matter how absorbed we were in the work, when Mr. Gierig stuck his head out of his office door everyone snapped to attention.

"Funke!" he would bellow, and Mr. Funke would jump up and slink into Mr. Gierig's office like a beaten dog. Sometimes Mr. Gierig would command several people to come in at a time and, even though his office had two extra chairs, staff members had to stand while he delivered rants that often lasted as long as a quarter of an hour. The only exception was Mrs. Binting, who was permitted to sit down when she took dictation. Still, every time the phone rang, Mr. Gierig would give Mrs. Binting an imperious wave with the back of his hand to signal that she should leave and shut the door behind her.

Not surprisingly, whenever Mr. Gierig was out of the office, which happened quite often, the atmosphere in the Purchasing Department became quite relaxed. During those times, Mr. Funke and Mrs. Binting took me into their confidence.

"If you don't mind, Frau Binting," I asked one afternoon, "do you have any idea why Herr Gierig doesn't let you stay in his office when he's on the phone?"

"That's easy. He's probably negotiating a bribe. It can't be company business, that's for sure, because, if you ask me, he doesn't have the foggiest idea what we do around here. He'll listen for twenty minutes to calls from one of our chemists or an engineer and then refer the person to someone like Herr Funke. Come to think of it, I honestly don't know why anyone at Arminius AG bothers to call him in the first place if they need to order something. It's like talking to a wall. But with suppliers, that's a different story. He's on a real gravy train."

"You mean gifts from suppliers, like a bottle of cognac? My father gets gifts like that all the time at Café Nitsch, like when he puts in an especially big order for canned fruit or flour."

Mr. Funke had been listening to our conversation. "Let me explain to our young apprentice how these things work," he said. "Take Herr Auer, for example. Just like your father, he may get small thank-you gifts from our suppliers from time to time, things like a case of wine or a two-pound box of fancy chocolates, but he would never let that influence his purchasing decisions. I actually think the man is incorruptible. He doesn't even keep the stuff for himself; he shares it with the whole department."

"But there's someone else around here, who will remain nameless," Mrs. Binting chimed in, "who doesn't hesitate to accept big-ticket items like a refrigerator, or a television set, or a leather living room set, or twenty-four porcelain place-settings. And what he can't use himself he gives away to his family or his friends. You'd have to be naïve to believe gifts like that don't affect purchasing decisions."

Mr. Funke nodded in agreement. "The worst part is that top management must know what's going on but they figure he's going to retire in two years anyway so why bother."

"By the way, Herr Nitsch, when you mentioned your father's café it made my mouth water," Mrs. Binting suddenly remarked. "Since our 'Company Commander' isn't at his post, would you mind biking into Bergheim to buy all of us some cake? I'll just copy down everybody's request and get you the money."

"I don't mind in the least, Frau Binting! It would be my pleasure."

CHAPTER 30

*I*n late August 1957, with only one month remaining before the end of my apprenticeship, I hitchhiked to Salzburg, Austria, with Hans Schürmann, a former classmate from the Commercial School, whose vacation time coincided with mine. During the first few days after our arrival we explored the massive castle overlooking the city, visited museums, and went to a wonderful concert at the Mozarteum University. The very first 45 RPM record I had bought for our record-player back home had been Mozart's "Eine Kleine Nachtmusik" but I had never before heard it performed in a concert hall.

"Maybe it's a good omen," I confided to Hans after the performance. "I buy a record by Mozart and get to hear the same music live in Salzburg. So I was thinking, the second record I got was Louis Armstrong's version of 'Mack the Knife.' What do you suppose my chances are of ever getting to hear *him* sing live?"

"You come up with some strange ideas," Hans retorted. "How you can even *think* about Louis Armstrong in the middle of Austria beats me."

On Sunday morning I accepted Hans's invitation to attend Mass with him in a Baroque church and was fascinated by the chanted sounds of the Latin liturgy even though I couldn't understand a word of it. When several violinists joined the choir in a selection by Franz Josef Haydn I was sure that the music resonated all the way to heaven.

"You know," I confided to Hans as we walked back to the youth hostel after the service, "my father claimed it's a waste of time to study Latin. His exact words were, 'The Romans are all dead anyhow. So why bother?' But now I can see why it might be a good thing to know."

"I struggled with it for five years in the *Gymnasium* but it is nice to be able to understand the Mass," Hans agreed.

Early the next morning we took a bus to Hallein, twenty kilometers south of Salzburg to visit the Schaunbergwerk Dürrnberg, an ancient salt mine that had been converted into a tourist attraction. After buying our tickets we donned white coveralls and then took turns perching on burlap sacks atop a forty-two meter long wooden slide that whooshed us at breakneck speed deep down below the surface. When we had all regrouped in a small, dome-shaped cave, our guide began his explanation.

"People have been mining salt in this area for thousands of years. The Celts were here, followed by the Romans. But it was around the year 1600 that salt mining was commercialized on a grand scale. In those days salt was called 'white gold' and it made the city of Salzburg and the Catholic Church very rich." He waited to see if there were any questions and then continued. "And now we're going to explore a short distance down one of the many long tunnels. If there's anyone who wants to leave us at this point please let me know now." Several claustrophobic tourists took up his offer to abandon the tour and took an elevator to the surface, but Hans and I decided to stick it out.

The deeper we walked into the tunnel, the more the guide talked about the deplorable working conditions of the miners in the Middle Ages who had faced the prospect of tunnel fires, cave-ins, and suffocation on a daily basis while working twelve-hour shifts. I contrasted the lives of those poor souls with the lives of the well-fed nobles and clergymen whose portraits hung in the history museum we had visited the day before. I thought again of the forced laborers who had toiled in the factory at Arminius AG during the war. Were the fat cats who lined their pockets with the resulting profits any better than the nobles of three hundred fifty years earlier? For that matter, was *I* any better for celebrating Carnival with the administration while "the poor slobs in the factory worked themselves to death," as Mr. Kohlhofer had put it?

"Boy, aren't you the gloomy Gus?" Hans chided me when we reached the surface. "Cheer up or no one's going to want to give us a ride."

We only had to flag down two cars to get to Berchtesgaden where we booked a few nights in the youth hostel. American military personnel mingled with tourists as Hans and I walked to a souvenir shop to buy postcards. I chose one with a view of the snow-capped 2,713 meter-high Watzmann, whose imposing double peaks towered over the town. Someone had told me that Adolf Hitler had lived in the town during the war, but there was no trace of him anywhere; Allied bombing raids in April 1945 had seen to that. For the tourists, the mountain was the attraction.

Hans looked over my shoulder at the postcard and read my mind. "What do you say? Let's tackle the Watzmann tomorrow! Who knows if we'll get another chance?"

Before heading back to the youth hostel for supper we each bought a few rolls and some fruit and packed them into our rucksacks. By 10 P.M. we crawled into our cots, and along with our ten roommates, all of whom apparently shared our plans, we were soon sound asleep. The next morning, awakened by the other hikers, we rose shortly after 5 A.M., filled our military canteens, and set out for the summit. It took us more than five hours to pass the tree line and continue up the trail in the blazing sun to the top but the spectacular view of the surrounding mountains made it all worth while. We lingered up there for two hours before starting our descent.

Over the next three days a steady rain blocked out the view of the mountain and we passed the time playing board games with some high school girls who were stuck like us in the hostel. But by the fourth day, worrying that the soggy weather would make hitchhiking difficult, we cut our trip short and headed back home to Bergheim. Neither of us wanted to risk getting back to work late.

****

I found the required daylong apprenticeship completion test at the Cologne Chamber of Commerce surprisingly easy, and on October 1, 1957, I became an official employee in the Arminius AG Transportation Department at triple my previous salary. To my astonishment, my parents agreed to let me keep the money.

"Why don't you register for that English class at Berlitz you've been telling us about now that you can afford it?" my father asked. "From what I hear, their method really works."

Days later I took a written and an oral test in the Berlitz School near the Cologne Cathedral and was placed into a class with six other students ranging in age from twenty-two to fifty-five. Our teacher, a bespectacled English lady in her early forties, only spoke English during each two-hour session.

At the same time that my prospects for learning English were improving, I could foresee a bright future at Arminius AG. Mr. Kopf was already talking about getting me a paid three to six month internship with the Rhenus Shipping Company in Cologne. He even dangled the prospect of my having another paid internship after that with a shipping company in Hamburg.

But all that was about to change. A few days later while Mr. Miele and I were working, Mr. Kopf was flipping the pages of the *Kölner Stadt-Anzeiger* when he suddenly gave a low whistle. "Gentlemen, this is big news. Listen up!" He put his reading glasses back on and found the spot he wanted on the page. "Here it is. 'Young men who were born between July 1, 1937 and December 31, 1937, have to report to the local draft board to be inducted for one year of service in the *Bundeswehr*.' When did you say your birthday was, Herr Nitsch?"

For a moment I was too stunned to reply. Germany had not had a draft since the end of the war. "That's my age group," I finally said. "I guess I'm going into the army."

"Well, wouldn't you know it," Mr. Miele mocked. "Our Prussian's going to be a soldier! So, Herr Kopf, how long do we have until we're shorthanded in the department again?"

"The draft starts in April 1958 and runs for six months but it's also possible to volunteer from April 1st on, instead of waiting to be called up." He handed me the paper. "I guess you'll want to keep this as a souvenir," he added with a smile. "Anyway, look on the bright side. At least we're not at war!"

The strange part of it was that I was secretly excited by the news. Even though I would turn twenty in December, I was still living at home with my parents where tension had been running high ever since Hubert started his apprenticeship with my father. The two of them were like a programmed disaster. Hubert never met my father's expectations and my father smacked him at least once a week. Mutti also suffered in the explosive atmosphere as her attempts to be an intermediary between Hubert and my father always ended in failure. But even if all had been well at home, after seeing the world from the top of the Watzmann, Bergheim now seemed way too small. With the exception of my class at Berlitz, every place I needed to go – Arminius AG, Oma's apartment, the Lutheran church, scout meetings – could all be easily reached on foot or by bicycle. I felt fenced in. The army could be my way out.

Since Oma had come over to the shop to join us for supper that evening, I waited until we'd finished eating before taking the newspaper out of my briefcase. "Herr Kopf found this story in today's paper. I'm going to be drafted into the army!"

Oma gave a little gasp. Then she burst into tears. "I don't believe it! The last war nearly killed us all and now they're starting the madness again? After all we've been through, hasn't our family sacrificed enough?"

"Now, Mother," Mutti said gently. "It's peacetime and this could be a wonderful experience for Günter."

"Don't talk to me about peacetime. It was peacetime when your three brothers joined up, too. And then the war started and two of them got wounded and one never came home."

"It would only be for a year, Oma," I explained, "and then I'll be right back here in Bergheim. You'll see!"

In the meantime my father had reread the newspaper story. "Have you thought about the timing? If I read this correctly, you could choose to start on April first if you wanted to."

"That's just what I was thinking of doing. What do you think?"

"Well, Stretch, you're a healthy guy. You're bound to pass the physical and you're going to get drafted sooner or later, no matter what. So you might as well get your service behind you. Don't you agree, Gretel?"

Mutti nodded and gave Oma a hug. "Sorry, Mother, but Willi's right. The sooner Günter gets started, the sooner he can get his career at Arminius AG back on track."

First thing the next morning I talked to Mr. Kopf and to Mr. Schmelzer in personnel to ask for a few hours off so that I could travel to nearby Jülich to complete the paperwork and be interviewed at the draft board. Not long after that a letter arrived directing me to report to the Zur Krone Restaurant in Bergheim's largest hotel for my physical. In my first real taste of army life, we were divided into groups, ordered to strip naked, and then called in, ten inductees at a time, to a large party room with windows facing an alley so that anyone who happened to walk by at that moment could have looked in and seen us.

A team of three doctors and a dentist examined each of us in turn. Most of the young men in my group were desperately hoping to fail the physical; I wanted desperately to pass it. After being poked at and approved by the doctors, the dentist had the last word. Since I didn't have a single cavity, he gave the nod. I was classified 1A.

While the next group got ready to be examined, the ten of us dressed and headed to the hotel bar for a beer. A reporter from the local paper rushed over to interview us as a photographer snapped our picture. We were instant celebrities when our photo appeared the next morning in the *Kölner Rundschau*.

A few weeks later I received a call-up order in the mail informing me that I had to report to the Gneisenau Barracks in Koblenz on April 1, 1958. The news spread fast in Arminius AG and I was given all kinds of advice and recommendations, the gist of which was, "You're going to have a good time provided, of course, there's no conflict with the Russians."

When I went to pick up my paycheck at the end of November, Mr. Scharwerker's greeting puzzled me. "Well," he said, "your father must be very proud of you. I'd be proud too if my son did what you did!"

"Excuse me, Herr Scharwerker. What should I be proud of? What did I supposedly do, Herr Scharwerker?"

"Well, didn't you volunteer for the Army as befits a proper young Prussian like you? For how many years did you enlist?"

"I'm sorry, Herr Scharwerker, but there must be some misunderstanding. I didn't volunteer for the army. I was drafted. I just accelerated my starting date and I have no intention of serving any longer than I have to."

He put his hands on his hips and glared at me. "Oh, that's your game, is it? Just do the minimum? Well, with your education you'd never have become an officer anyway. You'd have needed to go to the *Gymnasium* for that. But at least you're not a draft dodger like some of the youngsters I've been reading about. I'll give you that much!" He handed me my paycheck and turned his back on me.

"What an arrogant bastard!" I grumbled when I got back to the Transportation Department. "I thought Herr Scharwerker never finished the *Gymnasium*. Herr Kopf, didn't you tell me he left school when he was sixteen?"

"Yeah, he's always bragged that his rise through the ranks was a reward for his bravery. Bravery, my foot! He probably just killed more partisans than the next guy. How brave is that? As for serving the minimum amount of time, I don't blame you one bit. I spent a few years in the army towards the end of the war and hated every minute of it."

Mr. Miele chuckled. "Well, I'm glad I'm a little too old to be drafted but I almost think I'd rather be in the German army than on 'Captain' Scharwerker's shit list. Good luck with that."

CHAPTER 31

*W*ith only a few months left until I was scheduled to report for military duty, I looked forward to 1958 with nervous excitement. Arminius AG closed early on New Year's Eve and I rushed home to help out in the café. My job was to pack six or twelve *Berliner Pfannkuchen* (jelly doughnuts) into a flat white carton and carefully mark the type of filling on each carton. That way the hosts at New Year's Eve parties could decide which of their unwitting guests, expecting a sweet jelly filling, would bite into a mustard-filled *Berliner* instead. Thinking back to the years when Mutti, Hubert and I had starved under the Russians in East Prussia, I considered it sinful to turn a perfectly good pastry into a practical joke, but the cash register jingled with each sale and my parents had no second thoughts.

I had celebrated the last two New Year's Eves at home with my parents and the Krienkes, but I was no longer a teenager and this year was going to be different. Wilfried Plath had invited me to a party given by Brigitte Emmenthal, who was a friend of Wilfried's older sister. I had seen Brigitte around Zieverich. Two years my senior, she had attended the Commercial School in Horrem during my first year there and was now working as a secretary in the headquarters of an international chemical company in Cologne. Tall, long-legged and aloof, Brigitte knew that she was pretty. I had never dared to speak to her.

Two hours after the last customer left the shop, I put on a dark blue suit, a white shirt, a red tie, and my winter coat, and feeling somewhat ill at ease, walked over to Brigitte's house clutching two bags. One contained an expensive bottle of Mosel wine given to us by one of my father's suppliers; in the other was "Jailhouse Rock," my favorite Elvis Presley 45 RPM record. The two-story brick houses in the development where Brigitte lived with her parents were only a year or two old. They had been built in Zieverich with some of the *Lastenausgleich* funds set aside for refugees from the East. The Emmenthal family, like mine, came from East Prussia.

The few parties I had been to before were dull affairs under the watchful eyes of parent chaperones, at which the girls would sit and giggle while the outnumbered boys gawked at them from the other side of the room. I expected this party would be no different. But when Brigitte opened the door she greeted me with a radiant smile and a firm handshake. Her closely cropped, ash blond hair shimmered in the bright light of the entranceway.

"I'm so glad you could make it," she said, putting me instantly at ease. "It's high time we got to know each other."

"I couldn't agree more. Thanks for inviting me!"

She took the bottle of wine and studied the label. "You have very good taste in wine. Thank you! I guess you know most of my other guests. Why don't you join them? We've still got some things to do in the kitchen." Wilfried's sisters waved from the kitchen and it was only as Brigitte turned to walk away that I noticed she was wearing an apron over her white blouse and her wide skirt puffed up with several layers of crinoline petticoats.

I wandered over to Wilfried who was trying his best to talk to three girls at once. Meanwhile guests continued to arrive over the next hour, two dozen in all, of whom I knew only half. There was no sign of Brigitte's parents. Pat Boone's "Love Letters in the Sand" was spinning on the turntable as we sat down wherever we could to eat little sandwiches, franks, and potato salad. But as soon as we had finished eating, I added "Jailhouse Rock" to the stack of records waiting to be played and the party came to life. From that point on until the last minute of 1957, we alternated between slow dances and "Jailhouse Rock."

To my astonishment, whenever the music slowed, out of all the people there Brigitte chose to dance with me. Even more amazing, at the stroke of midnight, we embraced each other and kissed. Even after most of the guests had gone home, she and I danced, scarcely exchanging a word the whole time. I finally broke the ice.

"If you don't mind my asking, what's that wonderful perfume you're wearing?" It was the first thing that came into my mind to say.

She pulled me even closer and whispered, "*L'air du Temps.*" Then she stopped dancing and led me over to a seat next to her on the couch. Someone had put on "Treat Me Nice" from the flip side of my Elvis record. "All the girls I know are heartbroken that Elvis is going into the army in three weeks," Brigitte confided to me. "Is it true that you're going soon too?"

"I start in April. Actually, I'm glad to be getting away from home for a year. My father's really strict."

Brigitte smiled. "What do you expect from an East Prussian father? Mine's the same way."

"He can't be all that bad. I can't imagine my parents letting me give a party like this when they weren't home."

"It's only because my parents are staying over with out-of-town relatives tonight. Actually, I'm just as eager to leave home as you are. That's why I'm going to England in April to work for a year as an *au pair* with a family in Leeds. By the time I get back, my English should be so good that I'll make enough money to move out and live on my own."

I bit my lip at this news. Even though we had just met, I really liked Brigitte. Now it seemed as though we wouldn't have all that much time to get better acquainted. She squeezed my hand. "Cheer up! Let's dance!" she said and she pulled me to my feet. By then it was five in the morning and everyone else had gone home. We put a stack of slow songs on the spindle – "Tammy" and "April Love" and some songs by Johnny Mathis – and clung to each other until Brigitte fixed me breakfast two hours later.

My father was in the kitchen eating breakfast by himself when I got home. Instead of the expected lecture, he got up and shook my hand. "Happy New Year, Stretch. That must've been one hell of a party!"

I tried not to blush. "The best I've ever been to."

Then he stood back and looked me over. "Yes," he said slowly. "I imagine it was."

****

Some of the restaurants in Bergheim had started to order their dessert pastries from Café Nitsch. To reciprocate, my father had gotten into the habit of taking the family to one of those restaurants for an early Sunday lunch before our café opened at one o'clock. Hubert and I hadn't been to many fancy restaurants in our lives and we enjoyed the white linen tablecloths, fine service, and delicious food. But even on those occasions, there was tension in the air because my father constantly criticized Hubert for lapses in decorum such as not sitting up straight, or slurping his soup, or using the bread knife instead of the fish knife.

On the other hand, my father usually tended to cut me some slack, which irritated Hubert even more. One Sunday we went into a restaurant and the owner, who hadn't seen me for several years, exclaimed, "How long has it been? You've gotten so tall!"

I have no idea what came over me but I pointed to my parents and replied, "Blame them! They must've worked extra hard twenty years ago!"

For a second my father's smile froze, but when the restaurant owner burst out laughing and Mutti started to giggle, my father joined in, much to my relief. I couldn't even imagine what would have happened had Hubert told a joke like that. But then again, no one would have remarked on Hubert's height. He was as short and flabby as I was tall and thin.

The following day I came home through the shop. Mutti was waiting on customers but she beckoned me to join her behind the counter.

"Is something wrong?" I whispered.

"It's a catastrophe. Vati caught Hubert stealing money from his locked desk!"

"Is he sure? How'd he find out?"

"Sorry I can't talk now! It's too busy in here. Why don't you go upstairs and ask Vati? He's doing the books and I know he wants to talk to you."

"Is Hubert...?"

"Hubert's not here. He went for a long walk."

While rushing up the two flights to our apartment I felt sorry for Hubert. He hated working for my father; he was ashamed of his horrible complexion, and he had very few friends. But stealing? I hoped there was some mistake.

Just as he ended every long workday, my father was bent over his desk in the corner of our living room filing away invoices. As soon as I came in, he swiveled his desk chair to face me and said in a hoarse voice, "Did Mutti tell you what happened?"

"Yes, but just the gist. She had customers. The café's still busy. How can you be sure Hubert did it?"

My father took a deep breath. "As you know, about an hour before Mutti closes the store, I bring the big bills from the cash register up here and lock them in my left-hand desk drawer. Then I run back down to help close up for the night. Once we've eaten supper, I bring up the loose change and the balance of the bills from the register. I have to wait to count the day's take until I've brought up all the money, but I always count the big bills, the twenties and the fifties, before I lock them up in the drawer. That gives me an estimate of how we've done during the day. Are you with me so far?"

"Yes, but I don't see how..."

"Bear with me. I'm getting to that part. About a week ago, I counted thirteen twenties and two fifties before I went down to supper. But when I came back up, one of the twenties was missing. I thought maybe I'd miscounted but the same thing happened the next four days in a row. A twenty was always missing. Today I decided to hide in our bedroom to see if I could catch the thief red-handed. As soon as I heard someone go into the living room I sneaked through the enclosed porch and into your bedroom and what did I see? Hubert was opening my desk with a skeleton key! He froze when he saw me in the doorway."

"Then what happened?"

"I asked him, 'How often have you been stealing twenty Marks a day?' and he stammered, 'I don't know.' My first impulse was to smack him but what good would it have done?" My father paused and gazed out the window for a moment before turning back to me. "Anyway, I'm through with him. I never want him back in my baking kitchen again. He can find himself another job as far as I'm concerned!"

"But he's only fifteen; he can't go on his own. Will you be taking him on interviews or will Mutti?"

My father's hands shook as he assorted some invoices. Without even looking up he said, "Mutti can't leave the store and there's no way I'm going to do it. Imagine! My own son a thief! How could I in good conscience persuade other master craftsmen to take him on as an apprentice after what happened?" He put down the invoices and looked me square in the eyes. "Actually, Stretch, I was hoping you would do it."

****

I still had eight precious vacation days left at Arminius AG before I would join the army. Spending them job-hunting with my sullen, pimple-faced brother would hardly have been my first choice of how to use them. But when Mutti begged me to help Hubert as a special favor to her, I couldn't say no.

First thing Tuesday morning I told Mr. Kopf that an emergency had come up at home and requested permission to take the rest of my vacation time. By the time I biked back home, Hubert was sitting in our kitchen under Mutti's watchful eye. Even though he had painstakingly glued down his unruly cowlick with Brylcreem and forced the middle button of his jacket to close over his bulging stomach, his drooping shoulders and scowling face did not inspire confidence. I had my work cut out for me.

As we rode the train to the government-run employment office in Cologne, my brother sat slumped in the seat next to me, listlessly gazing out the window.

"Hubert, listen to me!" I pleaded. "The most important thing is to make eye contact. Sound confident! Smile!" But my words fell on deaf ears. Although the employment office gave us leads to apprenticeships as pastry maker, baker, mechanic, retail clerk in a department store, and supermarket cashier, and we duly trotted from one job opening to another, each time I introduced Hubert and made a pitch on his behalf, he stood next to me staring down at his shoes. Over the course of four days, several employers actually offered *me* a job. But no one wanted Hubert.

Finally, on our fifth day of looking, we took the tramway to the Ehrenfeld Station and walked a few blocks to the shop owned by Josef Monke. Before going inside we stopped to admire the shiny brass saxophones, trombones, and trumpets in the window. Wilhelm Monke, the owner's son, greeted Hubert cheerfully, as though they were old friends. He needed an additional apprentice to learn musical instrument making and repair and he wasn't about to be put off by Hubert's attitude problem.

"Nice to meet you, young man. Let me show you both around the shop." Putting his arm over Hubert's shoulders he led us into a room in the back where several young men were hunched over their workbenches. The daylight streaming in through the windows reflected off the brass instruments they were cradling between their knees. "If you join us, by the end of your three years you will have learned how to make, clean and repair brass instruments for the members of the Cologne Philharmonic and the Cologne Opera orchestra," Mr. Monke explained. "By the way, in case you're wondering, we made all of the instruments in our store window right here in the shop." He paused to give Hubert time to think. "So, young man, do you want to become our apprentice?"

To my astonishment, Hubert looked up and smiled. "Yes, Herr Monke. I'd love to."

"All right then, that's settled! When can you begin work?"

"I could be here tomorrow, Herr Monke."

"Why don't we make it April first since that's the traditional time to start an apprenticeship? If you come back here tomorrow, I'll have the contract ready for you to sign." Then he turned to me. "I'll need you back here, too, Herr Nitsch, since your parents can't come. I assume you'll be willing to sign as Hubert's guardian?"

"Of course, Herr Monke, and thank you!" I replied, trying my best to sound enthusiastic. Being Hubert's guardian was a bit more than I had bargained for.

The next morning Hubert and I returned to Cologne-Ehrenfeld to sign the paperwork.

"Well, Herr Nitsch," Mr. Monke said when he handed me a signed copy of the agreement, "if I understood you correctly, you'll be reporting to the army the same day Hubert starts with us here. How long will you be in for? A year?"

"Yes, sir. I'll finish my service in the spring of 1959."

"You don't happen to like jazz, by any chance?"

"That's my favorite kind of music, Herr Monke. How'd you guess?"

"Remember yesterday I told you and Hubert that we do repairs for the Cologne Philharmonic and the Opera? I should have also mentioned that our shop serves world famous jazz musicians. When Louis Armstrong, and Jack Teagarden, and Harry James perform in Cologne or in Düsseldorf, chances are they'll drop by to see us. The reason I mention it, is that I think you'd make an excellent addition to our front-office sales force. When you're discharged from the army, keep us in mind. If you decide not to go back to Arminius AG, give me a call or, better yet, stop by."

"Congratulations," I said to Hubert as he and I walked back to the Ehrenfeld tramway station. "You've got yourself a nice job!"

"Not as good as the one Herr Monke offered you!" he grumbled. "Why are you always stealing my thunder?"

"The job wasn't my idea, and anyway, I have no intention of working there."

"Do you mean that?"

"Of course I do. But all the same, if you ever get to see any of those famous jazz musicians, I want you to write me in the army and tell me all about it. Deal?"

"Deal!"

CHAPTER 32

"**G**uess who's coming for a visit?" Mutti asked me when I got home from work the following week. "Your cousin Gerda!"

Of Aunt Liesbeth's four surviving children, the one I had missed most was Gerda, with whom I had spent more than two years in Russian-occupied East Prussia collecting, sawing, and chopping wood, and picking blueberries, mushrooms, and ears of grain from the harvested fields.

On Sunday morning Gerda visited us at the café. My childhood companion had grown up into a tall, attractive young woman. After she hugged Mutti, she turned to shake my father's hand.

"Hallo, Uncle Willi! How long has it been? I think the last time I saw you I had just turned eight. Is that about right?"

"Hard to believe, but I think so. Imagine that. Fourteen years!"

"Come!" Mutti exclaimed. "I want to hear the latest Reimann family news." My father brought an extra chair from the café into the kitchen so that all five of us could sit down for lunch.

"Let's see, where to begin?" Gerda said as she helped herself to some stuffed cabbage and mashed potatoes. "Have you been getting Ilse's postcards? She's so happy with Cemal and her two stepchildren.

Funny the turns life takes sometimes. Who'd ever have imagined she'd end up marrying a Turkish doctor?"

"Your mother hasn't visited her there yet, has she?" Mutti wanted to know.

"She's afraid to fly to Turkey on her own so I think she's waiting for me to go with her but with my new job it may be a while before I can take that much time off."

"Tell me, Gerda, did Cemal speak German when he and Ilse met?" my father asked.

"Fluently. And now the children are learning it, too. They call Ilse 'Mutti' by the way."

"I'm so happy for Ilse. After all she went through in East Prussia, it's nice that she's found a great husband and a ready-made family." Mutti paused for a moment, then added, "I'll never forget that, if Ilse hadn't joined me at night, I couldn't have stolen enough potatoes from the *Kolkhoz* (a Russian state-run farm) to keep all of us from starving. She showed such courage!"

"It's funny, Aunt Gretel. Ilse says the same thing about you!"

Mutti blushed at the compliment. "Tell us about Dieter and Helga!"

"Dieter's still going to Middle School and Helga is working in a bank."

Mutti glanced at her watch. "Sorry to interrupt but my salesgirls will be here any minute and I have to open the café."

"And I have to greet our customers," my father added. " Why don't you pick out a dessert and join Hubert and me at a table up front?"

"Günter, you're not coming, too?"

"Sorry, I already promised my friend, Brigitte, I'd meet her this afternoon."

"Oh, now there's a piece of news! How long have you known her? What's she like? Is it serious?"

"Just since New Years Eve so I'd hardly call it serious. Anyway, the same day I go into the army, she's leaving to work for a year in England. So who knows if we'll even still be in touch a year from now."

Brigitte and I had planned to see a movie but when we met in front of the Apollo Theatre, we changed our minds and instead walked over to a recently opened ice cream parlor on the hill near the elementary school. As we lingered over our chocolate sundaes, our imminent departures in opposite directions weighed heavily on my mind. Still, I didn't feel comfortable addressing the subject directly. What if Brigitte didn't feel the same way?

"Have you gotten your final orders yet from the *Bundeswehr*?" she asked, as if reading my mind.

"Not yet. But I know I'll be stationed in Koblenz. To be honest, I would've preferred some place a bit further away. Now my parents are hoping I'll come up to Bergheim once a month on weekend leave. Fat chance of that if I can help it." I fished a cherry out of the bottom of my glass and scooped up the last bit of ice cream. "I sure wish I could speak English like you, but I guess there's no way I'll have time to study it while I'm in Koblenz."

"Why don't you bring along a Langenscheidt English-German dictionary? That way if you buy an English-language newspaper or a magazine every once in a while, you can look up the words you don't know. And there's always AFN, the BBC, and good old Chris Howland on BFN. Hey, you might even meet American soldiers when you go on maneuvers. You never know."

"I guess your English is pretty good by now."

"It has to be. Otherwise I couldn't work in England and make some money!"

"Talking about money, does your father play Toto? Mine's been playing every week, but so far, whatever he's put in has gone down the drain. It sure would be nice to hit it big. That would solve a lot of problems!"

"You're wrong there! Remember when that policeman won 384,000 Deutschmarks?"

"Rudi's father? Sure I do."

"Did you ever hear what happened to the Meinertz family in the meantime?" I shook my head. "They had one tragedy after another. Rudi's sister's marriage ended in divorce. His brother bought a souped-up motorcycle and died in a crash. The old man started drinking and Rudi threw his money around in Paris nightclubs like there was no tomorrow. From what I hear, he's dead broke by now. So, what do you say now about winning the Toto?"

"I guess people are right when they say you have to be careful what you wish for."

"Say, before I forget. When I write to you from England, should I write in English or in German?"

"Either one would be fine," I replied. "Just so long as you write!"

We had both saved the waffle cookies from our sundaes for last. The waiter came by with the bill on a little tray. "I hope it doesn't sound silly," I finally blurted out, "because we've known each other such a short time. But I'm going to miss you!"

Brigitte reached over and took my hand. "I'll miss you, too," she said.

CHAPTER 33

*O*n the last day of March I stopped by Mr. Scharwerker's office for my final paycheck and then returned to the Transportation Department to say good-bye to Mr. Kopf and Mr. Miele.

"Well, well, well," Mr. Kopf said as he shook my hand, "I'm curious to know about this new German army of ours. Be sure to drop us a line from time to time to let us know how things are going. One thing's for sure. If basic training is anything like the way I remember it, you're in for a rude awakening over the next three months."

"Don't let Herr Kopf spook you," Mr. Miele chided. "You're not exactly going off to battle. If you ask me, I have a feeling you're going to have the time of your life. Women always prefer tall guys like you, so my guess is that fighting off the young ladies of Koblenz will be the only kind of combat you're going to see."

"And don't worry about your job," Mr. Kopf added as I left for home. "It'll be waiting for you when you get back!"

After leaving my bike at Café Nitsch, I went over to Oma's apartment near the Aachener Tor to walk her over to our place for supper. Oma was still spry at seventy-six. She loved window-shopping in Bergheim and taking walks over to her favorite bench near the public pool when weather permitted. She never missed the weekly Bible study at the

Lutheran Church in Zieverich. So that evening, when she clung to my arm, it wasn't for support. It was her way of holding on to me for a few hours longer.

As a special treat on my last evening at home my father had baked little *vol-au-vent* puff pastries filled with chicken à la king. Afterwards Mutti served Camembert cheese for dessert, and my father and I shared a bottle of wine.

"This is really a double celebration," Mutti pointed out. "After all, Hubert is starting his new job tomorrow, too."

To my relief, when I raised my glass to toast my brother, my father did the same. "To both of you then!" he said. "Good luck on this next stage of your lives."

"That was a fine meal you prepared, Willi," Oma said as Hubert and I helped Mutti clear away the dishes. "But I can't help worrying what kind of food Günter's going to get in the army." She tipped her head to one side, eyeing me critically. "You're way too skinny, my boy. Promise your old Oma you'll write to let me know if I should send you some canned sausage or sardines like I did for my sons during the war."

"Don't worry, Mother," Mutti assured her. "The army won't let him go hungry."

"All the same," Oma replied, "the boy could use a little more meat on his bones."

****

First thing the next morning I shook hands with my father and gave Mutti a hug before walking to the train station with Hubert in time to buy myself a one-way ticket to Koblenz. Since my instructions were to bring along as little as possible, I had packed one change of underwear, a pair of socks, a razor, some razorblades, a tube of shaving cream, toothpaste, a toothbrush, a comb, and a pocketknife in my large briefcase. The only luxury I allowed myself was a Langenscheidt English-German dictionary.

"Are you sure you know how to get to your job on your own?" I asked Hubert as we walked through the long railway tunnel at Horrem to board the through train to Cologne.

"I'll be fine. It's only a short walk from the station to Herr Monke's shop. Don't worry about me!" He sounded cocky, but when Hubert got off the train at Cologne-Ehrenfeld he stood forlornly on the platform until the train left the station.

A few minutes later I arrived at the main Cologne railroad station. The train to Koblenz wasn't due to leave for another half an hour so I rushed outside to have a last look at the massive, seven hundred year old cathedral across the street before pushing my way back into the station against the tide of jostling rush hour commuters. Every seat on the train to Koblenz was taken by the time I came on board, but even standing in the corridor, I had a wonderful view of the castles perched on hilltops overlooking the Rhine. We passed through towns I had visited on bicycle trips with the Boy Scouts – Bonn, Königswinter, Bad Honnef, Remagen, and Linz – reminders of how close to home I was still going to be, before finally arriving in Koblenz.

In front of the station, soldiers standing alongside tarp-covered military trucks barked out their intended destinations. I clambered aboard the truck heading for the Gneisenau Barracks and we soon pulled away from the curb in a long convoy. After crossing the Rhine, our driver turned to the right onto a steep road leading to a guardhouse. A barrier was raised and we pulled to a halt in front of a sprawling two-story building. A row of gabled windows jutted out from the slanted roof.

My assigned room had three metal bunk beds with thin gray mattresses, six enormous metal lockers, a wooden table, and six wooden chairs. I put my briefcase on a top bunk, poked my head inside one of the empty lockers, and sat on the edge of my bed to wait for the arrival of my roommates. The first to appear was Benno Schmitt who had boarded the same train I was on when we stopped at Bonn. Short and pudgy, Benno strutted in as though he owned the place.

"I'll bet you were drafted," he said after we introduced ourselves. "Just so you know, I wasn't drafted. I volunteered as soon as I finished the *Gymnasium*. That means I'm on track to becoming on officer and I'd be pretty upset if anything happens around here that derails my plans."

"Don't worry," I replied with a smile. "I won't stand in your way."

A few minutes later Rudi Beinhorn and Alex Wüterich joined us. I liked Rudi right away but Alex was another story. He had squinty eyes, black hair, and a narrow beak of a nose, but his most prominent feature was his scowl. As soon as he sat down he pulled out a pack of cigarettes, glared at the rest of us defiantly, and lit up. The fifth member of our group was a lumbering giant named Ludwig Dickmann, a good-natured coalminer from the Ruhr Valley north of Cologne. Although Ludwig was not as tall as I was, he weighed considerably more, an equal mixture of muscle and fat. If he had had Alex's mean streak, he could easily have flattened any one of us. Buck-toothed Heinz Vogel was the last to arrive since he had the farthest to travel. Heinz lived in Stuttgart and spoke the peculiar dialect of the region. It was the first time I had heard anyone speak Swabian but I would soon get plenty of practice.

"It's exciting, isn't it?" he exclaimed after we had all introduced ourselves. "Hard to believe only lascht week we were all civilians and now here we are in the army! I can't wait to get schtarted."

All six of us jumped to our feet when Corporal Möllenburg stopped by our room at midday. A husky man of average height with an easy smile, he wore his military cap pushed back off his forehead giving him a casual flair.

"So, gentlemen," he began. "You've only just arrived but I need to find out if any of you plans to reenlist after your year of service is up." Benno waved his hand wildly, but the Corporal shook his head. "I already know your plans, Schmitt. My question is for the draftees."

Alex Wüterich snuffed out his cigarette. "I ain't got the education of Schmitt here. I'm just a faktree worker, but if I was on an offsur track, I'd sign up agin."

Corporal Möllenburg hesitated for a moment, as if he were going to say something to Alex, but thought better of it. "What about the rest of you?"

"I was working as a surveyor," Rudi Beinhorn said, "and I'm planning to go back to my job when my service is over."

"My boss at the Arminius AG chemical plant is holding an office job open for me," I added. "I've already completed my apprenticeship."

Ludwig and Heinz also planned to return to civilian life, Ludwig to the coal mine, and Heinz to his job as a mechanic.

"Thank you, gentlemen. If you ever change your minds, be sure to let me know. Now, let's get down to business. As far as the army is concerned, all six of you are still civilians but after lunch that's going to change. Once you finish eating, I want you to go to supply room 022 in the basement where they'll issue your fatigue uniforms, boots, helmets, pajamas, in other words all the gear you'll need to be proper soldiers. Let me give you a heads up. The soldiers working down there have their hands full on a day like this so don't expect them to wait on you like you're in a department store. It's your responsibility, not theirs, to make sure everything fits. Take your time and do it right the first time. You don't want to waste precious time trying to exchange things later on. If everything's clear, I'll see you back here at 1600 hours."

Rudi Beinhorn and I ate lunch together in the military canteen and then walked back to our barracks to get our uniforms. "I'd say we've got a pretty good group," Rudi commented as we went downstairs to the basement. "Except for Alex maybe. He's got a rather high opinion of himself, don't you think?"

"What bothers me most about him is his smoking. I'm hoping we can all agree to keep our room smoke free."

"Good luck with that," Rudi replied. "I don't think our friend Alex cares much about anyone other than himself."

The scene in room 022 was chaotic as dozens of young men rushed about collecting their gear. First we were each given a giant olive-green duffle bag and then we were issued a battleship grey trench coat, two fatigue uniforms, a dress uniform, a peaked cap, a military cap, two grey dress shirts, one tie, three pairs of olive-green underwear, three pairs of white underwear, six pairs of socks, two pairs of vertically striped pajamas, one sweat suit, a rucksack, sneakers, a pair of dress shoes, boots, and a helmet. I hoisted my tightly packed duffel bag onto my right shoulder, put on the helmet, and returned to our room carrying the trench coat and my dress uniform over my arm, and my peaked cap in my hand.

While the six of us were putting away our clothes in our lockers, Corporal Möllenburg paid us another visit. "Okay, gentlemen, listen up. After you've put all your stuff away into your lockers you can change into your fatigues. Starting tomorrow you'll be members of an armored infantry rifleman company of the Fifth Panzer Division. A company has three platoons of sixty men each. Each platoon has four fifteen-man squads. I'll be your squad leader for the next three months. Questions?" He waited a few seconds before continuing. "Here's the schedule for the rest of the evening. After supper in the canteen feel free to relax in your room. But at precisely 2200 hours, I expect all of you to be in bed and quiet." Alex Wüterich raised his hand. "Yes, Wüterich?"

"That's only ten o'clock, sir. I'm used to staying up way later than that."

"And I'm sure you're used to sleeping in late, too. But this is the army, Wüterich, and you're going to get a friendly wake-up call at precisely 0600 hours. When you hear 'Company on your feet!' you're all going to spring out of bed, run to the washroom, brush your teeth, shave, take a shower, put on your fatigues and your boots, and come to the courtyard on the double. Then we'll walk over to breakfast together.

That'll be the last time we walk by the way. By Thursday I'll expect you to know how to march to your meals in formation." He looked around to make sure that everyone understood his instructions. "That's all for today. I'll be back at precisely 2200 hours to check the appearance of your lockers. Make sure everything's put away neatly."

By 2155 hours we were all in bed waiting, not knowing what to expect, when Corporal Möllenburg came back and walked from metal locker to metal locker. Each time he opened a locker door, he shook his head. "Not one of you would pass the official inspection. Tomorrow I'll show you what's expected of you. When I show up tomorrow night I want one of you to stand at attention and report to me like this: 'Room No. 8 occupied with six soldiers. This room has been cleaned and aired out!' Good night." He snapped off the lights on his way out.

We all lay quietly on our bunks waiting for sleep to come when, out of the darkness, Alex broke the silence. "What an idiot! A neat locker? He's not my mother. That rule is full of shit!"

"Shut up, Wüterich!" Benno Schmitt hissed under his breath. "You're going to get us all into trouble."

But Alex had the last word. "Don't try to order me around, Schmitt," he hissed. "We'll soon see which of us is gonna be an offsur."

The next morning right after breakfast a tiny, bowlegged man stepped up to the front of the military canteen. He had an egg shaped head, prominent ears, and pop eyes. With his hands on his hips he stood first with his feet flat on the floor, then up on his toes, then flat down again, as though he were trying to pump himself up to be taller. Yet, despite his small stature, all one hundred eighty of us stopped talking as soon as he appeared.

"My name is First Sergeant Gleinmann," he shouted in a surprisingly loud voice. "In the next five minutes I exbect the entire combany to assemble on the barade ground in three groubs of sixty men, shortest men on the right, tallest on the left." The Sergeant's heavy Saxon accent, which I had heard so often in East Germany and on the radio, made me cringe. He glanced down at his watch. "Your dime starts NOW!"

When the dust settled after the mad scramble that followed, I ended up in the last spot on the far left, the tallest out of one hundred eighty men. First Sergeant Kleinmann walked the entire length of our three groups of sixty, stopping occasionally to reposition two or three men according to height. When he was satisfied he nodded to a tall, middle-aged man with a narrow head and beady eyes and announced, "Gombany ready for inspegtion, sir!"

The older man stepped forward. "Good morning, men. I'm Captain Kretschmann," he began in a high squeaky voice. "I'm the Commander of this entire company. As you know, you're here to go through three months of basic training. At the end of that time you will participate in large field exercises and maneuvers. But first we have to get you into shape. That's why our rifle range is in Schmittenhöhe, a six-kilometer uphill march behind your barracks. We're going to do a number of forced marches, many of them at night. Since I spent most of my time during the last war fighting on the Russian front, I know firsthand that the Ivans are masters of night fighting. We have to be ready to beat them at their own game!"

Then Captain Kretschmann turned over the command to First Sergeant Kleinmann who screamed, "Gombany, left turn!" As a result, the two men to my left and I were now at the head of the entire company.

Captain Kretschmann walked over to me. "What's you name, soldier?"

"Günter Nitsch, sir."

"Nitsch, since you're the tallest man in the company, I'm appointing you right fugleman. You have a loud voice, I assume?"

"Yes, sir."

"Good! Here's what you have to do. Whenever First Sergeant Kleinmann or I tell you 'forward march' you start to march in place, counting loud enough for the last soldier in the last row to hear you, 'Left, left, left, two, three, four, left, left, left, two, three, four!' so that every one of the soldiers gets in cadence. Once everyone is marching, if I call out the name of a song, say for instance 'Westerwald,' you're to scream so loud that the three soldiers in the 60th row in the back can hear you 'Company! A song! Westerwald!' Then you count, 'Eins, zwei, drei!' and sing the first line at the top of your lungs. When you repeat the first line, I expect everyone to join in. Did you understand me, Nitsch?"

"Yes, sir!"

Captain Kretschmann, a hint of a smile in his face, said, "I just hope your voice is loud enough. In the next few weeks you and the company will have plenty of opportunity to practice when you march over to breakfast, lunch and supper!"

I was pleased with my new assignment. Until that moment my height had always been a handicap. I was sure Herr Direktor Müllmann would never have pulled me by the hair if I hadn't been taller than he was and I still suspected Little Uncle of spiking my drink during the *Weiberfastnacht* party at Arminius AG. Now, for the first time in my life, it was an advantage to tower over everyone else.

But as I soon discovered, having a loud voice wasn't enough to get the job done. Especially after a long day's march the bedraggled men behind me would sing with all the enthusiasm of sick cats. Whenever the singing wasn't loud enough, First Sergeant Kleinmann would scream, "Low flying blanes! Full gover!" and we had to fall flat on the ground as fast as possible. "Now," the Sergeant would boom as we lay face down in the mud, "Led's dry that song again! Dis dime like you really mean id!"

We didn't only sing when we marched to meals, but also every time we marched up to the rifle range at Schmittenhöhe. Singing while walking uphill with all of our gear would have been hard enough, but after the first week, First Sergeant Kleinmann usually added one and a half kilometers to the trek by taking us on a roundabout route through a residential neighborhood. No matter what other songs he had selected, just before we made the right turn up the steep hill to the rifle range, the Sergeant would shout, "Nitsch! Banzerlied!"

"Company! A song! Panzerlied!" I would yell and then start off with the first few lines at the top of my lungs: "*Ob's stürmt oder schneit, ob die Sonne uns lacht, Der Tag glühend heiß, oder eiskalt die Nacht....*" (Whether it storms or snows, whether the sun smiles upon us, the day glowing hot, or the night freezing cold...)

One evening a few days later we were back in our room cleaning our rapid-fire Belgian-made rifles and shining our boots. We had left the door open to let out the smell of the shoeshine.

"Did you hear what Kleinmann said to me during inspection this morning?" I asked my roommates. "'Shud your mouth when you sbeeg to me!' How on earth does he expect me to do that?"

"Speaking of Kleinmann, by any chance have you noticed the little house on the left side of the road right where Kleinmann takes us up the hill?" Rudi Beinhorn asked as he disassembled his rifle.

"You mean where that lady and her three little kids always lean out the window and wave at us? They must really like our singing," Heinz Vogel replied.

"I hate to disappoint you," Rudi said with a grin, "but it's not because of our singing."

"Out with it, Beinhorn!" Alex Wüterich snapped impatiently.

"I found out today that it's Kleinmann's house. That little fart takes us one and a half kilometers out of our way just to show off for his family."

Ludwig Dickmann spat on the tip of his boot and buffed it to a fine shine with his brush. "Can I ask you somethun? Why does Kleinmann talk so funny? I never heard nobody talk like that before."

"It's simple. He's from Saxony," Heinz explained. "They all talk that way."

"Speaking of accents, did I ever tell you my Saxon joke?" I asked, warming to the occasion. "Here goes! A man from Hamburg arrives at the railroad station in Leipzig and asks a Saxon midget, 'How do I get to the Leipzig Trade Fair?' and the midget answers, 'Easy! Dake dramway line B. B like Ball.'"

Ludwig scratched his head. "I don't get it. Who's Ball?"

"B like Ball. You know, Saint Ball, from the Bible?"

Rudi gave me a sharp poke in the ribs with his elbow and nodded towards the door where Sergeant Kleinmann stood glaring at me. Then, as suddenly as he had appeared, he turned on his heels and walked away.

"That's a relief. I guess he didn't hear me!"

"Don't be so sure, Nitsch," Alex Wüterich warned with obvious enjoyment. "Don't be so sure!"

I dangled between relief and fear for two long days until Corporal Möllenburg pulled me aside first thing Friday morning. "So, Nitsch," he said. "I'm sure you're looking forward to going into town tomorrow night. Unfortunately, First Sergeant Kleinmann has other plans for you. You've drawn latrine duty starting Saturday at 1750 hours. So you'll be confined to base for the weekend."

At the appointed time I reported to the maintenance office. After the corporal on duty checked for my name on his list, he looked up at me and smiled. "Nitsch, is it? Have you ever cleaned toilets before?"

"No, sir."

"Well, it's not as bad as you think. I'm going to assign you to one of the barracks and from now until tomorrow morning at 0600 hours all you have to do is inspect the bathroom every two hours throughout the night to make sure all twelve toilets and the urinals are clean. You could go back to your room to sleep in between times but I wouldn't recommend it. To keep awake, most men on latrine duty sit up all night on the bench in the corner under the clock. I'll provide you with the cleanser, some rags, and a brush. You provide the elbow grease. Is everything clear?"

"Yes, sir."

"What are you being punished for by the way?"

"I'm not exactly sure but it might have to do with a joke I told."

"I'll be damned. A joke! I guess it's not so funny now, is it?"

"No, sir. It's not."

"Oh, and before I forget, there's one more thing. It's Saturday night and some of the men will be drinking more than they should. In case anyone misses the bowl, you'll find a mop in the supply closet."

"Yes, sir."

Over the next twelve hours, when I wasn't rinsing vomit out of the mop, or kneeling down to scrub out toilets, or catnapping on the bench under the clock, I had plenty of time for reflection. In a way, Oma had given me my first latrine duty when I was only eight. Nearly ten years had passed since I made the last of those treacherous, early morning walks down the narrow staircase of our apartment in Goldbach as the smelly contents of the overflowing pail swopped from side to side. I thought of the many times I'd climbed back up those stairs as Oma waited to smack me with her wet dishrag at the top of the landing. What would Oma say if she could see me now, bending over a dirty urinal with an army-issued rag?

When I got back to my room, everyone was still asleep. I took a shower, climbed into bed, and quickly dozed off. An angry Saxon midget appeared in my dream. "Blease," he pleaded, "dond dell any more of dose joags!"

****

On a cloudless Sunday afternoon half way through our basic training Heinz, Ludwig and I walked down the long winding road from our barracks that led to the bridge across the Rhine. We still had two hours to kill until the start of the 4 P.M. Tea and Dance at the Trierer Hof Hotel in the old part of town so we settled in at a small café to pass the time.

"Three pots of coffee, please," Heinz told the waitress when she came for our order.

"Two pots of coffee for them and a beer for me," Ludwig corrected him.

Heinz lit a cigarette and leaned back in his chair. "So, gentlemen, for one day at least we get to chase a few skirts. But from what I hear, it won't be easy. The guys who went lascht week said there are always many more guys than girls."

"Well, I'm not fussy," Ludwig said. "I'll settle for anyone who can cook."

"How about you, Günter? Got a schteady girlfriend back home?"

"No, not really. I met somebody a few months ago but when I came to Koblenz she went to England as an *au pair* girl for a year." I reached into my pocket and felt the letter I'd just received from Brigitte. "Actually, I thought it might be the start of something but now I'm not so sure. She just wrote to tell me she goes to local dance clubs with the other *au pairs* and they don't have any problem meeting young men."

"Well, two can play that game, I always say," Heinz remarked. "Let's go meet some girls!"

The Trierer Hof was an old-fashioned hotel with dark red armchairs in the lobby. Blue clouds of cigarette smoke greeted us as we pushed open the double doors and stepped inside the dance café. Even though we had arrived punctually at 4 P.M., recruits in uniform and older soldiers in civilian clothes already occupied most of the tables on the two long walls. At the far end of the oval-shaped room a lackluster five-piece orchestra was playing a fox trot. The five balding, middle-aged musicians, all dressed in black trousers and beige jackets, had dark baggy circles under their eyes.

"We won't be hearing any rock and roll in this joint," Ludwig grumbled as we took our seats. From our vantage point in the far right corner, things looked far from promising. To begin with, the men, half of them in uniform, outnumbered the women at least five to one. As a result, the dance had attracted the kinds of women who would benefit from odds like that. They weren't exactly the blind and the lame, but they were, on the whole, old, wrinkled, and homely.

Heinz stood up to peer across the crowded dance floor. "Slim pickings wouldn't you say? Looks like any half-way decent-looking girl has already been taken."

Just then a waiter stopped by our table. "Two pots of coffee and a beer, please!"

"Sorry, sir. We have a fixed menu. If you order coffee, it comes with a slice of cake."

"The beer doesn't come with cake does it?" Ludwig asked.

"Not with cake, sir. It's beer and a schnapps. We don't serve them separately. It says so on the menu right here." Heinz took the menu from Ludwig and gave a low whistle. The prices were four times higher than those we were used to on our side of the river. "Will that be all for now?" the waiter asked impatiently before rushing off to the kitchen to fill our order.

"We'd better make our drinks last," Heinz said. "I can't afford another round."

"Well," Ludwig announced after pointing out a heavyset woman in a bright-red dress and dyed red hair to match, "I'm gonna take my chances on her."

"She's more than twice your age," I protested.

"Yeah, but then no one else seems to want her, so I've got a good chance," and a minute later Ludwig and the lady in red stepped out onto the dance floor.

"I can do better than that!" I boasted to Heinz. "See that tall girl with the long black hair?"

"The one in the sleeveless green dress?"

"Uh huh. She's already had three different partners and I aim to be next."

As the orchestra struck up a slow waltz I walked over, gave a slight bow, and asked, "May I have this dance?" She was wearing a sweet perfume, and in my mind, she and I were already twirling over the dance floor. But she didn't budge from her chair.

"Sorry. But I don't dance with soldiers!"

By the time I slunk back to our table, she was already dancing with someone else.

"They won't see me back here anytime soon," I grouched. "It seems soldiers aren't good enough for the ladies."

"Anyway," Heinz added, "this place is way too expensive. When Ludwig's finished dancing with his dreamboat over there, let's all grab a beer on the other side of the Rhine."

CHAPTER 34

A convoy of army trucks had just deposited us in a rustic campground at the end of a dirt road on the outskirts of Hachenburg, an hour's drive northeast of Koblenz. The primitive wooden barracks reminded me of the barracks in the Ammo Camp where Mutti and I had lived as refugees before joining my father in Cologne. We had a full week ahead of us of forced marches up and down the hills in the surrounding forests.

Heinz dropped his gear on the wooden floor and looked around the shabby room. "You know where I'd like to be right now? Eating an expensive piece of cake in the Trierer Hof Hotel."

"There's no satisfying some people," I joked. "Last week you couldn't wait to get out of there."

For the next five days we went up and down hills, often at a forced march pace, both during the day and in the dark of night, loaded down with our full gear. On the last day we loaded our rifles with blanks and moved forward across gently rolling hills alongside machine gunners riding on tanks, the tanks firing as we went. Surrounded by the deafening noise from the guns and clouds of thick dust from the tank treads, I could only hope this was as close to the real thing as I would ever get.

"Well, men," Corporal Möllenburg greeted us cheerfully as we returned to the base camp at the end of the mock battle, "you've earned your reward. We've arranged a maneuver ball for all of you so hurry up and make yourselves presentable."

The large hall at the edge of town lacked the elegance of the Trierer Hof. There were no armchairs and no uniformed waiters, just a large bare room with a wooden floor and three small windows, the sort of place they might have used for hog auctions during the week. But none of us minded one bit. On a raised platform at the far end of the hall a peppy eight-man band played one American pop song after another and the young girls waiting to dance outnumbered us nearly two to one. We forgot our sore feet and aching shoulders and danced until the trucks arrived to take us back to the base. Even Ludwig didn't have to compromise. He spent the entire evening dancing with a tall, willowy young woman with long brown hair and pretty dimples.

Back in Koblenz a few days later Ludwig joined me at lunch. "Hey Ludwig, how's truck driving school going?"

"Okay, I guess. I should get my license pretty soon. Did you hear what happened today, with the tank? This guy 'borrowed' a tank to drive to a barbershop for a haircut. What a dumb ass! The company commander asks him why he did it and he says because he was late and he dint have a jeep and a driver like you do."

"Sounds like a good candidate for latrine duty, if you ask me."

"I think he'll get a lot worse than that." Ludwig gave me a sheepish smile as he tapped his fingers nervously on the tabletop. Then he cleared his throat. "Günter, could I ask you somethun?"

"Sure! Fire away!"

He took a crumpled letter from his jacket pocket and put it in my hand. "Could you read this?"

I skimmed the first few lines and tried to hand the letter back. "Ludwig, this is a love letter. I don't feel right reading your private stuff."

Ludwig's face turned bright crimson. "Please read it. It's from the girl I was dancin' with at Hachenburg. Remember, with the brown hair? I need to ask you a favor. Could you write an answer for me?"

"Why don't you write it yourself?"

"I can't. I don't know how. I ain't never got a letter like that before." There was desperation in his eyes, a feeling I understood all too well. After all, when I was eleven, I had been barely able to read and write myself after having lived for nearly four years in Russian-occupied East Prussia. At that point in my life, I'd barely had two years of formal education. Still, in the years since then I had somehow managed to make up for lost time. But Ludwig had had the benefit of at least eight years in the German elementary school system and yet he was still functionally illiterate. Even though I had no idea how he could have slipped between the cracks, I made up my mind to help him.

After supper Ludwig sat beside me as I wrote an answer to the young woman's letter. Then he painstakingly copied it out in a childish handwriting and went outside to mail it off. A few minutes later he came back to where I was sitting and handed me a tall glass of beer.

"Thanks," he said as he reached across the table and vigorously shook my hand. "I really 'preciate what you done for me."

****

As our three months of basic training came to an end, the six of us who had roomed together since the beginning of April got our permanent assignments for the remainder of our time in the service. Benno, Heinz and Rudi stayed on with the infantry unit. No one knew what happened to Alex Wüterich, but we all agreed that with his attitude, he was not likely to get a promotion any time soon. That left Ludwig and me, and as it turned out, we were both transferred to the barracks of a tank battalion located behind the towering Ehrenbreitstein Fortress in the Niederberg district of Koblenz. After taking a qualifying test in shorthand, typing, and spelling with a dozen other hopeful candidates, I was one of the lucky three who managed to get a passing grade. My new assignment would be an office job. Ludwig, his hard-earned truck drivers license in hand, was assigned to transportation.

My new superior in the battalion office was First Sergeant Krüger, a tall, skinny man with dark eyes, thinning salt-and-pepper hair, and a friendly smile. "Good morning, Nitsch," he greeted me. "I'm glad to have you working here. You had office experience before you were drafted, I understand."

"Yes, sir. After I got my degree from a commercial school, I did my apprenticeship at the Arminius AG chemical plant near Cologne."

"Good, then you should do just fine. Why don't you take a seat at one of those desks and spend the day reading the latest service regulations in this ring binder. It covers how many carbon copies you need to make of each document, how many signatures are required, stuff like that. One of the jobs you'll be doing around here is filing updates to the regulations. They change all the time." He looked around at the empty desks. "You've probably noticed that there aren't many recruits around. That's because most of them have taken their annual vacations before starting their new assignments. I'd suggest you do the same. So when you finish here today, why don't you stay in the barracks overnight and take off for home tomorrow morning? You can take fourteen working days so I'll expect you back here bright and early on the 22nd of July."

Once again there were three bunk beds in my room, but that night at least, I had the place to myself. I made up my bed on a top bunk, laid out my civilian clothes for the morning, stowed the rest of my gear neatly in my locker and thought about how best to use my vacation. Having enjoyed three months of freedom, I had no intention of spending the whole time at home.

Early Wednesday morning, I took a bus to the Koblenz train station and boarded the train to Cologne. After switching to the local tracks, I arrived back in Bergheim shortly before lunchtime. Mutti gave me a quick hug and then turned back to her waiting customers. My father was in the bake room behind the kitchen, but when he saw me he took off his apron and asked me to join him for a few minutes in our living room. I got myself a thick slice of Black Forest cake and a cup of coffee and carried them upstairs on a tray. My father came up a few minutes later.

"It's nice to have you home, Stretch," he began, but then he stopped. "I just don't know where to begin."

"I didn't want to ask you in the shop. Is the business in trouble somehow?"

"No, thank heavens; the café is doing fine. It's Hubert again."

"Hubert? What did he do this time?"

"In a nutshell, while you were writing to us about basic training, he was telling everyone he knew in Bergheim that you'd been promoted to Lieutenant."

"Is he out of his mind? Does he even know what basic training means? They had me crawling through the mud. I was on my knees cleaning out latrines!"

"Stretch, hear me out. That wasn't all. Imagine this. He also bragged that you'd been given your own horse."

"A WHAT?"

"And an orderly to take care of all your needs. What do you say to that?"

"It's incredible! How'd you find out?"

"I didn't. Mutti did. Customers kept stopping by to express their surprise about your meteoric career in the army. They'd never heard of anyone getting promoted like that after such a short time. I don't have to tell you how embarrassing this has been for your mother and me. There's something wrong with that boy. He's a pathological liar living in a fantasy world and the worst is, I don't know what to do about it. Maybe you can knock some sense into him."

"I'll try my best, but I can't make any promises."

****

As my parents, my brother and I ate supper together in the kitchen behind the café, I struggled to find a tactful way to tell them about my travel plans.

"Remember that coalminer I told you about? The one who asked me to write his love letters for him?"

"You mean he asked you to write more than once?" Mutti asked.

"Would you believe it? The girl he met writes once or twice a week. Anyway, he and I are both going to be stationed at the same base for the next nine months, so I'll get to do plenty of ghostwriting."

"All things considered, I don't suppose he'll be working in the same office with you?"

"No, hardly. He'll be driving a truck. Actually I haven't met any of the people I'll be working with yet. They'd already left on vacation."

"I'm glad you landed an office job," my father said. "You'll learn a lot just by hanging around the high-ranking officers you'll be working for."

"That's the way I see it, too. By the way, speaking of vacations, I hope you don't mind but I've decided to hitchhike to Sweden."

Mutti didn't take the news well. "That's a shame! I was planning on spoiling you with some good homemade food. And Oma was hoping to see you while you're home. How soon are you planning to leave?"

"Sorry, Mutti. But two weeks doesn't give me very much time to get there and back. I'm planning on leaving tomorrow right after breakfast."

"Well, Stretch, you have my blessings, anyway," my father said. "In my book, there's no better way to broaden your horizons than travelling to a different country. So if that's what you want to do, it's fine with me. Just be damn sure to get back to your unit on time. The army doesn't fool around with soldiers who go AWOL!"

"I'll be careful!"

"Tell me, do you have enough money on you to come back by train if you have to?"

"Provided I make it all the way to Stockholm? I guess not."

My father scratched his head. "You've written us about all kinds of things you've been doing, but you never mentioned money. How much do they pay you?"

"Just sixty Marks a month. It's not much but I've managed to save most of it. We didn't get much of a chance to spend money during basic training."

"Sixty Marks, that's all?" Mutti said as she gave my father a significant nod.

He cleared his throat. "Well, Stretch, your mother and I are really proud of you so we've decided to match whatever you get from the *Bundeswehr*. From now on we're going to send you sixty Marks every month. Use it to enjoy yourself when you're off duty."

"That means a lot. Thank you both!" As I jumped up to hug Mutti and shake my father's hand, Hubert bit his lip and a single tear ran down his cheek. I was suddenly unsure whether I was being rewarded, or he was being punished.

****

As Hubert and I walked to the Bergheim train station the next morning he chatted away about his job. "I sometimes throw up when I clean a trombone and all that disgusting spit runs out. But Herr Monke says I'm the best worker he's ever had."

"Really? After such a short time?"

"And you know those musicians you mentioned? Louis Armstrong and Jack Teagarden? They've both come back to the workshop to shake my hand and thank me for doing such a good job."

"Your friends must be impressed when you tell them that."

"You bet they are!"

"Same way you impressed them by saying I'd been promoted to lieutenant and had my own horse?" Hubert didn't meet my gaze. "Listen Hubert, your friends may believe that you met Louis Armstrong…"

"I did! And Harry James, too."

"…but the customers at Café Nitsch know better than to think I got a promotion like that during basic training. How do you think it makes Mutti feel when customers ask her about it?"

"I dunno."

"Let me tell it to you straight. With my education, I'm never going to be more than a lowly private. So, if you want to share my stories with your friends, tell them what's in my letters, but promise me you won't make any more things up!"

Hubert gave me a limp handshake and said, "I promise," without much conviction. When he was about to leave for his job at the Ehrenfeld station he looked down at his shoes and mumbled, "Have a great trip, Stretch." Then he shuffled off the train without looking back.

****

From the main railroad station I took a tramway to Cologne-Mülheim and walked to the Autobahn on-ramp. Despite my grease-stained *Lederhosen* and my fat rucksack, I got six lifts in succession bringing me to a small village on the outskirts of Hamburg just after sunset. For want of a better option, I was preparing to spend my first night on a park bench when a hunched over old man hobbled up to me.

"Well, young man," he said. "I see you'rrre a strrranger here. Arre you in need of any help?"

"No, sir. I'm fine. I'm on leave from the German Army and I'm hitchhiking to Scandinavia. This is as far as I managed to get today. By the way, if you don't mind my asking, where in East Prussia are you from?"

"Rrrastenburg. How did you know?"

236

"Because you roll your 'r' just like my Opa used to do. I'm originally from Königsberg."

"So you're a *Landsmann*!" He looked at me with new appreciation. "Tell me, do you have a place for the night?"

"Actually, I was planning to put my sleeping bag down right here on this bench."

"I wouldn't think of letting you do that! Come home with me! My wife and I always have a welcome mat out for a *Landsmann* from the East."

"Thank you, sir. I'll gladly take you up on that offer. By the way, my name is Günter Nitsch."

"Albert Noruschat," he replied and we shook hands like old friends.

While Mrs. Noruschat fried up a supper of potatoes, minced onions, and scrambled eggs for me, her husband and I relaxed in the living room over two bottles of the local Holsten beer.

"So, tell me, Herr Nitsch, when did your family leave East Prrrussia?"

"Unfortunately the Russians caught us in April 1945 when I was seven. They kept us there until September 1948."

"In Königsberg?"

"No, sir. First we were in Palmnicken where they mine the amber but then we were transferred to Goldbach. The town was so small, you've probably never heard of it. The Kommandant in Palmnicken needed vodka. The Kommandant in Goldbach needed workers for the state-run farm, so they traded."

"I've heard other stories like that," Mr. Noruschat said sadly. "We were luckier. My wife and I left with our daughters at the end of 1944, just before the Rrrussians swept in."

Mrs. Noruschat brought in my supper on a tray and joined us. "I don't know if you could hear our conversation in the kitchen," her husband said. "This young man didn't get out of East Prrrussia until the end of 1948."

"You poor dear! It breaks my heart to think of what happened to our beautiful *Heimat*. How on earth did you manage to survive during all those years?"

"Well, it's a long story."

"We have all the time in the worrrld," Mr. Noruschat said. "Dear, please bring Herr Nitsch some of that delicious head cheese and I'll open two more beerrrs."

I told them about the things Mutti never wanted to discuss at home: the starvation, the forced labor, the rapes, the lack of schooling. Just before midnight Mr. Noruschat and I brought the tray and the empty bottles to the kitchen while Mrs. Noruschat made up a bed for me on the couch.

"Tell me," Mr. Noruschat said as we set the dishes down in the sink, "when we firrrst spoke you said I rrreminded you of yourrr Opa. How's he doing these days?"

"We buried him in Goldbach," I said, fighting back tears. "I was only eight when he died."

Mr. Noruschat took a moment to digest this information. Then he put an arm over my shoulder. "He'd be verrry prrroud of you, my boy," he finally said. "Verry prrroud indeed."

****

The next morning a young couple gave me a lift to Travemünde, a beach resort on the Baltic Sea, and from there, a French businessman brought me all the way to Copenhagen, which Jochen Krienke and I had failed to reach three years earlier. I made sure to send Jochen a postcard from the Tivoli amusement park where I spent three evenings in a row dancing with Danish girls to the Dixieland music of Papa Bue's Viking Jazz Band.

On my last night in Copenhagen, as I watched Papa Bue play his trombone, I wondered whether Hubert had ever cleaned out the spit from his slide. I was sure if I told Hubert that I'd seen Papa Bue perform, he'd tell me the two of them were the best of friends. My brother's absurd boasts about meeting famous jazz musicians reminded me of Alex, the childish young man who stood in front of the Apollo Theater in Bergheim bragging about the movie stars with whom he claimed to have slept. How could Hubert have turned into someone like that? He had been a handsome, outgoing, skinny child, Oma's darling, during the hard years when we'd lived under the Russians. But the two years he spent afterwards in a TB sanatorium starting at age six changed him. It wasn't just that he gained an enormous amount of weight from a diet swimming in fat. Since he'd been the youngest patient, the older children had used him as a punching bag. After he came back at the age of eight, if things went wrong he was always on the defensive, ready to blame anyone but himself. Ever since then, I'd taken whatever he said with a very large grain of salt.

Four days later as I slogged along on foot somewhere in the middle of Sweden, torrential rain dripping off my poncho and down my nose, I thought again about Hubert. Jönköping, the nearest town of any consequence, was twenty kilometers down the road and I had no hope of getting a lift in such wet weather. Still, for all I knew, Hubert was back in Bergheim telling everyone I had a uniformed chauffeur and was on my way to the largest suite in the finest hotel in Stockholm.

It was still drizzling as I reached the outskirts of Jönköping, but despite my wet poncho and squishy shoes, I decided to try again to thumb a ride. To my amazement, a blond, middle-aged businessman in a top-of-the-line Mercedes pulled alongside. He leaned over to roll down the passenger side window and greeted me in English. "Where do you want to go?"

"To Stockholm, sir."

"I can give you a lift as far as Nyköping."

"That would be great, sir, thank you!" I stowed my rucksack and my poncho on the floor in the back and then climbed in next to the driver who immediately began to cross-examine me.

"You from Austria? Germany?"

"Germany, sir."

"How old are you? Are you a student?"

"I'm twenty and I just finished my basic training in the *Bundeswehr*."

He gave a low whistle and suddenly switched to German, "That's what I figured when I saw you. What's your hometown?"

"I was born in Königsberg but I've lived the last seven years near Cologne."

"Was your father in the *Wehrmacht*?"

"The *Luftwaffe*."

"Ah! A pilot!" I was about to mention that my father actually spent most of his time in Berlin, Paris, and Vienna running the kitchens in military hospitals, but the driver went right on.

"You can tell your father you got a ride from a soldier in the *Waffen-SS* and I've got my blood group tattoo to prove it," he said.

"But you're Swedish!" I blurted out. "I thought Sweden was neutral."

"I didn't give a rat's ass about that. I joined up to fight with Hitler against the Communists. Switzerland was neutral, too. But in the 11th *SS* Division, we had men from Sweden, Switzerland, and France. Can you imagine how glorious it was to fight those red bastards alongside likeminded men from all over Europe? Those were the best years of my life, young man, let me tell you!"

"I hadn't heard anything about people from outside Germany being in the *SS*," I admitted.

"There were a couple of hundred thousand of us from as far away as India. Read your history books! And we were tough too, tough as steel." His eyes gleamed as he talked. "Don't you believe all the crap people write about the *Waffen-SS*. We were the elite of the elite. Ask your father. He'll tell you."

I shifted uncomfortably in my seat. "I'll ask him about it when I get back home," I promised.

"Now," he continued, "tell me all about basic training. I hope you boys are getting whipped into shape or God help us if the Ivans ever decide to attack!"

When we arrived in Nyköping, he actually got out of the car to say good-bye. He was as tall as I was and when he shook my hand he nearly crushed it. "Always be proud to be a German just as I'm proud to be a Swede," he admonished me. "We Nordic people have to stick together. Have a good trip. *Auf Wiedersehen!*" As his Mercedes screeched into a side street and disappeared, I shook my head in disbelief. Even Hubert couldn't have made this stuff up.

****

After spending the night in a youth hostel in Nyköping, I got a lift the next morning all the way to Stockholm. I explored the city during the afternoon and then I grabbed a quick supper and changed into khaki slacks before heading over to one of the open-air dance floors on huge elevated platforms at the Gröna Lund amusement park on Djurgården Island. As soon as I had purchased a strip of ten tickets, a young woman with strawberry blond hair touched my arm and said something in Swedish. Without another word she led me onto the dance floor. The orchestra was playing an English waltz, and before I knew it, she had pulled me close and we were dancing cheek to cheek. It was the first time I had danced that way with a girl who was nearly my height and I looked forward to spending the evening with her, but as soon as the music stopped, she wandered off in search of another partner. A minute later a tall blond university student asked me to dance. She was an English major but she was also fluent in German and French. We danced together six times in a row and I was sure I was making a conquest when my dance partner suddenly looked at her watch. "Sorry," she said without a hint of regret, "but my boyfriend is waiting for me over by the carousel!"

"And so," I told my family when I got back to Bergheim a few days later, "those tall Swedish girls don't seem to think the way German girls do. They get all dolled up and douse themselves with perfume but when they dance cheek to cheek it doesn't mean a thing. Still, I must admit, I probably would have had a better chance if I hadn't mentioned I was spending the night in the youth hostel."

Mutti smiled. "You told them that? I would have run away, too!"

"By the way, aside from those tall girls, there was something else that impressed me about Sweden. It was untouched by the war. I've been so accustomed to seeing bomb craters, and twisted rusty bridges, and machine gun pockmarked walls, and amputees, that I was surprised to find a whole country without any of them."

"Well, they were neutral so it's not surprising that they stayed in such good shape," my father said.

"Oh, 'neutral' reminds me. I got a lift from a Swedish businessman in a Mercedes. Would you believe he bragged to me that he had the blood group tattoo of the *Waffen-SS* under his left arm? Those were the best years of his life according to him. He made me promise to tell you that."

"Did he think I'd be impressed?" my father asked. "The man's a full-blown idiot as far as I'm concerned."

"I was sure you'd feel that way, but I didn't dare tell him! It was raining and I didn't think I'd get another ride."

Hubert had been listening to my story with great interest. His eyes glowed with excitement as he leaned forward to ask, "Did he actually show you the blood group tattoo?"

"C'mon Hubert! He was wearing a suit and tie. Do you really think he'd take off his shirt right there in the street?"

"Well, I would have asked him to prove it," Hubert shot back, "cause you never know when someone like that is just making things up."

CHAPTER 35

When I got back to my new barracks in Koblenz, a soldier with a blond crew cut was sitting at the table leafing through a magazine. As soon as he saw me he jumped up.

"We've all been wondering who the sixth man would be," he greeted me, extending his hand. "I'm Siegfried Reimold. You've got the bunk under mine!"

"I think you're mistaken," I replied in an icy tone. "I made up the top bunk for myself before I left for vacation."

"Well, in that case, we'll switch," Siegfried said cheerfully. "It makes no difference to me where I sleep."

As the color rose in my cheeks I decided I had better start over. "Sorry for sounding like such an idiot. My name's Günter Nitsch. I'm starting tomorrow as a clerk typist in the battalion office."

"Same here, so I guess we'll be working together."

"What have you found out about the other four?" I asked.

"I think they put us together because we all have unusual jobs. The top bunk next to ours belongs to Private Georg Sommer. He's the chauffeur of the battalion commander. Under him is Klaus Brünner. He's the battalion photographer."

"And the other two?"

"Gerhard Gregorius is also a clerk typist." He looked around to make sure no one had come in. "And then there's Dietrich von Powitz who runs the post office. He's a real piece of work, let me tell you!"

"How so?"

"Speak of the Devil," Siegfried whispered. "See for yourself!"

A tall beanpole of a man with an unusually small head had just walked in. He had thin lips, protruding ears, sunken cheeks, and just a hint of peach fuzz on his pimply chin.

"Well, well, well, the third pencil pusher has returned from vacation. I'm Dietrich von Powitz," he said in a high-pitched voice.

"I'm Günter Nitsch. Pleased to meet you!"

"Did Reimold here tell you about me?" I shook my head. "I come from an old Prussian military family. There've been von Powitz officers in the army for hundreds of years. You may have heard the name? No? How strange! My father was a lieutenant colonel in the last war and my uncle was a general. He led a *Waffen-SS* unit of Russian Cossack volunteers in Yugoslavia. He was hanged in Moscow after the war. Are you sure you never heard of us? Anyway I'm running the post office on the base right now but in a year or two I intend to become an officer and carry on the family tradition."

"So you're an officer cadet?"

"No, I didn't bother with that. I'm a von Powitz! That's all anyone needs to know," and with that, he grabbed a few things from his locker and left the room.

As soon as he was gone, I turned to Siegfried. "Is he serious?"

Siegfried grinned. "Don't say I didn't warn you! And just so you know, there's no way in hell he's going to become an officer, family name or not. He's only got an eighth grade education and he never even bothered to make an apprenticeship. I think he'd only done some odd jobs before he enlisted. Still, he may be a bit of a screwball, but I like him all the same."

245

****

First thing the next morning, Gerhard Gregorius, Siegfried Reimold and I walked over to the battalion office together. First Sergeant Krüger, whom I had met briefly before my vacation, was already at his desk. Next to him Sergeant Brettschneider, a short, pudgy man with a fleshy nose, thick lips, watery pop eyes, and a chest full of war medals sat slouched in his chair. "Good thing they put you to work here," he commented after looking me up and down. "I bet you'd be the first one the Ivans would pick off if you were in the infantry and you're way too tall to fit inside a tank."

As soon as Gerhard, Siegfried and I had pulled up chairs next to his desk, First Sergeant Krüger explained our duties to us. "Well, men," he began, "you all have a very important role to play here in the battalion office. You'll be answering the telephone, completing forms, and keeping card indexes. You'll also be taking dictation from our battalion commander, Lieutenant Colonel Kuhn, and his deputy, Major Count von Hohenberg, both of whom served as officers during the last war. By the way, in case you're wondering, Sergeant Brettschneider has his desk in this office, but his job is to teach the troops about atomic, biological, and chemical weapons."

First Sergeant Krüger may have tried to make our job sound interesting, but it soon became routine. Several times a day one of us would be called in to the battalion commander's office to take dictation from Lieutenant Colonel Kuhn or his deputy. Then we would return to our desks to type out the letters. Aside from dictation and typing and filling out forms, there was rarely enough to do to fill the nine-hour workday. All in all, we spent more time reading *Die Welt*, the *Frankfurter Allgemeine* and the local paper and typing private letters to our parents and friends, than we did actual work. In retrospect, we probably should have spent more of our time proofreading our typing, but since our mistakes were rarely criticized, it didn't seem worth the trouble. I could only imagine how Dr. Haubold would have flown off the handle back at Arminius AG if he had received a letter with even one typographical error. Compared to him, Lieutenant Colonel Kuhn and Major Count von Hohenberg were remarkably easy to work for.

On the other hand, thanks to Dietrich von Powitz, life outside of office hours was anything but dull. Because of our varying work schedules, the six of us were not required to march in formation with our company to lunch and dinner. However, at breakfast time we were expected to do so. But not von Powitz. He always wandered in to breakfast on his own after everyone else was already seated. When criticized by the NCO on duty, he would rise to his full height and squeak, "Why don't you go complain to the Battalion Commander?" and the intimidated NCO would always back down. His disdain for the rules was also apparent in his work. Although von Powitz was required to open the post office promptly at 0800 hours, we could count on the fingers of one hand the number of times he actually did so. Perhaps because of the exalted status von Powitz gave to himself, he never called any of us by our first names. In retaliation, we nicknamed him "Powitzer."

Yet for all his eccentricities, there was at least one thing about von Powitz that we all approved of – he was the only common soldier in the entire battalion to own a car, a 1953 two-door Opel Olympia Rekord. How he managed to get permission to park it on the base, we never dared to ask. What mattered to us was his willingness to drive us off base on evenings and weekends and his promise to stay sober while doing so.

Early on the first Sunday morning in August as a kind of test run, Powitzer, Siegfried, Gerhard, and I crammed into the Opel and headed for Winningen, a little town in a wine-growing region along the Mosel River, a twenty-minute drive away. In that short distance our driver displayed a bloodcurdling recklessness for the rules of the road, jamming on the brakes at the few stop signs he chose to obey, shooting forward as soon as traffic lights turned green, swerving in and out of his lane, and making last minute left-hand turns despite oncoming traffic.

As his three white knuckled passengers climbed back out on our return to base, Powitzer beamed. "That was fun!" he exclaimed. "We should do this more often."

As soon as he drove away to park the car, Siegfried said, "If that's how he drives when he's sober…" and he rolled his eyes heavenward.

"So you don't want to drive with him again?" Gerhard asked.

"Sure I do. He was probably having an off day."

"Count me in!" I added. "Anything beats hanging around here."

Our weekend road trips took us further and further afield, but Powitzer's driving did not improve with practice. If anything, he became more reckless as time went on. Yet even after we had to wade through the muck to push the car out of a dunghill at four o'clock one drizzly morning on our way back from a night on the town in Frankfurt, we still looked forward to the next excursion.

Right after breakfast on a Sunday morning a few weeks later, Powitzer suggested a return trip to Winningen. "That was our first excursion, remember?" he said enthusiastically. "And besides, I have something special to tell you!"

Powitzer whistled "Westerwald" as he drove down the long road towards the river. About halfway across the bridge over the Rhine, he suddenly let go of the steering wheel and clapped his hands. "Boys!" he exclaimed. "Today we're going to celebrate. I finally got my driver's license!"

CHAPTER 36

"**C**ompany, on your feet! Trucks leave in fifteen minutes sharp!" a sergeant bellowed from the hallway in the middle of the night.

"Are they nuts?" Siegfried grumbled as we all jumped out of bed. It was just past midnight on a cold, damp night in early November and we had only been asleep for two hours. I pulled on my long johns and my camouflage suit, grabbed my gear, and raced outside where rows of tarp-covered, open back trucks were waiting to take us on the all-night ride to the Munsterlager military training area in northern Germany for ten days of maneuvers.

"You know," I confided to Siegfried as we all huddled together during that long, icy ride, "I actually have a family connection to Munsterlager."

"How so?"

"While my mother, brother and I were starving in East Prussia, my father managed to get himself captured by the British and when they found out he was a master pastry chef, they put him in charge of all of the chefs in the Munsterlager officers' mess. He worked there for three years, and all that time he had access to cigarettes and coffee to barter on the black market. From what he's told us, he was pretty much living like a king."

"Well," Siegfried said with a sigh, "I don't expect the same will be true for us!"

A few days later as I lay shivering, fully clothed and curled up like an embryo in the tiny two-man tent that Gerhard Gregorius and I shared for three nights, I thought again about the life of ease my father had enjoyed in Munsterlager after the war, and I resented it.

****

After three miserable nights in our tents, we were moved into the barracks in Munsterlager. "Well, men," Lieutenant Colonel Kuhn announced to our battalion when we assembled before breakfast four days later, "you've been doing such a great job at maneuvers despite this awful weather that you've earned a reward. For our last three nights here, you have permission to go to the British military canteen after supper. It goes without saying that I expect all of you to be on your best behavior."

Nails stuck up from the cracked wooden floorboards in the vast canteen that could easily seat several hundred soldiers at long, rough-hewn wooden tables. At one end of the room ten bartenders in civilian clothes waited to serve us. Everyone ordered beer and I was quickly put to work translating jokes from German into English and vice versa. Before long we launched into endless choruses of "Westerwald", the "Panzer Lied", and "Erika" at the top of our lungs as the British soldiers beat time with their fists on the wooden tables and hummed along. The British soldiers reciprocated with a rousing rendition of "It's a Long Way to Tipperary."

But the last night things turned ugly when the British soldiers challenged some German soldiers to a drinking contest to see who could down the most "antitanks," a near lethal mix consisting of two shotglasses each of whisky, gin, rum, and cognac served in a water glass. I had learned my lesson about mixed drinks back in Arminius AG and wouldn't go anywhere near that stuff. I watched from a safe distance as, one after another, seven German soldiers tried the British concoction. Three of them passed out cold and from the looks of the other four, they probably wished they had.

"How about a real challenge?" a British soldier screamed out over the sounds of cheering and clinking glasses. "The losers get their heads shaved!"

At that moment, Powitzer staggered over to the bar and held up a brown earthenware bottle of Steinhäger gin. "Let's even the playing field," he slurred, "and drink something German this round!" He looked around the room defiantly and took a seat on a bar stool right next to the sink where the bartender was swishing water into the dirty beer glasses. "Anyone?"

As a rosy-cheeked British soldier sat down next to Powitzer and rested his right elbow on the bar, Ludwig Dickmann, my coalminer friend from basic training, came over to me. He cupped his hands and shouted into my ear, "This should be good! That Brit ain't drunk nothin' stronger than milk."

The contestants raised their shot glasses to each other.

"*Prost!*" yelled Powitzer, and he swallowed the gin in one gulp.

"Cheers," replied the Brit who, with a quick jerk of his arm, spilled the contents of his glass into the sink at the same time that he tossed back his head.

The one-sided contest went on for ten rounds until Powitzer slid, unconscious, to the floor.

"To England!" someone shouted and two British soldiers hoisted their triumphant comrade onto their shoulders and paraded him around the room.

"That wasn't no fair fight!" Ludwig yelled and fists began to fly. In the wild scuffle that followed Ludwig scooped up the unconscious

Powitzer and we beat a hasty retreat just steps ahead of the military police.

"So how come you didn't take on the dare?" I asked Ludwig as we wobbled unsteadily back toward our barracks. "You could drink any one of them under the table."

"I woulda but eight beers is my limit. I gotta drive my truck back to Koblenz in the morning."

After rolling Powitzer into his bunk the rest of us turned in for the night. We were all sound asleep two hours later when he woke us up and hiccoughed loudly.

"So," I asked him, trying my best not to sound sarcastic. "How'd you think it went?"

"You saw me boys!" he exclaimed. "Nobody out drinks a von Powitz! NOBODY!"

****

As 1958 drew to a close, Siegfried, Gerhard, Powitzer and I were determined not to spend New Year's Eve in Koblenz, but the question remained where to go instead. On the morning of the 31st of December, the four of us lingered over breakfast as we went over our choices.

"Nitsch, what about Cologne?" Powitzer asked me.

"C'mon, I was just there for Christmas."

"I'd be up for Essen," Gerhard chimed in. "It's my hometown so I know all the best dance places."

"And don't forget Frankfurt," Siegfried added. "There should be plenty of action there."

"Listen up!" I said. "At this rate, we're going to end up badly outnumbered in the Trierer Hof Hotel. I've got a crazy idea. How about Luxembourg? I think they speak German there, and anyway, it would be something entirely different."

To my amazement, all three of them agreed. So later that day we all changed into dark blue suits, white dress shirts, and red ties, and climbed into Powitzer's car for the two and a half hour drive along icy roads through the Mosel wine country to the capital of the tiny country of Luxembourg. It was four hours before midnight when we parked at a bar where we gulped down a quick supper of potato fritters, franks, and beer.

As we paid our bill, I asked the bartender to suggest the largest ballroom within walking distance.

"That would be the Cercle Municipal on the Place d'Armes. But my hunch is, it'll be sold out by now."

The Cercle Municipal was an impressive building of light yellow brick with three arched entrances. By the time we got there, the clock over the second-floor balcony read half past eight. A twenty Deutschmark bribe to one of the ushers got us into the high-ceilinged ballroom where several hundred elegantly dressed revelers, mostly family groups and couples, sat in the glittering light of crystal chandeliers at beautifully set tables. The scent of expensive perfume mixed with cigarette and cigar smoke as gentlemen in tuxedos and ladies in evening gowns chatted in French and Luxembourgish, a dialect closely related to the German spoken in the Mosel River valley.

"I feel like I've died and gone to heaven," I exclaimed to my companions as an obliging Italian waiter set a table for us. "I thought places like this only existed in the movies."

A moment later the orchestra struck up a Viennese waltz and I made a beeline for an unusually tall girl with long, dark-brown hair in a lemon-yellow floor-length ball gown who had just returned to the table she shared with her parents. Moments later, she and I were out on the dance floor together.

"Günter Nitsch, *Bundeswehr*, Koblenz," I introduced myself. "You do speak German I hope?"

"I'm Nathalie Bolieu and yes, I do. I'm taking it in high school. But my native language is French. *Parlez-vous Français?*"

"Sorry, no."

"I could teach you," she whispered in my ear.

As we twirled to the music, I caught glimpses of Nathalie's parents watching us admiringly from the far side of the room, and when I brought her back to their table, her father nodded approvingly when she asked me to fetch her again for the next dance.

"Who's the flat-chested kid in the yellow dress?" Powitzer asked me when I sat down between dances. "She's got a figure like an ironing board."

"She makes up for it in brains," I replied. "She speaks French, German and Luxembourgish, and boy, can she dance!"

Next up was a slow waltz. "My parents would like to meet you," Nathalie told me. "Come sit with us for a while."

Mrs. Bolieu was in her early forties and bore a striking resemblance to her daughter. Her husband, a bald, square-jawed man with rimless eyeglasses, was about twenty centimeters shorter than his wife and at least fifteen years older. He gave me a crushing handshake and invited me to sit down.

"So," he began, "I understand from Nathalie that you're in the German army."

"Yes, sir, I am."

"I'm in international sales myself so I spend a lot of time in Germany. Wonderful country! Nice people! I'd like to hear more about you. Tell you what! Why don't you join us here at our table? We plan to stay until an hour past midnight. Your army buddies won't mind, I hope?"

"No, of course not. Let me go tell them and I'll be right back."

I rushed over to our table. Siegfried and Powitzer had ordered some food. Gerhard was still out on the dance floor.

"It's a trap!" Powitzer exclaimed when I told him about the invitation. "Run for your life!"

"Don't be silly. They just want to talk, that's all. I'll see you back here around one o'clock."

At the stroke of midnight, I leaned over to give Nathalie a friendly peck on the cheek. Instead, she took my face in both hands and kissed me right on the lips as her parents looked on.

"I've enjoyed meeting you," Mr. Bolieu said as I walked the three of them to the exit an hour later. "You gave Nathalie your address I hope? Let me give you my business card. Come back and visit us. We have a guestroom in our house and we'd love to show you around Luxembourg!"

"That sounds great. Our battalion is going down to Baumholder for maneuvers pretty soon, so I'll call you after that if it's all right with you."

A deep fog blanketed the roads as Powitzer drove us back to Koblenz so the return trip took hours longer than expected.

"How old is she anyway?" Powitzer asked me. "She looked like a teenager to me."

"I didn't ask," I admitted, "and I really don't care. She's tall, beautiful and well educated. I intend to see her again."

"Well, don't say I didn't warn you," Powitzer replied. "From where I was sitting it sure looked like her parents were setting a trap for you."

"Oh, c'mon Powitzer," Siegfried said. "You're just jealous."

"How about this? I'll send all of you a postcard next time I'm in Luxembourg," I said, "and we'll see who's right!"

****

Towards the end of the following week, Powitzer stopped by the battalion office to personally deliver a letter to me from Nathalie, but before handing it to me, he held it up to show everyone the bright red lipstick kiss on the back of the envelope.

"Hey, it looks like Nitsch made a conquest!" one of the other clerks teased. "Who's the lucky lady?"

"Leave the guy alone!" Siegfried snapped as I slipped the sealed letter into my pocket to read during lunch. Two hours later Siegfried came over to me in the mess hall. "Powitzer is such an idiot. A guy like that shouldn't be running the post office."

"He shouldn't be running anything as far as I'm concerned. Still, I'm wondering if he was right about Nathalie. This is a mushy love letter and she's enclosed five pictures of herself. We were only together a few hours."

"Is her parents' invitation still open?"

"Yeah. If I come for the weekend, they'll pick me up at the railroad station and show me around."

"Well, then, what have you got to lose?"

By the time we left for maneuvers in Baumholder in mid-February, a smirking Powitzer had hand-delivered two more love letters from Nathalie. "Ah, the sweet smell of Luxembourg!" he teased as he handed me the scented envelopes. "When are you going to see your lady love again?"

"I'm going back the last Saturday in February, not that it's any of your business," I snapped, "and I'll thank you to cut out the special deliveries."

When Sergeant Brettschneider sat down next to me in the back of the truck for the two hour ride to Baumholder, I immediately thought back to the lesson he gave us a few months earlier about the little black strip inside our dog tags. "After an atomic attack," he had explained with sadistic pleasure, "that strip can be used to measure your exposure to radiation. That way, you'll know exactly how long you've got to live. Unless, of course, the tag has melted, in which case you'd already be dead. Any questions?" A chilled silence had followed. I reached up to finger my dog tag as the truck bounced along and wondered whether Sergeant Brettschneider's years as a POW in Siberia had made him so bitter. The man never cracked a smile. For him the glass was always half empty.

"Sergeant, did I ever tell you that the Russians caught my family and me in Palmnicken, East Prussia, when I was only seven years old?" I asked.

"That must have been rough," he replied.

"I was wondering, since you fought in Russia, whether you ever heard about the massacre at Palmnicken."

"I have no idea what you're talking about. What massacre?"

"The *SS* shot several thousand Jewish women on the beach there in January 1945. My Opa was one of the German men who had to dig out the bodies with his bare hands that spring. He died of grief a few months later."

"Hold it right there, Nitsch. I'm sick and tired of these Jew-killing stories. Every damn time the body of some poor German soldier was found after the war, the *SS* or the *Wehrmacht* got blamed for murdering another Jew. It's all propaganda to burden us with more guilt and I'm fed up with it!"

"With all due respect Sergeant, my Opa told us that a yellow Jewish star was sewn onto the clothes on many of the bodies."

"All stagecraft! I don't buy it. How old did you say you were when you heard this fairy tale? Seven? So what could you possibly know about what really happened?"

"My Opa was a deeply religious man. I have no reason to doubt what he told me."

"And I suppose he prayed about it, right? That's what some of our men did in Siberia, too, and they died like flies just the same. It was luck that got some of us through, pure luck. Not that Holy Trinity stuff." His voice was shrill and everyone in the truck had turned to listen. "Think about it logically. If there were a God, why would he sacrifice his own Son for the likes of us? And a Holy Ghost, c'mon! More fairy tales!"

At this point Master Sergeant Krüger leaned forward. "All right, Brettschneider, that's enough now. These boys don't have to listen to your atheist views."

It had started to rain and the headlights from the truck following ours shone directly into Sergeant Brettschneider's face. He had thrust his chin forward in defiance and his eyes smoldered with rage. I suddenly knew what Opa would want me to do and I said a quiet prayer for his soul.

****

Seemingly endless rows of long, solidly built barracks clung to the sloping hills overlooking the small village of Baumholder. Everywhere we looked, colorful American cars as big as ships – two-toned Ford Fairlanes with curving fins, golden grilled DeSoto convertibles with black canvas tops, and Chevy Impalas with glistening chrome stripes – shared the roads with American military vehicles. The stench of diesel fuel hung heavily in the air.

We didn't have our field exercises with the Americans, but during our free time in the evenings, we had plenty of opportunity to meet GIs in the crowded bars in town. Toward the end of our first week of maneuvers, Gerhard, Siegfried and I were seated at a table with a redheaded American private. After my second beer, I screwed up the courage to start a conversation in English.

"If you don't mind my asking," I began, "what's the story with all the girls here tonight? There weren't any around earlier in the week."

He glanced over at the bosomy girls in tight short skirts, revealing low-cut sweaters and high boots, who were clinging to GIs at the bar. "Them? They're all hookers!"

"You mean prostitutes?"

"That's exactly what I mean. Those gals know when we get paid. From what I hear, some of them come from as far away as Paris to get their hands on our money before it gets spent on beer." He grinned at us. "But if you want my advice, I wouldn't touch 'em with a ten-foot pole."

"Well," I replied, "I can't see how it would be worth their while for the lousy 60 Deutschmarks a month they pay us."

"Holy crap!" the American exclaimed. "Is that all you boys get? Our draftees get $110 a month; volunteers $220. What's that come out to in Deutschmarks?"

Gerhard did the math and gave a low whistle. "$220? That's 880 Marks! No wonder the *Amis* can afford such huge cars!"

"Yeah, it goes a long way over here but back home in Chicago it doesn't buy that much."

"You're from Chicago?" I couldn't imagine a better place to be from. "Is it really such a great city for jazz?"

"Are you a fan?"

"Am I ever! When Louis Armstrong or Jack Teagarden or Gene Krupa came to Cologne, I tried not to miss a concert."

"What about Count Basie? Ever hear of him?"

"Sure we have," Gerhard said. "They play his music on AFN all the time."

"Well then, you're in for a treat. Count Basie and his orchestra are coming to our canteen this weekend. If you like, I can help the three of you get tickets."

The scene at the American canteen that Saturday night was pure pandemonium. Siegfried, Gerhard and I had sampled our first hamburgers slathered in ketchup and served on gummy white buns before joining more than a thousand soldiers who greeted the appearance of Count Basie and his orchestra on stage with stamping feet and wolf whistles. When Joe Williams finished singing his "Every Day I've Got the Blues" we all jumped up to give him a standing ovation.

As the three of us walked back to our barracks with the wonderful music still ringing in my ears, I thought again of my dream of going to America. But it was no longer the "Wild West" America from my *Billy Jenkins* dime novels that I wanted to see. Now I longed to visit Harlem, and Chicago, and New Orleans where I imagined that musicians would gather on street corners in the evening to play their beloved jazz.

****

An American paratrooper company had left stacked duffel bags in front of our barracks, ready to move in as soon as we left for Koblenz. It was our last day in Baumholder, and after making sure the barracks were spotless and loading our trucks, we were gathered outside waiting for a few stragglers to join us. Meanwhile, the Americans, in three-soldier teams, were racing to see who could set up mortars the fastest. Each team member would grab either a plate or a tripod or a barrel, and then they would race with their heavy loads for one hundred meters before putting the three pieces together. The team that yelled, "Ready to fire!" first, won the round. The second-place team had to do twenty pushups.

"See that, men," a captain of one of our tank companies said, nodding in the direction of the GIs. "It's really true what they say. American paratroopers would rather run than walk. Just look at the great shape those boys are in! I'd love to drill you guys like that. Compared to them, you lazy bastards are nothing but shit!"

An hour later, as the trucks sped down the highway towards Koblenz, we were all still grumbling about the captain's insult. During basic training, a Lutheran pastor had quoted from the theologian Dietrich Bonhöfer: "In Germany, your spirit gets crushed twice, first in school and then in the army!" How true that was. From the time I was eleven, my classmates had taunted me with the awful nickname "Fathead." Throughout my school years my teachers had constantly humiliated me, none more so than Herr Direktor Müllmann in the Commercial School who had dragged me by the hair while reciting that awful camel poem. Now it was the army's turn.

CHAPTER 37

*E*arly on the morning of the 28th of February 1959, I took a vacation day and went by train to Luxembourg. As soon as Nathalie saw me at the station, she rushed over and wrapped her arms tightly around my neck. Then she grabbed my hand and walked me back to where her father stood, smiling, next to his big black Mercedes. Somewhere in the back of my mind, Powitzer's warning was flashing, but I chose to ignore it.

"So, young man," Mr. Bolieu greeted me. "There's still some time before lunch to show you around our beautiful city. I don't imagine you saw very much of it on New Year's Eve."

Luxembourg City was built on several levels atop steep cliffs overlooking two rivers far below. We drove past the Grand Ducal Palace and the Cathedral and zigzagged through quaint side streets before pulling into the driveway of the Bolieu family's ten-room villa. When Mrs. Bolieu came outside in her apron to greet us, I reached out to shake her hand but she embraced me instead.

"I'm making *coq au vin*," she said. I raised an inquisitive eyebrow. "That's French for chicken in red wine sauce. Oh, and if it's all right with you, we're going to skip the soup and salad courses so that you two lovebirds can have more time together this afternoon."

261

Right after lunch Nathalie and I walked around the old fort. "Can you say it in French?" she challenged me. "*La Forteresse de Luxembourg.*" I repeated the name a few times and she chirped, "*Très bien!*" and squeezed my hand. Our walk then took us past the Musée d'Histoire et d'Art and finally to the vast interior of the Notre Dame Cathedral. A strange mixture of scents from incense and the burning wax from hundreds of flickering votive candles greeted us as we stepped inside. Nathalie walked slowly over to the holy water font, genuflected, dipped her finger into the font, and crossed herself. Then she looked up at me expectantly. "You're not Catholic?"

"No, I'm not. I'm Lutheran."

"Well, that shouldn't be a problem for my parents. My mother rarely attends Mass and my father only goes on Christmas Eve." She grinned and added, "And it certainly doesn't matter to me!"

"Me neither," I said, but her comment made me suddenly uneasy.

We sat a while in silence before stepping back outside into the cold. "So," Nathalie said as she grabbed onto my arm, "if you like Luxembourg in this frosty weather, you'll like it even more in the summertime." Another warning bell went off in my head but I ignored it. Here I was with a tall, beautiful, well-educated girl who spoke French, German, and Luxembourgish, and who lived in an enormous villa. I was sure she could have had her pick of young men and yet she chose to be with me. Even though the situation was too good to be true, I let down my guard.

As we approached Nathalie's home on the walk back, she suddenly turned to me and asked, "By the way, do you still remember the French name of the fort we saw?"

I thought for a moment and said slowly, "*La Forteresse de Luxembourg.*"

"*Très bien!* Günter, *je t'aime.*"

Mrs. Bolieu had supper ready for us when we got back. The table was beautifully set with a green and gold embroidered linen tablecloth, sterling silver flatware, dishes trimmed in gold leaf, and sparkling candlelight. "Family heirlooms," Mrs. Bolieu explained with a modest wave of her hand.

"Tell me," Mr. Bolieu said as he lit a cigar after supper, "what did your father do during the war? Any chance he served here?"

"Oh, no, sir. He wasn't part of the occupying force in Luxembourg if that's what you mean. He was a chef in the *Luftwaffe*. After he participated in the Polish campaign, he was stationed in Vienna, Paris, and Berlin until he got captured by the British."

"I bet he hated the Communists. Am I right?"

"Yes, sir, he did."

"A man after my own heart! Europe went through some rough times in the thirties and I, for one, always considered the Soviets a worse threat than Hitler's Germany. Quite frankly, I wasn't particularly upset when the German troops invaded Luxembourg."

Mrs. Bolieu interrupted her husband. "Come on! Tell the truth, François. You openly welcomed them!"

"I guess you could say that," he conceded. "Don't get me wrong, Günter. My parents were French and I like the French people and their culture, but when it comes to their politics in this century, the Treaty of Versailles and their leaning towards the Soviet Union well, that was just too much for me. All things considered, had I been younger I would probably have volunteered for the *Wehrmacht*!" Mrs. Bolieu gave her husband a disapproving look and I was unsure whether she disagreed with him or whether she was upset that he had been so frank with me. I was still digesting his comments when he continued. "Considering your height and your blue eyes, the *SS* would have accepted you into their ranks with a hand kiss!"

"To be honest, sir, I'm glad I wasn't old enough. I was only seven when the war was over."

"Of course, I realize that." Mr. Bolieu poured himself another glass of cognac and leaned forward as he went on. "Still, we need strong young soldiers like you, my boy. I worry day and night that Western Europe won't be prepared to resist when the Soviet juggernaut rolls right through to the Atlantic coast of France!"

Mrs. Bolieu suddenly jumped up. "Now, François, we can't sit around talking politics all night. Why don't we bring Nathalie and Günter to a dance club?" Mr. Bolieu nodded and got unsteadily to his feet. "I'll drive," his wife added as she reached into her husband's pocket for the car keys.

The four of us drove to a dimly lit nightclub, thick with cigarette smoke, where a small combo was playing schmaltzy music. Nathalie had put on a pair of high-heeled shoes so that we could dance cheek to cheek as her parents watched us from a table in the corner of the room. At first, when I glanced in their direction, Mr. Bolieu lifted his wine glass to me and smiled, but after an hour or two he rested his head in his arms on the table and fell asleep.

"He's had a hard day," Mrs. Bolieu said by way of explanation when we returned to the table during a break in the music. She gently shook her husband awake. "Why don't we go home dear and leave the young folks alone?" Then she turned to me. "Please get Nathalie back home before midnight. She needs her beauty rest."

As the four of us walked towards the exit together, Mr. Bolieu suddenly pushed his bulging wallet into my hand. "This'll more than cover the bar tab and a cab ride home." I protested that I had enough money of my own. "I won't hear of it," he insisted. "Just give me back the rest in the morning."

As soon as her parents were out the door, Nathalie flashed me a smile. "Don't I have great parents? Oh, and I almost forgot to mention that my father can help you get a job in Luxembourg when you're discharged from the army. I think he may even have a few things lined up already."

"You do have wonderful parents," I replied, choosing my words carefully. "But shouldn't we slow things down a little bit?"

"Why wait?" Nathalie retorted. "I'm going to be eighteen in April, you know."

"Well, for one thing, I don't speak French," I said. It was a lame excuse but I needed to buy some time to think the situation through.

Nathalie squeezed my hand. "I'm going to teach you, remember?"

Shortly before midnight we took a cab back to the Bolieus' villa. After kissing Nathalie good night and walking her back to her room, I changed into my pajamas and crawled into bed in the adjoining guest room. The wind was rustling the branches outside the window and the moon lit up a big white patch on the floor near the door as I lay, wide awake, feeling very much like a fly trapped in a spider web as I contemplated the bizarre events of the day. A few minutes later I heard my door click open and Nathalie, dressed in a floor-length sheer nightgown, tiptoed over to me.

"Let's snuggle!" Nathalie whispered as she cuddled up beside me.

I propped myself up on my elbow and sized up the situation. A beautiful seventeen-year-old girl lay in my bed right across the hall from where her parents were sleeping. If I had let her stay, I would have had bragging rights back at the base for weeks to come. But at what cost? Did I really want to marry this girl whom I hardly knew?

"I'm sorry, Nathalie," I finally said, trying my best to convince us both. "But I have too much respect for you and your parents to do this now. Why don't we wait, at least until you're eighteen?"

"Promise me you'll come back to Luxembourg?"

"Of course I will. Why would you doubt it?"

"*Je t'aime*," Nathalie whispered. Then she kissed me again and slipped out of the room.

First thing the next morning, when I returned Mr. Bolieu's wallet to him and told him exactly how much I had spent for the dance club and the cab home, he stuffed the wallet back into his pocket without counting the money.

Right after breakfast, the four of us took a two-hour drive out into the countryside. Mr. Bolieu gave me a running commentary on the country's history and the sites of interest. I pretended to listen and even managed to ask a few polite questions now and then, but since Nathalie had stretched out beside me with her head nestled in my lap as she gazed up at me adoringly, I was finding it hard to concentrate on his remarks.

"So," Mr. Bolieu said as we finally pulled up at the railroad station fifteen minutes before I had to catch the train to Koblenz, "how did you like our beautiful little country?"

"Very much, sir. Thanks so much for everything."

"I'm sure Günter will feel at home here in no time," Mrs. Bolieu added as she reached into the front seat to hand me a package containing several ham and cheese sandwiches, a box of Belgian chocolate cookies, and two apples for the short trip back to the base. She cocked her head to one side as she looked at me. "Here's a question for you to think about on the train. If the two of you ever have children, do you suppose they'd have brown hair like Nathalie, or be blond like you?"

"Don't rush things," Mr. Bolieu scolded as I struggled to find an answer – any answer – to her remark. "Nathalie and Günter have their whole lives ahead of them."

"You're right, sir," I replied, "we do." To myself, I thought, *and I'm not going to spend mine here*. Then I glanced at my watch, gave Nathalie a quick kiss, and headed for the platform.

My mind was racing as the train took me back along the Mosel River. Was I an idiot? Why couldn't I just do what the Bolieus expected me to do? Would I really be better off going back to my parents and to Arminius AG in Bergheim instead of moving to a life of ease in Luxembourg? Granted, Mr. Bolieu was still proud of his cooperation with the Nazis. But then, my father had also been a Nazi. Had he changed? I wasn't so sure. And Nathalie was tall and beautiful and smart. Was I ever likely to find another girl like that? Did I even deserve her?

On the other hand, the Bolieu family was undeniably crazy. Why would they want me to marry their daughter after such a short time? From the first moment they'd laid eyes on me, they had trusted me with Nathalie and their money. Yet, they hardly knew anything about me. The whole family was from an entirely different educational background and income class. Never in my life had I been in a house with ten rooms. How would I fit in? Why would anyone want to hire me if I couldn't even speak French? These questions raced through my mind over and over again. My head was spinning by the time the train pulled into the station at Koblenz.

Siegfried Reimold was polishing his boots when I got back to the barracks. "How's the lovely Nathalie?" he greeted me with a broad grin.

"She is lovely," I conceded, "but…"

"Don't tell me Powitzer was right?"

"I actually think he was for a change. It was like being in quicksand. The longer I stayed, the more trapped I felt. They didn't really care who I was. The only thing I can figure is, they just wanted a tall German husband for their daughter."

"Aren't you selling yourself a bit short?"

"Not really. If you get right down to it, the whole thing didn't make any sense."

"So you're not planning to go back?"

"Not until hell freezes over! But do me a favor. Don't tell Powitzer I said so!"

As it turned out, Powitzer was in no condition to tease me about Nathalie. With less than a month remaining before we were to be discharged from the army, he spent most of the time in a drunken haze, constantly bemoaning the fact that he was not going to become an officer in the great tradition of his family. Several times he even spent the night passed out cold on the couch in the postal office, forgetting to open for business the following morning. But somehow he still managed to stagger over to our barracks once or twice a week to hand deliver the passionate, and increasingly desperate, letters that came for me from Luxembourg. On the last Sunday in March, I finally wrote back to let Nathalie know that I was leaving for home and that I wished her all the best. I did not include my forwarding address in Bergheim.

Right after breakfast on our last day in the service a wild, beer-filled celebration began.

The scene in the Koblenz railroad station was simply incredible. Hundreds of young soldiers wearing civilian clothes and New Year's Eve party hats staggered around clutching open bottles of beer as military policemen grimly oversaw the proceedings. The ruckus was even worse in Cologne where the platforms were overrun with brawling drunks who had poured out of trains from all over West Germany in search of connections to distant cities, many of them blowing noisemakers and spinning metal rattles. As three military policemen dragged away a bloodied young man, a well-dressed elderly gentleman standing next to me waved his cane in their direction and shouted, "This would never have happened under the *Führer*!"

CHAPTER 38

*M*y return home had a sobering effect on me. On the one hand, I was glad to be a civilian again and to see my family. On the other hand, I knew that I had to put up with my strict father since my salary wouldn't enable me to move to Cologne and live on my own. On April 1, 1959, I was back in Arminius AG and it was as if time had stood still. Within a week I was back in my old routine and Mr. Kopf and the other department heads were still suffering under Dr. Haubold.

Brigitte Emmenthal was back from England and we had a couple of dates, but I felt she had changed and when I asked her whether she had met somebody in England, she was evasive. Even so, I invited her over to meet my parents. She came by the café the following Sunday at 3:30 P.M. when the greatest rush of customers was over. Brigitte and I each selected a slice of *Sacher Torte* from the display case and then we joined my parents at the table. After one of the salesgirls brought over our cake and four small pots of freshly brewed coffee, my father, oozing with charm, began asking Brigitte question after question about her family and her time in England. Mutti and I barely managed to get a word in edgewise and I wasn't sure which of us was feeling more left out. When the table was cleared and my father took a pack of Stuyvesant cigarettes from his pocket, I reached over to take one for myself.

"Since when do you smoke?" Mutti asked in astonishment.

"I took it up in the army," I boasted as I struck a match and lit up. Out of the corner of my eye I glanced over at Brigitte, hoping for her admiration. My father took a deep drag on his cigarette and blew the smoke out towards the ceiling. I sucked in the smoke from my cigarette and began to cough uncontrollably.

"You know something, Stretch," my father said as he took another deep puff, this time blowing the smoke directly into my face, "you look just like a monkey playing the clarinet!" Brigitte and Mutti both burst out laughing, as did customers at nearby tables. I quickly snuffed out my cigarette and forced myself to grin. When I walked Brigitte home I tried not to sulk as she gushed about my father's wonderful sense of humor and his stylish clothes.

"What a charming, attractive young lady!" my father enthused later at supper.

"Well, if you want *my* opinion," Mutti retorted, "she's not right for Günter and she's way too old for him besides." Then she turned to me, her eyes blazing. "Stretch, do me a favor. Please don't bring her back to the café."

****

Right after work on a Monday evening in the middle of June, I took a train to a Dixieland jazz concert given by the Dutch Swing College Band at the University of Cologne. The next morning my father complained that I had awakened him when I got home shortly after midnight. More to the point, he grumbled that I was wasting my hard-earned money on "that shitty *Negermusik*." It was ironic, in a way, since most of the members of the band were blond, blue-eyed Dutchmen, but jazz was jazz as far as my father was concerned.

The following Saturday night my father saw me putting on a white dress shirt and my dark-blue suit.

"Where are you off to this time?" he snarled.

"On a double date with friends of Brigitte. We're going to the Tabu jazz cellar in Cologne."

"The hell you are!" he shouted. "You're staying right here!"

"Try and stop me!" I yelled back at him. "They're picking me up any minute now and there's nothing…" But before I could finish the sentence my father took a short step backward and then suddenly lunged forward, punching me so hard in my chest with his right fist that I fell down backwards onto the carpet with my arms and legs splayed out to all sides as he stood his ground, breathing heavily and shaking with anger. I got up slowly, watching him carefully in case he decided to punch me again. Once I was back on my feet, I looked my father straight in the eyes, took a deep breath, and said, as calmly as I could, "If you ever hit me again, I'll hit you back." Then I turned on my heels and stormed downstairs to the street where Brigitte and her friends were waiting for me.

My father and I avoided each other whenever possible over the next few weeks. On the rare occasions when our paths happened to cross, we never exchanged a word. To escape the tension at home, I often stayed longer at Arminius AG or went for a long swim at the Bergheim pool on my way home, or hung out until late in the evening with my friends. But whatever I did, I kept thinking about my father's explosive burst of anger. Here I was, twenty-one years old and fresh out of the army. I towered over my father by at least twenty centimeters. What dark, hidden side of his nature would possess a scrawny, forty-nine-year-old man to attack his grown son in that way? Anyway, why should he care if I went to two jazz concerts in one week? I was earning my own money, so what business was it of his how I spent it? One thing was for sure; I had to get away from home for a while to give things a chance to cool down.

"Jochen Krienke and I are going to hitchhike through England and Scotland in July," I announced to Brigitte later that week as we waited for a movie to start. "Maybe you can give me some pointers about what to see."

"Actually, now that you mention it," she replied, while avoiding my gaze, "I've been meaning to tell you that I'm going there, too. I'll be leaving in August for another year as an *au pair*."

"But what about your job here? It must pay more than babysitting does."

"I have my reasons," she said just as the lights dimmed in the theater, "but I don't really want to talk about it if you don't mind."

"You met someone in England, didn't you?" I whispered, but she just shook her head and stared straight ahead at the screen.

****

Since Jochen could only take two weeks off and I had the whole month free, we arranged to meet in mid-July at the YMCA cafeteria in London. Early in the morning of the fourth of July, I took the train to Cologne, stationed myself next to an Autobahn on-ramp, and stuck out my thumb. To my absolute delight, within five minutes a burly American in a checkered shirt and khaki trousers screeched to a stop in a cream-colored Porsche with American military license plates. A Porsche! Wow! For a hitchhiker, getting a ride in a Porsche was like winning the top prize in the soccer Toto. But as soon as I opened the door to climb in, my luck ran out. A bulging duffle bag occupied the passenger side and assorted pieces of luggage crammed every bit of space behind the seats. There was no way I could squeeze inside. Reluctantly, I watched the sleek Porsche zoom away carrying my bragging rights with it.

Lifts from four different drivers in quick succession brought me within an hour's ride of the Belgian coast by early afternoon. After scarfing down one of the Tilsiter cheese sandwiches Mutti had packed for me, I waited only ten minutes before a middle-aged man in a Peugeot pulled over.

The driver leaned over and rolled down the passenger-side window. "Where are you headed?" he called out to me in perfect German.

"To the Ostend ferry."

"Well then, you're in luck!" he replied. "Hop in. That's where I'm going, too."

"How'd you know I'm German?" I asked as soon as he pushed the gas.

He laughed. "Easy. Your *Lederhosen* gave you away."

As we drove towards the coast, the driver peppered me with questions about my age, my schooling, and my job, and like so many of the other drivers I'd met outside of Germany, he also wanted to know what my father had done during the war. Throughout our conversation, I detected only a slight foreign accent in his German. Finally, my curiosity got the better of me.

"If you don't mind my asking," I began, "am I right that you were born in Germany?"

"Thanks for the compliment," he replied with a chuckle, "but no, I've lived my whole life in Belgium. Fact is, I studied German in high school but I really became fluent during the years I spent as a soldier in the *Waffen-SS*." He glanced over to see my reaction. "Does that surprise you?"

"Actually," I admitted, "you're not the first person to tell me that. I hitched a ride in Sweden once with a man who had joined up just like you."

"You can't imagine how wonderful that experience was," the driver continued. "The training was tough but we all had such absolute trust in one another. I'm willing to bet your time in the army didn't come anywhere close to what we shared back then." He was lost in thought for a minute. Then he suddenly asked me if I had ever heard of a Belgian named Léon Degrelle. "He's a hero of mine. One of the top men in the *Waffen-SS*," he explained. "The *Führer* personally awarded him the *Ritterkreuz*. Be sure to look him up when you get back home."

"I definitely will, sir," I said to mollify him, although I had no intention of doing so. When he dropped me off at the youth hostel in Ostend twenty minutes later, I sat down on my cot and thought over what he had told me. I had supposed that the *SS* man I'd met in Sweden was an aberration. But it was now becoming clear that, more than fourteen years after the end of the war, there were still former *Waffen-SS* men scattered around Europe who wished they could turn back the clock. What struck me as even more strange was that they were willing to brag to me about it. I simply could not understand it.

To clear my head, I took a short swim in the choppy waters of the North Sea. Then, before turning in for the night, I purchased a picture postcard. To try to appease my father, I deliberately addressed it to *both* of my parents and to Hubert before dropping it into the mail.

A short walk from the Youth Hostel brought me to the ferry slip first thing the next morning, and four hours later we docked in Dover on the English coast. Within minutes of stepping off the gangplank my Berlitz English was put to the test. The lorry driver who stopped to give me a ride up to London spoke what sounded to me like an entirely different language. As we sped along on what, for me at least, was the wrong side of the road, only two words jumped out at me at first – *Luftwaffe* and the Blitz – for neither of which, to my great relief, he thought I was to blame. By the end of the two-hour journey, I was able to understand at least this much of his story: He had been living in London during the air raids. He was a socialist. And all of England's problems were the fault of the "bloody Queen."

After the lorry driver dropped me off on the outskirts of London, I found my way to the Salvation Army down near the Thames River harbor. Located in a former factory, the four-story brick building was unlike any youth hostel I had ever seen on the continent. One hundred bunk beds on each of the four floors provided overnight space for as many as eight hundred people. Three of the floors were set aside for young people like me; the ground floor was reserved for the homeless men who spent their daytime hours loitering, drunk and incoherent, among overturned trash cans in the adjacent alley. I hadn't seen poor underfed men like that since leaving Russian-occupied East Prussia in 1948. In Germany, Austria, Denmark, and Sweden I had thought nothing of leaving my rucksack on my bed during the day. Here I was advised that, for my own protection, I should check my possessions with the reception for a small fee.

"You must be a new arrival," a young Swedish man greeted me when I came upstairs to find my assigned bunk, "so let me give you some friendly advice. Don't lose your 'bed card' 'cause the staff comes by every night to make sure no one has sneaked in. And if you can afford it, try to eat breakfast at a Lyons cafeteria. The thin, salty excuse for porridge they serve in this dump won't get you through the morning. At Lyons you'll get two fried eggs, a slice of bacon, white beans in tomato sauce, toast, and coffee, at a reasonable price."

As I sat at breakfast a few days later, I addressed a picture postcard of Big Ben to Café Nitsch and wrote, "Dear parents and Hubert." I figured if I continued this for the next few weeks it would be up to my father to make peace. But with him one never knew. Just to be on the safe side, I avoided mentioning the evenings I was spending in jazz clubs where hitchhikers and *au pairs* from the continent mingled with local English boys in leather jackets and jeans, their slicked back hair glistening with Brylcreem pomade, and their English girlfriends whose stiffly lacquered beehive hairdos, false eyelashes, and bright lipstick made them look old beyond their years. We listened to Ottillie Patterson sing in her throaty blues voice alongside Chris Barber's band or swayed to the music of virtuoso clarinetist Acker Bilk in his trademark vest, bowler hat, and goatee.

Even after a night at a jazz club, I had no desire to sleep late at the Salvation Army hostel. Instead, I usually woke at sunrise and spent my days exploring the city. After my first week in London, I took in the oddball rants at the Speaker's Corner in Hyde Park for several hours before surreptitiously joining a guided tour at the British Museum where I was startled to learn that German-born George Frederick Händel was "one of the greatest of all British composers." Of course, I also saw the normal tourist attractions – the Houses of Parliament, Buckingham Palace, the Tower of London – but what impressed me most was Paul Nash's painting *Totes Meer* (Dead Sea) at the Tate Gallery. It depicted the mangled rubble from dozens of downed *Luftwaffe* planes piled, like motionless waves, against the sandy shoreline. As I stared at that enormous canvas, I thought about the young German pilots, including Mutti's beloved younger brother Walter, who had rained down death and destruction over the very city where I was now standing. Although my Uncle Walter had returned safely from that mission, he crashed and died in Bessarabia in September 1941. My earliest childhood memory was of the drawn curtains on Opa's farm in East Prussia as Mutti and Oma sat in the darkened house and cried for days and days at the news. The same story must have been repeated in countless homes both in Germany and in England. And what had been the point of it all when, only a generation later, the young people from both countries could dance together to the music of Chris Barber and Acker Bilk in the jazz clubs of London?

****

Before Jochen was due to join me in London, I went back to the YMCA to reconfirm our reservations. After checking in with the office, I joined the group of six young men from Austria, Germany, Holland, and Switzerland, who had gathered out front for an evening stroll. As we were discussing which direction to walk, a tall, skinny young man with thick horned-rimmed glasses and dirty blond hair approached me to ask if he could come along. Except for the slight accent in his German, he reminded me of the brainy *Gymnasium* students I envied in Bergheim.

"Sure, why not?" I replied. "The more the merrier!"

"Hey, buddy!" the redheaded German with a thick Berlin accent who was standing next to me suddenly piped up, "You don't sound German; where're you from?"

"From Israel."

"Oh yeah? I guess they must've forgotten to gas you!"

For a moment, no one said a word. Then I yelled, "Are you insane?" at the same time that a young Dutchman snapped, "Are you drunk?"

"I-I-I don't know why I said that," the redhead stammered as he backed away from the group to avoid the grasp of the big strapping physical education student from Cologne who had stepped forward to grab him. "I-I-I was just trying to be funny."

"Listen up, you crazy asshole," the student snarled. "Get the hell away from us, and I mean *now*!" We had never seen someone run quite that fast.

Once the redhead was out of sight, we all reached over to shake the young Israeli's hand. "I hope you still want to come with us," the Dutchman said with a welcoming smile. Then, with our newly constituted group, the seven of us, from Austria, Germany, Holland, Switzerland, *and Israel*, set out to spend the next two hours exploring the city and sharing a few beers and some laughs in a nearby pub.

****

As planned, Jochen met me in the YMCA cafeteria on July 18th and after two more days in London, the two of us headed north towards Edinburgh, Scotland, six hundred fifty kilometers away. Aside from dealing with the inevitable questions about where our fathers had fought in the war, hitchhiking in Great Britain also included frequent stops at roadside inns for a cup of strong, black tea. Up to that point, I had forced myself to drink the stuff even though I hated every drop of it, so it was a relief to discover that Jochen, who loved the taste of tea, was only too happy to exchange my full cup for his empty one whenever our host's back was turned.

On the other hand, Jochen was amazed that I had managed to survive for the past two weeks almost exclusively on two meals a day of greasy fish and chips slathered in tomato ketchup. Just the sight of

277

it made him gag. On the second morning of our trip we were standing along the road in southern Scotland discussing what else we could eat when a very old man in a silver Rolls Royce crept to a stop. "If you chaps are heading up to Edinburgh, my wife here and I would be happy to give you a ride," he said in a reedy voice. His hand trembled slightly as he pointed to the tiny, wrinkled lady crumpled like a rag doll on the seat beside him. We took a quick look at the spacious legroom in the back seat and didn't need to be asked twice.

For the next half hour our driver peered intently through the steering wheel as he poked along at a snail's pace. Still, since we were seated in splendid comfort on the rich leather seat, we were in no particular hurry, and when our driver pulled into the parking lot of a half-timbered country inn with a thatched roof, I was even willing to down two cups of the obligatory tea if necessary. Instead, we were invited to lunch.

All of the elderly, well-dressed patrons of the restaurant did a double take when we came in and I really couldn't blame them since both Jochen and I were wearing our greasy *Lederhosen*, rolled down woolen socks, and hiking shoes. Besides that, I must have looked like Gulliver in Lilliput as I bent over to avoid cracking my head on the low-hanging, wood-beamed ceiling. As soon as we were seated, the waiter gave each of us an oversized menu written in old-English script on which each entrée cost more than I had spent on food for an entire week.

After watching us attempt to decipher the day's offerings, our host spoke up. "Mrs. McNevin and I eat here often," he said. "So we'd like to recommend the trout if that would suit you."

Although neither Jochen nor I had the foggiest idea what trout was, we gladly accepted his suggestion. Following a first course of hearty vegetable soup, the waiter brought out four servings of broiled fish, which he skillfully deboned at our table. While we ate, Mr. McNevin peppered us with questions about our education, our jobs, and our families. To our immense relief, World War II was never mentioned.

"So," Mr. McNevin said as we enjoyed a traditional Scottish dessert of heavy cream, raspberries, honey, porridge, and whisky, served in a tall glass, "you've told me about yourselves. Now it's my turn." Mr. McNevin had spent several decades as a British civil servant in India followed by a stretch in Kenya. "Of course," he added as his wife looked up at him in silent admiration, "that meant dealing with all those awful colored natives, but a man has to do what's required in the service of the crown, don't you think?" I would have liked to say something in protest, but with our meal paid for and the Rolls Royce waiting out front, I took the cowardly way out and kept my peace.

The memory of that tasty meal faded fast after our arrival in Edinburgh. We found accommodations in one of the three large rooms with bunk beds rented out by a chain-smoking Scottish spinster over her restaurant. After two straight days of Miss Macauly's tough mutton sandwiches laced with yellow fat, even Jochen was willing to go out in search of fish and chips.

The next eight days passed quickly, and we had no trouble getting rides through the rolling Scottish countryside. We got as far north as the remote Dunnet Head lighthouse, considered by some to be one of the loneliest places on earth, before heading back towards home. But just south of Inverness, the rain came down in buckets and our luck ran out. Stranded and sopping wet in the middle of nowhere, we watched as a few cars passed by, but no one was willing to stop. At last, when we were just about ready to pitch our tents by the side of the road, a lorry driver pulled over, and yelling over the noise of his diesel engine, he invited us to join him up front in the cab.

"I can take you as far as Glasgow," the driver said, as he stared straight ahead watching the road while clenching his stinking unlit pipe between his teeth. Then he fell silent and the only sound was of the rain pounding against the windshield.

After a few minutes, Jochen leaned over to me and said, in German, "If our driver would light his damn pipe it might smell a bit better in

279

here. But I guess he's a typical stingy Scotsman who doesn't want to waste the tobacco."

"Or the match!" I added with a grin.

A few hours later we arrived at the outskirts of Glasgow and the driver pulled over to drop us off. As we reached down to pick up our gear, the Scotsman opened the window to tap out his pipe along the side of the cabin. Then he spoke for the first time since he had picked us up. "You know, young men," he began, before suddenly switching to flawless German, "I didn't appreciate your comments back there about my pipe, or my nationality for that matter. Just so you know, I was stationed in Germany for eight years and my wife is from Berlin. Next time someone gives you a ride in the pouring rain, I'd suggest you go easy on the insults." Then he tipped his cap and winked at us, before cheerfully wishing us a good trip home. Totally embarrassed, Jochen and I shook our heads in amazement as we watched the truck disappear in the distance.

After spending a few more days in London, Jochen and I hitched rides as far as the coast where we caught the Channel ferry. Since I had spent nearly every last pfennig on Chris Barber and Acker Bilk records in London, by the time I returned home I was subsisting on day-old bread spread with a tiny bit of English margarine scraped from the plastic container in my rucksack. All that remained in my pocket were 1.80 in Deutschmarks and a few English and Belgian coins. Uncertain about the success of my postcard campaign, I felt a bit queasy walking into Café Nitsch, not knowing how things would stand with my father. But as soon as I entered the shop, he rushed over from behind the sales counter to greet me with a broad smile. "Look who's here! Our Stretch, the wanderer, has come back home!" he exclaimed, and he shook my hand as if nothing had ever happened.

CHAPTER 39

When I ran into Rupert Mayer in the cafeteria at lunchtime a few days after I returned to work, he took me aside and asked me to drop by to see him since there was a matter he wanted to discuss with me in private. Mr. Stommel had left for vacation the day before, so Mr. Mayer had the office to himself for the time being. As soon as I got to Mr. Mayer's office, he shut the door and offered me a seat.

"So, Herr Nitsch," he said once he'd gotten back to his desk, "tell me honestly. Now that you've done your basic training and spent a month in Great Britain, how're you readjusting to life here in Arminius AG?"

I took a deep breath as I thought about his question. "Honestly?" I finally said. "I'm bored to death. The internship with the Rhenus Shipping Company in Cologne Herr Kopf promised me fell through and I'm back doing the same old stuff I always did. Besides, with what they're paying me, I'm probably never going to be able to afford a place of my own."

"That's what I thought you'd say," Mr. Mayer replied. Then he reached into his desk drawer and handed me a glossy brochure. "Do you know anything about the Höwi? It's a two-year junior business college on Lindenstrasse in Cologne."

I skimmed through the pages. The red, white, and black coat of arms of the city graced the front cover. On the second page was a black-and-white photograph of a massive school building. Thirteen different subjects as varied as cost accounting and French were listed in the curriculum. Mr. Mayer waited patiently until I looked back up and shook my head. "Can't say that I have."

"I picked up the brochure at the Chamber of Commerce in Cologne, and when I read it, I thought it might be something for you to consider. The next semester starts on October first so there's still time to apply if that's what you decide to do. Why don't you keep the brochure and read it over at your leisure." He winked at me and added, "I'm sure it goes without saying that you should keep our little conversation under your hat."

"You have my word, Herr Mayer," I quickly agreed as I tucked the brochure away in my pocket. "And thank you!"

Right after supper that evening I rushed upstairs to the room Hubert and I shared and studied the Höwi information in detail. If I were to start on October 1, 1959, by July 1961 I would have a degree that would help me land a job in midlevel management in a medium-sized company, or in an executive training program in a large corporation. Rupert Mayer was right. The Höwi could be my meal ticket out of Bergheim.

When both Mr. Kopf and Mr. Miele were out of the office for a meeting the next day, I called the Höwi to get more information. On the positive side, my diploma from the Commercial School in Horrem, combined with my completed apprenticeship at Arminius AG, would qualify me to participate in the program, although the time commitment would be daunting. Classes were held from 8 A.M. until 1 P.M. five days a week and students were expected to spend at least another five hours a day studying the materials at home. On the other hand, even though the tuition was free, if I left Arminius AG to attend the Höwi, that would mean that for the next two years, I wouldn't be earning any money and would have to rely on the generosity of my parents for my living expenses and the cost of my textbooks.

Over the next few days, I thought about how to broach the idea of Höwi to my parents. I was confident that Mutti would support the idea but I fully expected my father to laugh in my face. That, I decided, was a risk I had to take. After the café closed on Saturday afternoon I sat down with my parents in our living room and told them how much this opportunity would mean to me. Since I had tried to anticipate every objection my father could raise, his reaction left me speechless. Without even consulting Mutti, he smiled at me and said, "If you want to attend the Höwi, and I think you should judging from what you've told us, then by all means go ahead. We'll pay for your books and we'll give you sixty Marks a month again just as we did when you were in the Army." Then he looked over at Mutti. "Unless, of course, you disagree."

Tears welled up in Mutti's eyes. "Go for it, Stretch!" she exclaimed. "It can only lead to good things for you!"

I jumped up from my armchair to shake my father's hand and to give Mutti a hug. It was only later, as I lay in bed, that I wondered again what had come over my father. Would he have been so generous if he hadn't punched me? Did he have a guilty conscience because of that? Whatever the reason, it really didn't matter. I knew he would keep his word.

****

At the beginning of September, as soon as my enrollment in the Höwi was approved, I gave Arminius AG the required notice. To my great relief, despite the fact that I was quitting only a few months after my discharge from the army and after taking a month-long vacation in England, Mr. Kopf assured me that there were no hard feelings. In fact, on my last day at work, he even arranged a small good-bye party for me at which I was presented with a glowing letter of recommendation. When Rupert Mayer came by our office to wish me well, I shook his hand and promised to keep in touch. Although I didn't dare say so, I hoped he knew how much I appreciated his having opened this new door for me.

At long last, on October 1, 1959, I took an early train to Cologne for the first day of class. Instead of taking two connecting streetcars, I decided to walk from the main railroad station to calm my nerves. The route took me past the towering Cologne Cathedral on my left, then through the old part of town, rebuilt after the Allied bombs had flattened it. I continued across the wide Neumarkt Plaza with its leafy trees and elegant shops, once the site of Nazi party rallies in the years before the war. Finally, on the far side of the Habsburger Ring where the old city wall had once stood, I reached Lindenstrasse where I recognized the four-story building pictured on the Höwi brochure.

My walk had taken longer than expected so, with only five minutes to spare, I raced up three flights of stairs and took the remaining empty seat in the back of the classroom next to one of the large windows. At precisely eight o'clock a scowling, baldheaded man with dark horn-rimmed glasses strode into the room, clasped his hands behind his back, and glared at each of us in turn as we shifted nervously in our seats.

"Good morning, gentlemen," he finally said. "I am Director Hettinger!" Then, after waiting until all fifteen students had shouted back in unison, "Good morning, Herr Director Hettinger!", he launched into a speech that was more ominous than welcoming. "You all know the curriculum," he began. "There are twelve required subjects: business administration, accounting, statistics, math, tax accounting, advertising, law, economics, economic geography, German literature, the history of Cologne, and English. For those who don't think that's enough, you can also elect to take French." His eyes narrowed and a vein in his neck throbbed as he went on. "Now, let me be perfectly blunt. You've probably read that you will need to spend as much time on homework as you do in class. But don't be fooled. If that's all the time you plan to spend on homework, you won't do well here. And as for those of you who dare to think the Höwi will be your stepping-stone to getting admitted to a university, just take a look around; if past experience means anything, at most only one of you will do well enough to meet that high matriculation standard."

Just as Dr. Hettinger was finishing up his speech, he introduced us to Dr. Fabri, our homeroom teacher, a tall man with a massive head crowned with an unruly shock of black hair who had quietly entered the classroom and now stood patiently to one side of the door. "Well," the Director concluded, "that's all I have to say. Herr Dr. Fabri will take over for now." And with that, he briskly left the room without even a hint of a smile.

"So," Dr. Fabri began, "since we'll be spending a lot of time together over the next two years, let's start out by getting acquainted. When I call your name, please come up to the front of the room and tell us something about yourself. Why don't we start with Herr Buscheur?"

A slightly built young man with watery-blue eyes and ruddy cheeks rose from his seat in the front row and turned to face the class. "My name is Ferdinand Buscheur. I'm from a village near Bielefeld. I attended a *Gymnasium* for six years, made an apprenticeship in a bank, and then worked there for three years as an employee. My wife and I just moved to Cologne."

After Ferdinand Buscheur sat down, my fellow classmates and I took turns introducing ourselves. No one else had gone to a *Gymnasium*; the rest of us were commercial school graduates with apprenticeships under our belts. The only thing that distinguished me from the rest of my classmates was that I had already completed my military service. By the time the next-to-last young man was called to the front, the stories all began to blur together. That changed when Dr. Fabri called on Theo Schrick who took out the wad of bubble gum he was chewing and stuck it to the arm of his chair before swaggering up to face the class with his hands in his pockets and a broad grin on his face.

"Name's Theo Schrick. I'm a tax advisor. Since I'm already pretty good at what I do, I'm not so sure whether the Höwi can teach me anything I don't already know. But I'm willing to give it a try and see what happens!" As he returned to his seat, he covered his mouth with his hand and snickered.

Dr. Fabri, clearly rattled, tapped his pen nervously on his desk while waiting for the class to settle back down. Then he called on Mr. Zemke, who was last on the list. A husky young man with curly blond hair and two-day-old stubble on his double chin took his place up front.

"Good morning. I'm Schäng Zemke from Levverkuse," he said in the thickest Cologne dialect I'd ever heard. "You know, where Bayer Pharmaceuticals is. I made my apprenticeship in the administrative office of a brewery."

Dr. Fabri looked down at his class roster. "I have you down as Johannes Zemke from Leverkusen."

"That's what I said. Levverkuse. And no one calls me Johannes. Schäng will do just fine!"

Then he grinned sheepishly and ambled back to his seat.

"Thank you, Herr Zemke," Dr. Fabri said. "But we'll use last names in the classroom if you don't mind." Then he gave us a lesson plan for the whole week and a long list of textbooks to buy. "Now," he announced, "the real work begins!"

And begin it did. As Director Hettinger had warned, between the hours I spent commuting and in the classroom, and the hours I spent preparing for every subject at home, it was like having two full-time jobs. I was usually up in the morning by 6 A.M. and rarely got to bed until close to midnight. By the time school broke for Christmas vacation, I had developed a love-hate relationship with my coursework. I soaked up the liberal arts subjects like German literature, English, and French, and enjoyed my readings in subjects like advertising, economics, business administration, and economic geography. I even liked studying the history of Cologne, although I would have preferred to study German or European history. On the other hand, I detested subjects like law, math, statistics, and accounting. As for tax accounting, I dreaded every minute of it.

To make matters worse, one of my classmates, Wolfgang Opschepper, loved nothing more than to criticize the rest of us if we gave an incorrect response in class. Tall and skinny, with light-blond hair and a bad complexion, he was quick to mock anyone who mispronounced an English word, or who wore what he considered to be unfashionable clothes, or who, like me, struggled with math and accounting. To add insult to injury, he constantly bragged about the number of girls he had conquered and the many who wished he had. He was also ambitious. After nearly every test, he would approach the teacher to try to bargain his grade up. No one was as eager as Wolfgang Opschepper to achieve the matriculation standard.

Even though I was loaded down with reading assignments, after nearly three months at the Höwi, I welcomed the month-long Christmas vacation since it allowed me to catch up on sleep. On my second day at home, as I was heading upstairs after breakfast, I ran into Mrs. Graf, who lived with her husband, a retired Latin and Ancient Greek teacher from the *Gymnasium*, in the apartment across the hallway from ours.

"Hello, Herr Nitsch," she greeted me. "I've been meaning to talk to you." She glanced over her shoulder at the closed door of her apartment before continuing. "You've probably noticed that my husband's mind is failing, the poor dear. He gave up reading a while ago. So, I'd like to give you one of his books to keep, if you promise me you'll read it." She disappeared into her apartment, and a minute later, returned with a well-worn copy of *Mein Kampf.*

"Thank you, Frau Graf. But are you sure you don't want to keep it for yourself?"

"Me? I'm never going to read it. My husband told me it's all rubbish anyway. But I know you like history, so…"

As soon as I opened the book, my curiosity was whetted by Mr. Graf's sarcastic comments written neatly in dark pencil on the margins of nearly every page. Twenty-five years earlier, if his copy of *Mein Kampf* had fallen into the wrong hands, he would surely have wound up in a concentration camp. I put aside my textbooks, turned to page one, and began to read. In chapter after horrifying chapter, Hitler spelled out a crystal-clear blueprint of his evil intentions. How, I asked myself, could anyone, having read that book, have voted him into office?

I was eating supper with my family on a snowy evening in mid-January towards the end of my Christmas vacation, and at the first lull in the conversation, I turned to my father. "I was wondering," I asked, "did you ever read *Mein Kampf*?" To my amazement, he shook his head. "But you were a member of the Nazi Party. You're always bragging that your party number was in the low three hundred thousands."

"So?"

"But did you at least buy a copy?"

"We didn't have to. Mutti and I were given a copy by an official in the Königsberg City Hall when we got married in 1935."

"This is unbelievable. You had *Mein Kampf* but you never read it. How about you, Mutti? You're an avid reader. Did you read it?"

"No, I never bothered," she admitted. "We were too busy in our café."

I was quiet for a moment, trying to digest this information. Finally I turned back to my parents. "Did *anyone* you knew read the book?"

They both thought for a moment. "No one that I can recall," Mutti replied as my father shook his head in agreement.

CHAPTER 40

*I*n March 1960, I heard from Wilfried Plath that Brigitte Emmenthal was back from England, bringing with her a handsome, solidly built Scotsman ten years older than herself. The very next day my invitation to Brigitte's *Polterabend* arrived in the mail. From what I'd heard, these wedding-eve parties were joyous events, with plenty of music, good food, and drink, highlighted by the smashing of stoneware and tin cans against the bride's front door for good luck. Had the invitation come from anyone else, I would have accepted it in a flash but coming as it did from Brigitte, without any warning or word of explanation, it left me bitter and humiliated. I tore the invitation into a thousand pieces and sulked.

"You've been walking around here looking like seven days of rainy weather," my father said to me a few days later. "Try to look at the bright side. I'm willing to bet that once you have your degree from the Höwi and land a good job, the girls will be running after you! You'll have to fight them off."

"Your father's right," Mutti added. "You should go to that party and show the world that you can do better. I always said she wasn't right for you, didn't I?"

But it was no use. I vowed to throw myself into my studies and give up dating entirely. No girl was ever going to hurt me like that again.

Fortunately, there were plenty of diversions at school to help take my mind off Brigitte. Despite Wolfgang Opschepper's desperate quest to be at the top of the class, Ferdinand Buscheur was the one who always got the straight A's. But in my opinion, Theo Schrick was at least as bright as Ferdinand was and would have had a great chance to win a place at the university if it weren't for his outrageous behavior. He enjoyed being the class clown, much to the consternation of our teachers.

One teacher whom Theo liked to bait was Dr. Gernegross who taught advertising. The sharpest dresser on the entire faculty, the aroma of Dr. Gernegross's musk cologne would precede him into the classroom. Wearing extra-long trousers in a vain attempt to hide his elevator shoes, he would tilt his chin upwards to appear taller. Rumor had it that he had advanced with incredible speed to a university professorship during the Third Reich, only to be demoted after the war. He had earned our animosity early on when he criticized the haircut of a young man in the front row.

"You there! You look like a castrated Caesar. How can you run around looking like that? *When I was your age*, it wouldn't have been permitted!"

It was Dr. Gernegross's custom to rush into the room, wish us a breathless "Good Morning!" and drop his leather briefcase with a loud thump on his desk. Then he would pick someone at random to ask, "Where did we leave off last time?"

When Theo Schrick's name was called we leaned forward in anticipation as Theo shrugged his shoulders and turned around to flash his trademark grin at the class. "Well, Herr Dr. Gernegross, after all it's your class," he began before pausing for effect. "So if *you* don't know, why on earth should I?"

"Of all the impertinence!" Dr. Gernegross shrieked in response as the veins in his forehead pulsed madly. "For the life of me, I don't know why you're wasting everyone's time here!"

Theo Schrick, still grinning defiantly, winked at the class and replied, "As I've sat through each of your boring lectures, I've often asked myself why *you* are wasting *ours*!"

By contrast, since she rarely invited questions during her lectures, Dr. Rasch, who taught us German literature, gave Theo Schrick very little opportunity to liven up her class; a smile from Dr. Rasch was as rare as a gold nugget in the desert. A dour spinster who lectured in a droning monotone, her clothes hung loosely on her flat-chested frame. Rumor had it that she borrowed her dresses from a much larger neighbor. Compared to the other faculty members who now and then told us about themselves, Dr. Rasch never once discussed her personal life, but judging from her enthusiasm for Jewish writers like Heinrich Heine, Franz Kafka, and Kurt Tucholsky, whose works were banned during the Third Reich, I assumed that she had not been a supporter of Hitler. I had already read Kafka's *The Metamorphosis* during my time in the German army. Now, with Dr. Rasch's encouragement, I found the time to read three additional works by him: *The Castle, Amerika*, and *The Trial*.

The only other woman on the faculty was Dr. Vollmer who taught both English and French. With her olive complexion and her pitch-black hair sprinkled with gray, which she parted in the middle and pulled back into a tight bun, Dr. Vollmer reminded me of the Sicilian woman who owned the ice-cream shop on the main street in Bergheim. Short and plump, she was nearly as wide as she was tall, yet she had an extraordinary amount of energy for her size, always racing along the corridors at top speed and somehow managing to take the stairs two at a time. Her enthusiasm spilled over into the classroom where I was actually one of the best students. Of course, it helped that in spite of my busy schedule, I still managed to take an English class with the native speakers at Berlitz every Wednesday evening and I also made a point of listening to French radio stations for ten minutes every evening to get more of a feel for the language.

It was while listening to a French radio broadcast in the middle of May, that I was suddenly possessed by the idea of skipping school for a few days to go to Paris. With an inexpensive return bus ticket from the Gare de l'Est to Cologne for the following Sunday safely in my pocket, I left the Höwi before my afternoon accounting class on Tuesday the 17th, took an early train home, gulped down a fast lunch, changed into casual clothes, grabbed my rucksack, and set out to hitchhike to France. A series of rides brought me along the Rhine, past Koblenz, and directly through Luxembourg City where I scrunched down in my seat for the seventeen kilometers between there and the French border, somehow imagining that an irate Nathalie and her parents might turn up at any moment at the side of the road to take revenge on me.

About thirty kilometers before Metz, my intended destination for the first night, an old French farmer stopped to give me a lift the rest of the way into town. He was the first Frenchman I had encountered and I was surprised that he spoke to me in German.

"Learned it as a POW in Germany during World War I," he explained. "Had to use it again when the Boches occupied our village during the last war. Not much love lost for your countrymen on that account, sorry to say."

"I know how it is and I can't blame you for feeling angry," I replied, "since I lived for nearly four years under Soviet occupation in East Prussia when I was a child."

We were both quiet for a few minutes before he spoke again. "Of course I must admit that the Germans were even-handed when it came to dispensing justice. I'll give them that much. When one of their soldiers raped a young girl from a nearby farm, the authorities saw to it that the man was court-martialed and shot. That was something to their credit, believe you me." He glanced over at me. "Anyway, I'm glad that our countrymen get along now."

"So am I!" I readily agreed.

"And now," he added with a sigh, as he pulled to a halt in front of the youth hostel in Metz, "we all have to worry about the Russians."

Reaching over to shake the farmer's hand, I finally put my beginning French into use. *"Merci monsieur!"* I exclaimed. *"Et au revoir!"*

****

I didn't have to wait long the next morning before a young couple in a bright-red two-door Volkswagen convertible stopped to pick me up. The driver, a French doctor, and his Polish wife, were happy to offer me a ride all the way to Paris. I squeezed into the backseat and found a way to stretch my long legs out sideways. Since the top was down, at least headroom wasn't a problem for me.

"Hope you're comfortable back there," the wife shouted back to me in English as the silk scarf covering her long brunette hair fluttered wildly in the wind, "because we're in a hurry and don't plan to stop unless someone needs to use the loo. We've even brought lunch along to eat in the car."

"That's fine with me!" I replied enthusiastically, although I was secretly hoping I would still be able to walk when we got there.

About an hour before we reached Paris, the young woman pulled a crusty baguette filled with thick slabs of smoked ham from the cloth bag at her feet, and cut it into three equal parts. To wash down the salty lunch, she handed a bottle of sparkling mineral water to her husband. Then, to my astonishment, she popped open the cork on a bottle of Bordeaux and filled two small water glasses, one for me and one for her. By the time they dropped me off near a bus stop on the southern outskirts of Paris in the early afternoon, the bottle of Bordeaux was empty and after extricating myself from the backseat, I was a little unsteady on my feet. The French doctor got out to shake my hand; his wife, who by then had a bad case of the giggles, reached up to let me kiss her on both cheeks. It was only after they drove off that I realized I was stranded at a lonely bus stop without a single French franc to my name.

A young man from Switzerland on a motor scooter finally came to my rescue. Since we both spoke German, he explained that he was finding it difficult to ride and study the map at the same time. If I would be willing to hop on behind him and navigate, we could ride together to the Malakoff neighborhood where he was sure I would find room at the youth hostel. Twenty minutes later, after changing money in a bank along the Boulevard de Stalingrad, and checking into the shabby *Auberge de la Jeunesse* where one night's stay cost less than a ride on the Métro, I slipped my German-French phrase book into my pocket and set out to explore the city where my father had served as a chef and food administrator in a German military hospital for two years during the war.

Once in the center of Paris, I screwed up all my courage and approached a gendarme. "Excuse me, sir," I asked in halting French, "but would you please tell me where to find a church called Sainte Chapelle?"

To my astonishment, this simple question provoked a stern rebuke. Poking my chest with his index finger, the policeman criticized me for mangling the language. "Don't you know the difference, monsieur, between a church and a chapel? A *church* called Sainte Chapelle, did you say? Those words would hurt the ears of every self-respecting Frenchman!" Then, after waving rudely in the general direction I needed to go, he shouted after me, "*Mon Dieu!* Sainte Chapelle is a *chapel*, not a *church! Souvenez-vous!* A *chapel*, not a *church!*"

Intimidated by my encounter with the gendarme, when I met two young Swiss men at breakfast at the youth hostel the next morning and discovered that one of them was fluent in French, I asked if I could join them when they went out sightseeing. The three of us spent the next few days together walking along the Champs Elysées, reading the inscriptions on the Arc de Triomphe, and exploring the Louvre. Early Saturday evening, as I looked up at the Eiffel Tower, I realized that I was standing in the same spot where my father had stood when he was photographed in his *Luftwaffe* uniform in March of 1941. That particular picture of my father had always intrigued me since I had been wearing my father's high black boots and his jaunty military cap earlier that year on my Opa's farm in East Prussia when my father snapped my photo while he was briefly home on leave. Now, more than nineteen years later, I tried to imagine those peaceful streets swarming with occupying German soldiers, but the image that came to my mind instead was of Mutti's stony face whenever my father had bragged to his friend, Fred Krienke, after the two of them had finished off two bottles of wine, about the good times he had had there.

My Swiss friends and I walked back over the Seine and headed for the Champs Elysées where hundreds of tourists mingled with the Parisians who were out for an evening stroll. Had my father once walked along there with a pretty French girl on his arm while Mutti loyally waited for him back home? Had he and his buddies often stopped at one of the nearby cafés to smoke Gauloise cigarettes while lingering over a glass of wine? As I was trying to picture what life must have been like for my father back then, there were gasps from the crowd. We all looked on in horror as, wobbling towards us in four uneven rows of three, a group of inebriated, middle-aged German men were singing the "Horst Wessel Song." The song had been the anthem of the Nazi Storm Troopers and had been banned in Germany since 1945. When the men passed by, they belted out the second verse at the top of their lungs as the Parisians turned their backs or covered their ears in disgust:

"Clear the streets for the brown battalions,
Clear the streets for the Storm Troopers!
Already millions look with hope to the swastika
The day of freedom and bread is dawning!"

Whenever my father had heard the "Horst Wessel Song" played as part of a television documentary, his eyes had lit up. I now realized with a terrible sense of shame that my father must also have sung that awful song when he was a member of the Storm Troopers.

At half-past eight on Sunday morning I stopped by the Youth Hostel office to settle my bill but even though office hours were supposed to have started at eight o'clock, when I knocked on the door no one answered. After waiting a few minutes and politely knocking several more times, I tried the knob, and to my surprise, found the door unlocked. A revolting odor of old sweat, stale cigarette smoke, and beer escaped into the entry hall as I peeked inside. In a tangle of naked arms and legs jutting out from under the torn thin sheet on the couch on the left side of the small room, a redheaded woman was sound asleep in the embrace of a North African man. Snuggling under a moth-eaten blanket opposite them on the other couch, a young blond woman dozed in the arms of her snoring, brown-skinned lover. Being careful not to awaken the sleeping couples, I slipped the money I was holding back into my pocket and gently closed the door behind me on the way out. An hour later, as I waited to board the bus that would carry me back to Cologne, I wondered whether the four of them were lying there, still dead to the world, as overnight guests clustered outside the door, vainly waiting for the hostel office to open for the day.

CHAPTER 41

*A*lthough my somewhat lame excuse to Dr. Fabri for my absence from school was that I had been out sick, I privately confided the real reason to Dr. Vollmer in the short break after my next French class. "Actually," I added, "you're partly to blame since you got me so interested in the language."

"Just between us," she replied with a sly smile, "you probably learned a lot more in those five days in Paris than in a whole month here at the Höwi." Then, just before Dr. Gernegross arrived for our economic geography lesson, she quickly added under her breath, "All the same, I wouldn't tell anyone else about it. The other teachers aren't likely to see it that way!"

Dr. Gernegross strode briskly into the room as Dr. Vollmer was on her way out. "So," he said, as he dropped a newspaper onto the desk, "I trust that you gentlemen have been keeping up with the business news. Who can tell me how crude oil is transported? I'll give you a hint. It's an English word that's recently been added to our language." When no one bothered to dignify his silly question with an answer, he glared at each of us in turn. "Come now! Surely someone must know this."

Theo Schrick looked back to the left and then to the right so that we could all see his wicked grin. Then he slowly raised his hand. "Ah,

Herr Schrick thinks he knows. Tell us, please, Herr Schrick, what it is called."

"I think it's called a peep-a-LEEN-a, Herr Dr. Gernegross," Theo replied, somehow managing to keep a straight face as the rest of us suppressed giggles.

"It's not pronounced peep-a-LEEN-a," Dr. Gernegross shrieked. "Only an idiot would say it that way. Aren't you studying English? It's 'pipeline!' The word is 'pipeline.'" Ignoring the reaction of the class, Dr. Gernegross began to mumble to himself as he angrily flipped the pages of the fat black ledger on the desk in front of him. "Let me see, Herr Schrick, if you're as dumb in your English class as you are in mine!" He stared down at the page and we all held our breaths. "What's this? You're an A student in English? Do you take me for a fool?" To his credit, Theo chose not to answer the question, although he must have been sorely tempted to do so.

****

In late June, once the dreaded year-end exams were behind me, I went in search of Dr. Vollmer, just managing to catch up to her as she was crossing the schoolyard on her way home. "Oh, hello, Herr Nitsch," she greeted me with a broad smile. "Are you off to Paris again?"

"That's what I wanted to tell you, Frau Dr. Vollmer," I replied. "It's London this time. I managed to save up enough money from my job at Arminius AG to take a month-long English course."

"Well, in that case, cheerio! Don't forget your umbrella and be sure to tell me all about it when you get back in the fall."

My tuition at the London language school included five hours of instruction each day as well as bed and breakfast at the home of an elderly widow. Our faculty members, all graduates of Oxford or Cambridge, taught English grammar, English literature, and English history. Joining me in the program were eleven other students – seven young women and four young men – hailing from Denmark, France, Germany, Holland,

and Italy. In our first class one of our teachers, a Mr. Townsend, wrote the names of the books we had to buy on the blackboard. One was a grammar book. The other two were satirical novels by Kingsley Amis: *Lucky Jim* and the recently published *Take a Girl Like You.*

Turning back towards the class, Mr. Townsend asked if any of us had read something by Amis. "No? You'll def-def-definitely enjoy him," he assured us. "He-he-he is with-without a doubt one of the fi-fi-finest English writers in the last few de-de-decades!"

After class, when six of us went for lunch in a coffee shop, I couldn't help commenting. "I know repetition is important when you're learning a language," I quipped, "but is anyone else bothered that all of the men on the faculty stutter?"

As everyone else nodded, a Danish classmate spoke up. "I took a similar course in London last year and the same thing happened. They all stuttered, especially at the beginning of a sentence." She grinned before adding, "What, What, I, I, I, was go, go, going to say…"

When we stopped laughing, a French student named Isabelle spoke up. "From what I've heard, all of the upper crust men who study at Oxford or Cambridge learn to speak that way to prove that they went to the finest universities. Believe it or not, it's a status symbol."

I had noticed Isabelle the minute she first walked into class. A tall, elegantly dressed blond with dark-brown eyes, she managed a travel agency in Paris. Her English was so good that I was surprised she hadn't been placed in a higher level. Since I lacked her sophistication and polish and was several years her junior, the thought never crossed my mind to approach her for a date, so it came as a total surprise when she walked up to me during a break a few days later to ask if we could have dinner together that evening in order to get better acquainted. We chose a restaurant near Piccadilly Circus and set the time for 6 P.M.

I got to the restaurant ten minutes ahead of time. The place was enormous; there must have been several hundred diners. So, rather than take a table, I stationed myself just inside the door to make sure I wouldn't miss Isabelle on her way in. Six o'clock came and went. As the minutes ticked by at least five different waiters approached me to ask if I was ready to sit down and eat. I could sense dozens of eyes staring at me, pitying me, as I shifted uneasily from foot to foot. Finally, at 7 P.M., I slunk back outside and headed for a pub near my bed and breakfast where I drowned my sorrows alone.

As soon as I arrived in class the next morning, Isabelle stormed over to me. I had been expecting an explanation, an excuse, anything to make me feel better. Instead I got a tongue-lashing. "I've never been so angry," Isabelle snapped at me. "Where *were* you last night? I waited just inside the door for half an hour, and believe me, I'm not accustomed to being kept waiting like that. I felt like a fool!"

Only then did it dawn on me that a restaurant of that size might have more than one entrance. How could I have been such an idiot? Nothing I could say or do made any difference to Isabelle. For the rest of the month she and I remained part of a group of six classmates who ate together and who splurged on tickets to *My Fair Lady*. But it was clear that, when it came to anything more than a casual friendship, Isabelle had given me one chance to impress her, and I had blown it. It wasn't until I was on my way back to Cologne that I thought again about that night in Piccadilly Circus and realized that maybe, just maybe, she had been equally at fault.

****

I may have been a failure in the romance department, but even so, my trips to Paris and London still made me feel like a sophisticated world traveler. Cologne suddenly looked like a provincial backwater compared to those great cosmopolitan centers. During the remainder of the summer vacation, when I wasn't studying my textbooks or swimming laps in the Bergheim pool, I reread both of the Kingley Amis books as well as the copy of the *London Times* I'd brought back with me. I dreamed of moving far away – perhaps even to New York

City – where I somewhat naively imagined that people from all around the world lived and worked together in harmony. Surely, I thought, no one could ever feel bored in a place like that.

But September and the start of the new school year quickly brought me back to reality. Fresh from my travels, I would have liked to study modern European history. However, since the Höwi was financed by the City of Cologne, our history curriculum was limited to local events – starting with the founding of the city of Cologne by the Romans in 50 A.D., moving on to the construction of the Eifel Aqueduct in 80 A.D., and eventually, focusing on the power struggle between the Catholic church and local residents who favored a secular government. I didn't see the relevance of this material to my future career, and to his credit, neither did our history teacher, Dr. Ludwig, a doddery old man with squinty eyes, a deeply lined forehead, thinning white hair, and bad teeth. But the rules were the rules.

Dr. Ludwig also taught business law, and as I soon discovered, he had no mercy for the weaker students in the class. He made a point of calling on me regularly just to see me squirm and I wasn't the only one he singled out. With biting sarcasm he would personally insult and humiliate anyone who did poorly on his tests. When he was most frustrated, he would wring his hands and heave a sigh. We all knew by heart what he would say next. "Gentlemen, you just don't get it, do you? At times like this I wish I were back at my first job, teaching in the Leipzig *Gymnasium* where the little Jewish boys in my class were all smarter than any of you!"

Dr. Ludwig also talked about the Jews in our history class, pointing out that Jews had originally come to Cologne with the Romans and were mentioned in the official city records as early as the fourth century A.D. Whenever the subject came up I would turn to the window and gaze over the rooftops at the six-pointed star atop the newly rebuilt Roon Strasse Synagogue. Rededicated in 1959, it had replaced the nineteenth century building destroyed on *Kristallnacht*. What, I wondered, had life been like for that Jewish congregation back in the days when Dr. Ludwig had started his teaching career? And what had become of them in the terrible years that followed?

Just like the forced labor personnel files I had been ordered to destroy during my apprenticeship at Arminius AG, for the most part the events between Hitler's rise to power and the end of the war had been covered up or ignored since 1945. Adults were reluctant to discuss such things. If they had actively participated it was best to keep quiet about it. If they had been victimized, the memories were still too painful. As a result, since that entire shameful period of our history was deliberately omitted from the curriculum in German classrooms, young people had been kept pretty much in the dark. What little we knew we gleaned from occasional newspaper articles about post-war trials of concentration camp guards. So when it was reported in the second week of October that West German television would run a documentary on the Third Reich, the news created quite a buzz. The first hour-long segment was scheduled to air on Friday, October 21st, followed by thirteen more hour-long segments at two-week intervals. Now, fifteen years after the end of the war, together with fifty-five million of my countrymen, I was about to find out the details.

On that Friday, five minutes before the end of Dr. Ludwig's business law lecture, he suddenly stopped talking and poked his head out into the hallway. After looking right and left to make sure no one was within hearing range, he closed the door and turned back to the class. "As you know," he began in a barely audible voice, "there are certain historical topics we are not supposed to touch on. That makes it all the more important that you watch every episode of the television program that starts tonight. I have a feeling that what you are going to see will be only the tip of the iceberg, but at least it's a start. And that, gentlemen, for reasons of school policy, is unfortunately the last thing I'm going to say on this subject."

Later that evening, after the café was closed and our supper dishes put away, my parents, Hubert, and I sat down together in our living room to watch the opening segment of *The Third Reich*, which was a fast-moving overview of what was to come. As an unseen commentator provided explanations, a series of photographs flashed on the screen – young Hitler in a class photo, Hitler conferring with cabinet members, Hitler speaking to officers of the *Wehrmacht*, Hitler at Hindenburg's funeral. Next came black and white film clips the most startling of which showed rows of Storm Troopers in tight formation goose-stepping past their *Führer*, followed by Hitler himself giving a fiery speech in Königsberg, East Prussia. As he spoke in strangely accented German, his arms waved wildly and his face contorted into bizarre gestures.

"I know just where that was," Mutti whispered to my father. "Do you remember?"

Ignoring Mutti's comment, Hubert looked at me in amazement. *This* was the great Adolf Hitler? The man was clearly a lunatic. By the time the program ended, Hubert and I were barely able to suppress our laughter.

"Now that I've seen the man in action, could you please explain to me how you could have voted for him," I finally said once my father had turned off the television. "He sounded like a foreigner from the Balkans and even if you don't listen to what he's saying, just look at him. He was like a crazy wind-up clown!" Hubert nodded in agreement and in the silence that followed, we both waited for our parents to speak.

Mutti was still gazing at the blank screen and shaking her head. "I can't understand it myself," she said. "Somehow we all got swept up by it and didn't notice how odd he really was. I'm ashamed to admit that I used to brag about having seen the *Führer* on three different occasions when he came to speak in Königsberg, but in those days it was like a badge of honor."

"I'll try to answer your question, Stretch," my father said as he pulled out his swivel desk chair and sat down opposite us. "It's easy now with hindsight to blame us for supporting Hitler, but at the time there was massive unemployment and everyone was polarized into two camps. You were either for the Communists or you backed the National Socialists. The way we saw it, that left my brothers and me only one choice, which is why we all signed up early on for the Storm Troopers. We felt like the elite of the elite and I was proud that my party number was in the low three hundred thousands. Believe me, it was a thrill to dress in that uniform and protect people at party rallies from Communist hoodlums."

"That's not all you did, Willi," Mutti quietly reminded him.

"I was just getting to that," my father went on. "The best part was infiltrating Communist rallies to break up their meetings. Of course, everyone was frisked on the way in so we had to show up unarmed and in civilian clothes."

"But if you were unarmed," I interrupted, "how did you…"

My father held up his hand and grinned at us. "It was easy. Let me show you." He walked into the bedroom Hubert and I shared and brought out my sturdy wooden desk chair. "The element of surprise was extremely important. We would spread out in the meeting hall and quietly take our seats. At some point, usually about twenty minutes into the rally, our leader would signal us with a shrill, two-fingered whistle. As soon as we heard him, we'd jump up and lift our chairs like this." His eyes glowed with excitement as he raised the chair into the air. "Then, before anyone had time to stop us, we smashed one of the thick back legs against the floor until it broke off. That's all there was to it. Believe me, after a few people got their heads smashed in with a broken chair leg, the rest of them would be hightailing it for the door."

My father's face was still flushed with excitement as he carried the chair back to our room. In his brief absence I glanced over at Hubert and caught the look of terror in his eyes. As if someone had flipped a switch, my father's seething anger was suddenly so close to the surface that we both could look deep into his soul. That my father could still

304

bask in his own glory over what he had done as a Storm Trooper made me sick to my stomach.

"And don't forget," my father added with smug satisfaction when he returned to the living room, "that when the *Führer* came to power he locked up the Communist Party leaders; he created jobs; he built the Autobahn and all of that was just fine with me."

"How can you equate those things?" I protested. "From what I've read, Hitler didn't just round up the Communists leaders; he rounded up everyone in the opposition and either killed them or put them into concentration camps. And don't forget what he did to the Jews!"

"Good point, Stretch," my father said as he reflected on my comment. "I'll grant you that Hitler's treatment of the Jews went way overboard. If it'd been up to me, he should have just resettled the Eastern Jews in Poland or wherever they came from and left the German Jews alone. The Jews in Königsberg were tops in their professions. When I was growing up Jewish doctors were the best of the specialists, whether it was a cardiologist, or an eye doctor, or a neurologist. My father always insisted on being treated by them. And it wasn't just in Königsberg. Uncle Hermann told me the same thing about Berlin."

Around midnight, long after my parents had gone to sleep, as I lay wide-awake in bed trying to make sense of what I had just heard and seen, I could hear Hubert tossing and turning on the bottom bunk. "Psst, Stretch!" he finally whispered, "Are you still up? Can I ask you something?"

"Sure, what?"

"Which do you think was harder to digest? The TV program or Vati's reaction to it?"

"Actually, what's puzzling me is something altogether different. Did you notice how quiet Mutti was when he held up that chair? I've been wondering how much she could really have known about him when they got married in 1935."

"Shouldn't we just ask her?"

I took a deep breath. "No, I don't think so. To be honest, I'd rather not know the answer."

CHAPTER 42

With the approach of my 23rd birthday, I felt like a failure. My weekdays were spent in class at the Höwi followed by long nights studying and cramming for tests. I was still living at home with my parents, and worst of all, I didn't have a girlfriend. Since I desperately needed a break in my routine, I volunteered to bring cooked meals over to Oma during the month of November, much to the relief of the salesgirls, Mutti, and Hubert, who normally had this responsibility.

I usually made the short walk along Hauptstrasse to Oma's one-room apartment right after dark. If I had arrived at that late hour when we were living under the Russians, Oma would have towered over me in the doorway, ready to smack me with a wet dishrag. Because our lives had depended on it back then, she had been strict with all of her grandchildren, saving especially harsh words for me. But now, as her petite seventy-eight-year-old frame was nearly swallowed up in the cushions of a large armchair, Oma wasn't the least bit threatening. As I sat opposite her, she would reminisce about life in East Prussia before the Russians came. She never tired of repeating the same stories about the joys and the hardships of raising her five children on Opa's hardscrabble farm, a routine broken up by regular attendance at the

307

Lutheran church in Schippenbeil where Opa had once been a pillar of the congregation. If, while she was talking about long-ago weddings, and baptisms, and funerals, I happened to doze off in that dimly lit, stuffy room, she would call out to me, "Ginter, are you awake? Ginter? Are you listening to me?"

"Sorry, Oma, but it's much too warm in here and I've been up since early this morning."

"Nonsense! I was actually going to ask you to put another one or two briquettes on the stove to warm the place up, if you don't mind. And don't complain to me about lack of sleep, young man. I take three or four sleeping pills every night at bedtime and I still lie awake for hours at a time."

"Does Frau Dr. Klemm know that you take that many?"

"Oh, what does she know? If it were up to her, I wouldn't take more than one or two a day and I'd never get any sleep at all." She stopped talking and looked up at me over the rims of her thin metal eyeglass frames. "Did you forget the briquettes? And while you're up, would you please bring over my thick woolen shawl? I'm fairly chilled to the bone."

As I reached down to drape the shawl over Oma's shoulders she grasped my hand. "Can you stay just a few minutes longer? There's something I want to talk to you about."

"Sure, Oma. What's on your mind?"

"It's Hubert. I pray every day that your father will give him the approval he desperately needs. But your poor Oma mustn't be praying hard enough because your father continues to heap praises on you all the time while Hubert still can't do anything right by him. Just between the two of us, the situation is breaking your poor mother's heart."

"Even if Mutti doesn't talk to me about it, I'm aware of what's going on, Oma, believe me, but I don't see how I can change anything."

"That poor boy," Oma repeated, "that poor, poor child," and as she began to hum "Holy God, we praise Thy name," I bent over to give her a hug and wish her a good night before slipping out of the apartment.

I had spent most of Saturday, December 3rd, at my desk studying for a battery of upcoming tests at the Höwi when, around four o'clock in the afternoon, I looked up and saw Hubert standing morosely in the doorway, his chest heaving from the exertion of walking up the stairs. "Mutti asked me to tell you that Oma's here," he explained, "and everyone's waiting to celebrate your birthday."

As soon as Hubert and I joined the rest of the family in the café, we all sat down together to drink pots of steaming-hot coffee and eat extra-moist slices of Black Forest cake. One by one the shopgirls left their posts behind the counter to congratulate me, as did the customers at nearby tables. "We're all so proud of your accomplishments," my father said as he raised his cup to me. "I foresee a great future for you once you've finished your studies." As he spoke, Hubert was about to put a third spoonful of sugar in his coffee. My father reached over and grabbed him by the wrist. "That's the last thing you need!" he hissed under his breath. "You should let Stretch here teach you something about self-discipline." His outburst was followed by an awkward silence. Oma had turned deathly pale.

Finally Mutti spoke up. Her voice trembled as she chose her words carefully. "Be fair, Willi. It's a special day so let's relax the rules a bit, why don't we?"

"Speaking of special day," I rushed to add. "Would you be at all upset if I go out this evening? I've been waiting two years for *The Bridge on the River Kwai* to play in Bergheim and I'd like to take Hubert along to see it tonight, if you don't mind." My brother's eyes lit up at the suggestion, but no one at the table looked more pleased than Oma.

CHAPTER *43*

*A*t the beginning of 1961 my family and I watched the final nine segments of the TV series *The Third Reich*. Each program was disturbing, but none more so than the February 24th program dealing with the fate of the Jews. Starting with a series of film clips showing terrified Jewish men, women, and children being unloaded, gaunt and disheveled, from freight trains at Auschwitz, Sachsenhausen, Dachau, Mauthausen, and Buchenwald, the focus shifted to haughty camp commandants and nonchalant guards in their crisp uniforms. As we sat, silently glued to the television screen, we barely had time to absorb these contrasts before we came face to face with horrifying images of naked corpses being casually tossed into mass graves.

At the end of the hour, Mutti was the first to speak. Her voice was choked with emotion. "Hubert, I suppose you were much too young to remember when the Russians made Opa dig up the bodies of those Jewish women in Palmnicken in 1945. But you remember it, Günter, don't you?" I nodded as I thought again about how my beloved Opa had suffered during that time. "That was bad enough, but that these horrible things were done on such a scale, I could never have imagined. We'd heard rumors, of course, but this, this…"

As Mutti's voice trailed off, my father spoke up. "Devastating, absolutely devastating! It's high time we all got such a strong dose of reality. I wish I could believe that all those incorrigible old Nazis out there who were watching tonight will finally have some sense of shame."

As if in reply to my father's comment, in another program segment two weeks later a German reporter interviewed a former captain of the *Wehrmacht*. "Do I understand you correctly, sir?" the reporter inquired. "You maintain that as late as 1943 you had no clue about the death camps in Poland?"

"That's correct," the captain replied. "I had absolutely no idea about those camps."

My father jumped up from his seat and shouted at the screen. "He's lying through his teeth! Does he think we're all idiots? I was only an NCO, and even I knew well before then that people were being killed in those camps. What's he going to say next? That they were all being sent to Poland on vacation?"

"Calm down, Willi," Mutti soothed. "Can't we talk about this after the program?"

But my father stood his ground. "Just look at them! That's the third officer he's interviewed and they're all sticking to the same story. Arrogant pigs! Let me tell you something. Those freight trains ran day and night. Every German soldier who served in Poland had to have seen the emaciated prisoners packed inside with the fear of death on their faces. We may not have known *how* they were killed. We heard the wildest stories; we could hardly believe them. But we all knew that most of those poor slobs wouldn't get out alive. The worst of it was that there was nothing we could do about it, absolutely nothing."

The following Monday morning I bought a newspaper so that I could read the latest reports of the Adolf Eichmann trial while I rode the train to the Höwi. As I walked to class, Dr. Ludwig passed me in the hallway. He gave the headline a quick glance and angrily shook his head.

A few minutes later, with an air of grim resolution, he launched into yet another pointless lecture on the history of the City of Cologne.

****

In mid-July, as we started a daunting round of written and oral final exams at the Höwi, everyone expected Ferdinand Buscheur to get the coveted "matriculation standard," which would give him the right to study business administration or economics at the university. Everyone, that is, except Wolfgang Opschepper who was still smugly confident that he would be chosen in the end. Ignoring the smirks of his classmates, he constantly boasted about his chances. "And when they pick me," he'd say with a nasty laugh, "I'll enroll in a business administration program at the University of Cologne and I won't have to send out job applications like the rest of you losers!"

The results were to be announced on Monday, July 24th. Unsure whether I had passed both math and accounting, I tried to calm my nerves over the weekend by swimming extra laps in the Bergheim pool. As it turned out, I needn't have worried. The only one who didn't make the grade was Johannes Zemke.

"And now, gentlemen," announced a beaming Dr. Fabri, "I have some very good news to share with you. One student in this class has achieved the matriculation standard." He paused to build up the suspense and Wolfgang Opschepper licked his lips in anticipation. "And that student is...Ferdinand Buscheur!" As Dr. Fabri walked over to shake Ferdi's hand, Wolfgang turned red as a beet and slumped down in his chair.

When class was dismissed, I went over to cheer up Johannes. To my astonishment, he seemed to be taking the news that he had flunked out surprisingly well.

"Actually, I was kind of expecting it," he confided to me with a sheepish grin. "I guess it's back to the brewery for me!"

"Well," I consoled him, "at least you have a job waiting for you, unlike the rest of us."

Out of the corner of my eye I could see Theo Schrick approaching Wolfgang Opschepper who was still sitting forlornly at his desk. "Hey, Old Man," Theo called out cheerfully. "If you don't mind joining the rest of us losers, we're all going out to celebrate." In the end, all fifteen of us headed out together to a bar on nearby Beethovenstrasse where the waitresses served us the local Kölsch beer in traditional tall 0.2 liter cylindrical glasses not found anywhere else in Germany to wash down our thick open sandwiches of Westfalian smoked ham or salami.

Despite his quirky behavior, Theo Schrick and I had become friends during our two years together at Höwi. So, after his fourth glass of Kölsch, Theo turned to me to make a slurry confession. "You know, Günter, I actually hated every single minute at the Höwi. I would never have enrolled if my parents hadn't made me do it. What a total waste of two years! And of all those empty-headed old windbags on the faculty, Gernegross was by far the worst." He leaned even closer to me and added with his trademark grin, "I hope I helped to liven up his class a bit!"

"What upset me most about Gernegross," I said, "was his making us parrot his exact words back to him on every test. After a while I began to suspect that he couldn't recognize a correct answer in any words other than his own."

"You got that right," Theo agreed. "The guy's a complete moron!"

As we were talking we could hear snatches of the conversation at the adjoining table where Wolfgang Opschepper was once again bragging about his problems fighting off female admirers. "I don't believe a word of it," Theo said under his breath. "I doubt he's got a steady girlfriend any more than I do." He stopped and gave me a sly look. "But I'll bet a tall guy like you can find a chick any time you want to."

"Sorry to disappoint you," I admitted. "My first real girl friend dumped me more than a year ago and there's been no one new in my life since then."

An hour passed and Theo Schrick, Ferdinand Buscheur, Hans Stiefenhöfer, and I were the only classmates left in the restaurant. Hans was the other friend I'd made at the Höwi. The four of us moved to an outdoor table and ordered another round of Kölsch beer. While the rest of us talked, Theo, who had become uncharacteristically sullen, picked tiny crumbs from the remaining crust of his sandwich and fed them, bit by bit, to the chirping sparrows on the dusty ground at our feet. Suddenly, he lifted his glass and offered a toast. "To the sparrows!" he said bitterly. "They're so much nicer than people!" He gulped down his beer and beckoned the waitress to bring him another. "Did I ever tell you that my parents are divorced and my mother and my stepfather fight all the time? That's why I hate going home. I never want to end up like that!" He scattered the last of the crumbs and suddenly smiled. "I plan to live it up with wine, women, and song. And," he continued after putting his finger to his lips to swear us to secrecy, "if I'm still alive by the time I reach fifty, I plan to end it right there."

Ferdi Buscheur held up his hand. "Come on, Theo. Life's not so tragic. Besides, when you're fifty, you'll want to be fifty-five, and when you're fifty-five you'll want to be sixty, and so on and so on until you reach a hundred and die of old age like the rest of us!"

"Fifty-five and not one minute longer!" Theo conceded. Then he began to giggle and I reached over to take the glass from his hand. Since he had clearly reached a stage where he couldn't walk or use public transportation, we put him in a taxi and sent him home.

****

Ever since the middle of May, when I had bought the book Dr. Fabri recommended on how to write a résumé, I had been collecting the addresses of major corporations. Now I settled down to the task of writing to each company on my list to inquire about a position in its executive training program. Not long after graduation, while most of us waited vainly by our mailboxes for good news, Hans Stiefenhöfer phoned to let me know that both he and another classmate had already been accepted by C&A, a huge European-wide clothing store chain headquartered in the Netherlands. "Sorry to say that there's no point in your applying to C&A," Hans informed me. "The owners, a family named Brenninkmeyer, are Catholics. If you're not Catholic, you don't stand a chance of getting hired there. By the way, did you hear that Wolfgang Opschepper and Wilhelm Krause got hired by BULL, the French computer manufacturer?"

"With my lousy math skills, I didn't even bother writing to companies like that," I admitted. "Anyway, congratulations. I'll let you know if I ever get anything other than rejection letters."

Hans phoned again at the beginning of August. "Anything yet?"

"Nothing. Not a thing."

"That's what I thought when I didn't hear back from you. From the sound of it, you definitely need some cheering up. My sisters and I are having a party at our home on the 12th. That's a Saturday night. We were hoping you'd join us." I quickly accepted the invitation. "Great! We'll expect you in Siegburg sometime between 8 and 9 P.M."

It took me a full two hours on three different trains to travel to Hans's home in Siegburg the night of the party. Still, I had allowed myself plenty of time so I managed to arrive promptly at half-past eight. After greeting me at the door, Hans introduced me to several of his friends and then he waved over an attractive girl with curly blond hair tied back in a loose bun whom I'd noticed on the far side of the room. "And this is my sister, Doris."

Doris gave me a firm handshake and smiled. "You must be Günter. Welcome! I've heard a lot about you. The girls and I are getting the buffet ready in the kitchen but let's make time to talk later on!"

The party was such a huge success that with Hans's parents away for the night, the celebration went on until six the next morning. Doris and I had hit things off right away so that even when most of the other guests had long since dozed off, we continued to dance and talk. Around seven that Sunday morning, Doris made a large pot of strong, black coffee and woke everyone up to a hearty breakfast of scrambled eggs and toast.

After we ate, Hans suggested that we gather around the television to watch the program hosted by Werner Höfer, a jovial man who usually put a light-hearted spin on hot political topics. We all squeezed together wherever we could find space as Hans walked over to turn on the set. There, on the screen, was Werner Höfer with several other journalists, all of them dressed in black, as if they had just returned from a funeral. Shocking images followed of East German workers using heavy equipment and barbed wire to seal off the border between East and West Berlin.

Gloom descended on all of us as we watched in deadly silence. Finally, the young man seated on the floor next to me gave a low whistle. "My God! It's the beginning of World War III!"

"Let's not get carried away," Hans reassured him. "There'll certainly be repercussions, but no war! There *can't* be."

As soon as the program ended, I excused myself and hurried back to the Siegburg station, suddenly anxious to get home to my parents. Passengers all around me on the trains talked in hushed tones or shook their heads in disbelief. A few women were sobbing uncontrollably. It was strange, I thought. Ever since Mutti, Hubert, and I left the Bodenteich refugee camp located only a stone's throw from the East German border to join my father in Cologne, 400 kilometers further west, I'd finally felt secure. But now, I was no longer so sure.

Mutti and the shopgirls were getting ready to open the café when I got back to Bergheim. As soon as Mutti saw me, she rushed over and gave me a hug. Her red-rimmed eyes told me that she had already heard the news. "Your father was listening to the radio in the baking kitchen when some of the first reports came in from Berlin and he rushed upstairs to wake us up," Mutti told me. "Hubert and I have been glued to the television for hours trying to make sense of things." Then, forcing a smile, she wiped her hands on her apron. "Life must go on, I suppose, so why don't you go wash up and tell your brother to come down for lunch?"

As soon as Mutti, Hubert, and I had finished eating, my father called me into his baking kitchen and closed the door behind us. He put his hand on my shoulder and looked me in the eyes. "Listen carefully, Stretch," he began. "I'm afraid this whole mess will blow up into another war and you'll end up as cannon fodder for the Ivans. I couldn't bear to have that happen. So here's what I think. If you want to take off for Spain or maybe somewhere in North Africa, you have my blessings. In case you go, I'll give you a thousand Deutschmarks to start you off. But wherever you wind up, just write postcards to let us know you're all right. Never use a return address. And don't come back until it's all over!"

His eyes had become moist as he waited for my reply, and at that moment, I wasn't sure which surprised me more – my father's dire warning or his willingness to show how much he cared about me. "Why don't we give Khrushchev and President Kennedy a chance to work things out," I finally said, with as much conviction as I could muster. "I'm sure as soon as the dust settles, they'll come to an understanding."

"And if they don't?"

"They have to, or there won't be any safe place left to hide."

Despite my outward calm, my father's warning had terrified me. Months before when I was at the Amerika-Haus I had idly picked up a brochure about emigrating to the United States. Now I fished it back out of the pile on my desk and read it in earnest. First thing Monday morning, I phoned the American Consulate in Frankfurt to request more information. A packet from the Consulate arrived a few days later. All things considered, the whole process didn't sound too difficult. I would need to fill out some forms, get passport photos taken, and go for a personal interview. The goal, as I understood it, was to get something called a "Green Card." After that, all I'd need was a letter from an American family willing to sponsor me. Tucking the packet away in my desk drawer, I suddenly felt more confident about my future.

CHAPTER *44*

*T*he Soviet encirclement of West Berlin, which I had first thought could be easily resolved by diplomacy, had instead become more entrenched. At the same time, I began to have serious doubts about my ability to find an American sponsor. Up to that point the only Americans I'd met were a few soldiers in Baumholder and the staff members at the Amerika-Haus in Cologne. Since I hadn't yet received a single job offer, I decided to follow up on my father's advice by taking a trip to Spain to see what life would be like there. Fortunately, I could afford to go because I had taken Dr. Fabri's suggestion back in 1960 and borrowed 900 Deutschmarks from my father to buy VW stock when the company first went public. By the Spring of 1961, when I sold the stock, it had already doubled in value so that, even after repaying my father, I still had 900 Deutschmarks left for myself, enough to book a four-week trip by VW bus with ASTA, a German student organization, for September.

I met my fellow travelers in a hotel lobby in Barcelona on the last day of August. There were only five of us altogether. As the only one in the group who had never attended a university, and the only one who didn't speak any Spanish, I often felt a bit like an outsider. Eberhard, a tall, sandy-haired German lawyer who was studying Spanish law at the University of Madrid, was both our travel guide and the driver of the VW bus. The other members of our group were three bespectacled women in their late twenties, all doctoral candidates. Christa, a quiet blond, and Gisela, a garrulous redhead, were both from Germany. Elfriede, who was Viennese, would surely have been the prettiest of the three had it not been for her pitch-black teeth, the result of almost incessant candy eating.

Ours was definitely a low-budget tour. That meant that except in places like Barcelona, Madrid, and Toledo, we would be sleeping in tents, one shared by Eberhard and me, and one for the three young women. All of the camping supplies (which were far superior to any I had seen in the scouts or the *Bundeswehr*) were already stowed in the back of the VW bus when we set out the next morning. Not long after leaving the coast, we opened up all of the windows to get some relief from the oppressive heat. Although the breeze did nothing to cool us off, it did succeed in blowing dozens of Elfriede's empty candy wrappers around.

When I had visited Paris or travelled in Great Britain, I had been surrounded by tourists. By contrast, the interior of Spain in 1961 was largely undiscovered by outsiders. Since we would often be the only foreigners for miles around, that first evening Eberhard had taken me aside to suggest that I wear khakis instead of my usual shorts. "Spain's a very religious country," he explained, "and the sight of a man in short pants is likely to offend the locals. You did bring some long pants along, I hope?" I nodded. "Good! Then that's settled."

Every day was a new adventure: the Alhambra Palace, built by the Moors in Granada; the nearby Gypsy encampments in Sacromonte; a thrilling bullfight right out of a Hemingway novel in which six bulls were killed in under two hours; sherry savored after a tour of the Tío Pepe winery. In Algeciras, while the rest of my travel companions chose to take a day off, I hopped aboard a ferry for the crossing to Tangiers in Morocco where blinding sunlight reflected off the whitewashed buildings. I strolled among Arabs in white flowing robes the short distance from the ferry slip to the gates leading through the inner city walls to the bustling Casbah market. Just inside the gate I saw two elderly men squatting on the dusty ground on either side of a handmade checkerboard. Coca-Cola bottle caps, half of them turned up and half turned down, were their makeshift game pieces. As soon as the game ended, I squatted down beside them, and after explaining in my best French that I was German, asked if they could recommend a good restaurant nearby.

"You're German!" one of the men exclaimed. "Let me ask *you* a question. When is Adolf Hitler coming to kick the French out of Algeria?"

"Excuse me?"

"Hitler. When is Hitler coming to free Algeria?" the man inquired again with even more urgency than before.

"And so," I explained to my companions when I rejoined them in Algeciras, "it fell to me to break the news to those two crestfallen gentlemen that the *Führer* had been dead for sixteen years."

The four of them looked at me as though I had gotten too much Moroccan sun. "You're putting us on!" Gisela insisted.

"Actually, I thought they were putting *me* on for a minute. But you should have seen their faces when I told them. For those two old men, World War II ended just before noon today."

****

A square window the size of an extra-large postcard was set deep within the thick, white-painted walls of my tiny hotel room in Toledo. As I lay down with my long legs dangling off the end of the bed, the Roman-style earthenware water jug on the nightstand glowed a pale shade of orange in the dim light from the only lamp. I drifted off to sleep and dreamed that El Greco himself was waiting for me in the street below.

The next morning I actually came face to face with El Greco whose self-portrait formed part of *The Burial of Count Orgaz*, his striking painting in the Church of Santo Tomé where he had been a parishioner. Keeping her voice low so as not to disturb nearby worshippers, Gisela drew on her background in art history to explain that devout Catholics had been traveling to see El Greco's masterpiece for nearly four hundred years. What could I ever do, I wondered, to get recognition like that?

The answer came soon enough. When the five of us left the church, an elderly Spanish lady took one look at me, dropped to her knees, and made the sign of the cross. An hour later, as we were about to enter a museum, another woman did the same; Eberhard approached her to ask for an explanation.

"Mystery solved," he reported back to us. "They think you're Prince Juan Carlos." All three girls burst out laughing but Eberhard put up his hand. "Actually, I don't blame them. Günter does bear a striking resemblance to the Prince. Both of them have high foreheads, light eyes, and wavy blond hair. They both have – forgive me for saying so, Günter – long, pointed noses, and they're both unusually tall besides."

Shortly after lunch Gisela noticed a magazine cover photo of Prince Juan Carlos at a newsstand. "You know, Eberhard," she said as she casually flipped the pages, "you may be on to something." Then she curtseyed to me as she jokingly added, "There must be some way we can use Prince Günter to our advantage."

"Don't even think about it," Eberhard shot back, much to my relief. "We can't and we won't. The last thing we need is a run-in with Franco's Guardia Civil!"

Later that night I escaped the stifling heat in my room and went outside to sleep on the wooden rack attached to the roof of our VW bus. As I lay on my back and gazed up at the stars, I was sure that my Doppelgänger Prince had never been lucky enough to do the same.

****

Over the course of our weeks together, while the rest of us snacked on plump, juicy grapes, Elfriede continued to wolf down candies. That is not to say that she wasn't willing to share. Each time she returned to the bus with a new assortment she tried, without success, to entice us to taste them.

"These are even better than the last ones!" she would insist. Then, just before her ghastly black teeth chomped down on yet another colorful fruit pastille, she would enthuse, "They're simply divine!"

The girls and I did our best to ignore her, but Eberhard could barely conceal his disgust. "She hates the taste of olive oil. She won't touch grapes. Paella isn't quite to her liking. Why on earth did she bother to come to Spain?" he complained to me when he and I checked into our double room in Madrid. "She could've just stayed home and rotted her teeth in Vienna."

On our last day in Madrid, after spending the morning in the Prado Museum, we followed Eberhard on a ten-minute walk to the Edelweiss German restaurant. "Let's see whether the lovely Elfriede can finally find something healthy to eat here," he whispered to me.

After studying the menu Christa, Gisela, Eberhard, and I ordered traditional dishes like sauerbraten and Wiener schnitzel. But not Elfriede who, after a long deliberation, selected a stew of sour kidneys simmered in chopped onion and sour cream. Each dish was served together with thick slices of German rye bread and pats of bright-yellow butter.

"At last!" Elfriede exclaimed as she slathered the butter on her bread. "A meal without olive oil!"

About half way through the meal, Eberhard flashed me a wicked grin. Then, just as Elfriede was about to lift another spoonful of the soupy brown stew to her lips, Eberhard turned to her and looked her straight in the eyes. "Let me ask you something," he said, while somehow managing to keep a straight face. "How can a pretty girl like you eat those disgusting piss filters?"

Elfriede's eyes opened wide with horror. Dropping her spoon into the half-eaten stew she rushed to the bathroom. The rest of us had nearly finished eating by the time she returned, as pale as cottage cheese, and sat back down. Glaring at Eberhard, she reached into her purse and retrieved a large piece of almond brittle that crackled when she bit into it. Then, without offering any of us a taste, she defiantly snapped her purse shut and sulked for the rest of the afternoon.

By the time our trip came to an end in Barcelona a few days later, all three young women were no longer on speaking terms with Eberhard. Having defiantly banded together with Elfriede amidst the flurry of candy wrappers in the backseat, Christa and Gisela ignored me as well, pointedly speaking Spanish among themselves as a reminder of my inferior education. When we parted company to return home, there was no suggestion from any of them that we keep in touch.

CHAPTER 45

I reached the café late on Sunday, September 24th, just as my parents were about to close shop for the night. My parents exchanged glances and I knew immediately that something was wrong. Mutti wiped her hands on her apron and gave me a hug. "Welcome home, Stretch. Come let's all sit down in the kitchen. Are you hungry?"

"Something's changed around here," I said, looking to each of them in turn. "What happened?"

Mutti sighed. "It's your brother again. He up and quit his musical instrument job at Monke and moved to Siegen to be an assistant manager at a youth hostel."

"I've always predicted he'd never amount to anything," my father added bitterly. "But I actually hoped he'd stick things out just this once. Can you imagine him leaving a well-paying job with a future for who knows what? Scrubbing floors? Washing bed linens?"

Mutti flashed me a sad smile. "We really shouldn't burden you with all this right now. While your father brings the day's receipts upstairs let me fix you some scrambled eggs with home fries and bacon and you can tell us all about your trip while you eat." Then she called out to my father. "Willi, don't forget to bring down Günter's mail!"

Four letters had arrived for me while I was away. Three were flat-out rejections. The fourth came from EPK, a meat wholesaler in Cologne, inviting me to schedule an interview with the company president, Mr. Petermann.

"Way to go, Stretch!" my father exclaimed. "You're finally on your way!" Rather than spoil the mood, I decided not to confess that the wholesale meat business would hardly have been my first career choice. I had deliberately written to Mr. Petermann on the assumption that no one else would think to apply there. Apparently, my strategy was paying off.

First thing Monday morning, I telephoned EPK, and two hours later, I was sitting across from Mr. Petermann himself. "Well, young man," he explained, "let me tell you a bit about our operation. EPK is a subsidiary of a large conglomerate in Gütersloh that slaughters the hogs they buy from local farmers. Each animal is then split in half and the parts are cooled close to freezing. Our job is to sell the meat directly to large supermarket chains. It's a new concept that eliminates the middleman." The salary he offered was more than three times what I had been paid at Arminius AG. "Just to be clear, Herr Nitsch, if you accept our offer, we'd train you in different divisions of the company with the goal of your becoming a member of management in a year or so. At the rate we're growing, we need lots of new blood at the junior executive level."

As Mr. Petermann spoke, long-forgotten images flashed through my mind of the night back in November 1944, shortly before my seventh birthday, when I watched in horror as my Opa, with the help of the two French prisoners of war who were working on our farm, whacked a struggling hog over the head and then hoisted it up on an iron hook in the barn before slitting its throat and draining the blood into a waiting bucket. I suddenly become aware that Mr. Petermann was awaiting my response. "That sounds like a wonderful opportunity, sir," I managed to say. "How soon can I start?"

"Would Monday, October second work for you?"

"Yes, sir, I'll be here bright and early," I said, and we shook hands.

****

"Perfect timing!" my father said when I told my parents I'd gotten the job. "The ANUGA Food Show is running all this week at the Cologne-Deutz fairgrounds. Now that you'll be working in the food industry, why don't you come along with me on Thursday? While you snack on all the free samples, you might even manage to pick up some useful pointers."

Thousands of exhibitors from all around the world had set up displays in the giant halls and the two of us walked for hours among the mouth-watering exhibits, munching on tasty sausage and cheese tidbits, sampling freshly-baked cookies, and stopping every so often to chat with sales reps who lavished my father with gifts of boxed chocolate candies with nougat filling, or bottles of almond and cherry liqueur. They hoped to persuade him to select their line of aluminum bowls, modern electric mixers, imported whisks, expensive confectioneries, canned fruits, exotic nuts and spices, or fruit liqueurs for his café. By 4 P.M. my father's feet hurt and he was more than ready to take the next bus home.

"I can manage these bags," he assured me, "so if you want to stay longer, that's fine with me." He and I walked together as far as the main entrance and then I went back inside to catch some of the exhibits my father and I had missed. I hadn't gone more than a few steps before I thought I heard a familiar high-pitched voice from the next aisle over. "Ladies and gentlemen! Check out our high quality, triple-decker stainless-steel pots! You heard me right! Triple-decker! It's the latest thing in cookware!" And sure enough, as soon as I turned the corner, there was my old army buddy, Powitzer, as skinny as ever, hawking his merchandise at the top of his lungs.

"Nitsch, what are *you* doing here?" he shrieked when he saw me. "We have to catch up! I've gotta work until seven, but if you're free later, let me treat you to supper."

At the end of the day, Powitzer drove me in his brand new red Mercedes to a restaurant in the old part of town. Along the way, I decided that both his driving and his complexion had improved.

"Judging from your car, you must be doing very well!" I commented as soon as we were seated.

"No one would take a lousy job like I've got if the money weren't good. If you want to know the truth, I hate what I do and my father's never forgiven me for not becoming an officer. Except when I'm at the ANUGA, I have to move from town to town hawking those damn pots in second-class department stores." He leaned forward and lowered his voice. "Why anyone would actually buy that crap is beyond me."

By the time the waitress brought us our dinner, Powitzer had already finished his second liter stein of Munich Löwenbrau and had started on his third. The food on his plate was untouched.

After I brought him up to date, Powitzer suddenly slammed down his empty stein and beckoned the waitress for another. "That reminds me. What ever happened to the rich chick in Luxembourg?"

"She's ancient history. I never saw her again."

"Nitsch, that was a serious mistake. The money you marry is money you don't have to work for!"

"Maybe so," I countered. "But that money comes at a steep price!"

"Say!" Powitzer said as he wiped his mouth with the back of his hand. "Just let me finish this one last stein and I'll drive you to the railroad station."

I shook my head, determined never to set foot in a car with him again. "Sorry, but I've got to go now or I'll miss my train. Thanks for supper. *Auf Wiedersehen!*"

"Take care, Nitsch. Hope we run into each other another time!" he replied. Then he hiccoughed loudly and gave me a mock military salute.

CHAPTER 46

*O*n my first day at EPK, after Mr. Petermann introduced me to the other twelve members of his staff, I was issued a crisp white smock and put to work calculating prices for the hog halves to be sold to each supermarket chain. This tedious routine was interrupted several times a week when Mr. Petermann took me along to mind-numbing seminars for executives of the meatpacking industry. Although most of my time was spent in the office, I sometimes slipped outside during my lunch hour to watch the sweaty workmen in their bloodstained uniforms strain as they unloaded trucks filled with unwieldy, pinkish-white severed carcasses with strangely elongated hind legs, the result of the hogs having been hung from thick metal hooks pierced through their ankles. Watching those men work made me feel better about my desk job.

Even so, after two months I was already wondering whether EPK and I were going to be a good fit. The other young men in my department, who were resentful that I was the only one being groomed for an executive position, ostracized me. Since math had never been my strong point, I hated doing complex price calculations hour after hour. So, by late November, after I returned from lunch one day to find bloody slabs of liver in the pockets of my smock, I had had just about enough.

Later that afternoon, when Mr. Petermann asked to see me in his office, I was almost hoping he was going to fire me.

"Well, Herr Nitsch," Mr. Petermann said, "it's time for you to learn more about our company, so I'm sending you to spend a day traveling to sales meetings with our chairman, Herr Steinmeier. Have an overnight bag packed and ready first thing Monday morning."

"Thank you, sir. I look forward to the opportunity."

Mr. Steinmeier pulled up to EPK behind the wheel of a late-model Mercedes SL190 sports car and stepped out to greet me. With his finely chiseled features, dark suntan, and blond hair, he bore a striking resemblance to the movie actor Tab Hunter, who was one of Mutti's favorites. From what I'd heard, in addition to the car he was driving, Mr. Steinmeier also owned four other identical models, which he kept parked at the airports in Berlin, Düsseldorf, Hamburg, and Munich since he was a frequent flyer and didn't want to bother with chauffeurs or car rentals.

As we drove to our first meeting in Düsseldorf, Mr. Steinmeier was friendly and relaxed. He chatted about his wife and three young children and inquired about my background and education, and even told a few jokes. But once we sat down at the negotiating table, he turned into a cunning fox, conciliatory and charming one minute, ready to pack up his papers and storm out in disgust the next, all the while wearing down the opposition from the two supermarket executives sitting across the table. By mid-afternoon, with a favorable contract tucked away in his briefcase, Mr. Steinmeier walked with me back to his car.

"You see how it's done?" he asked, as he flashed me a triumphant smile. "It's all a mind game. They're the mice; I'm the cat. And I rarely lose my prey."

It was late afternoon by the time we reached Bremen for the last meeting of the day. At stake was the negotiated price for the sale of several million Deutschmarks worth of hog halves to the largest supermarket chain in Germany. By 1:30 A.M. the long conference table was littered with sandwich wrappers, cake crumbs, and empty coffee cups. The supermarket executives had long since removed their jackets. Sweat had wilted the starch in their crisp shirts and all four men had deep circles under their eyes. Looking as fresh and alert as he had first thing that morning, Mr. Steinmeier reached over to smile and shake each man's hand once the deal was concluded.

The streets were deserted at that late hour so we made good time driving over to the Park Hotel. Two uniformed bellhops carried our small overnight bags inside. "Ah, Herr Steinmeier!" the hotel night manager exclaimed as he rushed over to greet us. "I trust your meetings went well today? Please be sure to let me know if you need anything to make your stay with us more comfortable!"

After arranging for 6:15 A.M. wakeup calls, we followed the two bellhops into the elevator and went upstairs. My bellhop unlocked the door to my room, reached over to switch on the overhead light, and handed me the key. Until that time my only accommodations in Germany had been primitive tents, country haylofts, and barebones youth hostels. Still I had heard somewhere that bellhops expected to be tipped. The young man must have sensed my uneasiness. "Herr Steinmeier has taken care of everything, sir," he assured me before stepping back out into the corridor and gently closing the door behind him.

My "room" for the next four hours was actually a spacious suite. Soundproof double doors opened onto a large living room. Near the entrance, a small flap covered an alcove in the wall where guests were requested to leave their shoes to be shined while they slept, but worried that my shoes might be gone in the morning, I decided not to risk it. The adjoining bedroom was furnished with an oversized bed, a cozy armchair, and a mahogany writing desk. The tiled bathroom alone was bigger than the room Hubert and I shared over the café in Bergheim. All this luxury, I thought, as I dozed off under a thick down comforter, just from selling frozen hogs!

When my wakeup call came promptly at 6:15, I found that three newspapers, *Die Welt*, *The Financial Times*, and *Le Monde*, had been slipped under the door. I stuffed *The Financial Times* and *Le Monde* into my oversized briefcase and brought *Die Welt* down with me to the breakfast room. The waiter glanced at my room key and smiled. "Good morning, sir. You're the guest of Herr Steinmeier, I see. May I suggest the full breakfast?" A few minutes later he returned with an order of scrambled eggs, ham, toast, fresh rolls, butter and jam, and a steaming hot pot of black coffee. I ate slowly, soaking up the atmosphere and savoring every bite, as I skimmed the headlines in the paper.

I glanced up to discover several guests staring in my direction and the hair on the back of my neck began to prickle. Had I used the wrong fork? Was there a butter stain on my tie? But then I realized that all of the attention was actually directed at the corpulent man seated at the table next to mine who was engrossed in reading the sensational gossip and lurid stories in the *Bild-Zeitung*. When he put the newspaper down to take the last sip of his coffee, I recognized him right away; he was none other than Ludwig Erhard, the German Vice Chancellor and Minister of Economics.

Mr. Steinmeier joined me just as Ludwig Erhard was getting up to leave. "Good morning, Herr Nitsch, I trust the suite was to your liking?" He turned around to watch Mr. Erhard walk away. "First time you've seen the man in person, I suppose? If you ask me, he should skip breakfast, maybe lunch and dinner, too. The man's a blimp on two legs!" Then, as if to make his point, he ordered a spartan breakfast of black coffee, dry toast, and marmalade. "Now," he continued, after the waiter rushed back to the kitchen, "the schedule for today! We're going to a short meeting in Hamburg and then you can take the train back to Cologne. By the way, did I mention that Herr Petermann is planning to transfer you in January to Rendsburg up in northern Germany for three months? That way you can learn about our hog buying operation first hand. After that I'll want you to spend some time at our headquarters in Gütersloh."

****

When I arrived in Rendsburg on January 2, 1962, I reported to the branch manager, Mr. Donnermann, a tall potbellied man from Saxony with incredibly bad breath who had the manners of a drill sergeant. Leaning forward so that his face would nearly touch the person he was addressing, his voice harsh and angry, he hollered instructions as if they were military orders. "Nitsch," he shouted at me as I resisted the urge to back away, "let me tell you something about how to run a company! When I took on this position two years ago, every idiot here was doing whatever he damn pleased. There was no discipline! But as a former company commander in the *Wehrmacht* I shaped up the hopeless bunch of slackers around here." He leaned even closer to me and I prayed I wouldn't faint. "Herr Steinmeier was apprehensive about my methods at first but now even he realizes I'm irreplaceable!"

Mr. Donnermann assigned me a desk and I was once again put to work doing complicated pricing calculations. However, instead of just working with the frozen end product, as I had done in Cologne, the computations done by the fifteen of us in that office now involved everything from the ever-changing purchase price of the live hogs from the farmer to the end sale of the final product in quantities of hundreds and thousands to supermarket chains. While we slaved over the numbers, a dozen hog buyers in an adjacent office drove out into the countryside every day, traveling from farm to farm to secure the future delivery of hogs as of a certain date.

But the heart of the Rendsburg operation was the slaughterhouse where several dozen butchers put in twelve-hour days, even longer if necessary when the demand was great, and in late January, I was invited to watch them work. Amid the stench of live hogs, singed hair and bristles, intestines, guts, blood, and human sweat, the process moved forward with grim precision. Squealing hogs were herded into a v-shaped passageway that gradually narrowed until only one animal could pass through at a time. Standing just outside the low wooden wall, a worker with an electric stun gun knocked each hog senseless just as it fell onto a slow-moving conveyor belt where two workers were waiting to stick hooks into the hind legs and hoist the unconscious creature onto a moving belt which glided forward on roller bearers to the next station. In only a matter of seconds, the animal then moved past a workman who used a gas burner to singe off all the body hair and a second workman who sprayed the lifeless creature with scalding hot water, before reaching a station where another man quickly scraped the skin clean.

Since I had spent my early childhood on my Opa's farm in East Prussia, I didn't flinch when the next man in line deftly slit open the hog's neck, releasing a torrent of blood, which gradually slowed to a trickle. Next the abdominal wall was slit open allowing the steaming intestines to spill out into a large vat. A second washing cleaned off any remaining blood before a worker sawed the hog in half, starting between the hind legs and continuing down the exact middle of the spine. After a final wash down, the two halves were briskly moved into a freezing facility.

"There you have it, Herr Nitsch," the supervisor who had given me the guided tour said when we stepped back outside. "You must admit the process is efficient, clean, and almost painless."

Since my job was on the line, I complimented him on the speed of the operation. Secretly, however, I vowed never again to eat anything made from pork.

CHAPTER 47

By the 14th of February when I knew that Carnival was in full swing in Cologne, I resented more than ever my dull job next door to the slaughterhouse, and for the first time, I even felt a little homesick. Since Mr. Donnermann did not permit employees to make personal calls from the office, I walked over to the post office during my lunch hour to phone Mutti. When she answered on the second ring, I could hear the chatter of café customers in the background.

"Günter! I'm so glad you called. We were planning to call you anyhow." Mutti stopped talking for a minute to give instructions to one of the shopgirls. "Listen, as you can hear, I've got too many customers at the moment. I'll let you talk to Vati in the kitchen."

Less than a minute later my father came on the line. "Stretch, I've taken the liberty of opening a letter to you from the Konsum Food Co-Op. And guess what? A Dr. Schlohwitt wants to see you for an interview in Hamburg about a position in their next executive training program. Stretch? Are you still there? I hope you don't mind that I read the letter. When I saw the name Konsum I thought..."

"Do I mind? That's the best news I've had in ages! Let me write down the contact information and I'll call him right now." I took a pad out of my briefcase and jotted down the name, address, and telephone number. Then, as soon as I got off the phone with my father, I called Dr. Schlohwitt to set up an appointment for Friday, the 16th.

That Friday, after calling in sick, I took the train to Hamburg where I met with Dr. Schlohwitt and several other high-ranking Konsum executives. The end result was a contract for an eighteen-month executive training program starting on Monday, April second. The training would begin with a month-long seminar at the Hamburg training center, after which I would spend the next six months assigned to the Konsum in Göppingen near Stuttgart, followed by another month of training in Hamburg in November. "We'll let you know as the time approaches where you'll be assigned after that," Dr. Schlohwitt explained. Just then his secretary buzzed him on the intercom. "Excuse me just a moment while I take this call," he said, reaching for the receiver. After a brief conversation, he turned back to me. "This is a bit awkward, Herr Nitsch, but I was just advised that the manager in Göppingen is somewhat old-fashioned. Since you'll be his first executive trainee from this program, he's insisting on meeting you before he agrees to put you on his payroll for half a year. Mind you, it's only a formality, but we'd appreciate it if you'd go down there within the next two or three weeks to introduce yourself to Herr Altholz. Of course all of your travel expenses will be reimbursed to you by us here in Hamburg."

"Consider it done sir," I assured him.

****

"So, Nitsch, I see you've made a full recovery," Mr. Donnermann sneered on my return to Rendsburg on Monday morning. "Don't think I'm not wise to you! You went home for the Cologne Carnival didn't you? I can smell it!"

"Herr Donnermann," I replied sharply, looking him square in the eyes, "I'm not going to dignify that accusation with an answer," and I stormed back to my desk. All weekend long I had been wrestling with my conscience since EPK regulations required me to give a full month's

337

notice, which I had no intention of doing. Now, Mr. Donnermann had given me the opening I needed. An hour later I went to his office. "I just want you to know that February 27th will be my last day here," I announced.

He shrugged his shoulders. "Fine with me!" he snapped. "That's just fine with me!"

Right after work on the 27th of February I packed up my two suitcases and took the train to Bergheim. My father was upstairs doing his bookkeeping when I got home. "I hope you don't mind my switching jobs like this," I said, thinking of how he had reacted when Hubert did the same.

"Not at all. Mutti and I knew you only took the job at that pig factory when nothing else came through. At the Konsum, on the other hand, you'll have a real future."

I set out early the next morning for the six-hour trip to Göppingen, changing trains three times along the way. Mr. Altholz was a pudgy man of medium height with a crisply starched handkerchief in the breast pocket of his three-piece suit. He had a booming voice, a thick regional accent, and a habit of glaring over the top of his eyeglass frames like a strict schoolmaster. "So, Herr Nitsch," he said, after glancing over my résumé, "I see that you're not a university graduate."

"Is that a problem, sir?" I ask, suddenly anxious.

"Not for me it isn't. Those egghead types always hate to get their hands dirty. All theory and no practice, if you know what I mean." For the next twenty minutes he grilled me about my work experience and my time in the army. Then he leaned back in his chair. "I'm sure you'll work out fine, but before you go, I want to make sure you understand the ground rules around here. When you get to Göppingen on the first of May, we will have rented a no-frills furnished room for you. As an old Social Democrat and a former union man I expect our employees to maintain a modest life-style because we're not, as you hopefully know, some giant stock corporation; we're a co-op, and besides the unions, our customers own our company. Our customers are our final bosses, Herr Nitsch."

"Dr. Schlohwitt in Hamburg explained the Konsum organization to me," I assured him.

"Did he really? What does *he* know? Has he ever sold sauerkraut and pickles from a barrel or had to deal with salesgirls who don't show up because it's snowing? At the seminar in Hamburg you'll hear lots of fancy theories but there's a big difference between theory and practice." He picked up the phone and called his secretary. Giving up all pretense of speaking High German, he barked instructions into the phone in the Swabian dialect, which I only understood thanks to the year I spent with my army buddies from Stuttgart. As he talked, he jotted down some notes. "Here's the address of the inn where you'll be staying tonight," he said, handing me the slip of paper. "I'll give Dr. Schlohwitt a call to let him know that you can start here on the second of May. Now, unless you have any more questions for me, I have to get back to work!" The whole meeting had lasted less than an hour.

A far cry from the Park Hotel in Bremen, the room I'd been assigned at the inn was small and sparsely furnished. A bathroom and shower were two doors further down the hall. As I lay awake listening to my neighbors through the paper-thin walls, I got my first taste of Mr. Altholz's notion of a modest lifestyle.

****

Since I had to go through there anyway on my way home, I left Göppingen right after breakfast the next morning and stopped off in Frankfurt to bring my application for a Green Card and my passport photos to the American Consulate. Earlier in the month, the United States had declared an embargo on Cuba, heightening tensions with the Soviet Union. Perhaps that explained why American tanks were in position on every surrounding street ready to pulverize approaching vehicles if necessary and also why I was questioned by foot soldiers at several checkpoints and then thoroughly body-searched before being allowed to enter the Consulate. At long last I had my face-to-face meeting with a young consular official. After interviewing me and reviewing the paperwork, she smiled and asked if I had any questions.

"I do have one concern. I've heard that there's a German quota. Will that affect me in any way?"

"Don't worry about it," she assured me. "Until around 1955, we had to turn away German applicants but ever since then, we actually don't get enough Germans to fill the quota."

"That's strange. I didn't expect that!"

"It is strange," she admitted. Then she leaned forward and lowered her voice to a whisper. "Actually, the way things are right now, a Norwegian milkmaid with an eighth grade education would have an easier time getting a Green Card than an African scientist with a Ph.D. in physics." When I didn't respond she raised one eyebrow. "You *do* understand what I mean?" I nodded, trying to hide my discomfort. "Yes, I was sure you would," and she gave me a knowing wink. "Well then, back to business! There's one more thing you still need to do, and that is to find an American citizen willing to sponsor you. After that you'll be all set to go."

On the way back to Bergheim I once again let myself daydream about living in the America I'd seen in the movies. I envisioned a place where six people could sit comfortably in over-sized cars; where executives worked in towering skyscrapers; where cowboys like *Billy Jenkins* rode prancing palominos across the western plains; where teenagers lived on hamburgers and ketchup; where vibrant jazz clubs could be found in every major city; the America I'd read about in *Life* and in *Ebony* at the Amerika-Haus in Cologne and not the close-minded place described by the consular official. Now, if only I could find an American sponsor, I would have a safe haven should the Russians once again threaten to invade from the East.

CHAPTER 48

L ate on the afternoon of Sunday, April 1, 1962, I checked in at the Konsum Training Academy, a cluster of old, redbrick buildings on a quiet street in Hamburg, and was assigned a spacious single room for my first one-month training session. Before heading down to dinner, I dropped off my suitcase and after surveying the furnishings – a bed, a large wooden wardrobe, two chairs, and a sturdy office desk strategically placed in front of the window – I began to feel more confident about what my "modest" accommodations in Göppingen would be like.

When all fifty-five of us assembled in the dining hall to chat before dinner, I noticed to my disappointment that there wasn't a single female candidate in the group. As soon as we had taken our seats, Dr. Schlohwitt stood up at the head table to address us. "Welcome, gentlemen! You are all about to embark on an exciting adventure leading to challenging management positions. As you know, we currently have 80,000 employees serving our 2.6 million members in almost 10,000 Konsum retail shops and small supermarkets throughout Germany. Following the latest industry trends we plan to convert many of our smaller retail food shops into modern supermarkets and to expand the floor space of our existing supermarkets. So, when you leave here to work in our various regional offices, you'll be getting in on the ground floor of this exciting new undertaking. Well, that's all for now. We'll get down to business tomorrow morning in our lecture hall. Enjoy your meal!"

All of us knew that, barring extraordinary circumstances, we were each assured a junior executive position with the Konsum at the completion of the eighteen-month training period. There was, however, a big difference between a permanent assignment in a big city like Berlin and a post in a small town like Göppingen. So, for the first few days, we all secretly sized up our fellow candidates to see how we measured up. From my point of view, the results weren't encouraging. Six of the men in our group had already worked as supermarket managers for several years. Of the rest, except for one other business school graduate, they all had university degrees. Several even had doctorates and a few, like Hans Spiessmacher, who sat at my table, were lawyers. Competition would be tough.

The training was intense. Over the next four weeks, in addition to listening all day to faculty members and high-ranking Konsum executives lecture on marketing, sales techniques, advertising, administration, and cost accounting, we worked together in small groups for several hours each evening on case studies. By the end of April, we were all looking forward to our first fieldwork assignments.

****

All of the shops in Göppingen were closed in honor of Labor Day when I arrived there on Thursday, May 1st. Lugging my heavy suitcase I set out in search of the boarding house where Mr. Altholz's secretary had rented a furnished room for me. My landlady, Mrs. Häberle, owned a small brick house with a sloping roof on a leafy street not far from the railroad station. Daffodils were already peeking up in her fenced-in garden and a pleasing aroma of freshly cut grass and apple blossoms filled the air. Even so, there were also ominous signs like the black cat that hissed at me when I walked past the rusty iron pump and the wooden water trough just like the ones farmers had once used when I was a small child back in East Prussia.

A matronly woman with unruly tufts of gray hair opened the dark-green wooden front door as soon as I knocked. "You must be Herr Nitsch. Welcome to Geppinge! I'm Frau Häberle. If you'll just follow me, I'll show you where you'll be staying." She led me into a small corner room with two windows that looked out on the antique pump under the apple trees. An old-fashioned canopy bed was next to the far wall, and opposite it, an armoire that must have once belonged to Mrs. Häberle's great-grandfather, a tiny table with a vase full of wildflowers, one stool, and a small dresser. Doilies, yellowed with age, covered every horizontal surface except the wooden floor. Atop the dresser was a porcelain bowl decorated with hand-painted yellow flowers and green leaves and beside it, a matching porcelain pitcher filled with water.

"So, what do you think?" Mrs. Häberle gushed. "I've given you the prettiest and brightest room in the house. If you need more water for the pitcher when you wash up in the morning, the pump is right outside. There's even a flush toilet right down the hall. And Herr Nitsch, for all these wonderful amenities, I'm only charging you forty Deutschmarks a month!"

"That's certainly reasonable," I replied politely, while trying to hide my dismay. "But is there a reason why you haven't mentioned a shower or a bathtub?"

"Oh, I don't have either of those, of course. This house is over three hundred years old, you know, and the toilet I had installed two years ago cost me a small fortune. But on Saturdays after work you could always go to the Geppinge indoor swimming pool. From what I hear, they have lots of showers over there." Then, to add insult to injury, just as she was about to leave the room Mrs. Häberle turned suddenly serious. "There's just one more thing, Herr Nitsch. It should go without saying that I don't tolerate any female visitors in my house!"

****

First thing Friday morning, Mr. Altholz introduced me to several other staff members before assigning me to a desk in the large room where his secretary and his two female assistants had their workstations. After handing me a stack of files, he addressed me in his booming voice. "If you study these materials, you'll have an idea about the sales generated by each of the stores in our district. Starting tomorrow, you'll be accompanying one of our store inspectors, Herr Butka, when he visits store managers to talk to them about sales, marketing campaigns, pricing, personnel and the like. Oh, and before I forget, I hope you're happy with your furnished room! The low rent Frau Häberle is charging you is a terrific deal. And just so you know, she's a long-time member of our Konsum and one of our most faithful customers."

I hesitated before replying. "Well, sir, I was wondering about the lack of a shower or a bathtub..."

Mr. Altholz held up his hand. "Herr Nitsch, as I'm sure Frau Häberle has already told you, we have a wonderful indoor swimming pool here in town. On Saturdays after work you can go there and take all the showers you want."

"Yes, sir, she did mention it."

"Well, then, I'm glad that's settled," Mr. Altholz said and he rushed back to his office.

****

Mr. Butka, whose thick blond hair encircling a large round bald spot gave him the appearance of an escaped monk, shook my hand and greeted me warmly the next morning. "Nice to have you on board, Herr Nitsch. I'll do my best to show you the ropes!" Ten minutes later we were driving through a hilly, green landscape to a Konsum store in the village of Süssen. "You're single I suppose?" he asked me without waiting for a reply. "Me, I'm married with two teenage daughters. My wife and I spoil them rotten to make up for everything we missed in our own childhoods, I suppose. We've just built a new house not far from here with bathrooms on the first and second floors. Imagine that!"

"I certainly envy you," I said, and then I blurted out the whole story about my room at Mrs. Häberle's boarding house.

"Well, you are in a pickle, aren't you?" Mr. Butka said sympathetically. "You know, there's a brand-new ten-story apartment building in Göppingen where you could get yourself a studio apartment that would be much more suitable. Trouble is, the rent there would be substantially higher than what you're paying, and besides, it would mean hurting Frau Häberle's feelings. I'm willing to bet you'd never get Herr Altholz's approval."

Despite Mr. Butka's reservations, I decided to investigate further. The rental agent at the high-rise had a sunlit studio available on the seventh floor with a large window, a fantastic view over Göppingen, modern furniture, a compact kitchenette, and a full bathroom with a shower, all for a mere 110 Deutschmarks a month, less than sixteen percent of my monthly salary. If I hadn't needed Mr. Altholz's approval, I would have rented it on the spot.

Screwing up all my courage, I went straight to Mr. Altholz first thing on Monday morning to explain to him my reasons for wanting to move.

"Out of the question, Herr Nitsch! Completely out of the question!" he shouted. "Can you imagine the scandal if our members found out that a junior staff member on the Konsum payroll was living in the only luxury high-rise building in Göppingen? Our members and our customers come first, Herr Nitsch. There's no bending that rule! Besides, think of the money you can save where you are now. And if those aren't enough reasons, think of how your leaving would hurt that poor war widow, Frau Häberle. I won't stand for it!"

Although I was steaming mad, I tried desperately to work out a compromise. "I'm sorry, Herr Altholz, but I fail to understand why I shouldn't be allowed to spend a mere sixteen percent of my monthly salary on rent when most people I know spend a third or more. Still, out of respect for our members and customers, I'm willing to forget about the studio. However, just so you know, I can't stay in Frau Häberle's house and I intend to look for an alternative."

For a second I thought he would explode, but instead he simply said, "Just a minute; I'll be right back." From next door I could hear his muffled voice as he talked rapidly to his secretary in the Swabian dialect. A few minutes later he returned to his office. "I had to verify something. Would you by any chance consider living in the Catholic Student Home? They have common bathrooms and showers, a dining hall, a recreation room, and a small library. Of course, you'd have a roommate but the nuns would clean the room and give you fresh linen once a week and a daily breakfast is included. Unfortunately, they charge the exorbitant sum of 80 Deutschmarks a month. But if you want to be that extravagant, I think our customers would tolerate the idea." Before I could agree to this suggestion, he continued, "I'm cutting you some slack, Herr Nitsch, seeing as you're new to this area and you evidently don't have a clue about the mentality of the Swabian people. I was born and raised around here and let me assure you that there's a lot of truth in our proverb: 'In Swabianland our money-saving drive is stronger than our sex drive.'"

"That's good to know," I said, and we both laughed. Then, before he could change his mind, I quickly added, "Herr Altholz, about that Catholic Student Home. I really appreciate your suggestion. It might be just what I need!"

When I woke up early the next morning, the sun, streaming through the ancient gauze curtains covering my windows, was already warming up my room. On such a beautiful day it seemed a shame to wash up indoors. Besides it was a nuisance afterwards to have to wipe up the wet floor, empty the dirty water over the flowerbeds, and refill the pitcher. So, taking the chance that Mrs. Häberle was still asleep, I put on a pair of blue jeans and my slippers and went outside to wash up at the pump. The metal handle squeaked a few times as I pressed it up and down but I was rewarded with a refreshing flow of cool water. When I left for work a short time later I was the cleanest I'd been in four days.

Immediately after work I stopped at the Catholic Student Home. The office door was wide open but since no one was inside I peeked into the crowded dining room where dozens of young men were eating their supper. An elderly nun saw me standing in the doorway and walked over. "Excuse me, young man, are you looking for someone in particular?"

"Actually, Sister, I just started on an executive training program at the Konsum and I'm looking for a place to live."

"Well, in that case, I'm just the person you need to see. My name is Sister Maria and I'm in charge of the Residence. Why don't we go back to my office where it's a bit quieter so we can talk?" The more Sister Maria told me, the more I was determined to move in. As she explained, most of the boarders were German and foreign students, German apprentices, and junior engineers.

"How soon would a room be available?" I asked.

"Actually, we have several vacancies so feel free to move in any time," she assured me. "Just let me know when you'd like to start."

When I got home a little later than usual, Mrs. Häberle was watching for me in the doorway. She glared at me reproachfully as I came down the front walk. "So there you are, Herr Nitsch! I can't begin to tell you how appalled I am about your behavior this morning. Imagine my shock when my neighbors told me they saw you running around naked in the yard and washing yourself at the pump. I've been beside myself all day just thinking about it and I'm sorry to say if you ever do that again, you'll have to look for another place to live." Her face was flushed as she waited nervously for me to apologize.

But I saw the situation differently. On my way back from my talk with Sister Maria I had been wondering how best to terminate my lease.

Now, my landlady had given me the perfect excuse. "Frau Häberle," I replied calmly. "First of all, just so you know, I wasn't naked; I was wearing jeans. But since you feel so strongly about what happened, I'll move out tonight!"

"As you wish. It's probably better for both of us. But what about the first month's rent, Herr Nitsch?"

"Why don't you keep it, Frau Häberle?" I replied magnanimously. Then, without wasting another minute, I packed my suitcase and returned to the Catholic Student Home.

"Back already?" Sister Maria greeted me. "You're a young man who knows his mind!" She handed me a key to a room on the second floor. "Your roommate is a young barber but I don't think he's home tonight," she explained. "He only sleeps here a few nights during the week."

As it turned out, my roommate was a handsome young man in his mid-twenties who spent the weekends and several days during the workweek at his girlfriend's apartment in a neighboring village. On the rare nights when he stayed over in Göppingen, he always pulled up in front of the Student Home in a shiny new slate blue Karmann Ghia car with a white roof. Our paths rarely crossed and when they did, we had little in common to talk about. Even so, his obvious affluence piqued my curiosity.

"Mind if I ask you something?" I inquired the second time he stayed over. "I'm making pretty good money over at the Konsum, but not enough to afford a car right now. How do you manage it?"

He grinned. "Can you keep a secret? Promise me you won't tell anybody here?"

"You have my word," I said, suddenly uneasy about what he might reveal.

"You're right. I couldn't afford the car on what I earn at the barbershop. So after work and on weekends I go to private homes but mostly to funeral parlors and shave corpses. Sometimes I even give them a haircut. The dead have to look their best too, you know." He leaned back in his chair and waited for my reaction.

"I wouldn't have the stomach for it," I finally said.

"I was squeamish too when I started two years ago. But I don't think about it any more." He walked over to the window and pointed at his car parked in the street below. "The money's just too good! There's one drawback, though. Girls don't find the idea at all appealing and the job doesn't make for good dinner table conversation. Lucky for me I found a girlfriend who doesn't mind."

Since my roommate was rarely there, I made it my business to seek out different people to sit with at dinner every evening. On the fourth night as I walked around the dining room with my tray, I overheard four young men speaking English.

"Mind if I pull up another chair and join you?" I asked and they all moved their chairs closer together to make room for me.

Three of the men – Ravi from India, Hiroshi from Japan, and Paul from Germany – were engineers employed by Schuler Presses, one of the largest employers in Göppingen. The fourth was Robert Proctor, a young American from San Anselmo, California.

"Nice to meet you, Günter," Bob said. "We were just talking about a former resident named Jean Paul who went back home this morning." As Bob explained, since Jean Paul was from Senegal, his native language was French although he also spoke German quite well. A few weeks earlier, shortly after he'd arrived from Africa, he had wandered into a local bar frequented by white American soldiers from the Cooke Barracks.

Ravi picked up the story at that point. "They yelled at him to 'Get out!' but of course he didn't understand them. From what he told us later, some of the soldiers figured he was only pretending not to speak English. So what did they do? They beat him to a pulp! He spent weeks in the hospital."

"Why didn't the German barkeeper interfere?" I asked.

"The white *Amis* are his best customers, I suppose, and he didn't want to ruffle their feathers," Paul said. "It's not like he's going to offend any Negro GIs. They have their own places to hang out."

"I saw the same thing, white bars and Negro bars, when I was on maneuvers in Baumholder. Even at a Count Basie concert Negroes sat with Negroes; whites with whites. Funny, but I didn't think anything of it at the time."

"You have a lot to learn about America," Bob said sadly. "A whole lot to learn."

After that first meeting, the five of us met up in the dining hall nearly every evening, and from there, we all grabbed bottles of beer and headed over to the residence lounge where we spent the next few hours talking about current events and listening to Paul read aloud from *The Morgue and Other Poems* and *Flesh*, both by Gottfried Benn, a poet-physician who had specialized in treating venereal diseases and whose nihilistic writing was accordingly filled with genuine angst and despair about the human condition.

But the highlight of the week came on Sunday mornings when Hiroshi clacked his way down to breakfast in his flat-bottomed wooden-soled thongs dressed in an ankle-length black and white kimono with a grey obi sash. After having lived in Göppingen for five years, Hiroshi could speak Swabian as well as High German and so, after we finished eating, we all walked over to a nearby pub where, after one or two beers, Hiroshi regaled the local farmers with off-color jokes told in the local dialect.

Of the four young men, I eventually got to know Bob Proctor the best. A tall, slim curly-haired college student from Marin County, Bob was spending a year improving his German while working at a job in a local factory that his parents had arranged for him through their connections to a wealthy German businessman in California. Bob's mother owned a beauty parlor in San Rafael; his father was a U.S. customs official in San Francisco. Quite often Bob and I sat together in the lounge consulting on difficult words and phrases in English and German. One day he stumped me by asking for the German word for a university campus. "You know," he explained, "that big grassy area where the students go to sunbathe or to play Frisbee or to read their textbooks under a tree."

I tried my best to picture what he was describing. "As far as I know, nothing like that exists in Germany," I finally said.

"That can't be true," he said. "No campus?"

Paul had overheard our conversation and was quick to agree with me. "Bob, Günter's right. We don't have campuses and you want to know why? Because here in Germany the universities are government financed and there isn't enough money to buy all that real estate."

I turned to Bob and smiled. "So I guess *you* still have a whole lot to learn about Germany."

"Touché!" he conceded and we all had another sip of beer.

CHAPTER 49

*I*accompanied Mr. Butka on daily trips to the surrounding Konsum stores and admired the way he lavished praise when it was deserved but could also give constructive criticism if warranted, all in either High German or Swabian, depending on the person he was addressing. As we went from place to place, we talked about business, current events, and life in general. Yet after only a few days, his comments took an alarming turn because every time Mr. Butka noticed a curvaceous teenage salesgirl in one of our stores, he confided to me that he would like to go to bed with her.

"You know, Herr Nitsch," he told me in attempting to justify his undisguised appetite for young girls, "when you've been married to the same women for twenty-two years as I have, the desire for your own wife has long since faded away. To be honest, I barely touch my old lady anymore and then I really have to force myself. In my opinion monogamy isn't normal for most men. We only act like it is because the Catholic Church has been drumming the idea into our heads for almost two thousand years."

Clearly this was not a situation that had been addressed at the training seminar in Hamburg and I struggled to find the proper response. "I'm sorry you feel that way," I finally said. Then, after pausing for a few seconds, I nonchalantly added, "How old did you say your daughters are now, Herr Butka?"

For a moment he looked baffled and then he somewhat sheepishly replied, "They're seventeen and fifteen. A difficult age, I can assure you."

Apparently I had hit a nerve. If Mr. Butka lusted after the salesgirls after that, he never mentioned it to me.

****

After my training period with Mr. Butka was finished towards the end of July, I took a few of my vacation days before starting to accompany the other store inspector, Mr. Pietsch, for the second half of my Göppingen training. My father had often told me wonderful things about Vienna, where he had worked in a military hospital during the war, so I decided to economize by hitchhiking to Austria, before returning by train that Sunday. My plan was risky. If Mr. Altholz found out that one of his well-paid junior staff members was disgracing the company by thumbing a ride, it might well cost me my job. To be on the safe side, I took a bus and then a taxi to the Autobahn on-ramp early Wednesday morning before flagging down the first car. By that evening, I had checked into a youth hostel in the Austrian capital, and over the next two days I had seen all of the tourist attractions within walking distance. As had been the case in Paris, wherever I went – St. Stefan's Cathedral, the Prater amusement park, Schönbrunn Palace, or the famous open-air Naschmarkt – I wondered if my father, dressed in his crisp *Luftwaffe* uniform, had once strolled there arm-in-arm with one of the local girls while his family was a thousand kilometers away in East Prussia.

At the suggestion of an employee at the youth hostel, on my last night in Vienna I went by tram to Grinzing in the northwest part of the city, a district popular with tourists because of its many quaint restaurants and outdoor wine gardens. To my dismay, Grinzing was overrun with large groups of tipsy, middle-aged tourists at least double my age. The only young person I met there was Bianca, a beautiful young woman with pitch-black hair and light-brown skin who was the tour leader for a group of elderly, well-to-do Brazilians. She and I danced a few waltzes and then, after we both walked her group back to their hotel, we spent the rest of the night together. Had she lived in Germany, I would definitely have wanted to see Bianca again, but since she would soon fly back to Rio de Janeiro, there was no point in pursuing her. Someday, I vowed as I picked up my rucksack from the youth hostel and rushed to catch the train back to Göppingen the next morning, I would meet a local girl from Cologne and start a relationship with a future.

****

On Monday morning, August 6, 1962, Mr. Pietsch parked in front of the office to pick me up. At least a head shorter than I was and grossly overweight, he had a fleshy red face, stringy blond hair, a double chin, and the habit of gasping for air at the start of every sentence. Although he was only in his early thirties, he had already spent more than fifteen years with the Konsum, having started as an apprentice sales clerk at the age of fourteen.

"Let's go! We've got a lot of work to do," he snapped at me. "You know," he said as we drove out into the country, "I worked my way up to this store inspector job the hard way. There weren't any fancy training programs like yours when I started. I had to work my butt off to get this far." He took a deep breath before continuing. "I suppose you're being groomed for something even better. Let me ask you something, Günter Nitsch. Did you receive the matriculation standard when you graduated from that fancy business school of yours?" I shook my head. "Not that it matters. Education isn't the key to success, you know. All a man needs is drive and hard work. I barely made it out of the eighth grade myself, and look at me now!"

Mr. Pietsch let his words sink in before needling me again. "So, Günter Nitsch, I understand you know English. How good is your English anyway?"

"It's actually pretty good! I can read English newspapers and books, and where I used to work, I even wrote a few business letters to customers in England and America."

"Glad to hear it, because I need a translation of a brochure," he said.

While pressing his enormous belly against the steering wheel to hold it steady, he let go with both hands and fumbled to reach a colorful brochure on the floor behind his seat. Flipping it open, he handed it to me, grabbing on to the wheel again just in time to steer the car into a sharp curve. "So," he said, "read it to me in German!"

The brochure contained glossy photographs and technical specifications about Tyler walk-in freezers. "With all due respect, Herr Pietsch," I protested. "You must be joking. I'd have to be an engineer to translate this stuff."

"What a let down," he sneered. "And I thought you knew English!" Then chewing the fingernails on his right hand while steering with the left, he drove on in silence.

As I soon discovered, except when he was kowtowing to Mr. Altholz, Mr. Pietsch was just as nasty to everyone else as he was to me. No one he dealt with, from store managers to stockroom clerks, was spared his snide comments. The worst treatment was dished out to the store managers we visited during our first two inspections in the morning. After that, Mr. Pietsch gobbled down the thick sandwich of sausage or of cheese that his wife had packed for his second breakfast and his manner became somewhat more tolerable. Nothing, it seemed, was more important to Mr. Pietsch than food. In each store along our route he "tried a sample" as he put it. More accurately, he tried everything – slices of sausage, of ham, of cheese; herring salad, potato salad, bean salad, macaroni salad – whatever he could get his greedy hands on. Even half an hour after a big lunch he would start to salivate as he approached the supermarket meat counter. To his credit, Mr. Pietsch always paid for the ice cream, candy, and chocolate bars that supplemented his diet yet, whenever he brought those items to the cashier, he made sure she heard him grumble under his breath that, "I really shouldn't have to pay for this!"

Mr. Pietsch must have lain awake nights thinking of ways to make my life miserable. On two separate occasions, just to show off his power, he ordered me to stand outside a Konsum food market in the village of Süssen all day long selling new spring potatoes out of an enormous crate that ran the whole length of the storefront and extended half way across the sidewalk. But two could play that game. Rather than protest, I sold so many potatoes that, by the end of the afternoon, I had to bend way down to scoop the last ones out for a waiting customer. To my relief, Mr. Pietsch was more civil towards me after that, even promising to take me along to a typical "start the weekend" celebration in Göppingen's largest Konsum food store the following Saturday afternoon.

When we arrived for the party shortly after closing hours, Mr. Pietsch and I walked past three young apprentices who were busy mopping the floors, scouring the cheese-cutting machines, and wiping down the countertops, to join Mr. Novotny and his nine sales clerks over by the deli counter where they were already eating sandwiches and drinking beer. The closer we came to where they were standing, the more I was aware of a putrid odor that burned my nose and stung my throat.

I had met Mr. Novotny weeks earlier and knew that he was from Vienna, but of course I couldn't risk my job by talking to him about how I had sneaked off to spend a few days there. He greeted me warmly and then asked, "So how's Herr Pietsch treating you?" Then he winked to let me know that no reply was necessary; he already knew the answer. "Help yourself to a sandwich!" he said cheerfully, holding out a tray filled with small rolls. Mr. Pietsch, I noticed, was already on his second and starting on his third. "Just so you know, Herr Nitsch, I fixed the cheese spread myself. It's an old recipe passed down from my Sardinian grandmother."

As soon as I took the sandwich from the tray I knew the source of the pungent odor; it came from Mr. Novotny's cheese spread. Even with the help of a tall bottle of Dinkelacker beer to wash it down, the minced onions, tiny specks of red pepper, and thick black pepper in the cheese made my mouth burn. And all the while the smell, that awful smell, was worse than rotting meat. To make matters worse, out of the corner of my eye, I noticed Mr. Pietsch watching me like a hawk, relishing every second of my discomfort.

When I had forced down the last bite, Mr. Novotny rubbed his hands together expectantly. "So, Herr Nitsch, how'd you like it?"

"To be honest, sir, it's a bit too spicy for my taste," I confessed, trying not to hurt his feelings. "So, if you don't mind, I'll have a salami roll next."

"That's fine with me. Since I'm sure Herr Pietsch warned you in advance, I was surprised that you were even willing to try one."

Mr. Pietsch swallowed the piece of cheese he had just stuffed into his mouth and his lips curled into a wicked grin. "Oh dear!" he said, his voice dripping with sarcasm. "I guess I forgot to tell you the recipe, Günter Nitsch. The spread's made from chopped onions, paprika and lots of black pepper, of course. But the secret ingredient is a very ripe Camembert cheese full of maggots. It's the maggots that give it that special flavor!" and then he doubled over with laughter.

CHAPTER 50

O ne evening I finally got around to phoning Siegfried Reimold, my old army buddy. When he heard that I had been living and working in Göppingen for nearly half a year, he chuckled. "How're you managing to talk to those peasant folks out in the boondocks?"

"Thanks to the head start you gave me back in Koblenz, I'm actually getting pretty good at it," I assured him.

"Well it's high time you got to see the more civilized parts of Swabianland," Siegfried replied. "I'm having dinner with my parents next Sunday. Why don't you join us?"

Siegfried picked me up from the Stuttgart railroad station in a brand-new Mercedes. "Wow!" I exclaimed. "Your father has a really nice car!"

He shook his head. "This one's mine; my parents have their own." He glanced over at me and grinned. "It's not like we won the soccer Toto or anything. My father's a master mechanic at the Mercedes Benz plant so he gets the cars at a great discount."

Siegfried's mother had cooked up a traditional Swabian meal. We started with *Maultaschensuppe* – noodle dumplings filled with minced meat, spinach, onions, and bread crumbs, in a clear broth – followed by Swabian beef escalope with crispy onions, and to top things off, for dessert, we had *Nonnepfürzle* – the name literally meant "little nun farts" – sweet dough cakes fried in oil and dusted with powdered sugar.

"I don't dare ask about the origin of the name *Nonnepfürzle*," I said when we had just about finished eating. "But why on earth is the soup named after a horse's muzzle bag?"

Mrs. Reimold laughed. "The story goes that during the Middle Ages monks invented the little pockets to hide the fact that they were eating meat during Lent."

"My wife hasn't told you the whole story," Siegfried's father added. "Those little dumplings are also called *Herrgottsbscheisserle*. In High German you'd say 'little ones who cheat the Lord.'"

When his parents had disappeared into the kitchen, Siegfried told me that he had become a successful sales representative for one of the leading textile companies. From the commissions he earned selling fine fabrics used to make men's and ladies' suits, he had been able to afford his own apartment half a kilometer away. "That gives me an idea," he said and he excused himself for a few minutes to go upstairs to his old room. When he came back he was carrying two bolts of fine cloth, each one-meter wide, one of solid grey flannel and one of grey flannel with fine stripes. "Here!" he said. "Take these home and have a tailor make you two suits. You see the quality? There's nothing better."

I tried to protest, but Siegfried was adamant. "They're yours now," he insisted, "and I'm not going to take them back." Towards evening, as we drove back to the train station, Siegfried suddenly thought to ask me about Nathalie, the girl I'd met in Luxembourg.

"Maybe it was a mistake to drop her," I confessed, "because there's been no one serious in sight ever since. I move around too often, I suppose. How about you?"

"There's this girl, Renate, I met recently. She's from Saxony in East Germany. I'm hoping it turns into something serious. I'll keep you posted!"

****

Towards the middle of August, when I heard that Bob Proctor was going to take a two-week sightseeing trip to Munich, Berlin, Hamburg, Frankfurt, and Cologne, I arranged for him to stay two nights with my parents in Bergheim. As luck would have it, Hubert was going to be home at the same time, so I waited uneasily for Bob's return, hoping that my brother wouldn't tell any of his tall tales like he had when I was away for basic training.

The night Bob returned to Göppingen, he, Paul, Ravi, and I got together in the room Paul and Ravi shared, to drink beer and listen to the latest LP by the Modern Jazz Quartet. "Hello, Stretch," Bob greeted me with a big grin, "I finally found out your nickname from your parents. They send their best regards, by the way, and asked me to tell you that Hubert now owns a Vespa. He and I rode around on it both days I was there seeing all the sights. We even climbed to the top of the Cologne Cathedral. Isn't the view great from up there?"

"To be honest, I've never been to the top," I confessed.

Ravi chuckled. "Isn't that always the way? The first time I saw the sights in Bombay was when I took around relatives from out of town."

Paul walked over to flip the record to the other side. "I really dig this stuff," he said. "Too bad my parents can't stand it."

"So, Paul, if you like our music so much, have you ever thought about emigrating to the good old U.S. of A.?" Bob asked jokingly. "Seriously though, with your Masters Degree in Mechanical Engineering and your work experience at Schuler Presses, you could get any job you wanted with one of the carmakers in Detroit."

"Not really. I intend to stay right here in Europe."

"Paul could never marry an American girl," Ravi kidded. "He likes being the boss!"

"You've got a point there," Paul admitted, "but I haven't found the right one here either."

Bob turned to me. "How about you, Stretch?"

"Funny you should ask," I replied. "I actually have a Green Card waiting for me in my desk drawer at home."

"Really? Well, if you already have a Green Card, what's keeping you here?"

"I want to finish my training program with the Konsum first and then I'll decide. Anyway, I couldn't go without a sponsor."

Bob thought for a moment. "You know, Stretch, my parents once sponsored an Irish family. Let me contact them and see if they'd been willing to do the same for you."

"Wow!" I said, scarcely believing my luck. "That would be amazing!"

****

At the end of August I received a note from Theo Schrick inviting me to attend our first Höwi class reunion at a restaurant in the old part of Cologne on the 15th of September. Only Theo would have dreamed up a reunion so soon after our graduation. What, after all, would we even find to talk about after only a year apart? My first inclination was to ignore the whole thing, but at the last minute I decided to take a vacation day and go home for the reunion since I hadn't seen my parents for nearly five months.

I got home in the early afternoon and spent a couple of hours in the café with my parents before rushing back by train to Cologne where Hans Stiefenhöfer and Theo Schrick had reserved a place for me at the table. We had barely started our meal when the bragging competition began as each of my classmates tried to prove that he had been the most successful. As usual, Wolfgang Opschepper was the worst braggart, hands down. If he were to be believed, within a short time he would be running the German subsidiary of the BULL Computer Company pretty much single-handedly. The rest of us were lucky to get a word in edgewise.

Around ten o'clock, Theo whispered to me that he couldn't stand to listen to Opschepper one minute longer. "Why don't the two of us skip out and head over to the Sartory Dance Hall on Friesenstrasse? I happen to know that a girls' commercial school is holding a reunion there so maybe we can pick up some chicks." As we walked over to Friesenstrasse in the pouring rain, Theo suddenly grinned. "A pretty girl from my office is at that reunion," he confided. "She's turned me down every time I've asked her for a date, so I was hoping you'd have more luck with her."

"Is that why you arranged this whole...?" I began.

Theo flashed me another sly grin. "Now what makes you think I would do that?"

Just another one of Theo's crazy ideas, I thought. Why would he want to fix me up *now* with someone from Cologne when I was living 500 kilometers away in Göppingen and would soon start on another four months of training in Saarbrücken near the French border? It didn't make any sense. Why, I wondered, as we pushed our way past the crowds of teenagers who had taken shelter from the rain in front of the Sartory Dance Hall, had I wasted a precious vacation day for this?

As soon as we paid the admission price and stepped inside, Theo yelled, "I'll be right back!" before charging across the dance floor, nearly knocking down a few couples in the process. A few minutes later he reappeared in the midst of a group of young women on the far side of the room, waving his arms wildly for me to join him. I walked over, and before I knew what was happening, Theo had grabbed my arm and steered me towards an unusually tall, dark-haired girl. "Charlotte Sorge, this is Günter Nitsch, the friend from the Höwi I was telling you about!"

Charlotte had dark eyes and a pert little nose but what attracted me first was her flirtatious smile. She had just come off the dance floor and her face was flushed; a few loose strands of dark brown hair dangled from her chignon. I was so busy studying her face that I didn't notice at first that her left arm was in a sling.

"Let's dance!" Charlotte exclaimed as she grabbed my arm to pull me out onto the dance floor. "Theo Schrick has told me all about you and I've been dying to meet you." As soon as we began to dance I recognized her perfume. It was *L'Air du Temps*, the same one Brigitte had always worn.

"What happened to your arm?" I inquired, to get the conversation started.

"I fell off my bicycle. How can anyone be so dumb?" she replied and she giggled like a tipsy schoolgirl. The thought that she might be underage suddenly made me nervous.

"If you don't mind my asking, when did you turn eighteen?"

"Eighteen? Is that what you think? Actually I'm way older than that. I'm going to be twenty on the 29th of December."

"I suppose Theo told you I'm working in Göppingen until the end of October and then after some more training in Hamburg, I'll probably be assigned to Saarbrücken for four months after that?"

"That's life," she said. "We'll just have to get better acquainted when you come back home," and she squeezed my hand tighter.

When the music finally stopped, Charlotte and I walked back over to where Theo was waiting. He was grinning from ear to ear.

I offered to buy everyone a glass of wine but Theo declined. "It's getting late and I'm driving," he protested. "So, Fräulein Sorge, since we both live on the other side of the Rhine, I'd be glad to drive you home." Charlotte bit her lip and gave me a longing look before reluctantly accepting Theo's offer. "And," Theo continued, "if Fräulein Sorge doesn't mind, I could also drop Günter off in Bergheim first." I protested that it would take him out of his way but he was adamant.

It had stopped raining, and with Theo in the lead, the three of us walked the few blocks back towards the restaurant where he had parked his car. Suddenly Theo spun around and clapped his hand to his forehead. "I totally forgot that I left a huge pile of accounting files on the front seat to work on tomorrow," he said. "I hope the two of you won't mind squeezing together in the back." *Theo hasn't overlooked a single detail*, I thought, as Charlotte and I cuddled together during the half-hour ride to Bergheim where all three of us climbed out of the car so that Theo could move the files to the back. Charlotte gave me a hug and a kiss and whispered, "Please write to me," before she and Theo drove off in the direction of Cologne.

****

A few days after I returned to Göppingen, Paul, Ravi, Bob Proctor, and I were having a heated discussion in the lounge. I had started things off by observing that, so far at least, everyone I had met at the Konsum was a left-leaning Socialist in sharp contrast to some of the unrepentant Nazis I'd dealt with during my apprenticeship at Arminius AG. Paul chimed in that he had read several books about the Third Reich and as a result, he "didn't trust any German over forty." Although he didn't say so directly, that apparently included the older members of his own family as well. Bob Proctor admitted that everything he knew about the Nazis came from one-sided Hollywood movies.

"Hey, Günter," Paul said, abruptly changing the topic. "Have you written yet to that girl you met in Cologne?"

"She beat me to it," I said, pulling a letter from my jacket pocket and removing the three enclosed photos. I passed around one of the pictures in which she stood, smiling, in hip-high grass. Along the edge she had written, "What can I do for you?"

Bob looked at the photograph and whistled through his teeth. "So," he teased, "what *can* she do for you?"

"She's invited me to a party she's giving on October 6th." I neglected to mention how passionate the rest of her letter had been.

"I take it you're planning to go because you'd be crazy not to," he said as he took one last look before returning the picture to me.

"Are you kidding? My acceptance is already in the mail!"

****

On my way to Charlotte's party I stopped first in Bergheim to say hello to my parents. Mutti waved at me from behind the counter and signaled that she would join me in the kitchen as soon as she could. The delicious aroma of freshly baked cherry tarts wafted from the baking kitchen where my father, as usual, was hard at work. He put down his rolling pin and came over to greet me. "So, how many minutes are you going to spare for your old parents this time?" he asked, his voice dripping with sarcasm. Then he grinned at me. "Out with it! Only a beautiful girl could induce you to make this trip twice in three weeks."

"Her name's Charlotte. She's hosting a party in Cologne-Höhenberg. But it's nothing serious. We just met," I replied. "Anyway," I continued, trying not to blush, "I was wondering if you could recommend a good brand of liquor for me to bring along."

At my father's suggestion, I was carrying a black-glass bottle of Queen Anne Scotch when I rang the bell marked Sorge promptly at 7 P.M. A minute later, Charlotte came to the door to let me in. "I can't tell you how glad I am that you've come!" she exclaimed, her eyes sparkling. Then she stood back and spun around. "Notice anything different about me? I got the cast off my arm yesterday, and just in time too." And she flung both her arms around my neck and kissed me. My heart was pounding with excitement as I followed her back upstairs to the apartment on the second floor where she lived with her mother.

Charlotte led me into the living room through a small entrance hall. Three armchairs were at the far end of the room in front of the windows. A teenage couple sat in awkward silence on the long couch in front of a coffee table to my left. On the opposite wall, there was a large wooden cabinet filled with paperback romance novels and wine glasses. Schmaltzy German pop music was playing softly on the phonograph in the far corner. Gradually the other guests began to arrive. With the exception of Theo, who showed up last with a date at least five years his senior, all of the guests were well under the age of twenty.

"I feel like an elder statesman in this group," Theo whispered to me when his date excused herself for a minute to freshen up. "Why do I suspect that this party was arranged just for you?"

"What gives you that idea?" I asked, but Theo just shrugged his shoulders and grinned.

The guests stood around, shifting from one foot to the other, sipping glasses of soda pop and nibbling on the little open sandwiches Charlotte had prepared. The wine she had put out sat unopened on a sideboard next to the bottle of Queen Anne Scotch. Shortly after ten o'clock, when everyone had left except me, Charlotte beamed in triumph. "Normally I like long parties, but I'm sure glad this one's over. Now we just have each other."

"Yes, but for how long? You know my last train to Bergheim leaves at…"

She put her finger on my lips and said, "Don't even think about it! If you feel the same way I do, you'll stay right here."

"But what about your mom?" I asked lamely, knowing full well that I wanted to stay.

"Never mind her! If she doesn't like what she sees when she finally drags herself back home, that's just too bad." Without saying another word she disappeared into the bedroom, returning with her arms full of blankets and pillows, which she used to build a makeshift bed on the thick wall-to-wall carpet. She quickly undressed and I did the same. Then we crawled under the covers and got the real party started.

It must have been nearly dawn on Sunday morning. Charlotte was sound asleep, her head and her left arm cuddled against my chest, when I heard the apartment door open. A tall, slim woman was dimly silhouetted in the hallway light. "Charlotte!" she commanded in a raspy voice, "I want you to come to our bedroom *now*!" Charlotte woke up with a sigh and shook her head. "Young lady," her mother insisted, "I really mean business!"

"Leave us alone!" Charlotte finally hissed. "I'm not budging." Without saying another word her mother turned off the hall light and went into the bedroom, slamming the door behind her.

"Shouldn't I get dressed and leave?" I asked nervously, but to my utter amazement Charlotte disagreed.

"Don't you dare," she chided. "You're not going anywhere!" and she pulled me closer.

Charlotte and I got up around 9 A.M. and she hurriedly packed away our makeshift bed. Her mother emerged from the kitchen a few minutes later carrying a tray laden with buttered toast, orange marmalade, poached eggs, and coffee, and the three of us sat down to breakfast. Like Trappist monks, we started the meal in icy silence. I was torn between apologizing to Mrs. Sorge or bolting for the door when Charlotte suddenly began to talk about the party, smiling and chatting away as though nothing unusual had happened.

We had just had our second cup of coffee when Mrs. Sorge turned to Charlotte and spoke for the first time. "Who brought the bottle of Scotch I saw in the kitchen?"

Charlotte said, "Günter did," and she smiled at me.

Mrs. Sorge gave me a hard look. "If you don't mind my asking, Herr Nitsch, do you drink that stuff?"

"Not me, but my father does."

"So, so," she said and I didn't know what to make of it.

While Mrs. Sorge was busy doing the dishes in the kitchen, Charlotte got a photo album from the bookshelf and showed me pictures of her travels. At the same time, she tried her best to persuade me to stay for lunch but I declined. "Maybe next time. I don't want to upset your mother any more than I already have, and besides, I have to catch a train back to Göppingen."

"Well then I'm going to go with you as far as the main station in Cologne to see you off!"

"How about a compromise? You walk with me as far as the bus stop. It'll be much easier for you to get back home from there," and she saw my point and agreed. Having been caught spending the night on the living room floor with her daughter, I had decided it would be inappropriate to thank Mrs. Sorge for "her hospitality" and so, as Charlotte and I were leaving, I just poked my head into the kitchen to say good-bye.

The bus stop was right around the corner but since buses ran less frequently on Sundays we had to wait more than ten minutes for the next one.

"If you don't mind my asking, why did your mother want to know about the Scotch? Does she disapprove of hard liquor?"

"Quite the opposite. She's actually attracted to men who drink. My father was a lush. A few years after they got divorced, she started dating her current boyfriend. One thing she and her 'acquaintance' have in common is their love of cocktails and expensive French cognac."

"Is that where your mother was last night, with her boyfriend?"

"Hardly. He sees my mother two, three, sometimes even four times a week, but only on weekdays because he spends every weekend with his wife and his three children."

"You're kidding!"

"I wish I were! Well you'll see when you meet him one day. He's two years younger than Mom and not at all bad looking, but he's a real slime ball!"

As the bus approached, I kissed Charlotte and promised that I would visit her at the end of October before starting my next month-long training session in Hamburg. On my way back to Bergheim, I tried to reason with myself. What had I gotten myself into? How could this adventure go on? Things would be different if I lived and worked in Cologne but instead I would be moving around like a gypsy for at least another year and who knew where the Konsum would send me after that. And yet – and yet – I was already counting the days until I would see her again.

When I got home just in time for lunch, Mutti rushed over to greet me. "Stretch, we've been worried about you. Have you by any chance forgotten that you're due back in Göppingen today?"

"No, of course not. I can still catch my train if I leave again right after lunch."

My father took a deep drag on his cigarette. "So how was the party?"

"Very nice, very nice!"

"Are you going to see the girl again? Does she know how often you'll be out of town?"

"Yes, I'm definitely going to see her again and of course I told her."

My father grinned. "And she didn't mind? Well then, let's wait and see how long *that* lasts."

CHAPTER 51

*E*ven though Mr. Altholz varied my routine by letting me accompany him to several business meetings, my last few weeks in Göppingen crept by slowly. On the 31st of October my friends at the Catholic Student Home organized a farewell party for me. As it turned out, I wasn't the only one who was leaving. Bob Proctor would be returning to California in April; Ravi was going back home to India; and Paul was looking for another job.

After rushing back to Cologne to keep my promise to Charlotte, and then completing my next Konsum training seminar in Hamburg, I visited Charlotte for a third time before starting my new assignment at the Konsum in Saarbrücken near the French border on December 3, 1962. It was my 25th birthday.

My new boss for the next four months was Dr. Bogner, a well-built young man in his early thirties with wide shoulders, a thick neck, a cleft chin, and a dirty-blond crew cut. A firm believer in adopting the latest trends from the American supermarket industry, Dr. Bogner had traveled extensively in the United States. One of the first assignments he gave me was to read English-language industry studies and half a dozen American trade magazines, and under his tutelage, I learned all about the theory and practice of location analysis – where to build a new supermarket, and more importantly, where not to. I later found out that Dr. Bogner drew large audiences when he lectured on this topic, both in a clear High German and in fluent French, at the University of Saarbrücken. In other words, he couldn't have been more different from Mr. Altholz in Göppingen.

Once again the Konsum had rented a room for me. My new landlady was Mrs. Lafontaine, a middle-aged widow who lived on a hill on the northern side of the city, an easy one-kilometer walk from my office. She showed me my room and the common bathroom and explained the kitchen privileges, all the while clutching the small crucifix hanging from a thin gold chain around her neck. I was about to pay her the first month's rent when she suddenly held up her hand. "Before we go any farther, there's one more rule that I strictly enforce. I do not, under any circumstances, tolerate female visitors."

"Well in that case, Frau Lafontaine, I suppose I'll have to look somewhere else because my girlfriend may come down from Cologne on a Saturday once or twice a month and she'll certainly want to stay over for the night."

"She's your girlfriend you say? Well then, I suppose I could bend the rules a little bit. If she doesn't come too often, I'm willing to let her sleep on my living room couch, if that's all right with you."

"That's very kind of you," I replied, but to myself I thought, *we'll see about that.*

****

The week before Christmas, Dr. Bogner took me aside. "Herr Nitsch, I understand that you're thinking of taking the tram to Forbach on the French side of the border this weekend. If so, I can recommend a great little restaurant where you can get a delicious French meal. But if you're planning on buying any French cognac or liqueur while you're over there, keep in mind that we sell exactly the same things just as cheaply right here in our Konsum stores. No other province in West Germany has a deal like that!"

On Christmas Eve I travelled home to Bergheim carrying my clothes and a few special gifts in my overnight bag and also lugging a separate suitcase containing two bottles of Courvoisier, one bottle of Grand Marnier, and one bottle of Bénédictine. Hubert, who had come home for the occasion, had walked Oma over to the café a few minutes before I arrived.

"Hubert was just starting to tell us about his job at the Youth Hostel," Mutti explained when I joined them. With that introduction, my brother launched into a series of wild stories, each one more fantastic than the last. If he were to be believed (and I didn't believe him for one minute) he had become indispensable – single-handedly tossing out unruly guests, doing all the cooking, and running the reception desk, all the while fighting off the advances of the entire female staff.

When Hubert finally stopped talking, I presented Mutti with a bottle of Channel No. 5 and gave my father a bottle of Courvoisier and a bottle of Bénédictine.

"Oh, Stretch, you shouldn't have!" Mutti said. "Imagine spending all that money on perfume for a frumpy old lady like me."

I gave her a big hug. "Nonsense! You're an elegant businesswoman and you certainly deserve it."

"Where'd you get a crazy idea like that? Really, Stretch, why don't you give it to your new girlfriend instead?"

"I've already got something for her but in a different brand," I assured her.

For Oma I had brought a box of fancy French chocolates, and for Hubert, an extra-large dress shirt that I hoped would fit. While I was distributing the Christmas presents, my father had been studying the labels on the bottles. "Thanks, Stretch," he said. "This is the best of the best. It must've cost you a small fortune."

"Don't worry. In Saarbrücken there aren't any customs duties on French products."

My father opened the bottle of Bénédictine and filled four liqueur glasses for everyone but Oma, who didn't drink alcohol. He raised his glass to each of us. "Let's start with this one," he said. "*Prost!* Merry Christmas, everyone!" Then he closed his eyes and took a sip. "You know, Stretch, this brings back wonderful memories of my time in Paris during the war. Did I ever tell you...?"

Mutti stood up, ready to storm out of the room, but it was Oma who came to the rescue. "With all due respect, Willi, those aren't the kinds of stories we want to hear on Christmas Eve. Why don't we all sing 'Silent Night'?" My father glared at her for a moment, but when he relaxed his shoulders Mutti sat back down, and the moment passed.

****

Charlotte greeted me with a big hug when I arrived on Christmas Day. Her twentieth birthday was only a few days off and she had just gotten a big raise at the office, so she had two extra reasons to celebrate. As soon as we got upstairs, I presented the remaining bottle of Courvoisier and the bottle of Grand Marnier to Mrs. Sorge. Then Charlotte and I exchanged gifts – an amber pendant and a bottle of *L'Air du Temps* for her and a copy of *The Tin Drum* by Günter Grass for me.

While Charlotte and her mother were busy preparing lunch in the kitchen, I flipped the pages of *The Tin Drum* but I couldn't concentrate. Instead I thought about how beautiful and vivacious Charlotte was. But there was so much more to her than that. She was intelligent; she was a hard working secretary in Theo's CPA firm (a fact which Theo never failed to mention each time he and I spoke). She was even an excellent cook. I had to admit that Charlotte was beginning to appeal to me in so many ways that I considered asking her to marry me one day, even if it meant ditching my plans to go to America.

Right after lunch Charlotte and I went outside to take a long walk. "I'm curious. May I ask you a question? Your mother looked really unhappy when I arrived. Was it because of me?"

"No, not at all. It's her so-called acquaintance, Herr Rahmler. He's spending the whole week with his family so she won't see him again until after New Year's."

"How long have things been going on like this?"

"More than two years now. I don't know why she puts up with it. If I were her, I'd send him straight to hell!"

"There's something else I've been wondering about. I've told you about my own childhood, but what about yours? What brought you from East Germany to Cologne?"

"You're not going to believe this," Charlotte said, "because it sounds like the script for a B movie. I told you my father was a heavy drinker, right? Well, one night in 1951 he skipped out on our family. That left my mother with a farm to manage and eleven-year-old twin girls to feed."

"Wait a minute! You have a twin?"

"Bear with me. I'm getting to that part. It was all too much for my mother to handle so she sent me to live in Cologne with my Aunt Sophie and my Uncle Franz. And here's the really weird part. She decided to give up my twin sister, Ella, for adoption to an older childless couple who are somehow distantly related to our family. The way it was explained to me, the couple owned a farm near Lüneburg, just south of Hamburg, and they wanted an heir they could leave it to when they died."

"And your mother?"

"When I was thirteen she gave up the farm in East Germany and came to Cologne to take me back. That's when she divorced my father." She looked up at me quizzically, trying to judge my reaction, but I just shook my head in disbelief. "I didn't claim that it made any sense," she finally conceded.

"Are you and Ella identical?"

374

"She's totally different. Try to picture a plump, red-headed farm girl and you'll have a pretty good idea of what she looks like."

We didn't talk for a few minutes while Charlotte gave me a chance to digest what she'd told me. It was certainly disturbing. But was it really any worse than what my own family had been through? When we'd lived under the Russians in East Prussia, I had been a street urchin, begging for a few kopeks or a slice of bread. By the age of eleven, when Mutti, Hubert, and I reached West Germany, I could barely read and write. And my father, too, had abandoned his family until his mother and sisters pressured him to take us back. We were both survivors who had come through traumatic childhoods unscathed, or at least, so I thought. After all, it wasn't Charlotte's fault that her mother split up her family while Mutti risked everything to hold ours together. And besides, she was the most beautiful girl I'd ever met. I put my arm around her waist as we walked back to her mother's apartment.

****

Charlotte's twentieth birthday fell on a Saturday and since I knew that she was handy with a sewing machine, I presented her with the bolt of striped grey flannel that Siegfried had given me in Stuttgart. "Perhaps you can make some skirts from this," I suggested.

She felt the material between her thumb and her forefinger. "This is really too good to waste on a skirt," she said, giving me a big hug. "Let me surprise you!"

Together with Charlotte's mother, we were invited over to Mrs. Sorge's sister and brother-in-law's home in Cologne-Mülheim that afternoon for coffee and cake. Since Charlotte had lived with her aunt and uncle for two years while she was growing up, I was curious to meet them. Aunt Sophie was short and plump, just the opposite of her younger sister. Whereas Charlotte's mother worked on a production line in a garment factory and had a tendency to mangle her grammar,

Aunt Sophie was a lady of leisure who spoke a fine High German just like Charlotte.

Aunt Sophie's good fortune was due to the fact that Uncle Franz, who was as thin as his wife was fat, had a Master's degree in engineering and was a well-paid executive in a machine tool factory in Cologne. Yet you wouldn't know it by the way she treated him. "Franz!" she announced soon after Mrs. Sorge had parked her ancient Volkswagen Beetle next to her sister's brand new Opel in the driveway. "Why don't you make the coffee and set the table while I show everyone our newest acquisitions?" She beamed as she led us over to a mahogany cabinet in the living room and pointed to the objects behind the beveled glass diamond-shaped windows. "See those cordial glasses on the top shelf. That's Waterford! And all those figurines are from Rosenthal. I insist on only the finest quality and why not, when you have the money?"

From the kitchen, Uncle Franz called out, "I'll be ready in a minute, dear."

"Oh, take your time, Franz," she shouted back. "What's the hurry? I want to show everyone my new emerald necklace!"

When, at long last, the five of us sat down at the dining table, Uncle Franz turned to his wife and said, in a meek voice, "I hope everything's all right, dear."

"Well," she grudgingly conceded, "I suppose it'll do, but really Franz, would it have been too much trouble to bring out the sterling silver flatware for the occasion instead of this old stainless steel?" Aunt Sophie now turned to Charlotte. "If you don't mind my saying so, you two are a good match. I actually like Günter a whole lot better than that last fellow you brought around here."

I had just taken a bite of cake and was afraid I would choke on it. Uncle Franz covered his mouth with both hands, not daring to challenge his wife. Charlotte, meanwhile, had turned beet red. Finally, Mrs. Sorge dared to speak. "For heaven's sake, Sophie, you're embarrassing both of them."

****

Charlotte visited me several times while I was in Saarbrücken and each time she came she had to sleep on Mrs. Lafontaine's living room couch. But as soon as Mrs. Lafontaine left for Mass on Sunday morning, Charlotte hopped into bed with me. By the time my landlady returned home from church, she would discover the two of us seated demurely in my room perusing the newspaper or deciding which restaurant in Forbach we would go to for lunch.

By the time of Charlotte's second visit, since I had long since finished reading *The Tin Drum,* I offered to lend it to her to read on her train ride back to Cologne, but she turned me down.

"Oh, you've probably read it already, I suppose."

"No, I haven't, and to tell you the truth, when I bought it for you for Christmas I skimmed the first few pages and some from the middle but I just couldn't get into it. I'm glad you liked it, though."

"Well, what kind of books do you like?"

"No special preferences."

"But you must like to read *something*," I persisted.

"Well, you know, magazines with lots of pictures."

"How about *Der Spiegel*?"

"Definitely not *Der Spiegel.* It's much too political and the articles are way too long. Speaking of *Der Spiegel*, Theo Schrick reads it all the time. He's a bit of an odd duck don't you think?"

But my mind wasn't on Theo at that moment and I ignored her question. "Are you sure you don't want to borrow *The Tin Drum*?" I asked her one last time in the hope that she'd give in.

"No thanks!" she chirped, as she reached into the side pocket of her overnight bag. "See, I've brought along the latest issue of *Die Neue Illustrierte* for the return trip."

CHAPTER 52

*I*n April 1963 I was transferred from Saarbrücken to the Konsum District Office in Düsseldorf for the next two months. Together with a company executive, Hans Spiessmacher and I traveled all over the Ruhr Valley assessing Konsum stores against a lengthy checklist and then writing detailed reports suggesting where improvements needed to be made. After a day or two, I concluded that the Ruhr Valley had more soot-spewing smokestacks than trees. By noontime our faces and our shirt collars were smudged with coal dust, and since neither Hans nor I had brought along more than three or four white business shirts, we were spending an inordinate amount of money on hotel laundry charges. Being a lawyer, Hans tried to make the case that these charges should be reimbursed to us as a business expense, but in the end we had to absorb them.

The hotels where we stayed were selected and paid for by the local Konsum offices and that frequently meant that the toilets and showers were somewhere at the far end of the hallway. However, there was always a sink in our rooms. Once again, Hans became the self-appointed spokesman for the two of us. "It's outrageous," he complained to the Konsum executive over breakfast, "that we have to stay under such primitive conditions!"

"I don't disagree," the executive replied. "After all, I'm staying here, too. I'll put in a call to the District Office about it, but don't hold your breath. By the time they get around to doing something, it'll be long past Easter and you fellows will be working somewhere else. In the meantime, here's a word to the wise." He looked at each of us in turn and then lowered his voice to a stage whisper. "Don't touch the sinks in your room if you can avoid it, especially when brushing your teeth." He glanced over his shoulder to make sure no one was listening. "Just think about all of those generations of traveling salesmen who've used the sink as a urinal during the night because they were too lazy to stagger down the hall." I was hoping he would wink to let us know that he was only joking. But it didn't happen.

We'd been working in the Ruhr Valley for less than two weeks when we were given four days off for Easter. I rushed home that Thursday right after work and shamelessly presented Mutti with a crumpled pile of dirty shirts to launder. Charlotte had promised to come to Bergheim to meet my parents the day before Easter and I wanted to look my best.

At four o'clock on Saturday afternoon I walked over to the bus stop next to the post office to wait for her. When the bus door opened and she came down the steps, she was wearing a white blouse, a form-fitting grey suit with a skirt that came just to her knees, and a matching tailored jacket that showed off her narrow waistline. I gave a low whistle. "You look just like a fashion model! Where'd you buy that outfit?"

"Don't you recognize the material you gave me for my birthday?" she teased. "I made the suit myself!"

My father, who had put on his best suit for the occasion, was waiting for us with Mutti in the café. After the introductions were made, he stood back to admire Charlotte. Then he turned to me with a wink and an approving nod.

"So nice to finally meet you," Mutti said, extending her hand. "Do you mind if we call you Fräulein Charlotte? Fräulein Sorge sounds so formal."

"You can even leave out the 'Fräulein'," Charlotte assured her, but my parents didn't dare stretch the rules of etiquette quite that far. Not yet, at any rate.

I rushed upstairs to put away Charlotte's overnight bag, and when I came back down, Mutti asked me to join her for a minute in the kitchen. "The photos you showed us don't do her justice," she whispered. "She looks like a film star!" Then, after a moment's hesitation, "I just hope you haven't taken on more than you can handle."

"I'll be just fine!" I replied as she and I rejoined my father and Charlotte in the café, but Mutti had actually struck a nerve. To be honest, it made me angry that not just my father but all men – young, old, and in between – ogled Charlotte whenever she and I took a walk or went to a restaurant together. Of course, Charlotte couldn't help being beautiful, but even so, each time it happened, I wondered how long it would be before she dumped me for someone better.

Mutti tapped me on the sleeve. "Were you listening to what I said? I was admiring Fräulein Charlotte's suit. It could've been custom-tailored in Paris!"

"Did she tell you she sewed it herself?"

"You don't say!" Mutti exclaimed. "Whoever would've thought it?"

Later that evening, just as my landlady in Saarbrücken had done, Mutti insisted that Charlotte sleep alone on the living room couch. As she made up the bed for her there, Charlotte smiled and played along. However, around midnight, when the light went out in my parents' bedroom, I climbed down from my top bunk and joined Charlotte who, I knew, was waiting up for me. Hours later, long after she and I had fallen asleep, I had a horrifying nightmare that Herr Direktor Müllmann was once again dragging me through the classroom by the hair like a stupid camel. I awoke in a cold sweat to discover Mutti leaning over me with my hair grasped firmly in her right hand and her left index finger over her lips. Once she had my attention, she waited with her arms crossed against her chest until I had gently disentangled myself from Charlotte and returned, with evident reluctance, to my own cold bed.

****

At the end of May, before my last period of training with the Konsum began, I went with Charlotte and her mother to visit Charlotte's twin sister, Ella. The farm where Ella was still living with her adoptive parents was a five-hour drive northwest of Cologne. Located just fifty kilometers from the Bodenteich refugee camp where Mutti and I had lived for nearly two years, the nearby village was only a thirty-minute drive from the East German border.

Ella was as plump as her sister had described her, and her hair was even redder than I'd imagined it would be. But even if she had been taller and thinner, she wouldn't have been nearly as attractive as Charlotte, a fact of which Ella was only too well aware.

"Boy," Ella had repeated to her sister several times as she dug into her second helping of *Pinkelwurst* and green cabbage at supper, "what I wouldn't give to have your hourglass figure!"

Ella's steady boyfriend, a shy young man named Claas who had inherited a nearby farm, came by after supper to drive Charlotte, Ella, and me to the annual dance being held that evening in the village inn. When we arrived, nearly two hundred young people were either seated at long tables drinking beer or out on the dance floor twirling to a fast polka. To be polite, I asked Ella for the first dance while Charlotte and Claas went in search of four free seats. Just as the music stopped, a tall blond man pushed past us through the crowd, and when he reached Charlotte, he swept her off her feet, twirled her around, and gave her a kiss.

"Who on earth is that?" I asked Ella who was looking in the same direction.

"Oh, never you mind about Thorsten. He was her boyfriend for a while when he lived around here. They used to see each other every time Charlotte came to visit. But now he's off studying economics at the University of Hamburg."

Ella and I walked slowly back to the table where Charlotte was waiting with her usual charming smile. "Thorsten," she said, "I want you to meet my boyfriend, Günter. And Günter dear, this is Thorsten, an old friend of the family." Then she put her arm around me and I forced myself to shake Thorsten's hand before practically dragging Charlotte out onto the dance floor.

"You're not angry with me, are you?" she asked sweetly, although she clearly knew I was. Afraid I'd say something I'd regret, I just shook my head. But as we danced I wondered how many previous boyfriends there had been. Charlotte had, after all, just barely turned twenty. When I had once confronted her after she murmured the name of a former boyfriend in her sleep, she had assured me that there had been only two, a young man in Cologne and another in Northern Italy where she'd traveled several times on vacation with her mother. And now Thorsten made three. But was that all? Only a few weeks earlier, when Charlotte had asked me to stop with her in front of a jewelry store window in Cologne so that she could admire the gold wedding bands on display, I had even considered asking her to marry me, but now I was beginning to think that Mutti was right. Maybe Charlotte really would be too much for me to handle.

CHAPTER 53

*T*hat summer my Konsum training took me to Euskirchen, a sleepy
little town in the Eifel Mountains just forty kilometers southwest
of Cologne. Since I could easily get there by train from Bergheim, I
moved back in with my parents. Mr. Pallmann, the manager of the local
Konsum, was a wiry man of medium height whose enthusiasm was
contagious. As soon as I arrived for my first day of work, he took me
into the adjoining office to meet his secretary, Miss Braun. "She keeps
the wheels greased around here!" he explained with a smile. Seated
to her right was my new direct boss, Mr. Pütz, a jovial, fast-talking
Rhinelander, who worked as a district store inspector, and to her left
sat Mr. Pallmann's assistant, a short, elderly gentleman with curly white
hair, unusually large ears, sallow yellow skin, and mirthless, deep-set
eyes. "And this is my right-hand man, Herr Rosensaft," Mr. Pallmann
said cheerfully. "Herr Rosensaft, meet our new executive trainee, Günter
Nitsch." Mr. Rosensaft glanced up at me and gave an unfriendly grunt.
Then, reluctantly shaking my outstretched hand, he averted his eyes
and busied himself with some paperwork on his desk. "Well," said Mr.
Pallmann apologetically, "I didn't mean to interrupt," and turning to me,
he added soothingly, "We all have deadlines to meet, you know."

"So, Herr Nitsch," Mr. Pütz said when I came back over to his desk, "Herr Pallmann tells me you're commuting here every day from Bergheim. Starting tomorrow, would it be possible for you to get here as early as seven in the morning? Our workday officially begins at eight but I like to start my inspection tours early because none of the store managers have time for me around closing time."

"That shouldn't be a problem, sir. I've been an early riser ever since I went through basic training."

"Good! Then off we go!" I helped Mr. Pütz load his files into his Peugeot and then we headed for the first store on his list. "The Euskirchen region is probably different from the ones you've been in before because we don't have any supermarkets yet," he explained. "For the past year or so we've been supplying frozen meat to the mom and pop stores in the area. Trouble is, some of the store managers have been trying to avoid losses by selling packages that are past-date. They may think they're clever but what they're doing is downright dangerous. So our job is to ferret out the bad meat before a customer gets sick."

"I suppose all we need to do is check the expiration dates?"

"In theory, yes. But the date may not be legible. I even suspect that some store managers rub it out on purpose. But there's a simple way to detect spoilage. All you have to do is scratch away a tiny piece of the cellophane packaging. Then you scrape a speck of frozen meat off with your fingernail and roll it between your index finger and your thumb. I suppose you know what rotten meat smells like?" I nodded, thinking back to the foul odor that rose from the dead horses piled into the ditch near the Deime River in Goldbach when I had lived under the Russians. "Well, then, you'll know right away if a package needs to be thrown out."

Twenty minutes later I had the damning evidence on the tip of my finger. Out of the thirty-two packages of frozen beef I had tested in the first store, eight were spoiled.

"This is totally unacceptable, *totally* unacceptable," Mr. Pütz berated the embarrassed store manager as she glanced nervously over her shoulder to make sure her two customers could not hear him. "I'm warning you! The next time this happens, I'm going to write a report!"

Since the same evidence turned up in store after store, by the end of the week Mr. Pütz's patience finally ran out and he instructed me to fill out formal complaint forms. The original was for the office in Euskirchen and the carbon copy went to the Konsum District Office in Düsseldorf. Mr. Rosensaft glowered at me disapprovingly when I placed the complaint forms on his desk at lunchtime the next day. A few days later, when I dropped off another set of complaints, he pursed his lips and the veins in his neck began to throb.

As soon as I sat back down at my desk, Mr. Rosensaft turned to the boss's secretary and hissed, "How dare that snot-nose put charges like this in writing! When this reaches Düsseldorf, it may cost those store managers their jobs! What gives him the right...?" He stopped in mid-sentence when he saw me get up and approach his desk.

I drew myself up to my full height so as to tower over him as he shifted uncomfortably in his chair. "Excuse me, Herr Rosensaft, were you talking about me? For your information, I've only been doing what I've been told to do by Herr Pütz. And just to set the record straight, I won't be called a snot-nose, not by you, nor by anybody else in this office for that matter!"

Mr. Rosensaft's hands began to tremble and the color drained from his face. "I've got nothing to say to you!" he muttered between clenched teeth and he turned back to the forms he was filling out without another word.

First thing the next morning Mr. Pallmann called me into his office and asked me to close the door behind me. "Have a seat, Herr Nitsch," he said. "My secretary told me what happened yesterday with Herr Rosensaft. First of all, let me put your mind at ease. I think it's perfectly in order to file written complaint reports. It would be a catastrophe for us if our customers got sick from eating spoiled Konsum meat products and that may be the only way to get our store managers to comply. But I don't think Herr Pütz should have asked you to sign them. Between you and me, I think he didn't want to jeopardize his relationship with the store managers by signing them himself. Am I clear so far?"

"Yes, sir, Herr Pallmann. Perfectly clear and thank you."

"Good. Now let me explain about Herr Rosensaft. He started working for the Konsum long before you were born. But during the Third Reich he spent many years in a concentration camp. You did know that he's Jewish, didn't you?"

I suddenly thought about the beautiful names on the files I'd destroyed at Arminius AG – Goldsohn, Himmelfarb, Hirschberg. Until that moment I hadn't made the connection. "No, sir, I really had no idea."

"I've spoken to Herr Rosensaft and he apologized for treating you so harshly. So everything seems to be fine. Just keep on writing those reports. By the way, I've also spoken to Herr Pütz and he will be signing the reports from now on. I've seen to that." I was about to leave when he held up his hand. "Let me tell you something that crossed my mind last night. I was in the Hitler Youth. In the last months of the war I was actually drafted into the *Wehrmacht* and taught how to shoot bazookas at tanks. You'd think this would bother Herr Rosensaft, but he knows as well as anyone that I was only sixteen at the time and he doesn't blame me for it. So I've been trying to figure out why he resents you so much. You were only seven at the end of the war after all. The only thing I can come up with is that you must remind him of one of his tormentors in the concentration camp. It's only a guess on my part, but please try not to take any resentment he may have towards you personally."

Mr. Pütz was waiting for me when I came out of Mr. Pallmann's office. "We're getting a late start today for sure," he groused.

On my way out the door I wished Mr. Rosensaft a "good morning" as I passed by his desk on the way to the car and he rather grudgingly wished me the same.

CHAPTER 54

Now that I was living in Bergheim again, I enrolled in a business English course at Berlitz leading toward a proficiency certificate that I hoped would help me get a better job in the future. On class days my schedule was grueling. After waking up at 5:15 A.M. to arrive in Euskirchen by seven, I worked a full day with Mr. Pütz and then, instead of going straight home, I left the train at the main railroad station in Cologne and walked a short distance past the Cathedral to get to class. With luck and split second timing I barely made it to Berlitz in time. By the time I got back to the café and ate the sandwich Mutti had left out for me, it was half past ten at night.

The Berlitz School was close to Charlotte's office and she soon made a habit of rushing over to meet me near the Cologne Cathedral so that she could give me a hug before she caught her bus back home to Cologne-Höhenberg. Several times she was delayed for a few minutes at work and I felt obliged to wait for her. As I stood there nervously checking my watch, I began to feel that Charlotte was smothering me.

"Listen," I finally said to her the third time she got there late, "I really can't afford to miss any more class time. So if you don't see me when you get here, just figure I had to leave." Charlotte threw her arms around my neck and burst into tears. "Be fair," I said, pulling away from her and giving her a quick kiss. "You know how important this class is to me and we'll always have plenty of time together on the weekends." Then I hurried off to Berlitz, not looking back once.

"How about this?" Charlotte suggested in her sweetest voice the next time we were together. "Why don't we meet for supper on some of the workdays when you *don't* have class? That way neither of us will be in a rush." That seemed reasonable enough but her plan didn't end there. Her goal, it seemed, was to take control of my life. As soon as we sat down to eat in a restaurant, she would try to talk me into coming back home with her afterwards. I tried my best to resist, but despite all of my protests, she usually managed to persuade me to stay over. And each time I gave in, some of my self-respect withered away. I secretly thought of Charlotte as a Lorelei, irresistibly luring me to my downfall.

On one of those weekday evenings we skipped the restaurant altogether and headed straight over to the Sorge apartment. "Mom's boyfriend is coming over," Charlotte had explained, "and she's invited us to join them for supper." I had seen Mr. Rahmler several times before as he and Mrs. Sorge were on their way out, but this was my first opportunity to really get to know him.

Charlotte's mother had fixed a huge plate of fancy open sandwiches and was setting the table while Mr. Rahmler sat on the couch reading a magazine when we walked in the door. He rose with difficulty to greet us, pushing against the cushions with both hands until he was standing on his pudgy legs. The belt of his expensive suit was hidden somewhere under his bulging stomach and the roll of fat from his double chin hid the collar of his white dress shirt. As he walked over to Charlotte and me, he reeked of aftershave lotion.

"Well hello, Herr Nitsch," he said as he shook my hand with both of his, a habit I detested. "I'm so glad we'll finally have a chance to get better acquainted."

"The same goes for me," I replied, trying my best to sound sincere. Mr. Rahmler, I quickly discovered, was one of those annoying people who repeated the name of the person he was talking to as often as possible.

"Supper's ready!" Mrs. Sorge announced at that moment and the four of us sat down at the table.

"You've outdone yourself again, my darling," Mr. Rahmler said to Mrs. Sorge. "You're such a dear to go to all this trouble," and he reached across the table to squeeze her hand. As he continued to address Mrs. Sorge with "darling" and "dear" throughout the meal, I wondered whether he addressed his wife the same way on the weekends.

We were almost finished with our meal when Mr. Rahmler started to pepper me with questions. "So, Herr Nitsch," he said. "I understand you just got your driver's license. What kind of a vehicle do you have in mind to buy?"

"I'm actually not planning to buy a car right now," I said, although I wondered why it was any of his business. "First of all I don't need one for my work, and besides, I don't believe in buying something like that on installments."

"Well, let me ask you this, then, Herr Nitsch," he persisted. "What would you say your prospects are when you complete the Konsum executive training program? What I mean, Herr Nitsch, is do you have a choice of where you'll be assigned?"

"I really couldn't say. Time will tell," I replied, trying to keep my annoyance from showing and my answers as vague as possible.

"Specifically, what I'd really like to know, Herr Nitsch," Mr. Rahmler went on, "is what kind of a salary you expect to receive when you finish?"

By now I had reached the breaking point. "Why don't you tell me first how much *your* monthly salary is?" I shot back, and to my relief, he finally backed off. It was just as well because, if he had asked me one more question, I had already made up my mind to ask him all about his wife and children and see how *he* liked it.

"So what do you think of Rahmler?" Charlotte asked me when her mother had left with her boyfriend to see a movie.

I could no longer control my anger. "I can't stand the man! Who does he think he is asking me all that stuff?"

"Maybe we should take a nice walk until you calm down," Charlotte suggested.

"I'm way past that point. If I'm still here when they get back, I'm going to say something I'll regret." When Mrs. Sorge returned home with Mr. Rahmler later that evening, I was already on my way back to Bergheim.

****

On the last Sunday in June, Charlotte and her mother may have been the only people I knew who weren't still all abuzz about President Kennedy's defiant speech in Berlin earlier that week. "Never mind Kennedy! What's on *my* mind right now," Mrs. Sorge said to me when I brought up the subject, "are these documents that my ex-husband needs to sign. He's living in a village not far from Bonn and I expect you and Charlotte to come with me."

Charlotte dreaded the visit with her father whom she hadn't seen for several years. "What's so bad about him? You've never really explained it," I asked Charlotte when we were alone.

"You'll know the minute you see him 'cause he'll probably be drunk by the time we get there. He's just an awful, stupid man."

"There must be something good about him. He's your father after all."

Charlotte shook her head. "Let me give you just one example and you decide. He didn't even bother to come when I got confirmed, but he sent me a brand new bicycle, the first one I'd ever had. Three weeks later, what did he do? He showed up at our apartment to take back the bike because he needed the money." Then she started to cry and I took her in my arms to comfort her.

An hour later the three of us arrived at the farm where Mr. Sorge worked as a farmhand. Charlotte poked me. "You see that short man over there in work pants and an open shirt? That's my father." Waiting for us at the side of the road was a man with scraggly reddish-blond hair, a leathery, sunburned face, and the cratered bulbous nose of an alcoholic. He removed his cap when he saw us, revealing the white forehead of someone who always covers his head while working outdoors. But it was the blank look in his watery blue eyes that I found most shocking.

Mrs. Sorge introduced me to Charlotte's father. "So you're gonna marry my daughter!" he said in a slurred voice. "Nice to meet ya!"

"Herr Nitsch and Charlotte are just good friends," Mrs. Sorge quickly corrected him.

"Friends? Sure they are. Sure they are. That's what they all say," he muttered. "You ain't fooling nobody with that!" He moved closer to Charlotte to give her a hug but she took a step back. The smell of schnapps clung to his breath and his clothing.

Charlotte tugged on my sleeve and whispered, "Please come wait with me over by the car. I can't bear to be around him another minute."

We watched from a distance as Charlotte's father signed the papers her mother had brought along in a thin file. A few minutes later Mrs. Sorge suddenly waved to us to come back over to where they were standing. "I'm not budging," Charlotte said as she grabbed my arm to keep me there. Mrs. Sorge shook her head and hurried back to the car.

"Charlotte!" she announced breathlessly, "You're not going to believe this. Your father's gone and married a milkmaid and she's just had a baby. Won't you please come over to congratulate him before we leave? It'll only take a minute."

While she was talking, a young woman with rosy cheeks who couldn't have been much older than Charlotte had joined Mr. Sorge. She was cradling a baby in her arms. The scene could have come right out of one of those western movies I had seen where an old, grizzled farmer sends back east for his mail-order child bride.

After taking a deep breath to steady her nerves Charlotte walked back with her mother and me. "That's wonderful news," she said. "I'm very happy for both of you." Then she shook hands with her father and her newly discovered stepmother and peeked at her tiny half-sister who was wrapped up in a dingy pink blanket.

During the drive back to Cologne, while Charlotte and her mother talked about Mr. Sorge's new bride, my thoughts were elsewhere. What a family! Not that mine was perfect by any means, but we were nothing at all like this. Mrs. Sorge's long-standing relationship with the married father of three hadn't seemed to be any of my business, that is, until Mr. Rahmler began to pry his nose into mine. I had steeled myself to the idea that Charlotte, young as she was, had already had two steady boyfriends before she met me, until I met the third. And now I had come face to face with her father, an ignorant drunken little man newly married to a woman half his age. And what about the baby? Was that the reason he had married her? I was already feeling closed in by my relationship with Charlotte, but what terrified me most was the thought that she might get pregnant. I pictured her irate father showing up on my doorstep one day, shotgun in hand, to force us to get married. It was time, I decided, to break up with her.

But how to go about it? I gave this question some serious thought. The most effective way, of course, was to simply stop calling, or at least so I'd been told by my buddies in the army who had had plenty of experience with that kind of thing. Still, after dating Charlotte for nearly a year it seemed a heartless thing to do. Nor did I want to do it in writing. Brigitte had dumped me like that. The invitation she had sent me to her wedding eve party had broken my heart; it still hurt me to think about it. The only responsible thing, I finally decided, was to gather up my courage and tell her in person.

My Berlitz classes met on Monday and Wednesday evenings and I made some excuse not to meet Charlotte after work on Tuesday. That gave me three more days to think things through. By Wednesday afternoon, I had made up my mind. Before leaving the Konsum office, I told Mr. Pütz that I had a doctor's appointment in the morning and wouldn't get to Euskirchen until lunchtime.

My heart was pounding when I called Charlotte from the pay phone in the lobby of her office building the next morning. For three days I'd rehearsed exactly what I was going to say, but when I heard her voice, I just blurted out, "We've got to talk," and asked her to come downstairs for a minute. She hung up the phone and I leaned against the wall for support, waiting for the elevator doors to open.

A minute later she joined me. The color had drained from her face and she grabbed my hand. She clearly sensed that something momentous was about to happen. "Let's go in here," I suggested, as calmly as I could, and we sat down together in the stairwell on the far side of the lobby. "Listen, Charlotte, as I said, we really do have to talk," I began. "There's no easy way to say this. You're a wonderful girl but I just don't want to be tied down to a long-term relationship right now." Before I could say anything further, she burst out crying.

"But couldn't we still date each other?" she whimpered.

"A clean break would be best for both of us," I replied, "and I won't change my mind. I hope you'll understand."

"You'll come back to me. I know you will. You *have to*," she sobbed and then, wiping her eyes with her handkerchief, she gave me a quick kiss and returned to work.

As soon as I got to my office in Euskirchen, I reported to Mr. Pütz who had spent the morning at his desk compiling reports. "Oh, you're back, Herr Nitsch," he greeted me. "I have to leave early today so we won't be doing any inspections. Why don't you spend the afternoon verifying these figures?" He handed me several files. Then he caught hold of my arm. "I hope I'm not intruding but did everything go all right at the doctor's? You're looking rather pale."

"Thanks for your concern, Herr Pütz. I'm just fine," but of course, it wasn't true.

At ten minutes to five, my phone rang, and as I reached for the receiver, I hoped it wasn't Charlotte. "This is Rahmler!" a man said on the other end. "Listen, Herr Nitsch, I have no idea what happened this morning between you and Charlotte, but I thought you should know that she's tried to take her own life."

My hands began to shake and my mouth went dry. "Are you serious? What did she do?"

"Frau Sorge found her. She was dozing in the armchair near the window in the living room. She had cut her wrist with a razorblade and then taken some sleeping pills."

"Where is she now?"

"They just got back home from the emergency room." He paused and when he spoke again there was the sound of desperation in his voice. "Herr Nitsch, Charlotte's mother and I would appreciate it if you would come over and talk with her."

"I'm sorry, Herr Rahmler, but I can't do that," I said after only a moment's hesitation. "If what you're saying is true, I'm sure my visit would only make matters worse," and I slammed down the receiver without another word.

During the train ride home my resolve weakened. Had Charlotte really done such a crazy thing in the few short hours since I'd left her? Or was this just a cruel trick to get me back? What if Charlotte's life really was in danger and I was the only one who could help? I wasn't sure I could trust Mr. Rahmler, but on the other hand, could I afford not to?

Rain was coming down in buckets as my train pulled into the station at Bergheim an hour later. I was soaked through and I had a splitting headache by the time I reached the café.

"You look like a drowned rat!" Mutti said. "Why don't you get into some dry clothes and then we can have supper?" My parents were waiting to eat when I came back downstairs. "I know you too well," Mutti said as studied my face. "Was there a problem at work?"

"It's Charlotte," I said, and before I knew it, I was pouring out my heart to them, explaining everything that had led up to the call from Mr. Rahmler. "And now she's tried to kill herself and I don't know what to do."

"How awful!" Mutti exclaimed when I finally stopped talking. "Who would have thought she'd do such a crazy thing? Maybe it would have been better if you'd let her down gradually. It must've been an awful shock doing it the way you did. I wish you'd talked it over with us first. But I suppose it's too late now and it's a shame, too. Whatever your objections are, I'm really fond of Charlotte. She would've been quite a catch."

My father saw things differently. "If I were you I'd lay low and never see her again. The girl's clearly unstable and who knows what else she might pull in the future if things don't go her way. Let her mother look after her and keep your nose out of it, I'd say."

Sleep didn't come easily to me that night. I lay wide-awake for hours trying to decide what, if anything, to do. Maybe Mutti was right. What hope did I have of ever meeting another girl as smart and beautiful as Charlotte? Was it fair to blame her for her family? Her father had already caused her so much pain and now she probably thought I'd dumped her because of him. No wonder she had taken things so hard.

But then I remembered my father's warning. Lie low! Keep you nose out of it! If I were honest, I had begun to have doubts about my relationship with Charlotte long before I'd met her father. Whatever the reasons, I wasn't ready to be tied down. If I went back to her now, I'd be taking her life in my hands and I was sure there'd be no chance of escape.

CHAPTER 55

*A*ll throughout the next day, as I drove around to inspect five different stores with Mr. Pütz, I couldn't shake off a vague but persistent sense of guilt. I imagined Charlotte, practically at death's door, desperate for a soothing word from me. She had been willing to throw away her life for me. But what was I willing to do for her? My thoughts went round and round but all I got were questions and more questions. There were no good answers.

Towards evening Mr. Pütz looked at his watch. "It's getting pretty late and I don't want you to miss your train so I'll drop you off at the Euskirchen station and then I'll drive home from there."

With five minutes to spare before my train was due to arrive, I was glancing at the headlines in the newspaper kiosk to pass the time when someone came up behind me and tapped me on the shoulder. "Herr Nitsch," he exclaimed, "I'm so glad I caught you!" I whirled around and came face to face with Mr. Rahmler. "Frau Sorge sent me to beg you to come back with me and talk to Charlotte. The girl's totally dissolved and we have no idea what she might try next." He once again grabbed my right hand with both of his and begged me with his eyes as he spoke. "In our opinion, Herr Nitsch, you're the only person in the world who can talk some sense into her right now!"

"I really don't see how..." I began.

"Believe me, it's the only way," Mr. Rahmler pleaded. "She might not live through the night if you don't." As he spoke, my train pulled into the station and I was tempted to make a break for it, but as if he could read my mind, Mr. Rahmler tightened his grip on my hand and said the words that finally won me over. "Please, Herr Nitsch, please don't let Charlotte die!"

"Mind you, I haven't changed my mind about our relationship," I said meekly, "but since you put it that way, I'm willing to stop by for a few minutes and then I'll go home to Bergheim." Feeling thoroughly defeated, I watched as my train left without me and then I obediently followed Mr. Rahmler outside to his car.

****

In the forty-five minutes Mr. Rahmler needed to cover the distance from the Euskirchen station to Cologne-Höhenberg we hardly exchanged a word. If, during that time, Mr. Rahmler suspected that I was considering escaping from his car once we got to the outskirts of the city, he would have been right. With sickening clarity, I knew that a trap had been set for me and I was walking right into it. My father, who had more experience with women than anyone else I knew, had sounded the alarm. In my place, he would have washed his hands of any responsibility, just as he had once coldly walked out on Mutti, Hubert, and me when we came from East Germany fifteen years earlier. But did I really want to behave like that? What kind of role model had he been, after all, that I would choose to follow his example? And who knew better than Mutti how awful it was to be abandoned? For her sake, I finally decided that talking things through with Charlotte was the only right thing to do.

Mrs. Sorge gave me a tight-lipped smile when she came to the door. She made no effort to shake my hand as she stood aside to let Mr. Rahmler and me come in. Charlotte was sitting with her legs tucked under her on the living room couch. The color had drained from her face and her eyes were red. As I crossed the room she reached out her hand to me and smiled but made no effort to get up.

"We're going to leave the two of you alone for an hour or so, so that you can talk things over," Mrs. Sorge said.

"That's really not necessary," Charlotte said softly.

"I beg to differ," her mother replied. "Herr Rahmler and I would just be in the way."

As soon as the two of them left, Charlotte turned to me to apologize. "Sorry that Rahmler picked you up in Euskirchen. Believe me I begged him not to go." She motioned me to sit down next to her on the couch. "But now that you're here, I'm really glad you came."

I stared at the thin white bandage around her left wrist. "Why'd you do it?" My voice was barely above a whisper even though no one else was there.

"Without you I didn't want to live any more," she whispered back.

"Oh, come on, Charlotte. You can't really mean that. Of course you could. There are thousands of guys out there like me."

"But you're special."

"I'm not the least bit special. And besides, you're ready to settle down and I'm not. My career is just taking off. I don't even know where I'll be living a few months from now."

While I was talking she unwrapped the bandage, exposing three tiny nicks on her wrist, each one no bigger than a small paper cut. I didn't have to be a doctor to see that none of the cuts had actually severed a vein. If she had really meant to do herself harm, she couldn't have done a worse job. But if she deliberately cut herself to win sympathy and attention, she had succeeded all too well. It was a dangerous game she was playing and the next time, if there were one, the razorblade might slip.

"Promise me you'll never do such a foolish thing ever again, no matter what happens." I finally said.

"So you do care!" Charlotte exclaimed, and she threw her arms around my neck and hugged me.

"Let me help you put the bandage back on so you don't get an infection, and then let's take a walk," I suggested, and she was forced to release her hold on me.

After leaving a brief note for Mrs. Sorge to let her know our plans, we went out for our usual stroll along the tree-lined path leading to the nearby neighborhood allotment gardens. At first Charlotte walked slowly, leaning heavily on my arm, but after a few minutes she forgot herself and picked up the pace. As the color returned to her cheeks and her eyes began to sparkle, I started to wonder why I had decided to break things off. More to convince myself than to convince her, I tried again to explain all the reasons why things wouldn't work out.

"You know, Charlotte," I said, "it's one thing for us to date when I'm living nearby, but once my training ends in a few months, I have no idea where I'll end up. I could be half way across the country. I'm even thinking of going to America for a year or two if the Konsum doesn't have a good spot for me."

She broke into a smile. "So? Why should that matter? Ever since we've known each other, you've been away for weeks at a time anyway and I've never complained, have I? And if you do decide to go to America, I could always go with..."

I held up my hand to interrupt her. "Let me put it more bluntly. I'm just not ready to settle down right now and you seem to be in a hurry. You've got so much going for you. You're a beautiful, intelligent young woman who could have your pick of anyone you wanted. Why would you want to waste your time with me? I'm just a twenty-five-year old trainee with a lousy education and an uncertain future."

Charlotte put her hands over her ears and burst into tears. "Stop it! I don't want to hear it! I don't want to meet anybody else. I've already made my choice!" Then, as we turned back towards the apartment, she just as suddenly stopped crying. "You've talked about going to

America before. But it's not like you'd be leaving tomorrow or anything, right?"

"I already have my Green Card so all I'd need is a letter from a sponsor. I told you about Bob Proctor's parents in San Francisco, remember? They might still come through for me."

"You're not fooling me with that excuse. If you haven't heard from his parents by now, what makes you think you ever will?" We had turned the corner and could see Mr. Rahmler's huge Opel-Kapitän parked next to Mrs. Sorge's Volkswagen in front of the apartment building. "They're home," Charlotte said and she gave me her most enticing smile. "Please, please don't go just yet. Come up for a few more minutes!"

"I really can't stay," I replied, determined to hold my ground.

But she didn't give up. She had one more trick up her sleeve. "I almost forgot. My sister Ella and her boyfriend are coming to Cologne a week from tomorrow and they'd love to see you. How about it? Just that once for old time's sake?" She kissed me and stood back to wait for my answer.

Say no! Say no! I thought. *She's nothing but trouble!* But before I could help it, I heard myself saying, "I'll think about it," and I knew that I'd been snared.

"That means 'Yes!' See you on the 13th!" Charlotte exclaimed, and quickly kissing me again, she disappeared inside the building before I had a chance to protest.

****

The following Saturday, and very much against my better judgment, I joined Charlotte, Ella, and Claas, in a restaurant in the old part of Cologne. The four of us were seated at a table on an outdoor terrace on the second floor overlooking the Rhine River. Our conversation was awkward at first since none of us wanted to talk about the recent "incident" even though it was certainly on everyone's minds. Charlotte's wrist was no longer bandaged but she was wearing a wide silver bracelet to hide the telltale scars.

Claas squirmed uneasily as he studied the menu, most of which was written in French. "I'm just a simple farm, farm, farm…"

Ella rushed to finish his sentence. "Farm boy! C'mon Claas, we've been to fancy places like this before."

"Not very, very…"

"Not very often, that's true." Ella turned to Charlotte and me and smiled. "That's what I find so endearing about Claas. He's so unpretentious." I could see that Claas had no idea what "unpretentious" meant but he smiled and took it as a compliment.

We ordered a bottle of Liebfraumilch wine before supper and two more bottles to accompany our main course and our dessert. While Charlotte and Ella chatted away, I studied the picture of the Virgin Mary on the label. She reminded me of Sister Monika, the beautiful young novice I had kissed in the Maria-Hilf Hospital the second time I broke my leg. As the evening wore on, I failed to notice that everyone else at the table was letting me do most of the drinking.

"Günter! You're not listening!" Charlotte scolded after the dessert was served. "I'll bet you haven't heard a single word we just said." Then she winked at her sister. "I was telling Ella and Claas that my mother's best friend from work has gone away for the weekend with her husband and the four of us can use their apartment. So, what do you think?" When I didn't say anything right away she dangled a set of house keys in front of my face as an added enticement. Then she dipped her spoon into her dish of apricot ice cream and slowly licked it clean before offering the next spoonful to me. I could feel her hand pressing against my thigh under the table.

Ella had covered her mouth to suppress a giggle and Claas was avoiding my eyes. That all three of them were in on this plan I had no doubt. Clearly the only sensible thing for me to do was to get up and leave while I still could. But the wine had blurred my brain, and besides,

Charlotte had never looked more beautiful. While I considered my reply, I reached over and idly turned the bottle around so that Sister Monika couldn't rebuke me.

"As Charlotte's been telling us, there's just one problem," Ella hurried to add before I had a chance to speak. "It's a one-bedroom apartment so we'd have to decide who gets the big double bed and who has to make do with the living room couch."

"What do you think about this idea?" Claas asked as he grinned at his chubby girlfriend. "The couple that weighs the most gets the bed." It was the longest sentence he'd spoken all evening and I was sure he'd rehearsed it for hours.

All eyes turned to me as I took another sip of wine. The challenge was irresistible. "How about this?" I finally said. "I know there's a scale in the Cologne-Deutz railroad station. Let's drive over there right now."

"And may the best couple win!" Charlotte added.

My legs were a bit unsteady as we all walked the few blocks to where Claas had parked his car before we set out for the Cologne-Deutz station on the other side of the Rhine.

Sure of victory, first Claas and then Ella climbed on the scale. Their combined weight was 135 kilograms, higher than I had expected, and I already imagined Charlotte and me spending the night on the couch. Charlotte stepped onto the scale next. "Fifty-five kilograms!" she announced. "Your turn, Günter, and you'd better weigh more than eighty!"

"What do we do if it's a tie?" Ella asked as I put my coin in the slot. "Wouldn't that be something?" The three of them leaned over to see the result.

"Eighty-two! Do you see that? Eighty-two! We beat you by two kilos!" Charlotte gloated. When I stepped back down she gave me a hug. "It must've been your height that made the difference, *mein Schatz!*" she whispered. "I really thought they'd win, didn't you?"

In a happy daze, I held Charlotte close to me in the back of the car for the fifteen-minute drive to the apartment. By the time the four of us sat down to breakfast the next morning, it was understood that Charlotte and I were back together as though "the incident" had never happened.

CHAPTER 56

*W*hen my time with Mr. Pütz in Euskirchen was over at the end of August, I returned to Hamburg where I was reunited with Hans Spiessmacher and all of the other executive trainees for our last required seminar. Dr. Schlohwitt introduced the speakers, all high-ranking Konsum executives, who each shared his rags-to-riches success story. One had started as a lowly sales clerk; another had come up the ranks through his union. The message was clear. Regardless of what position we were going to be offered at the end of the month, we all had an equal chance of running one of the regional headquarters one day.

"I was surprised that no one mentioned starting out as a restroom attendant," I joked to Hans Spiessmacher, during a lunch break.

"Or by mopping floors," he agreed with a laugh. "Actually, what bothered me more than all those corny stories was how little they each have to say about the rule of supply and demand. It's as if capitalism is a dirty word around here. Social responsibility may be great and all that, but we both know that you can't grow a business if you don't focus on maximizing the profits from your annual sales."

On Friday, the 27th of September, Dr. Schlohwitt began to call the trainees into his office one at a time to offer us our permanent positions with the Konsum. Each private interview lasted no more than five minutes. As I waited uneasily for my turn, I watched as most of the young men, evidently pleased with their assignments, left Dr. Schlohwitt's office and rushed upstairs to their rooms to phone home with the good news. But several others stormed out and announced to anyone within earshot that they were so insulted by their offers that they had quit on the spot.

"Just between us," Hans Spiessmacher said to me under his breath when this happened for the third or fourth time, "I'm thinking of doing the same if I don't like what they give me. From what I understand, if you quit before you sign a contract you can just walk away and there's nothing they can do about it." He leaned even closer to me. "But please don't quote me!"

"As long as you don't charge me for the legal advice!" I agreed.

Finally it was my turn to enter Dr. Schlohwitt's office. I sat down and watched nervously as he took a thick sheaf of papers from my file. "You're being given a great opportunity, Herr Nitsch," he said as he leafed quickly through the contract he had ready for me to sign. "The Konsum in Saarbrücken wants to hire you as the assistant to the manager of their largest supermarket for a period of two years. After that you would be transferred to their Marketing Department. You can see the salary right here. Very few candidates are being offered this much money, but of course, unlike some of our other young executives, you'd be expected to put in eighty-hour weeks. That's the nature of the supermarket business." He turned the contract around so that it was facing me and reached over to hand me a pen.

For the past eighteen months I had dreamed of an executive position in a large city where I could do marketing – some place like Berlin, Hannover, Stuttgart, even Düsseldorf – but try as I might, I couldn't imagine myself stuck away for the next two years in a supermarket in Saarbrücken. Besides, what if my chance to go to America actually came through? Could the Konsum still hold me to the contract? I wished I had asked Hans Spiessmacher that question but it was too late now.

Dr. Schlohwitt put the pen back down and took a deep breath. "Do you have any idea, Herr Nitsch, how much we've invested in your training?" I could tell from the tone of his voice that his patience was running thin. "I need your decision and I hope you're not going to disappoint us."

"I'm sorry, Herr Dr. Schlohwitt," I said as I stood up to leave the office, "but if that's your best offer, I'm going to have to turn it down." An hour later I had packed my things and was on my way back home.

****

Within a few weeks I landed a new job as the assistant to Mr. Hautegen, one of the directors of Eklöh, a top-notch supermarket chain headquartered in Cologne. My starting date was November 1, 1963, and much to my relief, I wasn't asked to sign a written contract. Compared with the Konsum, the marketing principals followed by the Eklöh management were cutting edge. The owner, Herbert Eklöh, after travelling to the United States in the nineteen-thirties, had been the first to introduce the American concept of self-service stores into Germany. After the war, he had opened the Rheinlandhalle, a two thousand square-meter flagship store in Cologne-Ehrenfeld, adjacent to the headquarters of the fast-growing Eklöh chain.

My new boss, Mr. Hautegen, an overbearing martinet, was a man of medium height with a red face and a thick mane of white hair whose department was responsible for the modernization and streamlining of the Eklöh supermarkets as well as their in-house bakeries, butcher shops, and meatpacking stations. Mr. Hautegen had been a commanding officer in the *Wehrmacht* during the war, and the presentations he gave to employees were sprinkled with military terms. Staff members were "human material," and our "mission" was to engage our opponents and pulverize the competition. He was also a misogynist and his two long-suffering secretaries, both well-educated women in their early thirties, resented the way he talked down to them.

"You've heard the way he treats us, Herr Nitsch?" one of the secretaries confided to me a few days after I'd started work. "Is it any wonder that awful man's already been through two messy divorces? How any woman could marry someone like that I'll never understand."

When I reported to Mr. Hautegen, the first assignment he gave me took me by surprise. "Listen up, Nitsch!" he said as he kept me standing at attention in front of his desk. "I'm getting sick and tired of all those shoplifters who pilfer our merchandise. Every item they steal is an attack on our profits! So this is what you're going to do. Ditch that tie for the time being because I'm sending you to work undercover every afternoon this week in the Rheinlandhalle. Push a cart through the aisles, but while you pretend to shop you'll really be doing reconnaissance. Watch out for dishonest customers! But especially keep your eye on the women! They slip merchandise into their clothes, or they stuff it into their purses; some of them even hide it in their baby carriages. Be vigilant, but maintain a safe distance. Don't strike until the thief leaves the cash register without paying for the item. Then you pounce. Believe me, you're going to hear all kinds of heartbreaking excuses. But show no mercy! And don't let them out of your sight until you've brought them to the store manager's office." I stood there, not sure he was through with me. Mr. Hautegen glared. "What are you waiting for? I've given you your mission. Now go do it!"

"Yes, sir, Herr Hautegen!" I was tempted to salute him on my way out, but my better judgment prevailed.

For the first three afternoons, I kept a watchful eye on several unsavory looking characters who, I was convinced, were likely shoplifters, but in each case, they paid for all of their items at the register on their way out. But on the fourth day, I noticed a well-dressed woman who put several inexpensive items in her cart before glancing around to see if she was being observed. As I pretended to study the price on a carton of eggs, I watched her take a half-pound package of butter from the shelf. Then, reaching down to lift the hem of her long skirt, she slipped the butter into the cuff of her baggy underwear. When she had paid for the merchandise in her shopping cart but not for the butter, I asked her to follow me up to the manager's tiny office.

"How dare you accuse me of theft!" she protested as we walked up to the second floor. "You'll be sorry!"

"So, what do we have here?" the manager asked when I brought the indignant customer inside.

"I observed this lady leaving the store without paying for a package of butter, sir."

"It's all a terrible mistake!" the woman insisted. "I've been falsely accused. Just wait until my lawyer hears about this!"

"A mistake you say? Is it really?" the manager asked as he casually walked past us to switch on the electric heater in the corner of the room. "Well, if my associate here was mistaken, we would certainly owe you an apology. But madam if, as you say, you didn't take the butter, then how do you explain the melting butter that's dripping down to your ankle?"

Mr. Hautegen congratulated me when he received my report. "Well done, Herr Nitsch. You saw it for yourself. It's always the women you can't trust. It's the women every time!" He pulled a thick manual from his desk drawer. "Since you've proved to be such a good scout, I want you to study the operations manual I wrote on how to improve the efficiency of a meatpacking station. All next week I'll be sending you into the field again to watch the butchers at work to see how that operation is going down."

Starting first thing Monday morning, I took a stopwatch into the back service area of the Rheinlandhalle where four highly-trained butchers and their eight assistants, each with an assigned job, cut, boned, sliced, packed, sealed, and labeled slabs of fresh meat along a slow-moving conveyor belt. When my stopwatch beeped every five minutes, the twelve of them glared at me resentfully as I noted their activities on a long checklist. At the end of the week, after reviewing my data, I concluded that, by working more efficiently, nine people could easily do the meatpacking job just as well as the twelve people the company employed.

"Good job, Herr Nitsch," Mr. Hautegen said when I made my report, "but for my taste you were a bit too generous to the workers. I would have transferred out four of them not three, but we'll stick with your figures for now and see how it goes."

"They're not going to lose their jobs, sir, are they, because of me?"

"No, unfortunately I can't fire them, if that's what you mean. But right after Christmas I'm going to send three of them to one of our outlying stores where they'll do the least harm to our operations." He glanced again at my report. "Once I've prepared a new work-flow chart, I can decide which of them to reassign."

For my third week at Eklöh, I divided my time between preparing dreary statistical reports in the office and observing operations in the adjacent store. By now word had gotten around that I had been spying on the employees and some staff members eyed me with obvious hostility. Others, anxious to protect their jobs, did their best to get on my good side by offering me tasty samples of fruit or cake. A few of the young women even began to flirt with me. It was on one such store visit that I met Georg von Apselberg, the assistant to the Marketing Director of Eklöh. He was a big man, ten centimeters taller than I was and at least twenty kilos heavier, who had spent half a year each working in supermarkets in Boston and in Philadelphia.

"How'd you manage it?" I asked him at lunch the next day. "I'd give anything to spend a year in the U.S."

"My father's a big shot in a large German retail chain so he was able to pull some strings for me. Never underestimate the value of connections, I always say. But since you'll probably never get over there, you should thumb through some of my American supermarket magazines. Eklöh has a long way to go before we catch up to those guys. Just see for yourself. I have the latest issue right here." I flipped a few pages, which featured an American store double the size of the Rheinlandhalle with a whole long aisle devoted to frozen foods and another aisle just for breakfast cereals. "They even have aisles set aside for *pet food*, believe it or not. And don't think that store is anything special, either," von Apselberg said when I handed the magazine back to him. "They have stores like that all over the U.S." He took a sip of his coffee before continuing. "But do you want to know what I liked best about America? It was the tall stacks of pancakes smothered in maple syrup. There's nothing like that New England maple syrup!"

****

As I had quickly discovered, I wasn't much better off working for Eklöh than I would have been in the Konsum supermarket in Saarbrücken. Playing store detective and singling out employees for demotion was a far cry from the marketing position I had set my heart on. And Georg von Apselberg's enthusiastic report about America only served to remind me that that dream was also on hold. I had received one or two postcards from Bob Proctor after he returned to California, but I was still waiting for the hoped-for sponsorship letter from his parents.

Charlotte, on the other hand, was thrilled with my new job since she had immediately assumed that I had moved back to Cologne to be closer to her. And she may well have been right. Despite everything that had happened I was still attracted to her, and I hated myself for it.

On Friday, the 22nd of November, I went straight from my office at Eklöh to the Sorge apartment since Charlotte and I had planned to go to a carnival dance party later that evening. Mrs. Sorge had gone out so the two of us had the apartment to ourselves. We ate a light supper and then, under the streetlights, we took a brisk walk in the fog to the neighborhood allotment gardens and back. Later, while I waited for Charlotte to shower and wash her hair, I took the *Kölner Stadt-Anzeiger* from my briefcase, put up my legs, and switched on the radio to the American Forces Network to listen to American pop music. I had just taken a deep breath and started to unwind when the music suddenly stopped. "We interrupt this program with breaking news," the announcer said. "President Kennedy has just been shot in Dallas, Texas."

For the next twenty minutes or so I was glued to the radio, desperately trying to learn whether the young president who, only a few short months before, had spoken so forcefully in Berlin, was dead or alive. "Charlotte!" I yelled when I finally heard the bathroom door open. "Come in here! Hurry!" She rushed into the living room in her bathrobe. A towel was wrapped like a turban around her wet hair. "President Kennedy has been shot! They just announced it and I don't know if they mean just wounded or if..."

"Switch to a German station," Charlotte suggested. "Maybe it'll make more sense."

But just then the announcer, his voice choked with emotion, said the dreaded words. President Kennedy was dead. I turned the dial in time to hear the German newscaster give the same grim report. Charlotte sank down next to me on the couch. As we listened, all thought of the carnival party was forgotten.

Charlotte cuddled up closer to me when I finally switched off the radio. "You're not still thinking of going over there, are you?" she asked. "This might set off riots, maybe even a revolution. I've heard that everyone in America carries a gun."

"You've been watching too many movies," I chided. "And yes, of course I still want to go. I'm sure I'll be fine." Still, despite my bravado, during the coming days, especially whenever Charlotte and I were together, I had lingering doubts. A country where a president could be shot dead was a far cry from the America of my imagination.

CHAPTER 57

*O*n Christmas day I presented Charlotte with a multi-colored French designer scarf and another bottle of *L'Air du Temps* perfume. Her gift to me was a copy of *Dog Years*, Günter Grass's latest book. On the second page, in her neat handwriting, she had copied the following words of wisdom from Goethe:

> Man can roam wherever he chooses,
>
> He can undertake whatever he likes
>
> But he will always find the way back
>
> To the place he was destined to be.

It was, of course, a not so subtle hint that I would always find my way back to her despite my having told her, on at least five different occasions that, from my perspective at least, things were far from settled between us. "I really need to get away for a while to give myself room to think. But if we both still love each other after I've been gone for a year or two, then we can talk about the future," I had so often explained, but I might as well have been speaking Chinese. If my message was getting through to her at all, she deliberately chose to ignore it.

Since, as they say, "Discretion is the better part of valor," after reading the lines she had written in the book, I decided not to share some news with Charlotte. I could only imagine how much more pressure she would have put on me had I told her that Jochen Krienke, my old friend from the Boy Scouts, as well as my Army buddy Siegfried Reimold, had both recently married their girlfriends. Rather than spoil Charlotte's Christmas, I also decided to wait a few more days before letting her know that my long-awaited sponsorship letter from the Proctor family had finally arrived in the mail and my America plans had now reached a point of no return.

But it was only when I visited a travel agent in downtown Cologne during my lunch hour a few days after Christmas that the reality began to sink in. If I really intended to go to America, I would have to book a passage on a ship to New York and then somehow manage to travel nearly five thousand kilometers across the vast North American continent on my own.

When she heard my plans, Mutti told me I was crazy. "Why don't you just stay home and marry Charlotte instead of going to a country where people go around shooting the president?" she had asked me when I got the letter. "At least here you know what to expect!"

My father disagreed. "If I had just turned twenty-six and were unattached like Stretch, I'd go to America and never look back."

"How soon...?" Mutti started to say.

"I was thinking by the end of April. That's when the *France* is sailing for New York. But just in case she asks, I haven't told Charlotte yet. I'm still waiting for the right moment."

"You know better than that," my father said. "There's never a right moment for that kind of thing."

****

With only a few months left until the *France* sailed, it would have made sense for me to save money for my trip by living at home, but now that I could finally afford my own place in downtown Cologne, I couldn't resist the temptation. On New Year's Day I found a furnished studio apartment with a kitchenette on Kommödienstrasse that I could rent on a month-to-month basis. There was a fancy pastry shop on the ground floor of the building and a newly installed elevator. The apartment had been recently renovated and there was even a small desk next to the windows from which I could see the Cologne Cathedral. Unlike the previous places I'd rented, I had my own private bathroom with a shower. The rent was more than Mrs. Sorge was paying for her one-bedroom apartment in Cologne-Höhenberg, but I rationalized that it was only for a few months and besides, if I was going to leave for America soon, why not go out in style?

As I looked around, the elderly, white-haired landlady stood in the doorway nervously twisting a thick set of keys. "So, Herr Nitsch. What do you think?"

I quickly weighed the advantages. Aside from giving me a much shorter commute to Eklöh, I could now come home as late as I wanted without worrying about waking my father, and Charlotte could stay over with me for a change without Mutti acting as chaperone.

"I'll take it!"

"There's just one thing you need to know before you pay me the first month's rent." By now I had a pretty good idea of what was coming. "All of my tenants are around your age. Now I'm not like some of those old-fashioned landladies. I understand that young people like to do a lot of entertaining. You can party to your heart's content for all I care. But there's one rule I must insist on. All visitors of the opposite sex must be off the premises no later than ten o'clock at night."

"You needn't have any concerns on my account," I fibbed. "I understand the rules."

****

Shortly after moving into my studio apartment, Mr. Hautegen, apparently pleased with the success of my report on the Meat Department, "rewarded me" by assigning me to spend three days each in Hamburg, Kiel, Osnabrück, and Münster, doing another efficiency study. Since time was limited and there were so many locations to cover, Mr. Hautegen even decided to put me in command of a team of four women from the home office who would travel with me from city to city. Yet, even though I suppose I should have felt honored by this new responsibility, I dreaded the job. After all, it was bad enough that the employees in the Rheinlandhalle already hated me; now I would be despised at the Eklöh stores in four other cities as well.

For the next fifteen workdays my Eklöh team pressed forward from early morning until late in the evening during the week and an additional six hours on Saturday. Stopwatches in hand, we spread out throughout each store and noted our observations at five-minute intervals. Even though the employees were told in advance that we were going to "help make their jobs easier," they understood full well why we were there and they threw themselves into their work with an enthusiasm that skewed all of our measurements. Shelf stockers rushed in and out of the supply room with new merchandise. Cashiers stopped chatting with their customers about the weather. Spills were mopped up the minute they occurred.

When I got back to Cologne, I told Mr. Hautegen what had happened. "I'm afraid my report doesn't reflect the way things really are," I said as I placed my findings on his desk.

"Don't be naïve, Herr Nitsch. Do you think I didn't anticipate what would happen? I used your team to set a trap. The bottom line is, that by speeding things up while they were being observed, the employees were actually proving how inefficient they were the rest of the time."

My heart sank. "Then people will still be transferred, sir?"

"Oh, yes!" He rubbed his hands together and picked up his pen. "I can't wait to see how many!"

****

On the 6th of February, Cologne was once again celebrating *Weiberfastnacht*, that wild party on the Thursday before the start of

416

Lent. Over at Arminius AG, I was sure that Mr. Schmitz, the "Little Uncle" from the Accounting Department, had long since stockpiled massive quantities of booze for the occasion. But Mr. Hautegen, a Prussian from Potsdam, was cut from a different mold. Not a word had been said about a party for his staff although we knew that most Eklöh employees were already celebrating elsewhere in the building. Around lunchtime Mr. Hautegen came out of his office with his overcoat over his arm. His face was grim as he addressed my two female colleagues and me. "In my opinion, this Rhenish *Weiberfastnacht* celebration is a total waste of valuable work time and I, for one, have no intention of sticking around to watch our employees get drunk. I'm dismissing the three of you for the rest of the day since nothing's going to get done around here anyway."

As soon as Mr. Hautegen was out the door, I grabbed my coat, and after stopping off for a minute at the travel office, I headed over to Charlotte's accounting firm where a *Weiberfastnacht* party was well underway. Peppy music was blaring from a record player and several dozen half-empty bottles of wine were on top of the file cabinets in the corner of the room.

"Glad you're here," Charlotte greeted me and she handed me a glass of wine. She clearly had gotten quite a head start on me. "So how's the trip to San Francisco shaping up?" she asked in a voice tinged with sarcasm.

"Just look at these brochures! Would you believe that the *France* carries two thousand passengers? It's got dance clubs, a movie theater, even one or two swimming pools."

"Well I guess it won't take you long to forget me on that pleasure boat." Then she clung to me and pleaded, "Promise me that won't happen!"

"Don't be silly. How could I?"

Suddenly I recognized some familiar faces on the far side of the room, which gave me a chance to change the subject. "Isn't that Jes

Schmiedler over there with Theo Schrick and Ferdi Buscheur? I didn't know that three of my classmates from the Höwi worked here."

"Herr Buscheur only works here part time while he's studying at the University of Cologne. And Jes Schmiedler doesn't work for us. He's just a good friend of Herr Buscheur's. By the way, Frau Schmiedler just had a baby boy. Isn't that the most wonderful news?" Her eyes brimmed with tears. "Come, let's go over and he can tell you about it himself."

We walked over to where my three former classmates were standing. "I guess you already heard the news," Jes Schmiedler said. "Charlotte told me how much she'd like to see the baby so how about the two of you coming over next week to meet my wife and son?"

I sensed another trap, but before I could find a good excuse to turn him down, Charlotte quickly spoke up for both of us. "We'd love to, wouldn't we, Günter?"

While Jes Schmiedler and Charlotte made more definite plans, Theo pulled me aside. "Just so you know, Jes married the tramway driver he was fooling around with. That little fling derailed when she led him off on the wrong track, the baby track I mean. And he's not the only one from the Höwi who had to get married. Remember that brown noser Wolfgang Opschepper? You know, the one who was always bragging about his female conquests? He's another one who got a girl pregnant. It's actually getting to be quite a sizeable club."

I glanced over to where Jes was still talking to Charlotte about the baby as she beamed at him with occasional nods in my direction. "Well," I said as I turned back to Theo, "that's one club I hope neither of us ever has to join."

****

The Schmiedlers lived in a studio apartment with a small kitchenette. Two bed sheets hung from a clothesline strung across the middle of the room. On the side of the divider closest to the door were a table and four chairs, a miniature étagère holding a few well-worn books and several bottles of liquor. A small plastic bathtub rested on a wide stool next to the kitchen sink and several diapers were hanging up to dry on a wooden rack next to the stove. The mingled odors of deep-fried potatoes, dirty laundry, and urine hung in the air.

Jes introduced Charlotte and me to his wife, a stocky woman who stood a few steps behind her husband. She was cradling a tiny infant in her arms.

"Oh, what a darling baby!" Charlotte gushed after she had peeked inside the blanket.

"Where are my manners?" Jes said. "Let me show you the rest of our place." He pulled aside the sheets to reveal an armoire, a double bed, a wooden chair, and a small crib. In the meantime, the baby's face had turned a bright shade of red and he began to cry at the top of his lungs.

"Is something wrong?" I asked.

"You don't know much about babies do you? He's probably just hungry," Jes reassured me as his wife began to unbutton the top of her blouse. "Why don't the two of us wait over here while the baby gets fed and then we can all eat supper?" He slid the bed sheets back in place leaving his wife and Charlotte alone on the other side.

"Oh, Günter!" Charlotte said to me when we left the Schmiedler apartment two hours later, "she actually let me hold that sweet little boy for a few minutes. What a great feeling! Can't you just imagine how wonderful it would be to have one of our own?"

"And live like that? Not if you paid me a million Deutschmarks."

"Well, I'll admit that their place was a bit cramped. But I'd give anything to trade places with them just the same."

****

Two days after Charlotte and I visited the Schmiedlers, my parents invited us to have dinner with them in a Bavarian family restaurant on the Hohenzollernring in downtown Cologne. Like Charlotte, Mutti still hadn't given up hope that I would change my mind about going to America and I suspected that she would use the occasion to try to dissuade me.

The restaurant, which had a vaulted ceiling and rustic wooden tables and chairs, was in the basement of an old building that had survived the bombing during the war. As soon as we reached the bottom of the stairs, I glanced around the room at the other guests to see if there was anyone I knew. Families with young children occupied most of the tables, and with one exception, couples sat at the rest. The awkward exception was my boss, Mr. Hautegen, who sat, glum and alone, at a table against the far wall. He was drinking beer from a half-liter stein while waiting for his food. Much as I hoped to avoid being seen, Mr. Hautegen had already caught my eye so I felt obliged to introduce him to my parents and to Charlotte. Then, to spare him any further embarrassment, when the four of us reached our table some distance away, I deliberately sat with my back to him.

"You're not really serious about leaving us to go half way around the world, are you?" Mutti asked me once we had ordered our meals.

"Not so loud! I haven't said anything about it at work yet. But yes, I really mean to go. I'm going to get my boat ticket sometime in the next few weeks. By the way, since the *France* is only two years old, I'm getting a great introductory price."

"But that would only take you as far as New York. Have you figured out yet how you'll get to San Francisco?" my father asked.

"I guess I forgot to tell you. There's this bus company called Continental Trailways that's got a special promotion for visitors from abroad. For just ninety-nine dollars I can buy a ticket that will let me travel anywhere in the States that I want for ninety-nine days."

"And how many of those days will you need to go to California?"

"I figure it should take me eighty-four hours but at least I'll get to see a lot of the country along the way. I think it's better than flying over it, don't you?"

Mutti hadn't quite given up on me yet. "But what about your job? You could go far at Eklöh if you were willing to stick it out for a few more years. And who knows what kind of work you'd get over there?"

"It can't be worse that spending every day thinking up ways to eliminate other people's jobs. I sure don't want to end up like my boss, who's hated by everyone in the company."

"Perhaps you have point there," my father said as he glanced over at Mr. Hautegen. "That poor man just started on his fourth stein of beer. Looks to me like someone who's trying to drown his sorrows."

Until that point, Charlotte had remained silent but now she reached over and took my hand. "How long will you be gone, Günter?"

"I'm thinking a year; less than that wouldn't make sense."

She bit her lip. "I guess that should be all right then. I can't imagine you'd want to stay away any longer than that."

****

Despite what I had said in the restaurant about my plans, I was secretly worried that I might be making a mistake. After all, there were nearly two hundred million people in America and I knew only one of them. In Germany, on the other hand, I not only had my family and Charlotte, but also friends like Jochen Krienke and Wilfried Plath whom I'd known since shortly after Mutti, Hubert, and I had been reunited with my father nearly thirteen years earlier. And then there was Rupert Mayer at Arminius AG who had inspired me to start at the Höwi, and my scout leader, Friedel Meuser, and my old army buddy, Siegfried Reimold, with whom I was still in touch.

Pushing these thoughts to the back of my mind I suggested to Charlotte that we go on two successive nights to see *Anatomy of a Marriage*, a two-part French film that had just been reviewed in the *Kölner Stadt-Anzeiger*. Each part, *My Days with Jean-Marc* and *My Nights with Françoise*, had identical story lines and involved the same couple: a young man and a young woman who meet, fall in love, get

421

engaged, and eventually marry. After a while, their marriage sours and their relationship ends in bitterness and divorce. But since *My Days with Jean-Marc* is told from Françoise's point of view, and *My Nights with Françoise* is told from Jean-Marc's, the stories could not have been more different.

We saw *My Days with Jean-Marc* on February 15th and then we went to an Italian ice cream store on the Hohe Strasse afterwards to discuss it. Charlotte was incensed by Jean-Marc's behavior, blaming him for everything that had gone wrong in the marriage. I disagreed and tried to show her how one-sided the story was, but the more I argued, the more she stood her ground.

The following night we went to see *My Nights with Françoise*. "See what I told you?" I asked Charlotte as we warmed up after the movie over two steaming cups of cappuccino. "You didn't give Jean-Marc a chance. Now that you've heard his side, you have to admit that it was all Françoise's fault."

"Yes, I heard his side of the story but I didn't believe a word of it." The vehemence of her reply startled me.

"Maybe we should talk about something else," I said. "They're just silly movies after all." Still, even days later I couldn't stop reflecting on what had happened. How could any couple ever be sure that they wouldn't end up like Françoise and Jean-Marc? I thought about how shaky my own parents' marriage had been after the war; about the divorce of Charlotte's parents; and about Mr. Rahmler, Mrs. Sorge's married boyfriend. And then there was the image of the Schmiedlers, stuck together in an awful apartment with their unplanned baby.

Was there really enough to my relationship with Charlotte to hold us together if we ever did get married? I already knew that she was emotionally fragile and I worried that we really didn't have all that much in common besides the obvious physical attraction. I loved to read; she had little interest in books. I followed the news; she rarely glanced at the headlines. Would we simply run out of things to talk about over the years?

For several nights after we'd seen the films, I had nightmares in which Charlotte turned into Françoise and I was her Jean-Marc. In those dreams, we had bitter disagreements, but no matter how hard I tried to persuade her, she won the argument every time. By the first week in March I was sure that I needed to spend a year or two in America to sort things out. Exactly two weeks after I had seen *My Days with Jean-Marc,* I went into the travel agency on Hohe Strasse and bought my ticket for the *France*.

****

With only a few weeks until my departure for New York, and despite all of my misgivings about Charlotte, I decided to spend as much time with her as possible. Most nights when she came over to my apartment, she obeyed the rules and left shortly before ten o'clock. When she stayed over, we would creep out early in the morning, well before my landlady got up. But on the morning of April 3rd, my alarm clock didn't go off and we both overslept. We rushed to get dressed and eat breakfast and then, worried that we might meet my landlady in the elevator, we crept down the stairs to the street floor. But it was no use. The landlady was waiting for us before we could sneak out the front door.

"Aha!" she snarled. "I've suspected that you were breaking my rules, Herr Nitsch, and now I've caught you red-handed. This isn't the kind of house where women can come and go as they please. I want you out of here today or tomorrow at the latest!"

"If it means so much to you, I'll move tomorrow, provided of course that you return my April rent." Without a word, she unlocked the management office and handed me back the money.

Once we were outside Charlotte said, "Boy, is she holier-than-thou or what? And now you're stuck with another move. Should I call my mother to come by with her VW?"

"No, please don't bother your mother. Since I'll be moving back home anyway, I'll ask my parents to come by with a taxi."

"Mind if I come, too?"

"Sure, why not? Be here by five o'clock. I wouldn't mind annoying that self-righteous old prude one last time."

"You can count on me to help with that," Charlotte promised with a mischievous grin.

On Saturday afternoon I packed my clothes and my books into my two suitcases and went downstairs to wait for my parents. The taxi my parents had reserved pulled up shortly before five, and a few minutes later, Charlotte joined us. She was dressed in a bright-red miniskirt, a tight silk blouse unbuttoned at the top, and spiked heels. As soon as he saw her, my father gave a low whistle. "Maybe we should have brought smelling salts for the landlady," he said as, much to Mutti's annoyance, he ogled Charlotte's provocative outfit from top to bottom.

While the taxi driver parked in front of the building my parents, Charlotte, and I went upstairs together. My grimfaced landlady was standing disapprovingly in front of my apartment door. She wore a dark-blue dress and her silver crucifix reflected the light from the ceiling fixture in the hallway. She gaped in horror at Charlotte as we approached.

"You've already met Fräulein Sorge," I said cheerfully, "but let me introduce you to my parents. They've come to help me move out."

The landlady followed us inside and carefully inspected every corner of the studio, alternately checking for possible damage and looking over at the four of us in disbelief. Just to taunt her, Mutti waited until she caught the landlady's eye. Then she put her arms around Charlotte and gave her a big hug.

At long last, the landlady reached out her hand for the keys, one for the house door and one for my studio. She grunted, "*Danke,*" when I handed them over and then accompanied us downstairs. Once we were back outside, she banged the building door shut and glared until our taxi drove away.

CHAPTER 58

*A*fter all the efforts I had made since I was thirteen years old to get out of my parents' house and gain some independence, it was ironic that I ended up spending my last three weeks in Germany living back home in my old room over my parents' café in Bergheim. Perhaps it was just as well, since it gave me a chance to spend some time with Oma, to visit old friends, and to take familiar walks past Langnickel's bookshop where Mr. Poltermann had once borrowed books and then loaned them to me; past Café Meyer where we had eaten our first meal together; past the Stüssgen Food Market and Frambach's clothing store where Mutti still shopped; past the Maria-Hilf Hospital where I had startled Sister Monika with a moonlit kiss; then on through the Aachener Tor to the Lutheran Church, the scene of Jochen Krienke's drunken confirmation; and, finally, to the building in Zieverich where my father's boss had dropped the four of us off after a tense ride from the main railroad station in Cologne in December 1950.

Just as I had done when I was starting my apprenticeship at Arminius AG and if I wasn't staying overnight with Charlotte, I would leave Café Nitsch right after breakfast and would rejoin my parents in front of the TV in the evening after supper. Hubert was now living in a furnished room over a small restaurant on Hohe Strasse in downtown Cologne

where he worked as a cook. I stopped by there to see him a few times
and to say good-bye. According to Hubert, he was on track to get that
greasy little waffle shop a coveted five star rating. Remembering how
he had once boasted that I'd been promoted to the rank of Lieutenant
while I was still cleaning toilets during basic training, I didn't dare ask
him what wild stories he was telling the restaurant customers about my
own "golden prospects" in America.

On April 9th, with barely two weeks to go, I came home to the
café just in time to join my parents for supper. As soon as I sat down,
my father handed me a copy of the April 8th issue of *Der Spiegel*. His
expression was grim and I soon saw why. On the cover was a photograph
of a crumbling wooden shack. A family in ragged clothing stood on the
sagging front porch amid piles of broken furniture and heaps of rubbish.
The bold yellow headline read POVERTY IN USA.

"Had you seen it?" my father asked me. "One of our customers
brought the magazine to us this morning. I think half of Bergheim
stopped by today to talk about it. To be honest, Stretch, much as I've
supported your plans, even I'm getting second thoughts about your
going to America."

"Didn't I tell you?" Mutti added. "Just look at that picture. We lived
better than that under the Russians."

"Well, I've read *Der Spiegel* a lot more often than the two of you
have. Their writers love sensational stories with a negative slant so it's
probably only half as bad as it looks."

"Read it first!" my father said. "Then we can talk about it."

Relying on trustworthy sources like *The Wall Street Journal, The
New York Times,* U.S. Government statistics, and Harvard Professor
John Kenneth Galbraith, the gist of the article was that, out of a
population of one hundred ninety million, thirty-eight million Americans
–particularly Negroes in the rural south, migrant farm workers, West
Virginia coalminers, Appalachian whites, and people living on Indian
reservations – were desperately poor. Making matters worse, according

to *Der Spiegel* disaffected teenage gangs armed with knives and guns roamed the streets of America's cities, terrifying the inhabitants. This was certainly not the tranquil American life depicted in the *Life* and *Ebony* magazines I'd read in the Amerika-Haus library.

"So?" my father asked when I put down the magazine. "Are you still sure you want to go over there?"

I thought about all of the travel documents neatly stacked on my desk: my Green Card, my passport, my train ticket, my passage on the *France*, and my ninety-nine dollar Continental Trailways bus ticket. I'd dreamed about going to America for so many years that there was no way I was going to back out now. "Lots of other people have made it there," I finally replied, feigning more self-confidence than I felt, "and I intend to give it a try."

****

The previous week when I had given Mr. Hautegen notice that I would be quitting my job on the 17th of April, he had launched into a tirade. "What insubordination! You must have known when you started here that you'd be leaving after such a short time." And then he leveled at me the harshest insult he could think of, "In my book, Nitsch, you're nothing but a deserter!"

On my last day he refused to look me in the eye when he shook my hand. Once I was on the train back to Bergheim I thought how strange it was that, after all the weeks I had felt guilty about the jobs my efficiency studies might be putting at risk, in the end the only job at Eklöh I was sure I had eliminated was my own.

CHAPTER 59

O n the day I was leaving Bergheim, I would have preferred to say good-bye to my parents and travel into Cologne alone, but Charlotte had insisted on spending my last night with me in Bergheim so that she could accompany me to the railroad station. On the morning of April 23rd, I gave Mutti a big hug as she did her best to fight back tears. My father solemnly shook my hand and wished me all the best. "Behave yourself and do us proud," he said.

"And don't forget to write!" Mutti added as Charlotte and I left the café.

"Don't worry, Frau Nitsch," Charlotte said. "I've given him a box of stationery so he has no excuse."

Less than an hour later Charlotte and I walked up the steps to the platform in the main Cologne railroad station where the train that would take me on the first leg of my journey was waiting. When I went on board to stow my luggage in the overhead rack, Charlotte followed me. "I'm coming with you," she said half-jokingly. But as soon as I brought her back down to the platform and reached down to kiss her she started to sob. Just then the conductor blew his whistle and I jumped back on the train and rushed to the window as the doors closed. We waved at each other until Charlotte became a blurry speck on the platform.

When my train left the station, I took a deep breath and looked back one more time to catch a last glimpse of the massive Cathedral. It had been the first building I had recognized when we came to Cologne years earlier and now it was the last I would see as I left. And then, with mounting excitement, I faced straight ahead towards the West.

All I was bringing with me were my two heavy suitcases and the four crisp hundred dollar bills tucked into my wallet together with the address of the Proctor family in California. In a few hours I would be in Le Havre, and tomorrow my ship to America would sail.